Color Tab Index to Bird Groups

STOKES FIELD GUIDE TO BIRDS

Western Region

Donald and Lillian Stokes

Little, Brown and Company

Boston   New York   London

First Edition

Library of Congress Cataloging-in-Publication Data
Stokes, Donald W.
     Stokes field guide to birds: western region / by
Donald and Lillian Stokes. — 1st ed.
       p. cm.
    Includes index.
    ISBN 0-316-81810-0
    1. Birds — West (U.S.) — Identification. I. Stokes,
Lillian Q. II. Title. III. Series: Stokes, Donald W. Stokes
field guides.
    QL683.W4S76 1995
    598.2978 — dc20   95-6610

10 9 8 7

RRD-IN

Designed by Barbara Werden

Printed in the United States of America

Contents

A Bird Guide for the 21st Century

More people than ever are watching birds. In addition to having fun, they want their birding to be a meaningful experience that results in a closer relationship to birds. To help people accomplish this, we have produced the *Stokes Field Guide to Birds.* What led us to this project was a desire to improve upon existing guides and to make a useful tool that would help people become better bird watchers and gain a new appreciation and understanding of birds. That is why our book not only provides fast and easy access to all the birds you might want to look up, it also presents important information on breeding biology, vocalizations, behavior, and conservation — information we believe will be more relevant than ever in the years to come and that will enrich your experience of the birds you see.

THREE-DIMENSIONAL BIRDING: IDENTIFICATION, BEHAVIOR, AND CONSERVATION

The preservation of the environment depends on those who love it, watch it, and know about it. Bird watchers have a key role to play in the coming century. They are among the dedicated people actually observing the natural world closely. They experience firsthand the changes that are occurring in bird populations in their own yards, their states or provinces, and even nationally.

The 21st century needs bird watchers who can accurately identify a bird, who know its needs for survival and reproduction, and who are aware of its population status.

These are all aspects of what we call three-dimensional birding — identification, behavior, and conservation. A knowledge of all three is needed for the public to begin making well-informed decisions that will help preserve bird populations. And since birds are excellent indicators of the general health of the environment, if we work to preserve their populations we will also be helping the environment as a whole.

It is our hope that through this guide more people will be able to identify birds and will become aware of the habitat needs and conservation status of the species they watch. We hope all bird watchers will become three-dimensional birders — avid and informed enthusiasts of birds and advocates for the environment.

HOW TO BECOME MORE INVOLVED

It is up to those of us who know the importance of the natural world to take an active role in protecting it. In bird-watching, this can result in more fun and a more meaningful experience. Here are some ways that you can become more involved with helping birds:

- Learn to identify more birds.

- Learn more about the biology of the species you watch through reading and your own observations.

- Become aware of the population trends of the birds you see.

- Keep a notebook of your observations as a record of all that you learn.
- Share your love for and knowledge of birds with others, both young and old.
- Participate in bird surveys and censuses.
- Join birding organizations and bird clubs in your area.
- Join local, national, and international conservation organizations.
- Create good bird habitats in your own backyard by providing bird feeders, birdhouses, and plantings that attract birds.
- Help your local conservation commission acquire and manage town lands so that they support more birds.

All of these activities add up to an involved bird-watching public. This is what three-dimensional birding is all about.

Acknowledgments

Undertaking a task as huge as field guides to North American birds requires the help and hard work of many people. We would like to thank those who had a major part in the writing and producing of these guides.

First and foremost we would like to thank the photographers who have devoted so much of their time and energy to capturing these birds on film. Their names are listed in the photo credits.

Second, we want to thank the various experts who read early drafts and helped make them better. Four people read the entire manuscript and made extensive comments. They were Wayne Petersen, David Wolf, Paul Roberts, and Allen Baldridge. We also had others read special sections: Debra Shearwater reviewed seabirds; Bill Clark reviewed vultures, hawks, eagles, falcons; Claudia Wilds reviewed gulls and terns; Joseph Jehl, Jr., reviewed shorebirds; and Trevor Lloyd-Evans reviewed warblers. Of course, we take full responsibility for the accuracy of the final work.

We would also like to thank Paul Roberts for enjoyable initial discussions on the scope and format of the guides, Wayne Petersen for discussions on the Learning Pages and the careful review of all slides, and our son, Justin Brown, for help in researching some of the breeding and behavior accounts.

The conservation data were gathered from a variety of sources. We want to give special thanks to Bruce Peterjohn and Sam Droege for their assistance in getting the data of the Breeding Bird Survey and the Christmas Bird Count and John Sauer for his guidance in interpreting the data. We were also fortunate to have the Network of Natural Heritage Programs and Conservation Data Centers and the Nature Conservancy arrange for us to use their superb database on the conservation status of North American birds.

We had a wonderful production staff at Little, Brown and Company, and we worked closely with them in all aspects of production in order to make the best possible guides. We especially want to thank Donna Peterson in production, Barbara Werden in design, and Peggy Leith Anderson in copyediting, who knows the book, word for word, better than anybody but ourselves. We also want to thank John Kramer for his help in setting up our Power Macintoshes so that the material was essentially typeset during writing, and in such a way that we could draw our range maps more efficiently. In addition, we want to thank our hard drive, Merlin, for not letting us down.

We also want to share our appreciation of our editors, Jordan Pavlin and, especially, Bill Phillips, editor in chief, vice president, and associate publisher of Little, Brown, for his longstanding support of our writing, from the very first book to these field guides, and for his warm friendship.

The Basics of the Guide

Area covered by this guide

SPECIAL SECTIONS

This guide offers a number of useful tools for bird watchers at all levels of skill and interest. Spending a few minutes now to familiarize yourself with these features will help you take full advantage of them whether you are using the guide at home or in the field.

Quick Alphabetical Index

Right inside the front and back covers is a concise alphabetical index to the birds. If you know the kind of bird you want to look up, this is a fast way to find it.

Color Tab Index

Facing the front and back covers is the **Color Tab Index to Bird Groups.** This provides access to the birds by groups — heronlike birds, shorebirds, woodpeckers, sparrows, and so forth. The color tabs are a fast way to automatically turn to the right portion of the guide. In addition, this index and the Species Accounts are arranged in phylogenetic order, that is, according to their believed evolutionary relationships, thus familiarizing all users with the only order of birds generally agreed upon by

scientists and birders in North America.

Quick Guide to the Most Common Birds

Immediately preceding the Species Accounts is the **Quick Guide to the Most Common Birds.** These are help pages designed especially for beginners. Here, the species of birds most commonly seen at bird feeders and in backyards are shown in a special format for quick reference and easy comparisons.

These pages will help beginners successfully master the identification of common birds so that they can then go on to learn others. Next to each picture is the number of the page where a detailed description of the bird may be found.

Learning Pages

Interspersed with the Species Accounts are other special sections called **Learning Pages.** These provide beginning and intermediate bird watchers with a basic orientation to the more complex and challenging groups of birds: hawks, shorebirds, gulls, flycatchers, warblers, and sparrows.

Learning Pages occur at the start of each of these bird groups. They provide an overall introduction to identification of the group, helpful organizing concepts or tips, and pictures of the most commonly seen species within each group.

SPECIES ACCOUNTS

The main body of the field guide is composed of full-page accounts for each species. Photographs, text, and range map are all on the same page, along with other new, informative features.

Species, Names, Order

All regularly occurring species within the range of the guide are included. Their scientific and common names and order are in accordance with the July 1995 supplement to the 6th edition of the American Ornithological Union Checklist of North American Birds.

In a few cases, two species are placed on the same page. This is done when one species follows the other in the phylogenetic order and looks extremely similar, making the comparison helpful. It is also done to keep the guide slightly shorter and reduce the weight of the final book.

Bird Feeder and Birdhouse Symbols

Identifying symbols have been included next to the names of birds that use bird feeders and birdhouses. This will help you recognize the species you may see at feeders or birdhouses, and may also encourage you to provide appropriate food and housing for these species. In the section called **Feeding** we have listed the feeder foods these birds prefer. The symbols are generalized and not meant to show the specific type of feeder or house used by that species.

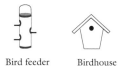

Bird feeder   Birdhouse

Range Maps

Up-to-date range maps show whether a bird is likely to be found in a particular area. The maps have 1–3 colors. Blue indicates winter range; yellow indicates summer range, which includes both breeding range and areas moved into in summer after breeding; green is year-round range.

There are several things to remember when using any range map. Ranges of birds are always changing in response to the environment and population of the species. At the edge of a range the bird is not seen in substantial numbers, but there are always some individual birds outside this edge, stretching the limits of the range. Also, maps may show a continuous range, but birds may live only locally within that range. This is particularly true of species that live in specialized habitats.

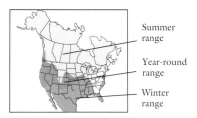

Summer range

Year-round range

Winter range

Photographs

Hundreds of color photographs have been carefully selected to show male, female, immature, and seasonal plumages of each species. For species in which male and female look almost identical, only one sex is shown. In many cases, such as hawks, gulls, and terns, we have also shown birds in flight, since this is often the most common way these birds are encountered. Photos for species that have only one adult plumage throughout the year have no identifying caption. All other photos are clearly captioned to identify age, sex, and season of the plumage shown.

Identification Section

The first information in the identification section is the average length of the species, measured in inches, from tip of beak to tip of tail. This allows rough comparisons of size between species.

In the identification clues for adult birds, some clues are in **boldface type.** These are the main clues to the identification of the species and, in most cases, are sufficient to distinguish this species from all others in the area. Additional clues in normal typeface provide further distinguishing marks that have proven helpful.

All descriptions of plumages refer to adult birds unless otherwise noted. There are separate headings for MALE and FEMALE when their plumages differ. If these headings are not included in a species account, then the sexes are alike.

Seasonal plumages are indicated by the headings SUMMER and WINTER. Summer is roughly from March through August and includes the breeding period; winter is roughly from September through February and coincides with the nonbreeding period. We vary from this approach only in describing the warblers, because traditionally their summer plumage is referred to as spring and their winter plumage as fall.

In preparing this guide, we had to choose what terminology to use to describe the various plumages of birds. Although there is general agreement among the scientific community to use the system of plumage terminology proposed by Humphrey and Parkes in 1959,

this system is still too complex for the lay public, more detailed than most bird watchers need, and not used in field guides.

Understanding any plumage terminology requires a basic knowledge of how and when birds acquire their various feathers. When a bird first hatches, it is covered with fine feathers called **natal down.** This is soon replaced by the first full set of feathers, which is called the **juvenal plumage.** In most North American birds, juvenal plumage is molted and replaced by new feathers in late summer. This new plumage may be like adult plumage or may be different. When it differs from that of the adults, we call it **immature plumage.** We continue to call it immature until it is like adult plumage.

In summary, we use the term **immature** to refer to any plumage between juvenal and adult plumages.

It is important to remember that sexual maturity and plumage maturity do not always coincide. Some birds can breed while still in immature plumage, and some birds may be in adult plumage but still not sexually mature.

In this guide, juvenal plumages kept only in summer are not described. This is because, in most species, they are only briefly held. Also, juveniles in summer are often still being attended by their parents and can thus be recognized by identifying the adults.

Any juvenal plumage kept into fall, and all immature plumages, are included in this guide. In most cases, we tell how long the bird stays in immature plumages; for example, "Imm. plumage kept until spring," or "Imm. plumage kept 1 year." This timing starts from the bird's first fall.

In a few instances, such as shorebirds, juveniles keep their plumage into fall and we see them gradually molting out of it as they migrate south. We have given them the heading FALL JUV.

In one case, we have varied from our system; this is in the hawks. Nonadult hawks in fall are technically in their juvenal plumage. We have called them immatures because there is such a strong tradition of referring to them in this way.

Feeding

This section describes the feeding location, method of getting food, and the foods eaten. Foods listed are the items that make up the bulk of the bird's diet. Most birds eat a wide variety of incidental foods and the complete list would be too long to include. When birds come to feeders, we mention the foods they prefer.

Nesting

Nesting and breeding information starts with a description of the nest, its materials, and placement. Many birds use a wide variety of nesting materials, and we have listed only the major items.

Under **Eggs** we have included a range of numbers for the clutch size. The majority of birds will lay the average of this range. Incubation period (marked by the letter **I**) is the time from the laying of the last egg until the first egg hatches. The fledgling phase (marked by the letter **F**) is the time from hatching to first flight (in precocial birds) or the time from hatching to leaving the nest (in altricial birds).

Following the time of fledging, there is the term **altricial** or **precocial**. These terms refer to the development of the young. Upon hatching, altricial young are dependent on the parents for food and warmth, for they cannot move well and are generally at first naked; they stay in the nest. Precocial young, upon hatching, are feathered and can generally feed themselves; they often leave the nest within a day or two of hatching.

The last information in the nesting and breeding section is the number of broods a bird has in a season. It is marked by a **B.** Shown is the number of successful broods a species will attempt in a normal season. It does not include cases of renestings after failed broods.

A question mark after one of the letters means that aspect of the bird's breeding biology, to the best of our knowledge, is not known and needs more study.

Other Behavior

This section deals with behaviors of the bird that you are likely to see or that are particularly interesting, such as flight displays, courtship activities, territory formation, and migration behavior, as well as other intriguing features about the bird's life. We hope you take time to watch and enjoy these aspects of birds.

Habitat

The major ecological habitats that the bird uses when within the United States and Canada are summarized in this section.

Voice

This section describes the main vocalizations of the bird. The term **song** refers to a partially learned, generally complex vocalization. The term **call** refers to short, instinctively given vocalizations.

Conservation

In the conservation section we share with you some of what is known about the population status and conservation of North American birds.

One way we do this is to say whether the bird is classified as federally endangered in the United States and/or Canada. Species or subspecies so designated are in danger of extinction in part or all of their range. Once a species is listed as federally endangered, the federal Fish and Wildlife Service may get funds and legislation to help protect it from further harm and foster its recovery.

We also tell you the bird's population trend (whether it is increasing or declining) and other pertinent information. Below is an example of the population trend information and a brief explanation of its symbols.

In cases where there are not enough data to suggest any population trend, you will see the phrase TREND UNKNOWN.

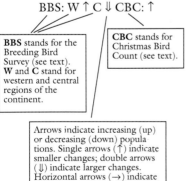

BBS: W ↑ C ⇓ CBC: ↑

BBS stands for the Breeding Bird Survey (see text). **W** and **C** stand for western and central regions of the continent.

CBC stands for Christmas Bird Count (see text).

Arrows indicate increasing (up) or decreasing (down) populations. Single arrows (↑) indicate smaller changes; double arrows (⇓) indicate larger changes. Horizontal arrows (→) indicate stable population.

Because this information is a key component of what we call three-dimensional birding, we want to explain it in some detail.

AN IN-DEPTH EXPLANATION OF THE CONSERVATION INFORMATION

There are two main programs used in North America to determine population trends of birds: the Breeding Bird Survey and the Christmas Bird Count.

The **Breeding Bird Survey** (BBS) was started in the United States and Canada in 1966 and was run by the U.S. Fish and Wildlife Service and the Canadian Wildlife Service; it is now administered by the National Biological Survey and the Canadian Wildlife Service. The survey is done by volunteers who drive a 24.5-mile route, stopping every half mile for 3 minutes during which they record all birds seen or heard. The route is fixed and driven only once, on a day during the height of the breeding season. There are over 3,000 routes all across the United States and Canada. In 1993, routes were also started in Mexico. The data from the survey are broken down into three regions of the continent: western (from the Rocky Mountains west), central (from the Rocky Mountains to the Mississippi River), and eastern (from the Mississippi River east). In this guide, BBS data have been reported for the western and central regions.

The **Christmas Bird Count** (CBC) was started in 1900 and is run by the National Audubon Society. It is the largest survey of birds in the world, with more than 45,000 volunteer participants. There are over 1,500 designated count areas in the United States and Canada, each 15 miles in diameter. Within a week or two of Christmas, each designated area is censused for one day, with participants seeking out and counting all birds in that area. CBC data are not broken down by region; they reflect population trends throughout Canada and the United States. CBC does not cover birds that winter south of the United States.

Other Surveys

Many species of birds are not covered well by either the Breeding Bird Survey or the Christmas Bird Count. To gather population trend information on these species, we have relied on other information and research that we believe is the best available. These sources are referred to in the text with different initials, which are listed below along with the organizations and people for which they stand.

CWS   Canadian Wildlife Service. The Canadian Wildlife Service, Ottawa ON K1A 0H3, publishes a regular report entitled *Bird Trends*. We used much of their information on shorebirds.

HWI   Hawkwatch International, personal communication, Steve Hoffmann. Hawkwatch International, Salt Lake City, is a nonprofit organization that concentrates on raptor conservation.

ICN   Ian C. T. Nisbet, unpublished manuscript.

The Meaning of the Arrows

The arrows used in the conservation information indicate increases or declines in the species' population; up arrows mean an increase, down arrows mean a decline, horizontal arrows mean a stable population. Arrows are based on the estimated average per-year change in the species' population for the period of the data analyzed. Single arrows ($\downarrow$) indicate a trend of less than 2% per year. Double arrows ($\Downarrow$) indicate a trend of 2% or greater per year. BBS data used are for the years 1966–1993; CBC data are for 1965–1989; CWS data are for 1974–1991; other data are for approximately the last 25 years.

We have used the double arrows to try to highlight those birds whose populations have gone through major changes in the last 2–3 decades.

If no arrow appears, the bird does not breed in that region or data are insufficient to indicate a trend.

Interpreting the Data

The data from the BBS and CBC provide us with a unique opportunity to track the populations of birds in the United States and Canada. The studies are the broadest of their kind in North America and are the ones most often relied on for population information.

However, they are not perfect. There are inherent problems with the collection and analysis of data. For example, habitats in count areas or along survey routes may change over time and affect the numbers and species of birds seen. Coverage has improved with more routes and census areas and more participants; in addition, observers are getting better and seeing more birds. In the CBC, census areas are not evenly spaced across the continent; also weather, such as stormy or sunny days, can affect the counts in the short run.

Other factors affect the analysis of the data. If the trend is based on the whole country, it may mask a change in one or more smaller regions. We are reporting the regional breakdown of the BBS data and the continent-wide analysis of the CBC data so that you can compare the two.

Another critical factor is the number of years from which data are taken. We have chosen to look at long-term changes by using the entire length of the study for which the data are adequately analyzed. If we had reported a recent 5–10 year span, the data might look different.

The information presented in this guide is the best available on bird populations and has not yet been made readily accessible to bird watchers or the public. Many organizations are working hard to pull together population data, for it is essential that we know the status of birds around us. We hope that more and better ways of censusing and tracking birds will be developed in the future and that many of you will be participants in gathering the data.

For More Information

More detailed information on BBS data can be obtained by writing:

> BBS Coordinator
> Patuxent Environmental
>   Science Center
> 12100 Beech Forest Road
> Laurel, MD 20708

More detailed information on CBC data can be obtained by writing:

> National Audubon Society
> Christmas Bird Count
> 700 Broadway
> New York, NY 10003

Parts of a Bird

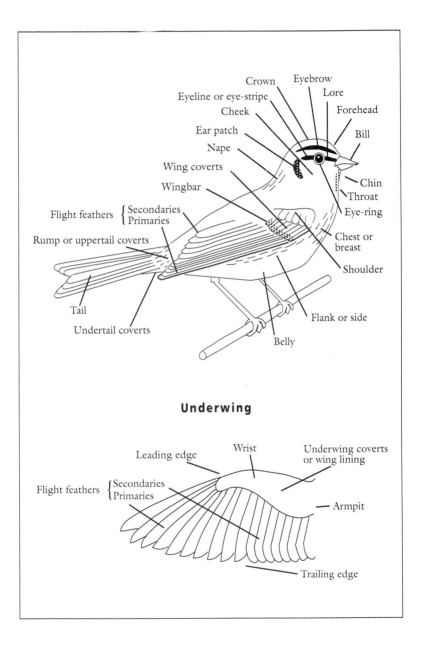

Crown
Eyebrow
Eyeline or eye-stripe
Lore
Cheek
Forehead
Ear patch
Bill
Nape
Wing coverts
Chin
Wingbar
Throat
Flight feathers { Secondaries Primaries
Eye-ring
Rump or uppertail coverts
Chest or breast
Shoulder
Tail
Undertail coverts
Flank or side
Belly

Underwing

Leading edge
Wrist
Underwing coverts or wing lining
Flight feathers { Secondaries Primaries
Armpit
Trailing edge

Quick Guide to the Most Common Birds

Backyard and Feeder Birds Grouped by Color

Scan these pages for the bird you have seen. If you find it here, go to the page shown for more information. If you don't see it here but have an idea as to the type of bird it is, turn to the Color Tab Index or the Quick Alphabetical Index and look for the group of birds that seems closest to your bird, then turn to that section and look through the pictures.

American Goldfinch, p. 505

Male

Female

Winter

Lesser Goldfinch, p. 503

Male

Female

Evening Grosbeak, p. 506

Female

Male

Female

Bullock's Oriole,
p. 492

Male

American Robin,
p. 380

Male

Anna's Hummingbird,
p. 259

Male

House Finch,
p. 499

Male

Purple Finch,
p. 497

Male

Female

Female

Song Sparrow,
p. 465

Pine Siskin,
p. 502

Fox Sparrow,
p. 464

White-crowned Sparrow,
p. 470

House Sparrow,
p. 507

Male

Chipping Sparrow,
p. 449

Female

House Wren,
p. 362

Red-winged Blackbird,
p. 480

Male

Female

Male

Female

Spotted Towhee,
p. 441

Brown-headed Cowbird,
p. 489

Male

Female

European Starling, p. 393

Winter

Summer

Brewer's Blackbird, p. 485

Male

Female

American Crow, p. 332

Dark-eyed Junco, p. 472

"Oregon" race

"Pink-sided" race

"Gray-headed" race

Chestnut-backed Chickadee, p. 347

Black-capped Chickadee, p. 344

Plain Titmouse, p. 349

Wrentit, p. 382

Tufted Titmouse, p. 350

Bushtit, p. 352

White-breasted Nuthatch, p. 354

Red-breasted Nuthatch, p. 353

Male

Male

Male

Female

Male

Male

Downy Woodpecker, p. 279

Hairy Woodpecker, p. 279

Acorn Woodpecker, p. 270

Northern Mockingbird, p. 384

Northern Flicker, p. 283

Mourning Dove, p. 225

Western Scrub-Jay, p. 326

Rock Dove, p. 221

SPECIES
ACCOUNTS

Red-throated Loon
Gavia stellata

Summer

Winter

Identification: 25" **SUMMER: Gray face and dark red throat;** nape striped with black and white lines **WINTER: Note gradual blending between white front and gray back of the neck.** (Border between light and dark areas is straight and lacks white triangular indentation seen in Common Loon.) **Thin bill** appears upturned; fine white spots on back may be visible. **IMM:** Similar to winter adult, but with grayish flecking on cheek. Imm. plumage kept 1 year.

Feeding: Feeds by diving underwater and pursuing fish. In winter, sometimes seen feeding in small flocks.

Nesting: Platform nest of grasses, twigs, and mud lined with finer materials, placed at the water's edge. Eggs: 1–3, olive-brown with dark marks; I: 24–29 days; F: 48–50 days, precocial; B: 1.

Other Behavior: Most loons need a running start of about 20 yd. on the water to take flight. This species can take off in less distance and is the only loon known to be able to take flight from land. During migration, flocks of hundreds may gather on the Great Lakes to feed. The birds migrate during the day in loose flocks.

Habitat: Summers on tundra lakes and arctic coasts; winters along coasts and in Great Lakes.

Voice: At start and end of winter gives short wailing call; otherwise quiet. Uses a variety of calls on the breeding ground.

Conservation: CBC: ↓

Pacific Loon
Gavia pacifica

Summer

Winter

Identification: 26″ SUMMER: **Pale gray crown and nape;** black-and-white checkered back; iridescent throat patch can appear purple, green, or black. WINTER: **Straight sharp border between the light and dark areas of the neck;** thin dark bill is held horizontal; eye is in the black cap. Some individuals have a thin dark line under the chin. IMM: Similar to winter adult, but with whitish scaling on back. Imm. plumage kept 1 year. ➤The rare Arctic Loon, *G. arctica,* is similar but larger and breeds in western Alaska.

Feeding: Feeds by diving underwater and pursuing prey such as fish, crustaceans, and frogs.

Nesting: Platform nest of stems, roots, and mud, placed near the water's edge. Eggs: 1–2, brown with dark marks; I: 23–25 days; F: 60–65 days, precocial; B: 1.

Other Behavior: One of the most numerous loons off the Pacific Coast, often feeding in flocks of hundreds or thousands along the coastline. The most commonly seen loon on winter pelagic trips in the West. It is rare, but regularly occurring, off the East Coast.

Habitat: Summers on tundra lakes; winters along coast.

Voice: Generally quiet in winter; summer calls include a sharp call like "kwao" and a wail that rises in pitch.

Conservation: BBS: W ⇓ C CBC: ⇑

Common Loon
Gavia immer

Summer

Winter

Identification: 32" The most commonly seen loon. **SUMMER: Black head and black bill;** black-and-white barred neck-ring; checkered back. **WINTER: The border between the white front and black back of the neck is irregular, with a white, triangular indentation at midneck.** Holds **thick bill** horizontal. **IN FLIGHT:** Feet trail behind tail and are larger than in other loons. **IMM:** Similar to winter adult. Imm. plumage kept 1 year. Immatures spend 1st year along coast.

Feeding: Feeds by diving underwater and pursuing fish. Feeding dives average 45 seconds long.

Nesting: Platform nest of aquatic vegetation, placed on the ground on an island or at the water's edge. Eggs: 2, olive-brown; I: 29 days; F: 2–3 months, precocial; B: 1.

Other Behavior: Listening to loon sounds can tell you about their behavior. The yodel-call is used for territory advertisement and defense; the tremelo-call is used during moments of alarm; and the wail-call is often used to help the pair keep in contact with each other. Loons may dive to escape danger and can remain underwater for up to 3 minutes.

Habitat: Summers on lakes; winters mostly along coast.

Voice: Wail-call: a drawn-out wail. Tremelo-call: a short tremulous call. Yodel-call: a wail followed by a long undulating call.

Conservation: BBS: W ⇑ C ⇑ CBC: ↑ Boats on lakes can disturb breeding birds.

Yellow-billed Loon

Gavia adamsii

Summer

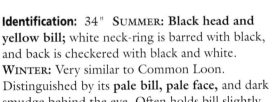
Winter

Identification: 34" SUMMER: **Black head and yellow bill;** white neck-ring is barred with black, and back is checkered with black and white. WINTER: Very similar to Common Loon. Distinguished by its **pale bill, pale face,** and dark smudge behind the eye. Often holds bill slightly uptilted.

Feeding: Feeds by diving underwater and pursuing prey such as fish, crustaceans, and marine worms.

Nesting: A saucerlike depression lined with twigs and grass, placed on islands, hummocks, or at the water's edge. Eggs: 2, brown with dark marks; I: 27–29 days; F: ?, precocial; B: 1.

Other Behavior: Generally only seen on its wintering grounds, the northwest Pacific Coast, where it most often feeds alone. Sexes may winter in different areas. It is the scarcest of the loons.

Habitat: Summers on arctic tundra lakes and coastal waters; winters along northwest Pacific Coast.

Voice: Generally quiet in winter; summer calls similar to those of Common Loon.

Conservation:
CBC: ↓
Has been a major victim of oil spills.

Pied-billed Grebe

Podilymbus podiceps

Summer

Winter

Identification: 12″ A small, stocky, brown grebe with a short stout bill. SUMMER: Obvious black ring around white bill; the chin is black. WINTER: The bill has a faint ring or no ring, and the chin is light.

Feeding: Feeds by diving underwater and catching fish, aquatic insects, frogs, and crayfish.

Nesting: A platform nest of decaying vegetation, attached to growing vegetation in shallow water. Eggs: 4–7, bluish green; I: 23 days; F: ?, precocial; B: 1–2.

Other Behavior: One of the earliest migrants among the grebes, often arriving on ponds before the ice is all melted. In territorial skirmishes males come together and tilt heads up while calling. Parents may do a distraction display of flapping their wings between dives when their young are in danger. Their white rear feathers may be flashed in times of alarm.

Habitat: Summers on lakes and ponds; winters also in sheltered saltwater bays.

Voice: During breeding, calls include a "cow cow cow cow cow," a loud "keck keck" in alarm, and a softer "cuk cuk cuk." It is generally quiet in winter.

Conservation: BBS: W ⇓ C ↓ CBC: ↑

Horned Grebe

Podiceps auritus

Summer

Winter

Identification: 14" SUMMER: **Golden ear tufts; reddish-brown neck.** WINTER: **White cheek patch is level with eye and extends almost all the way around the back of the head.** Also has white front to neck and whitish streaks along flanks.

Feeding: Feeds by diving underwater, eating small fish, crayfish, shrimp, and aquatic insects. Also eats land insects, frogs, and salamanders.

Nesting: Floating platform nest of plants and mud, anchored to vegetation. Eggs: 3–7, bluish white; I: 22–25 days; F: 44–60 days, precocial; B: 1.

Other Behavior: Like other grebes, this species can lower its body as it swims so that just its head shows; at other times it rides high on the water. In winter, often seen alone or in small flocks just outside the breaking waves, where it feeds. Tends to jump forward before diving down into the water.

Habitat: Summers on marshy ponds and lakes; winters mostly along the coast and on some inland lakes.

Voice: Makes a variety of loud croaks, chatters, and shrieks on the breeding ground; otherwise silent.

Conservation: BBS: W ↓ C ⇓ CBC: ↓ Vulnerable to oil spills.

Red-necked Grebe

Podiceps grisegena

Summer

Winter

Identification: 19″ SUMMER: Large grebe; long reddish foreneck; whitish chin and cheek; black cap. WINTER: Large and dusky, without sharp contrasts in plumage. The **long yellowish bill** helps distinguish it from the similar winter Horned and Eared Grebes. The **white on the chin extends up behind the grayish cheek.** IMM: Similar to winter adult, but without white mark behind cheek. Imm. plumage kept at least through winter.

Feeding: Feeds by diving underwater, eating fish, aquatic insects, marine worms, crustaceans, and mollusks. Also eats land insects and some vegetation.

Nesting: Floating platform nest of fresh and decayed reeds, rushes, and grasses, anchored to nearby vegetation. Eggs: 2–6, bluish white; I: 22–23 days; F: 50–70 days, precocial; B: 1.

Other Behavior: Adults eat their own molted feathers and even feed them to their young, as do some other grebes. All grebes avoid danger by diving underwater. Adults can dive underwater with young riding on their back — the young just hold on.

Habitat: Summers on lakes, ponds; winters mostly along coast.

Voice: Sounds include long wails, short vibrating wails, and chattering trills. Generally silent in winter.

Conservation: BBS: W ↑ C ⇓ CBC: ↑ May be subject to thinning eggshells and infertile eggs due to pesticides.

Eared Grebe

Podiceps nigricollis

Summer

Winter

Identification: 12″ SUMMER: **Golden ear tufts** and **black neck.** WINTER: **Small thin bill appears uptilted; grayish neck and cheek** with a whitish ear patch; **triangularly shaped head** due to elevated crest. Occasionally the cheek is whitish. In water, usually rides high in rear, low in front.

Feeding: Feeds by diving underwater, eating small fish, crustaceans, mollusks, aquatic insects, and the eggs of leeches.

Nesting: Floating platform nest of fresh and decayed vegetation, anchored to surrounding plants. Eggs: 3–9, dull bluish white; I: 20–22 days; F: 20–21 days, precocial; B: 1.

Other Behavior: Eared Grebes may nest singly or in colonies of several hundred pairs. Usually remain as flocks in wintering areas as well. On the breeding grounds they may be heard calling at dusk. Up to 1 million birds stage and molt at Mono Lake, Calif., and somewhat smaller numbers at other large saline lakes in the arid West. These large concentrations in small areas make them vulnerable to environmental changes.

Habitat: Summers on lakes and marshes; winters along the coast and on some inland lakes.

Voice: Breeding calls include a soft "pooeep" and a louder "hikarikup, hikarikup." Generally quiet during winter.

Conservation: BBS: W ⇑ C ⇑ CBC: ↓

Western Grebe
Clark's Grebe
Aechmophorus occidentalis   *Aechmophorus clarkii*

Western

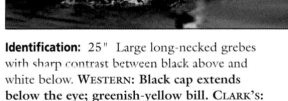
Clark's

Identification: 25″ Large long-necked grebes with sharp contrast between black above and white below. **WESTERN: Black cap extends below the eye; greenish-yellow bill. CLARK'S: Black cap stops just above eye; orange-yellow bill;** in winter, eye may have some light gray above and behind it.

Feeding: Feed by diving underwater, eating fish, mollusks, crustaceans, and aquatic insects.

Nesting: May nest in colonies containing hundreds of pairs; floating platform nest of decayed and fresh plants, placed in shallow water. Eggs: 2–7, pale blue-white; I: 23 days; F: 62–75 days, precocial; B: 1.

Other Behavior: As with all grebes, these species lack a long tail and use their lobed feet to help steer them underwater and in the air. During breeding the young may ride on parents' backs when in the water. Spectacular courtship displays occur on water and include running together over the water surface and presenting aquatic vegetation to each other. The 2 species winter in large flocks. Their ranges overlap and are not well known. Clark's is the less numerous of the 2.

Range for both species

Habitat: Summers on lakes and marshes; winters on coastal waters and some inland lakes.

Voice: Western's call is a 2-part "creek-creek"; Clark's call is an ascending "creek."

Conservation:
Western:
BBS: W ⇑ C ⇑
Clark's:
BBS: W ⇑ C
Hurt by oil spills.

Black-footed Albatross

Diomedea nigripes

Identification: 32" A very large bird seen only at sea. **Large bill; 7 ft. wingspan; body and wings dark overall;** light areas on face around base of dark bill, at base of tail, and sometimes on undertail coverts. Older birds may be paler on belly and underwings. IN FLIGHT: Long glides with stiff wings, then a few flaps.

Feeding: Feeds on the surface of the water, eating squid and whatever animal food it can find. Follows ships and eats garbage thrown overboard.

Nesting: Breeds colonially. Saucerlike nest scraped in bare sand. Eggs: 1, white with dark marks; I: 63–68 days; F: 4–6 months, altricial; B: most likely 1.

Other Behavior: Black-footed Albatrosses are wonderful dynamic soarers and are usually seen following fishing boats and pelagic birding trips and often alighting on the water as they feed. They may be attracted to fishing boats by the smell of the fish. Their large webbed feet are used to help them steer while flying. May be gregarious at food sources.

Habitat: Open sea when not breeding; breeds on remote islands near Japan and Hawaii.

Voice: Chickenlike squawk when competing for food.

Conservation: TREND UNKNOWN. Formerly hunted for eggs and feathers. With protection, populations recovering.

Laysan Albatross

Diomedea immutabilis

Identification: 32″ **Very large seabird; back and upperwings black; body white;** underwings white with variable black margins.

Feeding: Feeds on the ocean, eating mostly squid.

Nesting: Nest is a shallow scrape in the ground, with some debris around the rim. Eggs: 1, whitish; I: 65 days; F: 4–6 months, altricial; B: 1.

Other Behavior: Often follows boats for food. When on land, may need to run up to 100 yd. while taking off. Breeds in Hawaii.

Habitat: Open sea.

Voice: May squeal and scream when fighting over food with other birds.

Conservation: TREND UNKNOWN. Population decimated in early 1900s by feather collectors. Has started to recover, and species is now regularly seen off West Coast.

Northern Fulmar
Fulmarus glacialis

Light morph

Light morph

Dark morph

Identification: 19" A large gull-like bird generally seen only at sea. **Thick neck; stocky yellow bill; prominent rounded forehead;** pale "window" shows on upper outer wing. Varies in color from uniformly dark smoky gray (mostly in Pacific Ocean) to a white body with gray upperwings (mostly in Atlantic Ocean). **IN FLIGHT: Alternates flapping with gliding on stiff wings.**

Feeding: Feeds on the surface of the water, eating fish, jellyfish, shrimp, and other animal matter. Will occasionally dive as much as 6 ft. underwater in pursuit of food.

Nesting: Breeds colonially. Saucerlike nest on the shelf of a cliff or scraped in the ground, usually lined with fine material, and near or above the ocean; can also nest in holes or burrows. Eggs: 1, white with dark marks; I: 50–60 days; F: 46–51 days, altricial; B: 1.

Other Behavior: Often seen near fishing or seabirding boats. During breeding it feeds mostly at night. As a defense, both young and adults can vomit an oily substance on predators.

Habitat: Open sea; breeds along the far northern coasts. Occasionally blown to shore or found in harbors.

Voice: Usually silent at sea, but when competing for food may give a loud call like a low-pitched quack of a duck.

Conservation: CBC: ⇓

Pink-footed Shearwater
Flesh-footed Shearwater
Puffinus creatopus   Puffinus carneipes

Pink-footed

Flesh-footed

Identification: 19″ **PINK-FOOTED:** Largest of 3 regularly seen "white-bellied" shearwaters in West. **White belly and throat; grayish-brown upperparts; dark-tipped pink bill;** pink feet; white along center of underwings. **IN FLIGHT:** Wingbeat is slow and heavy, interspersed with some gliding. Wings are broad. **FLESH-FOOTED:** One of 3 regularly seen "dark-bellied" shearwaters in West. **Large; dark overall; pale bill and feet.** Flight like Pink-footed.

Pink-footed   Flesh-footed

Habitat: Open sea.

Voice: Pink-footed makes sounds when in flocks at sea.

Feeding: Feed on the surface of the ocean or through shallow dives, eating large squid, fish, and crustaceans.

Conservation:
Pink-footed:
CBC: ⇑
Flesh-footed:
TREND UNKNOWN.

Nesting: Colonial breeders. Pink-footed has shallow nest of grass at the end of a 6–10 ft. burrow. Eggs: 1, white; I: ?; F: 13 weeks, altricial; B: 1. Flesh-footed has shallow nest of bare earth at the end of a 1–2 ft. burrow. Eggs: 1, white; I: ?; F: 13 weeks, altricial; B: 1.

Other Behavior: Pink-footeds often follow fishing or bird-watching boats. They breed off the coast of Chile from Dec. to April, then stay north from late spring to fall. Flesh-footed Shearwater is usually seen in flocks of other shearwaters and is also attracted to boats at sea.

Buller's Shearwater

Puffinus bulleri

Identification: 18" One of 3 regularly seen "white-bellied" shearwaters on the West Coast. **Bright white below; dark slate-gray cap; bold gray and dark gray M-shaped pattern on its upperwings and back;** long wedge-shaped tail. IN FLIGHT: Slender wings and fast buoyant flight; long glides with very little flapping.

Feeding: Feeds on the surface of the ocean by alighting briefly and eating fish, crustaceans, and squid.

Nesting: Nests colonially. Saucerlike nest in a burrow. Eggs: 1, white; I: ?; F: ?, altricial; B: ?

Other Behavior: Seen mostly from midsummer to late fall. They often form flocks, but generally do not follow ships. On their breeding grounds, near New Zealand, they may share their nesting burrow with a large lizardlike reptile called a tautara; possibly both the bird and the reptile gain some benefit from the relationship.

Habitat: Open sea.

Voice: Generally quiet at sea.

Conservation: TREND UNKNOWN.

Sooty Shearwater
Short-tailed Shearwater
Puffinus griseus   Puffinus tenuirostris

Sooty

Short-tailed

Identification: 16" Two of the 3 "dark-bellied" shearwaters in the West. **SOOTY:** Most common of the 3. **Dark overall; dark bill and legs; silvery underwing linings,** which look like a flash of white as the bird lifts its wings in flight. **IN FLIGHT:** Quick wingbeats; some soaring and gliding. **SHORT-TAILED:** Difficult to distinguish from the Sooty. Best clues are its **shorter thinner bill, narrower wings, and rounder head.**

Feeding: Feed on the surface of the water, eating fish and squid. Sooty eats schooling anchovies. May dive for food and use their wings to help them swim underwater.

Nesting: Colonial breeders. Both have nests of dead leaves and twigs, placed at end of 3–4 ft. burrow. Eggs: 1, white; I: 52–56 days; F: 90–100 days, altricial; B: 1.

Other Behavior: Sooty Shearwater gathers in flocks of hundreds of thousands off the coast in late summer. Short-tailed Shearwater spends its summers off Alaska. It is seen off Calif. in winter, when it migrates to and from its breeding grounds, which are near Australia. Both species follow ships.

Sooty   Short-tailed

Habitat: Open sea.

Voice: Generally quiet on open sea.

Conservation:
Sooty:
CBC: ⇑
Short-tailed:
CBC: ↓

17

Black-vented Shearwater

Puffinus opisthomelas

Identification: 14" Smallest of the regularly seen "white-bellied" shearwaters in the West. **White below; dark brown above; grayish freckled face; dark bill.** Its name refers to its dark undertail coverts. **IN FLIGHT:** Being small, it has a more rapid wingbeat than the other, similar western shearwaters. Its flight is fluttery with little gliding.

Feeding: Feeds on the surface of the ocean and dives and swims underwater, eating fish, squid, and crustaceans.

Nesting: Colonial nester. Shallow nest of twigs and grass at the end of a 6–10 ft. burrow or in a cave. Eggs: 1, white; I: 51 days; F: 70–75 days, altricial; B: ?

Other Behavior: Often seen from shore along Calif. coastline summer through winter, for it prefers feeding in shallow water. Movements northward along coast vary from year to year.

Habitat: Open sea.

Voice: Generally quiet in open sea.

Conservation: TREND UNKNOWN. Vulnerable, since population breeds on only 2–3 islands off Baja Calif., Mex. Most of the population is on 1 island.

Fork-tailed Storm-Petrel
Oceanodroma furcata

Identification: 9″ The only light-colored storm-petrel in the West. **Pale blue-gray back and wings; pale belly; underwings dark in front and pale behind; dark patch around the eye. IN FLIGHT:** Flight is direct with rowing wingbeats.

Feeding: Feeds on the surface of the ocean, eating small fish.

Nesting: Colonial breeder. Nest on bare ground at the end of a 3 ft. burrow or in rock crevice on slope or at the bottom of a cliff. Eggs: 1, white with dark marks; I: 37–68 days; F: 51–61 days, altricial; B: 1.

Other Behavior: Breeds in summer on islands off the Northwest Coast. Largest colonies are in Gulf of Alaska. Like all N. Hemisphere storm-petrels, it comes to nesting colony after dark, to avoid gull predation. Sometimes visible from shore during stormy conditions, late fall to spring.

Habitat: Coastal islands and open sea.

Voice: Generally quiet when feeding at sea.

Conservation: TREND UNKNOWN. Introduced cats, rats, and foxes put island colonies at risk.

Leach's Storm-Petrel

Oceanodroma leucorhoa

Identification: 8″ **Triangular off-white rump patch** (sometimes narrowly divided in the center); **long forked tail.** Off S. Calif., some birds may have dark rumps; they are then distinguished from other dark storm-petrels by their flight behavior. **IN FLIGHT: Distinctive zigzag flight; alternates flaps with glides; wings narrow, pointed, and bent at the wrist.**

Feeding: Feeds by hovering just above the surface of the water, eating plankton, small fish, and squid.

Nesting: Colonial nester. Shallow nest of dry grasses and weed stems at the end of a 1–3 ft. burrow in a field or among rocks. Eggs: 1, white; I: 38–46 days; F: 63–70 days, altricial; B: 1.

Other Behavior: Does not usually follow ships and does not regularly patter its feet on the water when feeding. Nests on coastal islands and goes to and from the nest at night. This may help protect it from gulls, which rest at night. Feeds farther offshore than other storm-petrels. As in all storm-petrels, nestlings are fed a regurgitant of stomach oil. Introduced cats and rats put island colonies at risk.

Habitat: Coastal islands and far offshore; occasionally near shore during storms.

Voice: High purring and clucking notes given on breeding grounds at night; generally quiet out at sea.

Conservation: ICN: ↓

Ashy Storm-Petrel
Oceanodroma homochroa

Identification: 8″ One of the 3 **all-dark** storm-petrels in the West. Distinguished from the other 2 by its **medium size** and flight. In some lights, appears slightly grayer than Black and Least Storm-Petrels. **IN FLIGHT:** Often uses **rapid shallow wingbeat,** in which the wings move from just above to just below the body plane.

Feeding: Feeds on the surface of the ocean, eating small fish and crustaceans.

Nesting: Colonial breeder. Nest is bare ground in rock crevice or other natural cavity, such as piled rocks or driftwood. Eggs: 1, white; I: 44 days; F: ?, altricial; B: 1.

Other Behavior: Forms large mixed flocks (with Black Storm-Petrels) of thousands off the coast of Calif. near Monterey in late summer and fall; flocks often roost together on the water during the day. You may be able to smell the flocks from a distance because of their distinct, musky odor. In this and other storm-petrels, their well-developed sense of smell helps them locate their nesting burrow and food at sea.

Habitat: Coastal islands and open sea.

Voice: Generally quiet when out at sea.

Conservation: TREND UNKNOWN. Almost entire world population rafts up in Monterey Bay, Calif., each fall. This makes species vulnerable to oil spills.

Black Storm-Petrel
Least Storm-Petrel
Oceanodroma melania   Oceanodroma microsoma

Black

Least

Identification: Black 9", Least 6" **BLACK:**
Largest of the 3 **all-dark** storm-petrels on the
West Coast. Distinguish it from the others by its
large size and flight. IN FLIGHT: **Slow deep
wingbeats,** in which the wings move from high
above to far below the body plane. **LEAST:**
Smallest of the 3 **all-dark** storm-petrels seen on
the West Coast. Note its **sparrowlike size** and
flight. IN FLIGHT: **Quick deep wingbeats** as it
flies low over water. Appears tailless.

Feeding: Both species feed on the surface of the water,
hovering just above the waves at night. Black Storm-
Petrels eat small fish and crustaceans; Least Storm-
Petrels eat mostly plankton.

Nesting: Black Storm-Petrel breeds colonially. Shallow
nest of a few twigs in rock crevice, among boulders, or
in an abandoned burrow of Cassin's Auklets. Eggs: 1,
white; I: 18 days; F: ?, altricial; B: 1. Least Storm-Petrel
places nest on bare ground in crevice, on ledge, or
among stones. Eggs: 1, white; I: ?; F: ?; B: ?

Other Behavior: Breed on islands off the coast of
southern Calif. and Baja Peninsula.

Black   Least

Habitat: Coastal
islands and open
sea.

Voice: Generally
quiet when out at
sea.

Conservation:
Black:
TREND UNKNOWN.
Least:
TREND UNKNOWN.

American White Pelican

Pelecanus erythrorhynchos

Adult

Adult

Identification: 62″ Large white bird; large orange-yellow bill; orange-yellow throat pouch. Keellike growth occurs on middle of upper bill during breeding. **IN FLIGHT:** Trailing half of wings is black; soars gracefully. **IMM:** Similar to adult, but bill and throat pouch are gray and dark areas of wings brown. Imm. plumage kept 3–4 years.

Feeding: Feeds while swimming, dipping bill into the water to catch fish in its pouch. Usually feeds in small groups that may cooperatively herd fish toward shallow water where they are easier to catch.

Nesting: Nests colonially on large inland lakes. Nest a slight depression on bare ground, or a more elaborate mound of earth, brush stems, and debris. Eggs:1–3, white; I: 29–36 days; F: 21–28 days; B: 1.

Other Behavior: One of the largest birds in N. America; can soar for long distances and often flies in line or V formations. Over breeding grounds may do conspicuous flights involving soaring and diving.

Habitat: Summers on large inland lakes; winters along coast.

Voice: Generally quiet away from breeding grounds; young at nest can give loud whines or grunts.

Conservation: BBS: W ⇑ C ⇑ CBC: ⇑ Populations at some inland lakes are vulnerable to local drought.

Brown Pelican
Pelecanus occidentalis

Adult

Immature

Nonbreeding adult (l.), breeding adult (r.)

Identification: 45" A large coastal bird; gray-brown body and wings; large dark bill; dark throat pouch. Neck all white in nonbreeding adult; nape is brown in breeding adult. IMM: All dark with increasing amounts of white on head. Imm. plumage kept 3–4 years.

Feeding: Feeds by diving from the air into the water and catching fish in its throat pouch. This distinguishes it from the American White Pelican, which feeds while floating on the water. Imm. Brown Pelicans occasionally feed while swimming on the water.

Nesting: Nests colonially on coastal islands. Nest a rim of soil and debris 4–10 in. high on ground, or a saucerlike nest of sticks, grass, and reeds in the top of a mangrove tree. Eggs: 2–4, white; I: 28–30 days; F: 71–88 days, altricial; B: 1.

Other Behavior: Breeds, roosts, and feeds in flocks. Often flies in line formations high in the air or low over the water surface. When catching fish, scoops up fish and water, then surfaces and drains water out of pouch before swallowing fish.

Habitat: Coastal.

Voice: Adults usually quiet; at nest give a soft "check check." Young at nest can give loud barks and screams as they compete for food.

Conservation:
BBS: W ⇧ C CBC: ⇧ Loss of nesting habitat on coastal islands can threaten pop. Federally endangered in West.

24

Double-crested Cormorant

Phalacrocorax auritus

Adult

Immature

Identification: 33" Most commonly seen cormorant in the East and usually the only one seen well inland. **All black** with a **broad orange throat pouch.** "Double-crested" in name refers to crests that grow during breeding; they are hard to see. **IN FLIGHT: Neck is crooked** rather than straight as in other cormorants. **IMM:** Dark brown with light brown belly, light throat, and orange throat pouch. Imm. plumage kept 2–3 years.

Feeding: Feeds by diving and swimming underwater, eating mostly fish. May hold wings out to dry after diving in water.

Nesting: Nests colonially. Platform nest of sticks and seaweed lined with leafy twigs and grass, placed in a tree or on the ground. Eggs: 2–7, pale blue; I: 24–29 days; F: 35–42 days, altricial; B: 1.

Other Behavior: Can be seen soaring high, using rising thermals of air to gain altitude and then coasting on a long glide. May have trouble taking off from land and water, often needing to run along the water to gain speed. After fishing, often stands with wings outstretched to dry. Flocks often fly in line or V formations.

Habitat: Coasts, inland rivers, and lakes.

Voice: Silent away from nest; at nest can give a variety of deep croaks and grunts.

Conservation: BBS: W ⇑ C ⇑ CBC: ⇑ Populations rapidly recovering from pesticide-caused declines.

Brandt's Cormorant

Phalacrocorax penicillatus

Adults

Immature

Identification: 34" **All dark** with a **patch of beige feathers on the chin;** throat pouch turns bright blue during breeding. Distinguished from Double-crested Cormorant by lack of orange throat pouch and in flight by its straight neck. **Imm:** All dark brown with a pale whitish patch on chin. Imm. plumage kept 2–3 years.

Feeding: Feeds by diving and swimming underwater, eating small saltwater fish.

Nesting: Colonial nester. Saucerlike nest of seaweed and other marine vegetation, placed on rocky ground. Eggs: 3–6, pale blue; I: ?; F: ?, altricial; B: 1.

Other Behavior: Stays in flocks throughout the year. May be seen engaging in "feeding frenzies," in which a flock cooperatively pursues a large school of fish. Often feeds just offshore. Like many other cormorants, it may be seen flying in long line formations as it moves from roosting to feeding areas. The most frequently seen cormorant offshore.

Habitat: Coastal.

Voice: Silent away from nest; at nest can give a variety of deep croaks and grunts.

Conservation:
BBS: W ⇓ C CBC: ⇑

Pelagic Cormorant

Phalacrocorax pelagicus

Summer

Winter

Identification: 27" The smallest and slenderest of the western cormorants; lacks a visible throat pouch. **SUMMER:** During breeding has **white patch on flanks** and develops **2 distinct crests — on the crown and the nape;** red facial skin. **WINTER: All dark with a lack of any obvious facial markings. IMM:** All dark brown with no facial markings and no contrasting lighter areas. Imm. plumage kept 2 years. ➤On southwestern Alaska coast, the similar Red-faced Cormorant, *P. urile,* has red facial skin and a partly yellow bill.

Feeding: Feeds by diving and swimming underwater, eating mostly fish but also crabs and crustaceans.

Nesting: Nests colonially. Platform nest of sticks, seaweed, and moss, placed on high, steep cliff above water or seaside building. Eggs: 3–7, pale blue; I: 26–31 days; F: ?, altricial; B: 1.

Other Behavior: Pelagic Cormorants have been known to dive 180 ft. underwater. Nests are used year after year, with new material added each time, making some nests several feet high.

Habitat: Rocky shores with cliffs, and other coastal areas.

Voice: Silent away from nest; at nest can give a loud groan.

Conservation: BBS: W ↑ C CBC: ↓ Because of their deep dives after fish, cormorants are sometimes caught in fishing nets.

American Bittern
Botaurus lentiginosus

Identification: 25ʺ A stocky bird with **brown streaking underneath** and a sometimes visible **black streak extending down neck from base of bill.** IN FLIGHT: Brown back and dark outer wings. IMM: Similar to adult, but lacks black streak. Imm. plumage kept into winter.

Feeding: Solitary feeder. Stands or walks extremely slowly, then strikes prey with lightning stab. Diet includes lots of fish; also reptiles, amphibians, insects, and small mammals.

Nesting: Nests singly, but nests have been found within 40 yd. of each other. Platform nest composed of cattails, sticks, grasses, placed in dense marsh vegetation a few inches above water. Eggs: 2–7, buffy olive-brown; I: 28–29 days; F: leave nest at 14 days, time of first flight unknown, altricial; B: 1.

Other Behavior: When standing or when alarmed, bitterns often assume a posture with neck elongated and bill pointed straight up so that they appear camouflaged, blending into the vegetation around them. Sometimes they gently sway while holding this position. Males may be polygamous. Secretive birds.

Habitat: Freshwater or brackish marshes with tall vegetation.

Voice: During breeding male gives a booming "pumper-lunk" call. Sounds like an old-fashioned hand pump. Alarm call is "kok-kok-kok."

Conservation: BBS: W ⇓ C ⇓ CBC: ↓ Loss of wetlands is causing declining populations.

Least Bittern

Ixobrychus exilis

Male

Identification: 13″ Our smallest heron. **Dark crown and back; rich buff underparts. MALE:** Crown and back are black. **FEMALE:** Crown and back are rich brown. **IN FLIGHT:** Note **buffy inner wing patches**. Flies weakly with quick wingbeats.

Feeding: Stalks through the reeds in crouched posture or stands in place, and sometimes sways neck. Eats small fish, frogs, insects, small mammals, and sometimes bird eggs and chicks.

Nesting: Small platform of sticks and live or dead vegetation, placed in cattails, bulrushes, or bushes 8–14 in. above water. Eggs: 2–7, pale blue or greenish white; I: 19–20 days; F: up to 25 days, altricial; B: 2.

Other Behavior: This is a secretive bird. Will flutter briefly above reeds. Climbs in and even runs through reeds 2–3 feet above water. Alarm posture with bill pointing skyward like that of American Bittern. In courtship, males give cooing sounds.

Habitat: Marshes that include dense vegetation, like sedges and cattails; salt marshes.

Voice: Male gives guttural "uh-uh-uh-oo-oo-oo-ooah," female makes ticking sound. Both give "tut-tut."

Conservation: BBS: W C ⇓ CBC: ⇑ Declining due to loss of wetlands.

Great Blue Heron
Ardea herodias

Dark morph

White morph

Identification: 50" Our largest and most widespread heron. **Grayish-blue body; white head; black stripe over the eye.** IMM: Similar to adult, except head has solid black cap, which gradually changes to white. Imm. plumage kept 2 years. ➤Rare white morph of Great Blue Heron, the "Great White Heron," is entirely white with legs and bill orangy yellow; it is limited to S. Fla.

Feeding: Feeds in shallow water by standing or walking slowly, then grabbing small fish, frogs, birds, and aquatic insects with its bill. Can feed in deeper water by plunging or swimming. Also hunts on land for small mammals. Individuals may form temporary feeding territories up to several hundred yd. in diameter which they defend.

Nesting: Breeds in generally small colonies in isolated areas or singly. Large platform nest of sticks lined with finer twigs and vegetation, placed in trees or shrubs 30–70 ft. above ground. Eggs: 3–7, pale bluish green; I: 28 days; F: 55–60 days, altricial; B: 1.

Other Behavior: Males display from nest sites with neck arched over back, bill pointing up.

Habitat: Marshes, swamps, river and lake edges, tidal flats, mangroves, other water areas.

Voice: Harsh guttural "frahnk" or short "rok-rok" call given during aggression. Both sexes do bill clacking.

Conservation:
BBS: W ↓ C ⇑ CBC: ⇑

Great Egret
Ardea alba

Identification: 39″ **A large white heron** with a **yellow bill** and **black legs.** Immature is similar to adult. In breeding season adults of both sexes have long white plumes growing on their back.

Feeding: Primarily feeds by walking slowly, head erect, then striking prey. Forages in shallow water for small fish and amphibians, but also on land for insects, reptiles, and small mammals. May feed solitarily and defend feeding areas by displaying aggressively and supplanting intruders. Also feeds in large groups when food is concentrated. Has been known to steal fish from other birds.

Nesting: Nests in colonies with other herons, ibises, and cormorants or singly. Nest is flimsy platform of sticks, twigs, and reeds, placed in tree or shrub 8–40 ft. above ground or in cattails 1–4 ft. above water. Eggs: 1–6, pale bluish green; I: 23–26 days; F: 42–49 days, altricial; B: 1.

Other Behavior: Among this and other herons, greeting ceremonies between pair include calls, head stretched up and over back with bill skyward, and bill clacking, in which mandibles are snapped open and shut.

Habitat: Marshes, swamps, seashores, lake margins.

Voice: A deep, rattlelike croak.

Conservation:
BBS: W ⇑ C ⇑ CBC: ↑
At turn of century, hunted for plumes used in feather trade. Since decline of hunting and ban on DDT, which had led to eggshell thinning, population has increased.

Snowy Egret
Egretta thula

Adult

Immature

Identification: 24″ **White body; black bill; black legs with bright yellow feet.** During breeding, the feet and facial skin in front of the eye turn orange or red. **IMM:** Like nonbreeding adult, but legs black in front and yellow in back. Bright yellow facial skin at base of bill clearly distinguishes it from the similar imm. Little Blue Heron. Imm. plumage kept 1 year.

Feeding: Very active. Often feeds in flocks and in aggregations with other species. Has diverse foraging techniques: walking slowly or quickly, running or hopping, and using its feet to stir, rake, or probe food from bottom. Can vibrate bill in water to attract fish. Eats shrimp, fish, crabs, amphibians, snakes, and insects.

Nesting: Nests in large colonies of thousands, singly or with other herons in small colonies. Sticks and twigs compose a platform, which is placed on the ground or in tree or shrub 5–10 ft. high. Eggs: 3–5, pale bluish green; I: 20–29 days; F: 30 days, altricial; B: 1.

Other Behavior: Aggressively defends nest and feeding sites with calls, displays such as raising crest, and fights. Communal nighttime roosts outside breeding season.

Habitat: Coastal areas, marshes, river valleys, lake edges.

Voice: In breeding colonies, "wah-wah-wah"; during aggression a harsh "aah."

Conservation: BBS: W ⇑ C ⇑ CBC: ⇑ Hunted to near extinction in late 1800s, for plumes. With protection, population now expanding.

Little Blue Heron

Egretta caerulea

Immature (l.), adult (r.)

Identification: 27" **Dark overall; purplish head; blue gray body and wings; bill two toned** blue-gray at the base with a darker tip. **Imm:** All white with greenish-yellow legs and a two-toned bill like the adult's. Gray facial skin at the base of the bill distinguishes it from the similar imm. Snowy Egret. White becomes blotched with blue-gray as bird changes to adult plumage. Imm. plumage kept 1 year.

Feeding: Stealthily walks through shallow waters and peers down looking for prey. Eats fish, insects, amphibians. May follow other birds and catch prey stirred up by them.

Nesting: Nests colonially, often with other heron species. Nest of sticks and twigs is placed in tree or shrub 10–15 ft. above the water. Eggs: 2–5, pale bluish green; I: 20–24 days; F: 42–49 days, altricial; B: 1.

Other Behavior: Males may mate with females on neighboring territories.

Habitat: Swamps, inland marshes, and coastal areas.

Voice: During courtship a rattling chatter; low-pitched "aarh" during aggressive interactions.

Conservation:
BBS: W ⇓ C ↓ CBC: ↓ Spared during plume trade because it does not have long breeding plumes.

Tricolored Heron
Egretta tricolor

Identification: 26" **Dark blue-gray heron** with a **white belly and underwings;** white stripe down the front of the neck. Bill color varies from dark on top and yellow beneath to gray at base and darker at tip. **IMM:** Similar to adult, but brown mottling on neck and wings. Imm. plumage kept 1 year.

Feeding: Wades belly-deep in water. In addition to stalking prey by walking, it also runs or hops with wings open. Eats fish, amphibians, insects.

Nesting: Nests in large colonies, often with other herons. Platform nest of sticks and twigs lined with finer vegetation, placed in tree or shrub 6–15 ft. above the ground. Eggs: 3–7, pale bluish green; I: 21–25 days; F: 35 days, altricial; B: 1.

Other Behavior: Courtship involves circle flights, chases, and displays during which neck feathers, back feathers, and crest are raised. Bill clacking is frequent.

Habitat: Marshes, shores, mudflats, tidal creeks.

Voice: Guttural "unh" and "culh-culh" given during courtship displays. High-pitched "aah" given during aggression.

Conservation: BBS: W C ⇑ CBC: ↑ Spared by plume trade because its plume color was not popular.

Cattle Egret

Bubulcus ibis

Identification: 20" Common small heron. **White overall; short, stocky, yellow-orange bill;** legs vary from orange to yellow-green. Breeding adult has buffy-orange plumes on head, back, and breast. **IMM:** Similar to nonbreeding adult, except with dark gray legs. Imm. plumage kept until next spring.

Feeding: Typically seen away from water, feeding in fields, lawns, and along highways. Eats insects, amphibians, reptiles, mollusks. Often follows cattle or horses, watching for insects they stir up.

Nesting: In same-species colonies or with other herons. Platform nest of sticks, twigs, and reeds, placed in shrub or tree 3–30 ft. above the ground. Eggs: 2–6, bluish white; I: 21–24 days; F: 30 days, altricial; B: 1.

Other Behavior: Originally most likely from Africa, this species has widely expanded its range. It first flew across the Atlantic and spread to S. America in 1880. By 1942 it was seen in Fla. and was nesting there by the early 1950s. Deforestation and cultivation have continued to provide it with favorable habitat. It is now widespread across the country.

Habitat: Open dry areas, lawns, fields, pastures with livestock.

Voice: In colonies, a "rick-rack" call. When alarmed, gives "kok" call.

Conservation: BBS: W ⇧ C ↑ CBC: ⇧ May displace some native species of herons at breeding sites.

Green Heron

Butorides virescens

Adult

Immature

Identification: 19″ Small all-dark heron; compact shape; blue-green back; reddish-brown neck and chest; short bright yellow to orange legs. Looks short-necked because it holds its head close to its body. **IMM:** Similar to adult, but with brown streaking on neck and belly; wing feathers may have buff dots at tips. Distinguished from imm. night-herons by smaller size, darker back, and longer pointed bill. Imm. plumage kept 1 year.

Feeding: Crouches in branches on shore and waits for prey or wades stealthily. May also plunge or jump or stir up bottom with foot. Has been known to place an object such as a twig or insect on water to lure prey to surface. Eats fish, insects, crabs.

Nesting: Nests singly or in small colony. Nest of sticks, placed in tree or grass hummock. Eggs: 3–6, pale blue-green; I: 21–25 days; F: 34–35 days, altricial; B: 1–2.

Other Behavior: Does crest raising and tail flicking when excited. Courtship involves pursuit and circle flights. Duets of "skow"call occur between the sexes.

Habitat: Shores and water edges with dense vegetation, salt marshes, streams.

Voice: "Skow" call is commonly given when flushed and in flight. Aggressive call is "raah."

Conservation: BBS: W ⇑ C ↑ CBC: ↑

Black-crowned Night-Heron

Nycticorax nycticorax

Adult

Immature

Identification: 25 " **Gray-and-white stocky heron; black cap; black back.** Short pale yellow legs turn reddish in breeding season. **Imm:** Brown with white streaks below; large buffy-white spots on back and wings. Told from imm. Yellow-crowned Night-Heron by its greenish-yellow lower bill (Yellow-crowned has all-dark bill); Black-crowned also has a comparatively longer, thinner bill. Imm. plumage kept 2 years.

Feeding: Although it can feed by day, this species feeds mostly at night or at dusk, either on individual feeding territories or in aggregations. Diet consists of fish, amphibians, insects, and small mammals. Eats the young of other bird species such as terns, herons, and ibises.

Nesting: In colonies or singly. Nest consists of coarse twigs, reeds, and finer material and is placed against a tussock, or in reeds, shrub, or tree up to 160 ft. high. Eggs: 3–5, pale blue-green; I: 24–26 days; F: 42–49 days, altricial; B: 1.

Other Behavior: In greeting ceremony, birds stretch necks horizontally with breeding plumes on head raised and they touch bills. Roosts in trees during the day.

Habitat: Diverse — freshwater streams, lakes, rice fields, dry grasslands, salt marshes.

Voice: Low, hoarse "quok" often heard at dusk. During nesting, "rok-rok."

Conservation: BBS: W ⇑ C ⇓ CBC: ⇑

Yellow-crowned Night-Heron

Nyctanassa violacea

Adult

Immature

Identification: 24" **Stocky gray heron; black head; buffy-white crown.** Also has a white cheek patch, a dark stocky bill, and yellow legs. **Imm:** Grayish brown overall with fine white streaks on breast and fine white dots on back and wings. Best told from imm. Black-crowned Night-Heron by its stocky all-dark bill (Black-crowned has yellowish lower bill). Imm. plumage kept 2 years.

Feeding: Feeds mostly at night, but sometimes during day. Eats a large number of crustaceans, particularly fiddler crabs and crayfish. Also eats fish, insects, mammals, and small birds.

Nesting: Solitary or in small colony with other herons. Substantial platform of coarse sticks lined with finer twigs and leaves, on ground or in tree or shrub up to 40 ft. high. Eggs: 3–5, pale bluish green; I: 21–25 days; F: 25 days, altricial; B: 1.

Other Behavior: Greeting ceremonies include crest raising, calls, bill clacking. Lots of display flights and chases occur in colonies. Roosts in tall trees or shrubs.

Habitat: Coastal as well as ponds, swamps, rivers, parkland.

Voice: Has many calls. "Quack" call is higher pitched and less harsh than Black-crowned Night-Heron's; flight call is "scaup"; a whoop is given during nest displays.

Conservation:
BBS: W C ↓ CBC: ↑

White Ibis
Eudocimus albus

Adult

Immature

Identification: 25″ **Large, white, long-legged bird; long, downcurved, reddish bill.** During breeding, bill, facial skin, and legs turn bright red. **IN FLIGHT:** Wings show black tips. **IMM:** White belly and rump; brownish head and back; dark wings. Dark areas gradually change to white. Bill is pink. Imm. plumage kept 1 year.

Feeding: Feeds in groups or alone in shallow fresh or salt water. Probes the bottom with its bill. Eats crayfish, mudcrabs, frogs, and aquatic insects.

Nesting: Nests in large colonies of thousands. Loose nest of sticks and twigs, placed in tree or shrub, occasionally in low vegetation such as sawgrass and bulrushes. Eggs: 3–5, greenish white with dark marks; I: 21–23 days; F: 28–35 days, altricial; B: 1.

Other Behavior: Flies with neck outstretched. Flocks go to large nocturnal roosts at sunset in long lines or V's. This bird can also soar in circles. Other birds, such as Little Blue Herons and Great Egrets, may follow feeding White Ibises and snatch prey they have scared up.

Habitat: Salt and freshwater lakes, marshes, swamps, tidal mudflats, shores.

Voice: Mostly quiet. Alarm call is nasal "hunk, hunk, hunk."

Conservation: BBS: W C ⇑ CBC: ⇑

White-faced Ibis

Plegadis chihi

Summer

Winter

Identification: 23″ Large, dark, long-legged bird with a long downcurved bill. SUMMER: Chestnut head and neck; red facial skin around base of bill; thin line of white feathers surrounding the back of the reddish eye. WINTER: Streaked gray-brown head and neck; reddish eye; dark facial skin. IMM: Similar to winter adult, but duller. Indistinguishable from imm. Glossy Ibis. Imm. plumage kept 1½ years.

Feeding: Prefers to feed in freshwater marshes. Wades and probes in shallow water. Consumes crayfish, crabs, frogs, insects, snails, fish.

Nesting: In small colonies, usually with other herons. Nest is deep cup of dead reeds and sticks lined with grass, on floating mat of dead plants or attached several ft. above water to bulrushes, shrub. Eggs: 3–4, bluish green; I: 21–22 days; F: 28 days, altricial; B: 1.

Other Behavior: Flies in lines or compact groups. Direct flight with short intervals of gliding. May circle high in air, then rapidly plunge down with feet dangling.

Habitat: Freshwater and brackish marshes.

Voice: Nasal grunting.

Conservation: BBS: W ⇑ C ⇑ CBC: ⇑ Loss of wetlands and pesticide use is leading to declines in population. Populations now recovering in Ore., Calif., and Nev.

Wood Stork
Mycteria americana

Adults

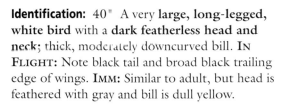
Adult

Identification: 40" A very **large, long-legged, white bird** with a **dark featherless head and neck**; thick, moderately downcurved bill. **IN FLIGHT:** Note black tail and broad black trailing edge of wings. **IMM:** Similar to adult, but head is feathered with gray and bill is dull yellow.

Feeding: Feeds in shallow, often muddy water by wading and groping along the bottom with its bill. Food includes small fish, frogs, snakes, small alligators, and other aquatic animals.

Nesting: In colonies. Many nests can be in same tree. Flimsy platform of sticks lined with finer material and placed in tree, preferably large cypress or mangrove, several feet above the water. Eggs: 3–4, dull white; I: 28–32 days; F: 55–60 days, altricial; B: 1.

Other Behavior: Breeding cycle may be triggered by food supply. After rains decrease and marshes dry, fish are concentrated and more available to storks, and breeding starts. If there is too much rain, and high water precludes concentration of prey, storks may skip breeding or desert eggs.

Habitat: Swamps, coastal shallows, ponds, flooded pastures.

Voice: Mostly quiet. Young have gooselike flocking note.

Conservation:
CBC: ↓
Endangered in U.S. Declines due to loss of nesting and feeding sites. Restoration efforts are under way.

41

Black Vulture
Coragyps atratus

Adult

Immature

Identification: 25" IN FLIGHT: In all plumages, **large black bird; pale whitish primary feathers; short tail.** Soars with wings held in a slight dihedral; does not rock from side to side as does Turkey Vulture; periodically gives 3–4 rapid flaps. PERCHED—ADULT: A **large black bird; naked, wrinkled, gray head;** pale bill. IMM: Similar to adult, but head black, smooth, and covered with fine down; bill all dark. Imm. plumage kept 1 year.

Feeding: Feeds by scavenging on carrion in the wild or in urban areas. Finds food by sight alone, whether perched or in flight; flies higher than Turkey Vulture and may watch it and follow it to prey.

Nesting: Nest on bare ground in cave, on cliff ledge, in hollow stump, or under vegetation. Eggs: 1–3, pale greenish white with dark marks; I: 37–48 days; F: 70 days, altricial; B: 1.

Other Behavior: Roosts communally, sometimes at same spots as Turkey Vultures. When perched, may hold wings out in the sun as does Turkey Vulture.

Habitat: Open country, dumps, urban areas.

Voice: Hisses, grunts, and snarls heard near the nest site and when birds are competing over food.

Conservation: BBS: W ⇓ C ↑ CBC: ↑

Turkey Vulture
Cathartes aura

Adult

Immature

Identification: 26" IN FLIGHT: In all plumages, large all-dark bird; trailing half of wings silver. During soar, wings held in a V; bird rocks side to side and rarely flaps. Has a smaller head and longer tail than Black Vulture. PERCHED—ADULT: Large all-dark bird; naked red head; pale bill. IMM: Like adult, but small head is gray; bill at first all dark, changing to pale with a dark tip. Imm. plumage kept 1 year.

Feeding: Feeds by scavenging on carrion, fresh or decayed. Finds food by sight and smell while soaring.

Nesting: Nest a scrape on bare ground, in hollow stump, cave, cliff ledge, or old building. Eggs: 1–3, dull white, occasionally with dark marks; I: 38–41 days; F: 70–80 days, altricial; B: 1.

Other Behavior: Turkey Vultures are often seen coming to and from nightly communal roosts, which may be located on tall buildings or towers and in large trees. The birds use thermals of warm air and updrafts off ridges to stay aloft; when these are no longer available and they need to flap, they usually stop flying and land.

Habitat: Open country and dumps, occasionally roosts in urban areas.

Voice: Grunts and hisses heard at nest site and often during competition over food.

Conservation:
BBS: W ↑ C ↑ CBC: ⇑

Fulvous Whistling-Duck

Dendrocygna bicolor

Identification: 20″ **Rich buffy head and body; dark back and wings; dark bill.** White feathers create lines along the flanks. In Flight: Note buffy belly, black wings, and white patch on rump. Flies with head and feet lower than body, and feet extended well beyond the tail, as does Black-bellied Whistling-Duck.

Feeding: Primarily feeds at night in marshes and rice fields. Eats aquatic plants, grass and weed seeds, alfalfa, and waste grain.

Nesting: Nest of reeds lined with grasses and weeds is placed on the ground in dense vegetation or grass hummock, rarely in tree cavity. Eggs: 12–14, dull white; I: 24–26 days; F: 55–63 days, precocial; B: 1.

Other Behavior: Highly social. Usually found in groups. Female may lay eggs in other female's nest. Up to 100 eggs laid by several females were found in 1 nest. Often the duck will desert the nest. This intraspecific brood parasitism occurs in many duck species.

Habitat: Wet agricultural land, ponds, and marshes.

Voice: Flight call a whistling, loud "kaweee."

Conservation: BBS: W ⇓ C ⇑ CBC:→ Population declines in parts of its range due to habitat destruction and pesticide use.

Black-bellied Whistling-Duck
Dendrocygna autumnalis

Identification: 21" **Gray head; broad white eye-ring; bright red bill;** dark reddish-brown body; contrasting buff and white on wings. **IN FLIGHT:** Broad white streak down the center of upperwings; dark belly. Flies with head and feet lower than body. **IMM:** Similar to the adult, but bill is dark gray and rich brown areas of adult are gray and brown. Imm. plumage kept until following spring.

Feeding: Does much terrestrial grazing. Eats mostly sorghum grain, Bermuda grass seeds, and other plant material. Rarely mollusks and insects.

Nesting: Nest of rotted wood chips in tree cavity or nest box 8–30 ft. above the ground. May also nest on ground among vegetation. Eggs: 12–14, white; I: 25–30 days; F: 53–63 days, precocial; B: 2.

Other Behavior: Seen in large flocks. Tree nest is placed next to herbaceous plants so ducklings have soft landing spot when they jump from nest at 1 day old.

Habitat: Woodland ponds and marshes.

Voice: A series of 3–4 whistles, often given in flight.

Conservation:
BBS: W C ⇑ CBC: ⇑

Tundra Swan
Cygnus columbianus

Identification: 53″ Body all white; bill black with a small yellow dash before the eye; yellow dash not always present. The black facial skin narrows to a point before touching the eye, leaving eye more isolated on face than in the larger Trumpeter Swan. Head and neck may appear rusty due to iron staining in northern lakes. **IMM:** All-white body and neck; brownish head; pink bill with a dark tip and nostril. Imm. plumage kept until following spring.

Feeding: Eats aquatic vegetation, mollusks. In winter also eats grain.

Nesting: Platform nest of grasses and mosses, placed on an elevated hummock on small island. Eggs: 2–7, dull white; I: 35–40 days; F: 60–70 days, precocial; B: 1.

Other Behavior: Assembles in large flocks, sometimes in the thousands, to feed or rest.

Habitat: Summers on tundra; winters on lakes, ponds, open marshes.

Voice: High-pitched whistling "kow-wow."

Conservation: CBC: ⇑

Trumpeter Swan
Cygnus buccinator

Adult

Immature

Adult bill detail

Identification: 65″ **Body white; bill all black.** The black facial skin broadly touches the eye, making the two seem more connected than in the similar Tundra Swan. **IMM:** Grayish brown overall, with a pink bill that is dark at the tip and broadly dark at the base. Imm. plumage kept through following spring.

Feeding: Feeds by plunging its head and neck underwater, or tipping body bottom-up, like a duck, so that it can reach plants on the bottom. Can also dig a hole with its feet on pond bottom to get at roots of plants. Eats aquatic vegetation, mollusks.

Nesting: Platform nest of reeds, grasses, and sedges, placed along the shore, or on muskrat or beaver house. Eggs: 2–9, creamy white; I: 33–37 days; F: 91–120 days, precocial; B: 1.

Other Behavior: Defends nesting territory from other swans but will let ducks nest nearby. May, at times, have to compete with introduced Mute Swan. Named for the loud trumpeting "koo-hoo" call, which can be heard for a mile or more.

Habitat: Summers on lakes, ponds, and large rivers; winters also along the coast.

Voice: A resonant trumpeting "koo-hoo."

Conservation: BBS: W ⇑ C CBC: ⇑ Once nearly extinct; populations now recovering.

Mute Swan

Cygnus olor

Adult

Immature

Identification: 55″ **Body white; bill pink to orange with black knob at base.** Swims with unique posture of neck in an S-curve and often with wings slightly raised over back. **Imm:** Light brownish with an all-dark bill. Imm. plumage kept 1 year.

Feeding: Eats leafy parts of fresh- and saltwater plants, algae, waste grain.

Nesting: Nest is a large pile of herbaceous vegetation lined with feathers, placed near water. Eggs: 4–8, pale grayish green; I: 35–38 days; F: 115–155 days, precocial; B: 1.

Other Behavior: Usually seen in city parks, but also seen in the wild. This native to Europe and Great Britain was brought to the U.S. in 1800s and stocked on estates and parks. Escapes developed into the wild population. The name "mute" was given because this swan is usually silent. It does not have the same vocal structure as our native swans and can only make hissing and snorting sounds. In flight, its wings make a repeated droning sound; our other swans have quiet wingbeats.

Habitat: Lakes, parks, coastal bays.

Voice: Usually silent.

Conservation: CBC: ⇑ In some coastal areas, Mute Swans are beginning to aggressively compete for food with native species of waterfowl.

Greater White-fronted Goose

Anser albifrons

Identification: 30″ A dark-headed goose with a pink or orange bill. "White-fronted" refers to the ring of white feathers at base of bill. Variable black barring on the light brown belly; legs and feet orange. **In Flight:** Note black patches on belly and dark upperwings. **Imm:** Also dark-headed goose with a pink bill. Lacks the white on face and barring on the belly. Imm. plumage kept through following spring.

Feeding: Feeds on grasses, sedges, and grains such as wheat, rice, and barley, and on new growth in burned meadows.

Nesting: Nests in open wet tundra on hummocks or elevated ground. Nest of sticks, grasses, mosses, and down is placed in hollowed-out depression. Eggs: 4–7, creamy white; I: 22–28 days; F: 42–49 days, precocial; B: 1.

Other Behavior: Flocks may contain thousands. May also mix with Canada Geese on migration and in wintering areas, feeding in fields with them. Courtship and aggressive behavior can be seen in wintering flocks.

Habitat: Summers on tundra lakes and rivers; winters on wetlands, fields, and agricultural land.

Voice: High-pitched "leek-leek" call.

Conservation:
CBC: ⇑
Declining in Pacific flyway.

Snow Goose

Chen caerulescens

Dark-morph adult (l.), light-morph immature (ctr.), light-morph adult (r.)

Adults

Identification: 29″ **White goose with a pink bill.** Best distinguished from much smaller Ross' Goose by proportions; it has a **longer neck and bill** and **flatter head.** The two are often seen together on wintering grounds. **IN FLIGHT:** Black wing tips are prominent in flight, less so when bird is at rest. **IMM:** Light morph is light gray with dark legs and bill. Dark morph is all dark. Imm. plumage kept until following spring. ➤Dark morph, called "Blue Goose," has a pink bill, white head and upper neck, and dark body and wings. Larger eastern form, "Greater Snow Goose," winters along Atlantic Coast and often has orange (due to iron staining) on head.

Habitat: Summers on tundra; winters on agricultural fields and wetlands.

Voice: A high-pitched honking.

Conservation: CBC: ⇓

Feeding: Digs up the roots and tubers of aquatic plants. Also feeds on waste grain and tender shoots of grasses.

Nesting: Highly colonial. Nest of grasses and down is placed near the water. Eggs: 3–5, white; I: 23–25 days; F: 40–49 days, precocial; B: 1.

Other Behavior: Winters in large flocks that can number in the tens of thousands.

Ross' Goose
Chen rossii

Light-morph adults

Identification: 24″ **A small white goose with a stubby pink bill.** Best distinguished from the larger Snow Goose by proportions; it is 25% smaller, with a **shorter neck and bill** and **rounder head.** The very rare "blue" morph has a pink bill, a white face and belly, and a dark body and wings. **IN FLIGHT:** Black wing tips are prominent in flight, less so when the bird is at rest. **IMM:** Light morph is similar to adult, but with a grayish wash on the head. Imm. plumage kept until following spring.

Feeding: Feeds on grasses and waste grains.

Nesting: Nests primarily on islands in lakes as a protection from mammalian predators. Concentrated nests average 15 ft. apart. Nest of grasses and mosses, concealed under vegetation. Eggs: 3–5, white; I: 21–24 days; F: 45 days, precocial; B: 1.

Other Behavior: Mostly seen in small numbers amid larger flocks of Snow Geese on wintering grounds.

Habitat: Summers on tundra; winters on agricultural fields and wetlands.

Voice: Higher-pitched honking than Snow Goose.

Conservation: CBC: ⇑

Brant
Branta bernicla

Western subspecies *(B. b. nigricans)*

Eastern subspecies *(B. b. hrota)*

Identification: 24″ The **all-black head and bill** distinguish this **small goose** from others. Black neck, back, and wings; white rump; whitish sides with gray barring; and a belly that is white (in East) or dusky (in West). Thin white markings on either side of neck can be hard to see at a distance; they meet in front of neck in western subspecies. IN FLIGHT: Note black head, neck, and chest; large white rump patch.

Habitat: Summers on high arctic coast; winters on coastal waters.

Feeding: Feeds on sedges, grasses, arctic plants, sea lettuce and other algae, and eelgrass.

Voice: Soft "ruk-ruk" calls.

Conservation: CBC: ⇓

Nesting: Semicolonial. Nests along shore of pond or stream, or on small island. Nest of seaweeds, grasses, and down is placed in low cover. Eggs: 3–5, dull white; I: 22–26 days; F: 40–50 days, precocial; B: 1.

Other Behavior: Highly social. Flocks fly low over water in long wavy lines. Courtship occurs on wintering areas. Early spring storms on breeding grounds can cause nest desertion and consequent population drop since females do not renest. Pacific populations now heavily dependent on Mexican (Baja Calif.) lagoons for wintering.

Canada Goose

Branta canadensis

Identification: 25–45 " The most widespread and commonly seen goose. Look for its **black head and neck** and **white chinstrap.** Otherwise, brownish gray except for white rump. Varies greatly in size, with smallest forms living farthest north. **IN FLIGHT:** Note black neck and white chinstrap.

Feeding: Feeds on the ground and in the water. Eats submergent vegetation, grasses, winter wheat, clovers, and waste grain, especially corn.

Nesting: Nests at edges of ponds, lakes, or swamps, on rocks or grass hummocks out in the water. Nest made of sticks, mosses, and grasses lined with down. Eggs: 4–7, white; I: 28 days; F: 2–3 weeks, precocial; B: 1.

Other Behavior: Breeding range has increased due to management programs. Some birds that used to migrate now overwinter because food is provided for them by people at local ponds. Although this is a pleasant activity, it creates a major problem in many parks, golf courses, and public lands where the geese foul lawns, overgraze the grass, and may become aggressive during breeding.

Habitat: Summers on lakes, marshes; winters on lakes, bays, fields, parks.

Voice: Male gives "ahonk." Female duets with higher "hink" call.

Conservation: BBS: W ⇑ C ⇑ CBC: ↑ Subspecies Aleutian Canada Goose is endangered in U.S. All other populations increasing.

53

Wood Duck

Aix sponsa

Male

Female

Identification: 18″ **Male: Distinctive colorful head; white throat, partial neck-ring, and chinstrap** all connected. Large crest is green, bill is pink, and eye is red. In eclipse plumage, male is similar to female but retains a suggestion of the white facial markings. **Female: Brownish gray** with a darker crown and **broad white eye-ring** that tapers to a point in back. **In Flight:** Large head; long square tail; distinctive flight call.

Feeding: Feeds on the surface of the water, eating mostly aquatic plants like duckweed. Also eats insects, minnows, frogs, and feeds in wild rice marshes.

Nesting: Nest of wood chips and down is in natural tree cavity or human-made box 5–50 ft. above the ground or water. Eggs: 10–15, dull white; I: 27–30 days; F: 56–70 days, precocial; B: 1–2.

Other Behavior: Watch for many courtship displays, which take place through fall and winter. In inciting, female repeatedly flicks bill back over shoulder. Done near her mate and directed at intruding male. Her mate responds by raising wings and tail, turning the back of his head to her, and swimming away. She follows him.

Habitat: Wooded swamps, rivers.

Voice: "Oo-eek" flight call given by female. Male gives high whistle in courtship groups.

Conservation: BBS: W ⇑ C ⇑ CBC: ↑ By 1900s was almost extinct due to hunting and habitat destruction. Now recovering due to nest-box programs.

Green-winged Teal
Anas crecca

Male

Female

Identification: 14" Our smallest dabbling duck. **MALE:** Gray body with white vertical stripe on side at start of wing. **Reddish-brown head; iridescent green patch extending behind eye.** In eclipse plumage, male looks like female. **FEMALE: Mottled brown; dark streak through eye; green speculum, which is usually visible; small bill.** IN FLIGHT: Small duck, light belly, and green speculum. ►A similar male without the white vertical stripe may be the Eurasian subspecies, *A. c. crecca.*

Feeding: Feeds by dabbling along the edges of ponds and waterways, eating the soft parts of aquatic plants and their seeds. In the fall it visits grainfields and eats seeds, waste corn, wheat, oats, and buckwheat.

Nesting: Nest of grasses, weeds, and down is placed in depression in ground, concealed in grass or brush. Can be up to a mile from water. Eggs: 7–15, pale olive-buff; I: 21–23 days; F: 34–44 days, precocial; B: 1.

Other Behavior: One of earliest spring migrant ducks. Does courtship displays from winter through spring.

Habitat: Summers on freshwater ponds and lakes; winters also on rivers and sheltered coastal marshes.

Voice: Male gives piping "krick'et" whistle. Female gives high-pitched decrescendo quacking call of about 4 notes.

Conservation:
BBS: W ↑ C ↑ CBC: ↑

55

Mallard
Anas platyrhynchos

Female (lower l.), males (top and r.)

Identification: 24" MALE: **Iridescent green head; yellow bill; chestnut breast.** White neckring can be hidden or exposed. Eclipse plumage is like female's, but with unmarked yellowish bill and reddish-brown breast. FEMALE: **Brown-streaked; orange bill broadly marked with black in the center; whitish tail feathers.** IN FLIGHT: Dark blue speculum bordered by white; underwings and body the same color.

Feeding: Male defends small feeding area in open water while female is building nest. Eats mostly aquatic vegetation, but also grain and insects.

Nesting: Nest of reeds and grasses lined with down, placed on ground near water. Eggs: 8–10, pale greenish white; I: 26–30 days; F: 50–60 days, precocial; B: 1.

Other Behavior: Mallards and other ducks in the genus *Anas* have similar complex courtship displays, and these occur fall through late winter. In inciting display, female follows her mate while repeatedly flicking her bill back over one side of her body. During head-up tail-up display, male stretches head, wing tips, and tail upward, then lowers them.

Habitat: Lakes, rivers, bays, parks.

Voice: Male does not quack; gives "rhaeb, rhaeb" call during aggression and short whistle during courtship. Female quacks in a decrescendo when uneasy or separated from male; gives "quegegege" call during inciting.

Conservation:
BBS: W ⇑ C ↑ CBC: ⇓

Northern Pintail

Anas acuta

Male

Female

Identification: 25″ **Long-necked** slender duck with **long pointed tail.** MALE: **Dark brown head; white breast and neck; gray flanks and wings.** Thin white line extends up sides of neck. In eclipse plumage, male looks like female, but has darker back. FEMALE: **Long neck; pointed tail; plain light brown head and neck; gray bill.** IN FLIGHT: Long neck; long thin tail; white streak on neck of male.

Feeding: Eats seeds, roots and shoots of aquatic plants, small crustaceans, corn and other grain.

Nesting: Concealed nest of leaves, grasses, and sticks lined with down is placed close to, or sometimes farther away from, water. Eggs: 6–12, greenish buff; I: 22–25 days; F: 36–57 days, precocial; B: 1.

Other Behavior: Large flocks of wintering birds often fly to cornfields to feed. Pair formation starts on wintering areas in Dec. and continues into spring migration. Head pumping by pair precedes copulation.

Habitat: Summers on open marshes and ponds; winters on coastal bays, lakes, and agricultural fields.

Voice: Female quacks. Male gives a fluty whistle.

Conservation: BBS: W ⇓ C ⇓ CBC: ⇓

Blue-winged Teal
Anas discors

Male

Female

Identification: 15" MALE: **Gray head; broad white crescent in front of eye.** Eclipse plumage, kept from late summer into midwinter, very similar to female's. FEMALE: **Small brown duck** with a **green speculum.** Differs from similar female Green-winged Teal in having **light spot at base of relatively large dark bill** and **dark eye-stripe that is darker behind eye.** IN FLIGHT: Light blue patches on forewing.

Feeding: Rarely dives. Skims the water surface with bill or reaches below the surface with head and neck. Eats seeds and vegetative parts of aquatic plants.

Nesting: Nest composed of grasses lined with down, placed in grassy cover not far from water. Eggs: 6–15, dull white; I: 23–27 days; F: 35–44 days, precocial; B: 1.

Other Behavior: Pair formation takes place midwinter through spring. Males do aggressive chin-lifting displays to one another. The female's primary display, as is the case with many surface-feeding ducks, is inciting (see Mallard for description).

Habitat: Summers on small lakes in open grasslands; winters on marshes and protected coastal areas.

Voice: Female gives a high-pitched quacking. Male gives a peeping "tsee" note.

Conservation:
BBS: W ↓ C ⇓ CBC: ⇑

Cinnamon Teal

Anas cyanoptera

Male

Female

Identification: 16″ MALE: **Head, neck, and body dark cinnamon**; wings and back blackish. In eclipse plumage, male is similar to female, but has rustier plumage and a yellow or orange iris. FEMALE: Similar to female Blue-winged Teal, with **green speculum** and **light area at base of bill.** Differs by having a **darker, more uniformly colored head; little or no eye-stripe,** especially past the eye; and a **faint light area at base of bill.** IN FLIGHT: Light blue leading edge to wing, as in Blue-winged Teal.

Feeding: Prefers shallow water surrounded by grasses and herbaceous cover. Eats seeds of aquatic plants.

Nesting: Nest formed of grasses lined with down, placed in grassy or herbaceous cover, sometimes on islands. Eggs: 7–12, pinkish buff; I: 21–25 days; F: 49 days, precocial; B: 1.

Other Behavior: Hybridizes with Blue-winged Teal. Molts into breeding plumage relatively late, and courtship continues through spring migration. Nesting densities can be up to 100 pairs per square mile.

Habitat: Open shallow lakes and marshes.

Voice: Female sounds like Blue-winged Teal. Male gives series of "chuk" notes.

Conservation: BBS: W ⇑ C ⇑ CBC: ↑

Northern Shoveler
Anas clypeata

Female (l.), male (r.)

Identification: 19" Long bill widens considerably at the tip. MALE: Dark green head; white breast; reddish-brown flanks. Eclipse plumage is similar to female's, but with darker back and more reddish-brown breast and flanks. FEMALE: A brown-streaked duck with a spatula-shaped bill that is gray on top and orange along the opening. IN FLIGHT: Large bill; pale blue forewing; green speculum.

Feeding: Feeds at water's surface by straining out small organisms with comblike edge of large bill. Eats aquatic insects and other invertebrates. Also eats duckweed and submerged aquatic plants.

Nesting: The concealed nest of grasses lined with down is placed in a depression in the ground and can be more than 100 yd. from the nearest water. Eggs: 6–14, pale greenish buff; I: 21–28 days; F: 36–60 days, precocial; B: 1.

Other Behavior: Usually found in small flocks or pairs. Much aggression is shown during displays and territorial defense.

Habitat: Summers on open shallow lakes and marshes; winters also on protected coastal areas.

Voice: Females do quacking and a decrescendo call of 5 notes, with the 1st note the loudest. Male gives low "took-a" note during courtship.

Conservation: BBS: W ↓ C ↑ CBC: ⇑

Gadwall

Anas strepera

Male

Female

Identification: 21" MALE: A grayish duck with a light brown angular head and a black tail. White speculum is often visible. In eclipse plumage, looks like female. FEMALE: Brown with a white belly and white speculum; bill grayish with orange along the opening. IN FLIGHT: Note white belly and speculum.

Feeding: Feeds by tipping body tail-up and by diving for food. Eats seeds and vegetative parts of aquatic plants.

Nesting: Often nests colonially on islands with good habitat. Nest of plant material and down is well hidden under dense herbaceous cover. Eggs: 7–13, white; I: 26–28 days; F: 48–60 days, precocial; B: 1.

Other Behavior: The complex courtship displays of this species are similar to those of other ducks in the genus *Anas*. Females do the inciting display. Males respond by turning the back of their head toward inciting female. Males do a number of displays. These include grunt-whistle, in which male points his bill down, raises the back of his neck, and gives a short high-pitched whistle. Gadwalls were primarily western until 1950s and 1960s, when they were introduced to the Northeast.

Habitat: Open lakes and marshes.

Voice: Female does quacking and a higher-pitched decrescendo than Mallard. Male gives whistle and "raeb-raeb" call.

Conservation: BBS: W ⇑ C ⇑ CBC: ⇑

Eurasian Wigeon
Anas penelope

Male

Female

Identification: 19" A rare but regular winter visitor along both coasts, sometimes found inland. MALE: Look for the **reddish-brown head** with a **cream-colored crown,** and **gray sides and back**. Notice the white patch next to the dark rump. FEMALE: **Uniformly brown; small rounded head; darkish eye patch; light gray bill with black tip.** Gray morph of the female very similar to female American Wigeon.

Feeding: Feeds along the edges of ponds and waterways, eating aquatic plants such as pondweeds and eelgrass and also insects.

Nesting: Grassy nest hidden under low shrubs. Eggs: 7–10, white; I: 24–25 days; F: 40–45 days, precocial; B: 1.

Other Behavior: Breeds in Iceland and the British Isles and across northern Europe and Asia. Winters in those areas as well as around the Mediterranean and in China, Japan, and Africa. Is a regular winter visitor to the U.S. Social behavior is the same as American Wigeon's.

Habitat: Lakes, bays, estuaries.

Voice: Female gives abbreviated decrescendo call of 1–3 syllables. Male's calls are louder than American Wigeon's and are of 1 or 2 syllables.

Conservation: CBC: ⇑

American Wigeon

Anas americana

Female (l.), male (r.)

Identification: 21" MALE: White forehead and crown; gray head; iridescent green patch through eye; white patch before black tail. Male in eclipse plumage similar to female. FEMALE: Brownish sides, grayish head and neck, dark eyespot, and light gray bill with black tip. IN FLIGHT: White forewing; green speculum; light belly.

Feeding: Feeds on the stems, leaves, and buds of aquatic plants such as pondweeds, water milfoil, wigeon grass, wild celery, and eelgrass. May eat vegetation stirred up by diving ducks like Canvasbacks.

Nesting: Concealed in rushes or sedges, or under tree clumps, the grassy nest is generally placed rather far from water in upland meadows. Eggs: 6–12, white; I: 23–25 days; F: 36–48 days, precocial; B:1.

Other Behavior: Usually found in small flocks. As early arrivals on their southern wintering grounds, they immediately begin courtship, which lasts until March. By then, most females have paired. During courtship, competing males repeatedly give whistling calls and lift folded wings nearly vertically above back.

Habitat: Summers on lakes and marshes; winters on wet meadows, lakes, protected coastal waters.

Voice: Soft, growling "quegegege" by female during inciting. She also quacks. Male gives soft, descending 3-syllable whistle.

Conservation: BBS: W ↓ C ⇑ CBC: ↓

63

Canvasback
Aythya valisineria

Male

Female

Identification: 21" A long-billed duck with a long sloping forehead. MALE: Reddish-brown head; black breast; white body; bill and tail black. In eclipse plumage is slightly browner but retains reddish-brown head and black breast. FEMALE: Grayish body; brown head and neck; long black bill; long sloping forehead. IN FLIGHT: Black bill; long sloping forehead.

Feeding: Dives to 30 ft. underwater to get roots, buds, and tubers of aquatic plants, especially pondweeds and wild celery. Also eats aquatic insects, small fish, and crustaceans.

Nesting: Bowl-shaped nest of reeds and sedges lined with down, attached to surrounding vegetation or placed on floating mass of vegetation. Eggs: 7–12, greenish olive; I: 24–29 days; F: 56–77 days, precocial; B: 1.

Other Behavior: Concentrates in large numbers on migratory and wintering grounds. Courtship continues during spring migration and includes aerial chases. Males leave females during incubation and gather in large flocks to molt. Females molt when young fledge.

Habitat: Summers on prairie lakes and marshes; winters on lakes and sheltered coastal waters.

Voice: Female gives soft "krr-krr." Male gives cooing note during courtship.

Conservation: BBS: W ⇓ C ↓ CBC: ↓ Populations declining due to drainage of marshes and prairie potholes where ducks breed.

Redhead
Aythya americana

Male

Female

Identification: 20″ Both sexes have **short bluish bills with black tips** and **steep rounded foreheads. MALE: Reddish head; black breast; grayish body.** In eclipse plumage has brown body but retains reddish head and dark breast. **FEMALE: Plain, warm brown body; darker brown back and wings; darker brown crown; buffy eye-ring; black-tipped bill. IN FLIGHT:** White belly; gray wings; small rounded head.

Habitat: Ponds, lakes, bays.

Voice: Male has catlike call during courtship. Female gives soft growling note.

Conservation:
BBS: W ⇑ C ⇑ CBC: ⇓

Feeding: Eats aquatic vegetation, including the roots, stems, and leaves of submerged plants. Also eats insect larvae, mollusks, and small crustaceans.

Nesting: Basketlike nest of rushes, reeds, and cattails lined with down is attached to surrounding vegetation. Eggs: 9–13, pale buff; I: 24–28 days; F: 56–73 days, precocial; B: 1.

Other Behavior: A substantial portion of females do not attempt to nest; rather they "dump" their eggs in the nests of other Redheads or other species of ducks, especially Canvasbacks. The hatching success of these parasitically laid eggs is low because the host female often deserts the nest and then renests.

Ring-necked Duck

Aythya collaris

Male

Female

Identification: 16" In profile, **crown comes to a point**. MALE: All dark except for **white vertical mark in front of light gray sides; broad white band encircles grayish bill** just before black tip; a thinner band encircles base of bill. Brownish "ring" on neck is barely visible. In eclipse plumage, male like female, but with yellow iris. FEMALE: **Grayish brown with white eye-ring** and faint white line behind eye; **bill has white ring at tip;** poorly defined light area on face at base of bill. IN FLIGHT: White belly and gray speculum.

Feeding: Dives for tubers, leaves, and seeds of submerged vegetation. Also eats mollusks and insects.

Nesting: Nest of grass and mosses lined with down, placed near water's edge. Eggs: 6–14, olive-buff; I: 25–29 days; F: 49–56 days, precocial; B: 1.

Other Behavior: Found in small, often single-sex flocks during fall migration. Courtship peaks during spring migration. Copulation is preceded by bill dipping.

Habitat: Summers on open lakes, marshes; winters on large lakes and coastal areas.

Voice: Females give soft "rrrr" notes. Males give loud whistle during displays.

Conservation:
BBS: W ↑ C ⇓ CBC: ↓ Populations have increased considerably in East over last 50 years.

Greater Scaup

Aythya marila

Male

Female

Identification: 18″ Head shape and bill size are best characteristics for distinguishing this species from Lesser Scaup. Greater Scaup's **head is like a rounded rectangle** and never comes to a peak in the center; **slightly larger bill**. MALE: **Dark head and breast** and **dark tail** separated by gray back and **white flank**. In excellent light, note **greenish gloss on head**. FEMALE: **Dark brown; extensive white patches on either side of base of bill.** Distinguish it from female Lesser Scaup by head shape and bill size. IN FLIGHT: Long white band on inner wing extends onto wing tip.

Feeding: Dives as deep as 25 ft. underwater for up to 1 minute, eating submerged plants, crustaceans, mollusks, and snails.

Nesting: Often on islands. Nest is made of matted vegetation, grasses, and down. Eggs: 8–11, olive-buff; I: 24–28 days; F: 35–42 days, precocial; B: 1.

Other Behavior: In fall and winter often found on deeper lakes and in more saltwater habitats than Lesser Scaup.

Habitat: Summers on tundra lakes; winters on salt water and coastal ponds.

Voice: Male gives a soft "wa-hooo" note and a triple-note whistle. Female gives a growling "arrr" call.

Conservation: CBC: ⇓

Lesser Scaup
Aythya affinis

Male

Female

Identification: 17" Head and bill shapes are most useful characteristics distinguishing this species from Greater Scaup, but differences are subtle. On Lesser Scaup the **head comes to a peak at the top or near the back; bill is slightly shorter and narrower.** MALE: **Dark head and breast** and **dark tail** separated by gray back and **white flank.** In excellent light, note **purplish gloss on head.** FEMALE: **Dark brown with small white patches on either side of base of bill.** Distinguish from Greater Scaup female by shape of head and bill. IN FLIGHT: Long white band on inner wing usually does not extend to outer wing.

Feeding: Dives for submergent plant seeds, snails, insects, and crustaceans.

Nesting: Concealed nest of grasses lined with down is placed on ground, in cover within 100–200 ft. of water. Sometimes nests in tern colonies. Eggs: 8–14, olive-buff; I: 21–28 days; F: 49 days, precocial; B: 1.

Other Behavior: Highly social. Winter flocks, or "rafts," may number in the thousands.

Habitat: Summers on prairie lakes and marshes; winters on lakes, sheltered coastal areas, freshwater ponds.

Voice: Male gives faint "whee-ooo" note, a single-note whistle, and a quacking sound. Female makes a purring "kwuh" sound.

Conservation: BBS: W ↑ C ⇑ CBC: ↓

Common Eider

Somateria mollissima

Male

Female

Immature male

Identification: 25" A large duck often seen in large flocks floating along the coast. **MALE:** Distinctive **white back and black flanks** easily seen from a distance. Long sloping "Roman nose." **FEMALE:** All **brown with profile like that of male.** **IMM:** Female much like adult; male dark with white areas of adult plumage developing first on breast and then elsewhere. Imm. plumage kept 3 years.

Feeding: Dives in sea as far as 60 ft. underwater for whelks, sea urchins, crustaceans, and mollusks, especially blue mussels.

Nesting: Prefers boulder-covered islands. Nest of seaweeds, grasses, sticks, and mosses lined with down is placed on ground. Eggs: 3–5, pale greenish olive; I: 25–30 days; F: 56–70 days, precocial; B: 1.

Other Behavior: In Iceland, down from nest is collected during incubation and is used commercially; female usually does not desert nest. Cooing sounds accompany a lot of male courtship displays. Males often winter farther north than females and immatures.

Habitat: Coastal waters.

Voice: Female gives several hoarse-sounding calls. Male gives dovelike cooing sounds.

Conservation: CBC: ↑ Susceptible to oil spills.

69

King Eider
Somateria spectabilis

Male

Female

Immature male

Identification: 23" Stays farther north than Common Eider and so is only occasionally seen. **MALE: Orange shield over base of bill;** black back and flanks; white breast. **FEMALE: Brown duck with a Roman nose** similar to that of Common Eider but **frontal lobes of bill shorter and more rounded;** otherwise hard to distinguish. **IMM:** Female similar to adult. Male dark with no shield on bill at first; develops white of adult plumage first on breast, then on other areas. Imm. plumage kept 2–3 years.

Feeding: Dives as deep as 200 ft. underwater for mollusks, crustaceans, sea urchins, starfish. Also eats algae, eelgrass, sedges, and aquatic insects.

Nesting: Nest of feathers and down is placed on the ground near water, but can be some distance away. Eggs: 4–7, olive-buff; I: 22–24 days; F: up to 50 days, precocial; B: 1.

Other Behavior: After hatching, broods merge and "nurseries" of up to 100 ducklings are attended by several females. Stays in large flocks during winter.

Habitat: Summers on tundra; winters along subarctic coast.

Voice: Female gives hollow-sounding notes. Male makes cooing sounds.

Conservation: CBC: ↑

Harlequin Duck

Histrionicus histrionicus

Male

Female

Identification: 17″ A small compact sea duck with a short bill. **MALE:** A slate-blue head, breast, and back boldly patterned with white. Also has red-brown flanks. In eclipse plumage similar to female but with some white on wings. **FEMALE:** All dark brown; unstreaked; 3 white patches on each side of face. **IN FLIGHT:** Dark belly; white face patterns; long tail; small bill.

Feeding: In summer feeds on insects found in streams. In winter moves to coast and dives for mollusks.

Nesting: Concealed nest of grasses lined with down. Eggs: 4–8, light buff; I: 28–30 days; F: 40–70 days, precocial; B: 1.

Other Behavior: Has the ability to swim in torrential currents and rapidly moving streams where it forages for insects. Male's color and white spotting may provide camouflage in this environment.

Habitat: Summers on mountain rivers and streams; winters on rocky coasts.

Voice: High-pitched peeping sounds.

Conservation: BBS: W ⇑ C CBC: ↓ A major victim of oil spills, with sharp declines in population.

Oldsquaw

Clangula hyemalis

Summer male

Winter male

Female

Identification: 19″ A sea duck best recognized by its **variable light and dark plumage** and **pointed tail.** Plumage varies since adults molt 3 times each year and there is an immature plumage as well. SUMMER—MALE: **Black head and breast; large white patch surrounding eye.** FEMALE: **Dark wings; light flanks and head; large dark smudge behind cheek.** WINTER—MALE: **White head; large dark patch on side of neck.** FEMALE: **Similar to summer, but lighter.** IN FLIGHT: Note light eye patch of both sexes and long, pointed tail of male. IMM: Similar to the adult female, but variable. Imm. plumage kept 1 year.

Feeding: Can dive to 200 ft. deep. Eats crustaceans, mollusks, and larval insects.

Nesting: Concealed grassy nest. Eggs: 5–11, yellowish buff; I: 24–35 days; F: 35–40 days, precocial; B: 1.

Other Behavior: Very social. Much courtship and territorial displaying done winter to summer. Very vocal throughout year.

Habitat: Summers on tundra lakes, coastal inlets; winters along coast.

Voice: In winter males give yodeling calls. In courtship males give "ah-har-lik" call with a bill toss. Females give guttural calls during chin-lifting display.

Conservation:
CBC:→
Suffers in oil spills.

Black Scoter

Melanitta nigra

Males

Female

Identification: 19" **MALE:** All black with a large orange knob at base of bill. **FEMALE:** Brown; small-billed; cheek noticeably lighter than crown and nape. **IN FLIGHT:** All dark with silvery wing linings; male with orange knob on bill. **IMM:** Female similar to adult female; male similar to adult female, but with yellow knob on bill showing in first winter. Imm. plumage kept 1 year.

Feeding: Usually feeds in shallow water just outside breaker zone. Sometimes frequents deeper water. Eats aquatic plants, crustaceans, and mollusks, especially mussels and limpets.

Nesting: Concealed nest of coarse grasses lined with down, on ground close to water. Eggs: 5–8, pale pinkish buff; I: 27–31 days; F: 45–50 days, precocial; B: 1.

Other Behavior: Formerly called Common Scoter. The least common of the scoters. They do not breed until their second spring, when they reach sexual maturity.

Habitat: Summers on tundra lakes; winters along the coast.

Voice: Female gives grating notes. Male gives mellow whistle during courtship.

Conservation: CBC: ⇓

Surf Scoter
Melanitta perspicillata

Male

Female

Identification: 20″ MALE: **Black; orange, yellow, and white bill; white patches on forehead and nape. FEMALE: Brown; large dark bill; darker crown; 2 white spots on side of face.** The forward spot ends in an abrupt vertical line where it meets the bill. This can help distinguish it from the similar female White-winged Scoter. **IN FLIGHT:** Lighter belly on female; male with white patches on head. **IMM:** Females like adult female; males have colorful bill, but lack full white head markings. Imm. plumage kept 1 year.

Feeding: Dives underwater and feeds primarily on mussels and crustaceans. Eats some insects and plants.

Nesting: Concealed nest of weeds located some distance from water. Eggs: 5–8, pale buff; I: ?; F: ?, precocial; B: 1.

Other Behavior: Has the habit of diving through the breaking surf. Scoters gather into huge flocks along the coast during fall migration. Traditionally, they were hunted at this time.

Habitat: Summers on semiwooded arctic lakes and rivers; winters along the coast, very infrequently found inland.

Voice: A low guttural sound. During mating season male gives a low whistle.

Conservation: CBC: ↓

White-winged Scoter
Melanitta fusca

Male

Female

Identification: 22″ **White wing patch** on all-dark male and female is a good clue, but not always visible when wings are closed. **MALE: Black; small white mark around eye;** multicolored bill tip. **FEMALE: Brown; large dark bill; 2 whitish spots on face.** The forward spot is ovate; the shape of this spot and the white wing patch can help distinguish it from the similar female Surf Scoter. **IN FLIGHT:** All dark with bright white speculum. **IMM:** Female may have more distinct facial spots than adult; male browner and lacking eye patch of adult. Imm. plumage kept at least 1 year.

Feeding: On the coast, birds concentrate in water that is less than 20 ft. deep and feed on mussels, clams, and scallops.

Nesting: Concealed nest of sticks, leaves, and feathers, on ground near water. Eggs: 5–12, pink-buff; I: 26–29 days; F: 63–77 days, precocial; B: 1.

Other Behavior: Most widespread scoter. Migrates in flocks, often flying in long line formations.

Habitat: Summers on lakes and ponds; winters along the coast.

Voice: Females give a thin whistling note. Males give a bell-like call during courtship.

Conservation:
BBS: W ⇓ C   CBC: ↓

Common Goldeneye

Bucephala clangula

Male

Female

Identification: 18" MALE: **White flanks; dark head; rounded white spot in front of and below eye.** In perfect lighting, head looks glossy green. FEMALE: **Grayish; white collar; dark brown head. Bill dark with small area of yellow at tip.** Note **thicker bill** and **more sloping forehead** than similar female Barrow's Goldeneye. IN FLIGHT: Large white speculum area; white patches on male's face. IMM: Both sexes similar to female at first. Male gradually develops adult wing and facial pattern. Imm. plumage kept 1 year.

Feeding: Dives underwater to feed on crustaceans and mollusks. Also eats aquatic insects.

Nesting: Nest in tree cavity or man-made nesting box is lined with feathers from female's breast. Eggs: 5–15, olive to light green; I: 28–30 days; F: 56–66 days, precocial; B: 1.

Other Behavior: Has spectacular and complex courtship with numerous displays. When nesting sites are scarce, female may lay eggs in another female's nest.

Habitat: Summers on lakes and marshes; winters on interior and coastal waters.

Voice: Relatively silent. Male gives nasal "eeent" during courtship. In flight, wings make whistling noise.

Conservation: BBS: W ↓ C ⇑ CBC: ↓

Barrow's Goldeneye
Bucephala islandica

Male

Female

Identification: 19" MALE: **White flanks; dark back and head; clear white crescent in front of the eye.** In perfect lighting, head looks glossy purple. FEMALE: **A grayish duck** with a **white collar** and **dark brown head. Bill mostly yellow-orange** in western birds; dark with yellow tip in eastern birds. Note **thinner bill, darker head,** and **more vertical forehead** than similar female Common Goldeneye. IN FLIGHT: Large white speculum area bisected by dark bar, and note facial crescent of male. IMM: Both sexes similar to female at first. Male gradually develops adult wing and facial pattern. Imm. plumage kept 1 year.

Feeding: Eats mollusks, crustaceans, fish, aquatic insects.

Nesting: Uses tree cavities or nest boxes, but also can nest in rock crevice or on the ground. Eggs: 8–10, olive-green; I: 30–32 days; F: 56 days, precocial; B: 1.

Other Behavior: Male display behavior and vocalizations differ from Common Goldeneye's. Hybridization with Common Goldeneye rare.

Habitat: Summers on wooded lakes and rivers; winters on estuaries or coastal lakes.

Voice: Males give grunting and clicking notes. Females mostly silent.

Conservation: BBS: W ⇑ C CBC: ⇑

Bufflehead
Bucephala albeola

Male

Female

Identification: 14" A small duck with a large rounded head. **MALE:** Note **conspicuous white wedge at back of dark head;** white breast and flanks. **FEMALE: Gray-brown duck; dark head; long white dash behind eye. IMM:** Female similar to adult; male has larger white dash than female, and this gradually develops to the full white wedge. Imm. plumage kept 1 year.

Feeding: Dives underwater and eats small mollusks, fish, snails, and crustaceans. Also eats aquatic insects.

Nesting: Nests in tree cavity 5–50 ft. high or nest box, which it lines with down. Eggs: 8–10, ivory to buff; I: 28–33 days; F: 49–56 days, precocial; B: 1.

Other Behavior: Winters in small flocks. Courtship, which begins in Jan., has high level of aggression.

Habitat: Summers on wooded lakes and rivers; winters on lakes and coastal waters.

Voice: Generally silent; female makes guttural sounds during courtship.

Conservation: BBS: W ⇓ C   CBC: ↑

Hooded Merganser

Lophodytes cucullatus

Male

Female

Identification: 18" Note the **short thin bill** and **crested head** on this smallest of the mergansers. MALE: **Black head; white fan-shaped patch within crest** (when crest is raised); flanks brown; back is black. Black vertical line cuts diagonally down through white breast in front of flanks. FEMALE: Plain brown with a **darker back; red-brown crest; darker upper bill.** IN FLIGHT: Note thin bill, grayish wing linings, and rapid wingbeats. IMM: Female like adult; male like female, but with some white in crest. Imm. plumage kept 1 year.

Feeding: Dives underwater. Eats small fish, frogs, crustaceans, mollusks, and aquatic insects.

Nesting: Nest of grasses and down, placed in tree cavity or nest box. Eggs: 6–18, white; I: 32–41 days; F: 70 days, precocial; B: 1.

Other Behavior: Courtship begins in midwinter, usually occurring in mixed groups of 3–10 birds. Females do head bobbing and pumping. Most male displays involve crest raising.

Habitat: Summers on wooded rivers and lakes; winters on similar locations as well as along the coast occasionally.

Voice: Male gives froglike note. Female makes a hoarse "gak."

Conservation: BBS: W ⇑ C CBC: ⇑

Common Merganser
Mergus merganser

Male

Female

Identification: 25" This merganser has a **long bill that is thicker at the base,** making its **forehead appear more gently sloping** than that of the Red-Breasted Merganser. **MALE: Dark green head; creamy white breast and flank; dark back;** red bill. **FEMALE: Gray; red-crested head sharply delineated from white chin and breast;** red bill. **IN FLIGHT:** Thin bill, white breast on male. Flight strong and direct. **IMM:** Female resembles adult; male looks like female at first, but begins to develop adult male plumage by first spring. Imm. plumage kept 1 year.

Feeding: Dives underwater and eats mostly fish, also crustaceans and mollusks. Serrated bills of all mergansers aid in holding slippery fish prey.

Nesting: Down-lined nest of weeds and roots in tree cavity, nest box, or rock crevice, or on ground. Eggs: 8–11, buff; I: 28–35 days; F: 70–84 days, precocial; B: 1.

Other Behavior: Displays involve much chasing on water and in air, and underwater attacks.

Habitat: Summers on wooded lakes and along rivers; winters on large lakes and estuaries, usually on fresh water.

Voice: Male's courtship call is a guitarlike note. Female gives harsh sound.

Conservation:
BBS: W ⇑ C ⇓ CBC: ↑

80

Red-breasted Merganser
Mergus serrator

Male

Female

Identification: 23" This merganser has a **long bill that is thin at the base,** making its **forehead appear more abrupt and vertical** than that of Common Merganser. **MALE: Dark green crested head; white neck-ring; rusty breast;** red bill. **FEMALE: A brown duck** with a **red-crested head that gradually shades to the white breast;** red bill. **IN FLIGHT:** Thin bill; dark breast on male. Flight fast and direct. **IMM:** Female resembles adult; male looks like female at first, but begins to develop adult male plumage by first spring. Imm. plumage kept 1 year.

Feeding: Dives for fish, mollusks, and crustaceans.

Nesting: Nest lined with vegetation and down is sheltered under shrubs, logs. Eggs: 5–11, greenish buff; I: 29–35 days; F: 59–65 days, precocial; B: 1.

Other Behavior: Courtship begins in winter. Males do elaborate posturing and give distinct catlike call.

Habitat: Summers on rivers and lakes; winters along sheltered coastal waters, preferring salt water.

Voice: Male gives catlike "yeow-yeow." Female gives harsh double note.

Conservation: BBS: W ⇓ C CBC: ↑

81

Ruddy Duck
Oxyura jamaicensis

Summer male

Winter male

Female

Identification: 16″ Small stocky duck with a broad bill and a stiff tail that is often held straight up. SUMMER—MALE: Reddish-brown body; black head; white cheek; light blue bill. FEMALE: Brown; head appears 2-toned, having a dark crown and a lighter cheek with a line through it. Keeps same plumage all year. WINTER—MALE: Similar to female, but with no line through cheek. IMM: Like adult female. Imm. plumage kept 1 year.

Feeding: Dives and feeds on aquatic plants, crustaceans, aquatic insects.

Nesting: Well-concealed nest of plant material is attached to marsh plants. Eggs: 6–10, dull white; I: 23–26 days; F: 42–52 days, precocial; B: 1–2.

Other Behavior: Birds are in large winter flocks. They start courtship on spring migration. Male's tail cocking and neck enlargement is most obvious display. Females dump eggs in nests of other females and in nests of other duck species such as Canvasbacks and Redheads.

Habitat: Summers on open lakes; winters also along coast.

Voice: Mostly silent. Males make drumming sound by beating lower mandible on breast.

Conservation: BBS: W ↑ C ↓ CBC: ↓

The term *hawk* refers to several related bird groups, including eagles, falcons, kites, and ospreys. Vultures, not closely related, are often included because they look similar and soar with hawks.

To identify hawks, start by learning the fairly distinctive silhouette and flight behavior of each group. Then learn the most common species in each group. The Learning Pages will help you do this with adult hawks; immature hawks are more difficult to identify, but have essentially the same size, shape, and flight behavior as the adults. For each hawk shown on these pages there is the name, a brief description, and the range of wingspread (W), from the smaller male to the larger female (a sexual difference typical of hawks). For complete information on adults and immatures, see the Species Accounts.

Most hawks are not commonly seen; the ones that are, are listed below. The best way to see other hawks is during fall migration, when large numbers move south on clear days with generally north winds. Along ridges or the coast are good places to look for them.

Commonly Seen Hawks: Which Ones and Where

- **Perched along roads:**
  Most large hawks are Red-tailed Hawks, p. 102
  Most small hawks are American Kestrels, p. 107

- **Perched or soaring near water:**
  Most are Ospreys, p. 87
  Some may be Bald Eagles, p. 90

- **Soaring over land:**
  Black Vulture, p. 42, or Turkey Vulture, p. 43
  Red-tailed Hawk, p. 102

- **Perched near or attacking birds at bird feeders:**
  Sharp-shinned Hawk, p. 92

Eagles

Very large; mostly dark; very long wings; soar continuously.

Bald Eagle Dark with white head and white tail. W 71–89". P. 90.

Golden Eagle All dark with golden mantle. W 72–87". P. 105.

Buteos

Large hawks; broad wings; short tails; soar a lot; seen in open areas.

Red-tailed Hawk Red tail; usually a belly band; dark line at front edge of wing. W 47–56". P. 102.

Swainson's Hawk Brown bib extending onto light chest; pale wing linings; dark flight feathers. W 47–54". P. 100.

Rough-legged Hawk Dark square patches on wrists of wings. W 48–56". P. 104.

Red-shouldered Hawk Whitish wing windows next to dark wing tips. W 37–42". P. 98.

Ferruginous Hawk White underwings with chestnut mottling on wing linings; dark-feathered legs form a V underneath. W 53–60". P. 103.

Vultures

Large birds; mostly black; soar continuously, rarely beating wings.

Turkey Vulture All black with trailing half of wings light gray. W 63–71". P. 43.

Black Vulture All black with pale whitish primaries. W 55–63". P. 42.

Accipiters

Small-to-large hawks; short rounded wings; medium-to-long tail; in flight, alternate several quick flaps with glides ("flap, flap, flap, glide"); catch other birds in the air.

Sharp-shinned Hawk
Small; square-tipped tail with thin gray band at tip; looks short-necked. W 20–26". P. 92.

Cooper's Hawk
Crow-sized; long tail rounded at tip with whitish terminal band; heavyset head and long neck. W 28–34". P. 93.

Northern Goshawk
Red-tailed Hawk size; long wings; wide tail; soars more than other accipiters. W 38–45". P. 94.

Northern Harrier

Large hawk; long thin wings held in a V over back; long tail with white rump patch; tilts from side to side when soaring. W 38–48". P. 91.

Osprey

Large hawk; dark above, white below; when soaring, forms a shallow M, with wings arched forward at the wrists and bent down at the tips. W 59–67". P. 87.

85

Falcons

Small-to-large hawks; pointed wings; direct flight with little gliding.

American Kestrel Small falcon; thin wings with light spots on trailing edge. W 20–24". P. 107.

Merlin Medium-sized dark falcon; heavier than kestrel; angular wings; very direct flight. W 21–27". P. 108.

Prairie Falcon
Large falcon; long wings; long tail; thin dark bar on cheek; dark wing linings. W 36–44". P. 111.

Peregrine Falcon
Large falcon; long wings; broad tail; broad dark bar on cheek; whitish wing linings. W 37–46". P. 109.

Kites

Medium-sized hawks; long thin wings; long thin tails; graceful and buoyant fliers that often catch insects in the air.

White-tailed Kite Light gray above, white below; white tail. W 37–40". P. 88.

Osprey
Pandion haliaetus

Female

Male

Identification: 24" IN FLIGHT: In all plumages, **dark above, white below; white head; prominent black streak through eye**. When soaring and gliding, forms a **wide shallow M,** with wings bowed (wrists up and forward and wing tips pointed down). Females generally more streaked on breast than males. PERCHED— ADULT: **Dark back and tail; white head; dark streak through eye.** IMM: As adult, but pale tips to wing and back feathers; streaked crown. Imm. plumage kept 2 years.

Feeding: Eats mostly fish, usually caught by hovering over water, then diving down and catching them in its talons. Fish are carried headfirst as bird flies off.

Nesting: Large platform nest of sticks lined with moss and grass is placed on a tree, cliff, or human structure 5–200 ft. high. Eggs: 2–4, whitish with reddish-brown blotches; I: 34–40 days; F: 49–56 days, altricial; B: 1.

Other Behavior: Male brings female all of her food during breeding. Immature birds stay on wintering grounds for 2 years before returning north.

Habitat: Large lakes, rivers, coast.

Voice: A down-slurred chirp given in mild alarm; an ascending squeal given during sky-dance display

Conservation: BBS: W ⇑ C CBC: ⇑ First studies leading to 1972 ban on DDT done on declining Osprey populations, which are now recovered.

87

White-tailed Kite

Elanus leucurus

Immature

Adult

Identification: 15″ IN FLIGHT—ADULT: **Light gray above, white below; black shoulder patches; black wrist patch on underside of pointed wings.** Distinguished from Mississippi Kite by white rather than black tail. Hunts by hovering. IMM: Similar to adult from below, but narrow dusky band near tip of tail. PERCHED— ADULT: **Gray back, white belly, black shoulders.** IMM: Black wings, brown back, rufous wash across breast, dusky band on tail. Body feathers like adult's in 2–3 months, but tail band kept 1 year.

Feeding: Eats almost exclusively small rodents, catching them by hovering above ground and dropping down.

Nesting: Platform nest of sticks and twigs lined with grass, weeds, and rootlets, placed in tree 5–60 ft. high. Eggs: 3–6, white with dark marks; I: 30 days; F: 33–37 days, altricial; B: 1–2.

Other Behavior: Gregarious with communal feeding and roosting areas from fall through spring, and communal roosts of nonbreeding birds during breeding season.

Habitat: Grasslands with scattered trees, near marshes, along highways.

Voice: A repeated short "chip chip chip"; a longer "kree-eek" given during mild alarm.

Conservation: BBS: W ⇑ C ⇑ CBC: ⇑ Disappeared from original Midwest range by 1900; now increasing and expanding range.

Mississippi Kite

Ictinia mississippiensis

Adult

Immature

Adult

Identification: 14" IN FLIGHT—ADULT: Gray with **black tail** and **whitish head.** Distinctive white patch on inner trailing edge of wings seen from above. Black tail distinguishes it from similar White-tailed Kite. IMM: Long, pointed brown wings; heavily brown-streaked belly changing to gray with small white blotches in spring; 2–3 thin white bands on black tail. PERCHED—ADULT: **Whitish head; gray underparts and back; black tail.** IMM: Body and tail as described above. Imm. plumage kept 1 year.

Feeding: Eats mostly insects caught on the wing. Catches them in its talons; and eats them while flying.

Nesting: Flat nest of twigs lined with green leaves, placed in tree 4–135 ft. high. Eggs: 1–3, bluish white; I: 29–31 days; F: 34 days, altricial; B: 1.

Other Behavior: Previous nests are often used in following years. First-year birds may become helpers at the nest of breeding birds. Migrates in flocks. Increasingly seen wandering north of its range into S. New England. Expanding range into West.

Habitat: Open woodlands, wooded streams, swamps.

Voice: Generally quiet, but gives a "kee kew, kee kew" when disturbed at the nest.

Conservation:
BBS: W C ↑

89

Bald Eagle
Haliaeetus leucocephalus

Adult   Immature   Immature

Identification: 31" IN FLIGHT—ADULT: Very large dark bird; white head; white tail. Massive head and bill equal to one-half or more length of tail. Soars on flat wings. IMM: Very large dark bird; white armpits; white mottling on wing lining; undertail, if whitish, has dark edges; variable amounts of white on belly after 1st year. PERCHED—ADULT: White head and tail. IMM: Told from Golden Eagle by lack of gold on head and nape, longer bill, and presence of white on belly. Imm. plumage kept 4 years.

Feeding: Eats mostly fish inland and mostly birds along coast; also carrion and some mammals, such as rabbits.

Nesting: Massive platform nest of sticks and vegetation lined with moss and grasses is placed on cliff ledge or in the fork of a tree 10–180 ft. high. Eggs: 1–3, bluish white; I: 34–36 days; F: 10–12 weeks, altricial; B: 1.

Other Behavior: Eagles congregate at feeding areas in late winter and early spring. During their soaring, look for chases and even passing of sticks between birds; these may function in courtship.

Habitat: Along coasts, lakes, and large rivers.

Voice: Has a repeated piercing scream given between pair, and a rapid series of chirps given at nest.

Conservation: BBS: W ⇑ C CBC:→ Most populations are recovering from serious declines due to use of DDT.

Northern Harrier
Circus cyaneus

Immature

Male

Female

Identification: 18" In FLIGHT: In all plumages, long slender wings held in a V; long tail; rectangular white patch on rump. When soaring or gliding it may **tilt from side to side**. PERCHED—MALE: Gray above; white below. FEMALE: Larger than male; brown above; streaked brown below. IMM: Brown above; reddish brown to creamy brown below, with streaking only on chest. Imm. plumage kept 1 year, gradually changing to adult.

Feeding: Feeds by coursing close to the ground and quickly swooping down on its prey. Eats mice, rats, birds, snakes, frogs, and other small animals.

Nesting: Platform nest of sticks and grasses lined with fine materials is placed on the ground. Eggs: 3–9, bluish white, sometimes with dark marks; I: 31–32 days; F: 30–35 days, altricial; B: 1.

Other Behavior: Often hunts at dusk and catches prey by sound as well as sight. Their owllike facial disk of feathers may function to help them locate sounds. Males are polygamous, mating with up to 3 females. Birds may roost communally in winter.

Habitat: Open fields, grasslands, prairies, marshes.

Voice: Variety of shrill alarm calls when disturbed at nest, otherwise quiet.

Conservation: BBS: W ↓ C ⇓ CBC: ↓

Sharp-shinned Hawk
Accipiter striatus

Adult

Immature

Immature

Identification: 11" IN FLIGHT: In all plumages, **small; short rounded wings; long narrow tail.** Uses short flaps followed by glides and is often **buffeted about by wind.** Differences from Cooper's Hawk: **tail squarish at corners,** sometimes notched; **tail narrowly tipped** with off white; bird looks **short-necked.** IMM: Heavy streaking on breast *and* belly makes it look darker than imm. Cooper's Hawk. PERCHED—ADULT: **Blue-gray above,** light below with **reddish-brown barring; tail as described; crown similar to back in color.** IMM: Dark brown above, light below with thick brown streaking. Imm. plumage kept 1 year.

Feeding: Feeds by catching small birds in midair and carrying them off to eat. May hunt around bird feeders.

Nesting: Platform nest of sticks lined with bark, placed in tree 10–90 ft. high. Eggs: 3–8, whitish with dark marks; I: 30–32 days; F: 21–28 days, altricial; B: 1.

Other Behavior: Largest numbers seen on spring and fall migrations as it flies along coasts or mountain ridges.

Habitat: Summers in mixed deciduous and coniferous woods; winters in woods and near bird feeders.

Voice: A rapid series of high "kek kek kek kek" notes given during alarm.

Conservation: BBS: W ↓ C CBC: ↑ Recent declines in Northeast noticed during migration counts.

Cooper's Hawk

Accipiter cooperii

Adult

Immature

Immature

Identification: 16" IN FLIGHT: In all plumages, "crow-sized"; relatively short rounded wings; very long narrow tail. Uses short flaps followed by glides and is **steady in the wind.** Differences from Sharp-shinned Hawk: **longer tail rounded at corners, often with wide white band at tip; neck wider and longer.** IMM: Fine streaking mostly on breast makes it look lighter bellied than imm. Sharp-shinned. PERCHED—ADULT: **Blue-gray above;** light below with **reddish-brown barring; crown darker than back;** tail as described. IMM: Dark brown above; light below with thin brown streaks. Imm. plumage kept 1 yr.

Feeding: During breeding season has regular feeding routes where it hunts for common medium-sized birds such as Mourning Doves, jays, and starlings.

Nesting: Platform nest of sticks lined with bark, placed in tree 10–70 ft. high. Eggs: 3–6, pale blue-green with dark marks; I: 32–36 days; F: 27–34 days, altricial; B: 1.

Other Behavior: May show up at bird feeders, especially in winter, when it roams more widely for food.

Habitat: Mixed forests and open woodlands.

Voice: Loud, repeated, high "kek kek kek kek" call given during alarm or during pair interactions.

Conservation:
BBS: W ⇑ C ⇓ CBC: ↑
Populations may be slowly recovering after declines in the 1940s and 1950s due to use of DDT.

Northern Goshawk

Accipiter gentilis

Immature

Adult

Immature

Identification: 21" IN FLIGHT: In all plumages, large; long "muscular" wings, tapered at tip; long wide tail. Flies with **deep powerful wingbeats;** less "flap and glide" than is typical of Sharp-shinned and Cooper's Hawks. ADULT: **Dark gray above; light gray beneath; dark cap; white eyebrow.** IMM: Dark brown above; lighter below with thick brown streaks on breast *and* belly, making it look darker than imm. Cooper's Hawk. PERCHED: See adult and imm. clues above. Imm. plumage kept 1 year.

Feeding: Feeds on birds by catching them in air, mammals by swooping down on them. Eats medium-sized birds and mammals such as grouse and squirrels.

Nesting: Platform nest of sticks lined with bark, placed in the crotch of a tree 18–75 ft. high. Eggs: 2–5, bluish white; I: 35–38 days; F: 35 days, altricial; B: 1.

Other Behavior: Birds do flight displays over territory: slow exaggerated flapping between glides; undulating flights, as bird repeatedly flies up and swoops down. Can be aggressive to humans near nest site.

Habitat: Deep woods with mostly conifers.

Voice: Short, harsh, repeated "kek kek kek kek" used during pair interactions, and a down-slurred wail like "keeaah" given when the male brings food to the nest.

Conservation: BBS: W ↓ C CBC: ↑

Common Black-Hawk

Buteogallus anthracinus

Adult

Immature

Adult

Identification: 21″ IN FLIGHT—ADULT: **Black hawk; wide rounded wings; tail appears short and has wide white band through middle** and fine white band at tip. Small light areas may show at base of outer primaries. IMM: Streaked brown below; short wide tail has thin wavy black and white lines and wider black terminal band. PERCHED—ADULT: **Black;** tail as described; **yellow legs; prominent yellow-orange facial skin and black-tipped bill.** IMM: Dark back and wings; streaked below; buffy eyebrow and long dark streak off base of bill; tail as described. Imm. plumage kept 1 year.

Feeding: Hunts reptiles, amphibians, crabs, and insects by perching above wet areas or standing on bank or sandbar.

Nesting: Nest of sticks lined with grass and leaves, placed in tree 15–100 ft. high. Eggs: 1–3, white with dark marks; I: 34–37 days; F: 43–50 days, altricial; B: 1.

Other Behavior: Undulating display flights and dives may occur over the nest site. Usually seen perched.

Habitat: Wooded streams, rivers, and swamps; dry canyons

Voice: A series of harsh whistles increasing and then decreasing in intensity.

Conservation: HWI:→

Harris' Hawk
Parabuteo unicinctus

Adult

Immature

Adult

Identification: 20" IN FLIGHT: In all plumages, a **dark hawk** with **reddish-brown shoulders and wing linings; long black tail has broad white band at base** and **white band at tip.** ADULT: **Dark underparts; dark flight feathers.** IMM: Light streaks on belly; whitish flight feathers. PERCHED—ADULT: **Dark brown hawk with reddish-brown shoulders;** reddish-brown leggings; long tail; white undertail coverts. IMM: Like adult but with whitish streaks on dark breast.

Habitat: Desert scrub and mesquite woodlands.

Voice: A drawn-out alarm call like "kirrrrr."

Conservation: BBS: W ⇑ C ⇓ CBC: ↓

Feeding: Feeds by swooping down on prey. Eats wood rats, gophers, rabbits, squirrels, lizards, insects, and some birds.

Nesting: Platform nest of sticks and weeds lined with grass and green mesquite is placed in mesquite, cactus, or tree 10–30 ft. high. Eggs: 1–5, bluish white with marks; I: 33–36 days; F: 40–45 days, altricial; B: 1–2.

Other Behavior: A cooperative breeder with additional adults often attending a pair's nest, helping with feeding, and defending the nest. There can be up to 5 helpers at the nest. Can be polygamous, with either 1 male and several females or 1 female and several males.

Gray Hawk

Buteo nitidus

Adult

Immature

Identification: 17" IN FLIGHT: In all plumages, small buteo; long tail; thin, U-shaped, white band at base of tail. Flies like an accipiter, with rapid flaps followed by a glide. ADULT: Much like a gray version of a Broad-winged Hawk. **Black tail has 2 white bands, the wider one near the tip;** light unmarked underwings. IMM: Brown with very heavily streaked underparts; tail has thin dark bands with the last widest. PERCHED— ADULT: **Gray back and head; underparts barred gray;** tail as described. IMM: Dark eyeline; barred leg feathers; tail and breast as described.

Feeding: Birds perch in trees scanning for prey and then fly out to catch it. They eat lizards, snakes, small birds, and small mammals.

Nesting: Small platform nest of sticks, placed in tree along riverbed. Eggs: 1–3, pale bluish white; I: 32 days; F: 42 days, altricial; B: 1.

Other Behavior: May do roller-coaster flights near nesting area.

Habitat: Wooded rivers in semiarid areas.

Voice: A loud call like "creeee" given at disturbances around nest.

Conservation:
HWI:→
Streamside trees in which it nests are being cleared for agriculture, threatening its already small population.

Red-shouldered Hawk

Buteo lineatus

Adult

Immature

Adult

Identification: 17" IN FLIGHT: In all plumages, a **long-tailed long-winged** hawk with **thin crescent-shaped wing windows parallel to the dark tips of the wings.** May alternate flaps with glides like an accipiter. ADULT: Tail has **3–4 thin white bands between wide black bands.** IMM: From below, tail whitish with many narrow dark bands of equal width. PERCHED—ADULT: **Cinnamon breast; reddish shoulders; bold white spots on dark wings.** A pale race lives in S. Fla. IMM: Brown above, streaked brown and white below; tail as described. Imm. plumage kept 1 year. Imm. of Calif. race is similar to adult.

Feeding: Spots prey when perched. Eats small mammals, snakes, lizards, frogs, insects, and a few birds.

Nesting: Platform nest of sticks lined with finer materials is placed in tree 10–120 ft. high. Eggs: 2–6, bluish with dark marks; I: 28 days; F: 35–49 days, altricial; B: 1.

Other Behavior: Birds return to same nesting area repeatedly; do roller-coaster flights and dives as displays.

Habitat: Woodlands and swamps.

Voice: A down-slurred scream often given in a series during displays near nest.

Conservation: BBS: W ⇧ C ⇧ CBC: ↑

Broad-winged Hawk
Buteo platypterus

Adult   Immature   Adult

Identification: 15" IN FLIGHT—ADULT: **Broad black and white bands on tail;** wings broad, held flat during soar; wings white underneath with **conspicuous black border along tip and trailing edge.** IMM: Tail light brown with 4–5 thin dark bands, the last widest. PERCHED—ADULT: **Dark brown above; reddish-brown barring underneath.** IMM: Brown upperparts and brown streaking below; tail as described. Imm. plumage kept 1 year.

Feeding: Feeds by swooping down on prey from a perch. Eats mammals, birds, reptiles, and amphibians.

Nesting: Platform nest of sticks lined with greenery and bark, placed in tree 3–90 ft. high. Eggs: 1–4, white with dark marks; I: 30–38 days; F: 35–40 days, altricial; B: 1.

Other Behavior: Broad-wings are best known for their spectacular migrations, when they gather into flocks of thousands, rising on thermals and then gliding on to the next thermal. These migrations can be seen from various hawk-watching sites in fall. Spring migration is more dispersed except in S.E. Tex. and along the southern shores of the Great Lakes.

Habitat: Dry woodlands.

Voice: Most common call is a very high-pitched whistle with a short preceding syllable, like "sigeeee."

Conservation: BBS: W ⇑ C ↓ CBC: ↓ Up until the 1930s, migrating hawks were shot for sport by the thousands. Now they are all protected by law.

99

Swainson's Hawk

Buteo swainsoni

Light-morph adult   Light-morph immature   Dark-morph adult

Identification: 19″ **IN FLIGHT:** In all plumages, **long wings; long tail; pale wing linings; dark flight feathers.** Soars with wings held in a V, often tilts side to side. Dark morphs have all-dark bodies; rufous wing linings; and light undertail coverts. **PERCHED—ADULT: White chin; brown bib extending onto light chest.** Dark morph all dark. **IMM:** Dark brown above, streaked below; thick streaking on upper chest suggests biblike pattern of adult. Dark morph similar, but more heavily streaked below. Imm. plumage kept 2 yr.

Feeding: Often feeds by hopping on ground, eating insects such as grasshoppers and crickets. Also soars and catches mice, rabbits, lizards, frogs, and birds.

Nesting: Nest of sticks lined with plants, placed in tree, on cliff, or on ground. Eggs: 2–4, bluish white with dark marks; I: 28–35 days; F: 30 days, altricial; B: 1.

Other Behavior: Migrates in groups, rising on thermals, then gliding to the next thermal. Similar to Broad-winged Hawks in the East, although flocks are smaller, generally only in the hundreds.

Habitat: Prairies and open arid land.

Voice: A long high-pitched whistle.

Conservation: BBS: W ⇑ C ↑ CBC: ↓ Significant declines in S. Calif., where populations may be down 90% since 1940s.

100

Zone-tailed Hawk

Buteo albonotatus

Adult

Immature

Adult

Identification: 20″ IN FLIGHT: Looks like a Turkey Vulture, having a paler trailing half of the wings, flying with wings in a V, and tilting from side to side while soaring. **Distinguished from it by the thick white bands on its black tail and darker trailing edge of wings.** Also has a yellow cere. Imm. similar to adult, but with numerous thin dark tail bands. PERCHED: **Adult and imm. similar to adult Common Black-Hawk. Distinguished in flight by narrower wings and, when perched, by gray facial skin.**

Feeding: Feeds by swooping down on prey from the air. Eats mostly squirrels, lizards, birds, and frogs.

Nesting: Platform nest of large sticks lined with twigs, placed in mesquite or other tree 25–100 ft. high. Eggs: 1–3, bluish white with occasional marks; I: 35 days; F: 30–40 days, altricial; B: 1.

Other Behavior: This hawk may have evolved to mimic the Turkey Vulture and thus gain access to prey that have become accustomed to seeing the harmless vulture and not fleeing.

Habitat: In open rugged country near canyons or cliffs.

Voice: Alarm call is a long whistle.

Conservation:
HWI:→

Red-tailed Hawk

Buteo jamaicensis

Adult

Immature

Dark-morph adult

Adult

Identification: 19″ Extremely variable plumage. **In Flight—Adult: Long broad wings held in shallow V; reddish upper tail; dark mark on inner front edge of underwing; white chest; usually a belly band. Imm:** Distinctive upperwing paler on outer half; finely banded gray-brown tail; may show rectangular wing windows. **Perched—Adult: Red tail; white chest; usually a belly band;** white mottling on back. **Imm:** Similar except for tail. Imm. plumage kept 1 year.

morphs: "Krider's Hawk" (in Great Plains) — Pale version of above, may lack belly band. "Harlan's Hawk" (in Northwest and Midwest) — Body, upperwings, and underwing coverts dark with white spotting; tail streaked gray with dark tip. Intergrades of all morphs.

Feeding: May perch, hover, or hold still into wind when hunting. Eats small mammals, birds, reptiles.

Nesting: Platform of sticks lined with bark and greenery, in tree 15–120 ft. high. Eggs: 1–5, bluish white with dark marks; I: 28–35 days; F: 44–46 days, altricial; B: 1.

Other Behavior: Most commonly seen hawk.

Habitat: Variety of open habitats.

Voice: A down-slurred scream like "tseeeaarr" often directed at intruders; a harsh up-slurred "klooeeek" given by fledglings and adults; and a piercing "chwirk" during courtship or territorial encounters.

Conservation:
BBS: W ⇑ C ↑ CBC: ⇑

Ferruginous Hawk
Buteo regalis

Adult

Immature

Identification: 23" In Flight—Adult: Very large; white body; white underwings with chestnut on wing linings; dark-feathered legs form a V underneath. From above, note light rectangular patch on outer wings and light area at base of tail. Soars with wings in a shallow V; may also hover or hold still in wind. Imm: Similar, but lacks chestnut on wing linings and has white-feathered legs. Perched—Adult: White breast; pale head; reddish shoulders; dark-feathered legs. Often perches on ground. Imm: Dark brown above; light below; white-feathered legs. Imm. plumage kept 1 year.

Feeding: Feeds by swooping down on prey from the air. Eats mostly medium-sized mammals, reptiles, insects.

Nesting: Platform nest of sticks, bones, and cow dung lined with grasses, placed on ground, cliff edge, or in tree 6–55 ft. high. Eggs: 2–6, bluish white with dark marks; I: 28–33 days; F: 44–48 days, altricial; B: 1.

Other Behavior: In breeding territory, maintains up to 5 nest sites, only 1 used. Roosts communally in Calif.

Habitat: Arid open land and grasslands.

Voice: Alarm call of a down-slurred scream used near the nest.

Conservation: BBS: W ⇑ C ⇑ CBC: ⇑ Breeding range has shrunk drastically in the last few decades; by 60% in parts of Can.

Rough-legged Hawk

Buteo lagopus

Light-morph immature

Dark-morph adult

Light-morph adult

Identification: 21" IN FLIGHT—ADULT: From below, **light morphs have distinctive black rectangular patch on wrist; white tail with wide dark band at tip.** Male has darker chest than belly; female darker belly than chest. **Dark morphs have dark bodies and wing coverts; silvery barred flight feathers with dark trailing edge.** Male has black tail with 3–4 narrow white bands; female has silvery tail with dark band at tip. IMM: Similar to adult female in both morphs, but with dusky terminal band on underside of tail. Light-morph imm. has solid dark belly. PERCHED: Bodies and tails for morphs as described above.

Feeding: Often hovers while hunting, but may also hunt from perch. Eats primarily voles and lemmings.

Nesting: Platform nest of sticks and grass placed in open tundra or on cliff. Eggs: 2–7, white with dark marks; I: 28–31 days; F: 39–45 days, altricial; B: 1.

Other Behavior: Adults and immatures migrate south in winter, and both color morphs are seen.

Habitat: Summers at the arctic tree line; winters in open country.

Voice: Generally silent on its wintering grounds.

Conservation: CBC: ↓

Golden Eagle
Aquila chrysaetos

Immature

Adult   Adult

Identification: 30" In Flight—Adult: Very large; long broad wings; all dark. Soars with wings in shallow V; head projects beyond wings less than one-half length of tail. Imm: Dark, with white areas limited to base of primaries and outer secondaries on wings (imm. Bald Eagles have white on armpits) and at base of tail. Perched: Adult and imm. dark with golden feathers on crown and nape. Imm. plumage kept 4 years.

Feeding: Hunts by soaring and then diving down on prey such as rabbits and rodents and some birds. Feeds on road-killed deer in the West.

Nesting: Large platform nest of sticks and roots lined with finer materials is placed on cliff ledge, on ground, or in tree 10–100 ft. high. Eggs: 1–4, creamy with dark marks; I: 43–45 days; F: 72–84 days, altricial; B: 1.

Other Behavior: Starts nest building anytime during nonbreeding season when site is clear of snow. May build nest on high-power electric poles. Breeding success often tied to populations of prey such as rabbits.

Habitat: Mountains, foothills, and adjacent grasslands.

Voice: Generally quiet; repeated series of chirps when approaching the nest with food.

Conservation: BBS: W ↑ C ↓ CBC: ↓ Federal protection has curtailed some of the aerial hunting and poisoning of this species.

105

Crested Caracara
Caracara plancus

Adult

Immature

Identification: 23" IN FLIGHT: In all plumages, **checkered white patches at tips of bowed black wings; long white neck; long whitish tail with wide dark terminal band;** black cap; black belly. Flight usually low and direct with deep rowing wing beats. PERCHED—ADULT: **Black cap; orange-red base of bill and face; white head and neck.** IMM: Like adult, but browner with streaking underneath. Imm. plumage kept 3 years.

Feeding: Feeds on the ground, eating mostly carrion, but also turtles, small mammals, fish, crustaceans, and insects.

Nesting: Bulky platform nest of sticks and vines lined with finer materials, placed in branches of cactus, palmetto, and other trees 8–80 ft. high. Eggs: 2–4, pinkish with dark marks; I: 28 days; F: 30–60 days, altricial; B: 1.

Other Behavior: Caracaras may fly along highways in the morning looking for animals killed by cars. They often displace Turkey Vultures from food and even harass them into regurgitating what they have eaten. Increasing and expanding range in Tex.

Habitat: Dry scrubland, prairie.

Voice: A cackling call can be given early in the morning. The bird's name comes from this.

Conservation: BBS: W C ⇑ CBC: ⇑ Populations are declining, especially in Fla., due to habitat loss.

American Kestrel

Falco sparverius

Male

Female

Male at nest

Identification: 9″ IN FLIGHT: Small colorful falcon; long tail; thin sickle-shaped wings. MALE: **Blue-gray wings; reddish-brown tail with broad black tip.** A line of translucent spots is visible along trailing edge of wings. FEMALE: **Wings, back, and tail reddish brown; thin dark brown bars on tail.** Spots along trailing edge of wings less conspicuous. PERCHED: **Two black sideburns on each side of face.** Male has blue-gray wings; female has lightly barred brown wings. Imm. almost identical to adults.

Feeding: Hunts by perching or hovering, then diving to catch prey. Eats voles and mice, birds, and insects.

Nesting: Natural cavity, nest box, woodpecker hole in cactus or tree, or in cliff nook, no nesting material. Eggs: 3–7, pinkish with dark marks; I: 29–31 days; F: 29–31 days, altricial; B: 1.

Other Behavior: Male does all hunting for 8–12 weeks during the breeding period; female remains at the nest. Male and female do fluttering flights when exchanging food that the male has brought to the nest.

Habitat: A wide variety of open habitats, including urban areas.

Voice: Most common call is a series of sharp staccato notes like "klee klee klee" given during disturbances at the nest.

Conservation:
BBS: W ↓ C ⇑ CBC: ↑

Merlin
Falco columbarius

Female

Immature

Identification: 10″ IN FLIGHT: In all plumages, **small dark falcon.** Heavier than a kestrel, with **thicker angular wings** and **powerful direct flight** that is usually low over vegetation; also has darker underwings. Sideburns indistinct. Often aggressive to other birds in flight. PERCHED— MALE: **Blue-gray above;** appears **light below** due to fine brown streaking. FEMALE: **Dark brown above** with **heavy brown streaks below** — the "chocolate falcon." IMM: Similar to adult female. Imm. plumage kept 1 year.

Feeding: Catches birds in the air, feeds secondarily on rodents, lizards, snakes, and insects.

Nesting: Uses abandoned nest of other bird, a cavity in a tree or cliff, or on the ground with no nest materials except a few sprigs of greenery. Eggs: 2–7, white with dark marks; I: 28–32 days; F: 25–35 days, altricial; B: 1.

Other Behavior: A wide variety of elaborate aerial maneuvers and calls are used in courtship displays. Food collected primarily by the male may be passed to the female in midair.

Habitat: Summers in a variety of habitats, including forest edges, farmland, urban areas; winters on coastal lowlands, prairies, marshes.

Voice: Alarm note is a high "kikikikiki."

Conservation: BBS: W ⇑ C ⇑ CBC: ↑

Peregrine Falcon

Falco peregrinus

Adult

Immature

Adult

Identification: 16" IN FLIGHT: In all plumages, large falcon; relatively long tapered wings; long broad tail; dark crown, broad sideburn on cheek extends below eye. Flight is direct with steady rowing beats on swept-back wings. Plumage varies from the Tundra form, which is bluish gray above with a white chest, to the Peale's form, which is darker above with a heavily spotted chest. As in most falcons, females noticeably larger than males. PERCHED—ADULT: **Bluish-gray back; barred belly; white bib; wide dark sideburn. IMM:** Brown back; streaked brown breast and belly; dark sideburn. Imm. plumage kept 1 year.

Feeding: Catches birds on the wing; eats some insects.

Nesting: A scrape in the ground on a cliff ledge 50–200 ft. high. Eggs: 3–4, creamy white with dark markings; I: 28–33 days; F: 30–42 days, altricial; B: 1.

Other Behavior: Spectacular fliers with tremendous speed when pursuing other birds. Some have been introduced into cities, where they nest on buildings.

Habitat: Open country near cliffs, urban areas, coast.

Voice: A series of harsh high-pitched sounds like "ki ki ki ki ki" given as an alarm near the nest.

Conservation: BBS: W ⇓ C ⇑ CBC:→ Extirpated in the East but now recovering slowly through protection of nests and restocking.

109

Gyrfalcon
Falco rusticolus

Gray-morph adult

Gray-morph immature

Gray-morph immature

Identification: 22″ IN FLIGHT—ADULT: **Large heavy-bodied falcon; long broad wings; long wide tail that tapers toward tip.** White morph all white except for lightly barred back and tail. Gray morph has gray upperparts, whitish body with gray spotting on breast and belly. Dark morph is dark with pale streaking on breast. From below, gray and dark morphs show darker wing linings than flight feathers. IMM: Similar to adults but browner; more streaked below. PERCHED—ADULT: **White morph mostly white; darker morphs have gray or brown back and streaked breast.** IMM: Similar to adults, but darker and with a bluish, rather than yellowish, base to bill.

Feeding: Hunts by catching other birds in midair, such as ptarmigans and grouse; eats some small mammals.

Nesting: Scraped depression on cliff ledge or uses abandoned nest in tree. Eggs: 3–8, pale yellowish with dark marks; I: 28–36 days; F: 49–56 days, altricial; B: 1.

Other Behavior: Gyrfalcons that range into southern Can. and northern U.S. in winter are usually immatures.

Habitat: Arctic tundra to tree line.

Voice: Alarm note is a harsh "kikikikiki."

Conservation: CBC: ↑ There is pressure worldwide on these birds, for they are collected from the wild and sold to falconers in other countries for large sums of money.

Prairie Falcon
Falco mexicanus

Identification: 16" IN FLIGHT: Large falcon; long pointed wings; long tail. From below, note **prominent dark wing linings and armpits that contrast with its light-colored body and light translucent flight feathers.** These traits distinguish it from the similar Peregrine Falcon. From above, has dark back and wings and lighter tail. PERCHED: **Brown back and brown-streaked front. Dark cheek bar is thinner than in most Peregrine Falcons.** IMM: Similar to adult, but more streaking on breast and a blue-to-yellow cere (rather than orange as in adult).

Feeding: Catches birds in midair or on ground, and mammals after swift swoop.

Nesting: Scrape in a cliff ledge 20–400 ft. high. Eggs: 2–7, pinkish white with dark marks; I: 28–32 days; F: 35–42 days, altricial; B: 1.

Other Behavior: Strongly territorial during the early stages of breeding; less so later.

Habitat: Plains, grasslands, and other open country.

Voice: Alarm notes include a harsh series of short notes like "kikikikiki."

Conservation:
CBC: ↑
This species, owing to prey differences, was not as adversely affected as Peregrines by pesticide residues.

111

Gray Partridge

Perdix perdix

Identification: 13″ **Rusty face and throat; gray breast; brown barring on flanks.** Male has large brown patch on whitish belly; female lacks patch. IN FLIGHT: Note chestnut tail feathers.

Feeding: Eats grain, weed, and grass seeds; also leaves and insects.

Nesting: Nest is a scraped depression lined with grasses, weeds, and feathers, near rocks or taller vegetation. Eggs: 15–17, olive; I: 23–25 days; F: 13–15 days, precocial; B: 1.

Other Behavior: Native to Europe and Asia, but introduced into N. America and now widespread. In fall, forms covey of about 10–30 birds, which remain together throughout winter.

Habitat: Open farmlands and hedgerows.

Voice: Unmated male gives rusty-gate "kee-uck" sound to advertise for female.

Conservation:
BBS: W ↑ C ⇑ CBC: ↓

Chukar

Alectoris chukar

Identification: 13" A bold black necklace encircles its white chin. Back and breast are grayish; white flanks boldly barred with black; bill and eyes are red.

Feeding: Feeds on weeds, seeds, and grasses, especially cheatgrass.

Nesting: Concealed nest lined with feathers, placed in a scraped depression near shrub or rock. Eggs: 10–20, yellowish with dark marks; I: 22–24 days; F: 7–10 days, precocial; B: 1.

Other Behavior: Introduced from Asia to U.S., mainly in the West. Winter covey consists of 20–40 birds. The "chukar" call is given by both sexes as a signal to reassemble a scattered covey. In addition, it is used as an advertising call of unmated males, or as an aggressive call by paired males.

Habitat: Arid rocky slopes and canyons.

Voice: Both sexes give "chukar" call.

Conservation:
BBS: W ⇓ C CBC: ↓

Ring-necked Pheasant

Phasianus colchicus

Male

Female

Identification: 33" A large chickenlike bird with a **long pointed tail. MALE: White neck-ring; green head; red wattles.** Body is a mixture of iridescent greens, browns, and golds. Two other forms can be seen: one with white on the wings and another lacking the white neck-ring. **FEMALE: Rich brown with dark markings on wings and back.**

Feeding: At bird feeders, eats cracked corn and mixed seed from the ground. In the wild, eats waste grain, weed seeds, acorns, berries, and insects.

Nesting: Nest of grasses and leaves placed on the ground is concealed among grasses or shrubs. Eggs: 10–12, brownish olive; I: 24 days; F: 10–11 weeks, precocial; B: 1.

Other Behavior: One of the most conspicuous aspects of pheasant behavior is the crowing of the male. It sounds like "skwagock," and is accompanied by an audible wing whir. This is territorial advertisement, and it is most frequent in the spring, in the early morning and late afternoon. Some males have just 1 mate, but 45% of males have a harem of females with whom they mate.

Habitat: Farmlands with woods edges and hedgerows.

Voice: Male gives "skwagock" call. Female responds to him with "kia-kia" call.

Conservation: BBS: W ↓ C ↓ CBC: ⇊ First introduced into N. America in 1850s. Now widespread.

Spruce Grouse

Dendragapus canadensis

Male

Female

Identification: 15" **MALE: Black chin and breast; red eye combs. Tail is black with a reddish-brown tip** except in the Northwest, where the so-called Franklin's Grouse form has an all-black tail. **FEMALE: Brownish overall with black barring on breast and belly;** tail as in male. Females come in reddish and grayish color phases.

Feeding: Feeds on the ground and in trees, eating needles and buds of conifers; also wild berries, grass seeds, and insects. In winter exclusively eats conifers.

Nesting: Grassy nest is placed in well-concealed location in brush or thicket. Eggs: 6–7, buff with dark marks; I: 23 days; F: 10 days, precocial; B: 1.

Other Behavior: In territorial display males do nearly vertical flutter flights, producing a drumming sound by rapidly beating wings. In western race called Franklin's Grouse, the males twice clap their wings above their back during this display. Often very tame.

Habitat: Dense coniferous forests with occasional clearings.

Voice: Male may make hissing sound when female is near. Female makes low warning calls to chicks.

Conservation:
CBC: ⇑
As with many grouse, populations fluctuate cyclically.

115

Blue Grouse

Dendragapus obscurus

Male

Female

Identification: 18″ MALE: **Unmarked gray chin and breast; yellow-orange eye combs.** Tail is black with gray tip, except in northern Rockies, where lighter area at tip is absent. During displays, males may expose yellow-to-red air sacs on either side of the neck. FEMALE: **Brownish overall with gray-and-white mottled breast;** tail is as in male.

Feeding: Feeds on the needles, buds, and seeds of firs and hemlocks. Also eats insects.

Nesting: Well-concealed nest of grasses and pine needles, placed at base of tree or rock. Eggs: 7–10, buff with light marks; I: 26 days; F: 7–14 days, precocial; B: 1.

Other Behavior: Male attracts female with "hooting" display. He spreads tail while inflating colorful neck sacs, which help amplify his calls. May be very tame.

Habitat: Open woodlands, mountain slopes, brushy lowlands.

Voice: Male gives series of low-pitched hooting calls.

Conservation:
BBS: W ⇓ C CBC: ↓

Willow Ptarmigan

Lagopus lagopus

Summer male

Summer female

Identification: 15" SUMMER—MALE: Reddish-brown head and neck; brown body; white on wings and belly. FEMALE: Mottled brown with black tail; heavier bill than similar female Rock Ptarmigan. WINTER: **All white except for black tail.** •Willow and Rock Ptarmigans are very similar. The **females are hard to distinguish in the field;** both are mottled brown with black tails in summer and all white with black tails in winter. Their **black tail in all seasons** distinguishes them from the otherwise similar White-tailed Ptarmigan.

Feeding: Buds from woody plants, seeds, insects.

Nesting: Nest a shallow depression in ground lined with grass, moss, and feathers, placed by grass clump or base of log. Eggs: 6–7, yellowish with darker marks; I: 21–22 days; F: 9–10 days, precocial; B: 1.

Other Behavior: Red eye combs of males are swollen during displays. Songs are given by males at end of courtship display flights. Females cover the nest with vegetation when they briefly leave it during incubation.

Habitat: Summers on shrubby alpine areas; winters at lower elevations.

Voice: Call a loud "tobacco tobacco."

Conservation: TREND UNKNOWN.

Rock Ptarmigan
Lagopus mutus

Summer female

Winter male

Summer male

Identification: 13″ SUMMER—MALE: **Grayish-brown head and neck; brown body.** FEMALE: **Mottled brown with black tail;** smaller bill than similar female Willow Ptarmigan. WINTER—MALE: **All white except for black tail and black streak through eye.** FEMALE: **All white with black tail.** •Rock and Willow Ptarmigans are very similar. The **females are hard to distinguish in the field;** both are mottled brown with black tails in summer and all white with black tails in winter. Their **black tail in all seasons** distinguishes them from otherwise similar White-tailed Ptarmigan.

Feeding: Leaf and flower buds and catkins from woody plants, seeds, insects.

Nesting: Nest a shallow depression in ground lined with grass, moss, and feathers, placed in rocky area. Eggs: 6–9, buff with dark brown splotches; I: 21–24 days; F: 12–14 days, precocial; B: 1.

Other Behavior: Nests in barren areas. In spring males develop red eye combs, which are used in courtship displays. Migrates from north when snow covers food.

Habitat: Tundra and barren rocky slopes.

Voice: Gives a long snoring call.

Conservation: TREND UNKNOWN.

White-tailed Ptarmigan

Lagopus leucurus

Summer male   Summer female

Winter

Identification: 13″ Ptarmigans molt 3 times per year. This is the only species in N. America with **white on the tail in all plumages.** This shows best when the bird is flying. SUMMER—MALE: **Mottled brown and black with white on wings, belly, and tail. FEMALE: Underparts barred black; upperparts brown with thin yellow barring on back and uppertail.** FALL AND SPRING: Patches of brown and white on head and back; mostly white on wings, belly, and tail. WINTER: Both sexes **completely white except** for black bill and thin red eye comb.

Feeding: Eats the catkins of alders, and the buds, flowers, and twigs of alpine willows and other shrubs.

Nesting: Nest lined with grasses, lichens, and feathers, placed in depression on alpine turf or under shrub. Eggs: 4–16, buff with darker marks; I: 22–23 days; F: 10 days, precocial; B: 1.

Other Behavior: Male attracts female with song-flight display and calls from 15–50-acre breeding territory. Pair bonds last until chicks hatch. Female defends nest.

Habitat: Summers on rocky mountain tundra; winters at edge of tree line.

Voice: Cackling and clucking noises.

Conservation: TREND UNKNOWN. Has been introduced into Sierra Nevada.

Ruffed Grouse
Bonasa umbellus

Male

Identification: 17" MALE: **Note brown or gray tail with dark subterminal band;** sides of neck (the ruff) black; belly and chin light. Crest on head erected when bird is alarmed. FEMALE: **Browner and more barred below; central brown gap in the dark tail band;** black ruff is smaller.

Feeding: Feeds on berries, leaves, buds, seeds, and insects.

Nesting: Nest lined with leaves, twigs, and feathers, placed in scraped depression and concealed under brush or shrub. Eggs: 6–15, buff with light marks; I: 21–28 days; F: 10–12 days, precocial; B: 1.

Other Behavior: Male advertises his territory to prospective mate by drumming from a favorite spot, usually a fallen log. Drumming sound is made by bracing tail against log and giving a series of strong wingstrokes. He also struts before female with tail fanned and neck ruff raised. Female raises brood. She will feign injury if disturbed during incubation. Ruffed Grouse can at times be very tame. They occasionally approach humans and may even act aggressively.

Habitat: Forests with mostly deciduous trees.

Voice: A sharp "quit-quit" alarm note. Female gives cooing and clucking notes.

Conservation: BBS: W ⇓ C ⇓ CBC: ↑

120

Sage Grouse

Centrocercus urophasianus

Male in display

Female

Identification: 31″ **Very large** grouse with a **pointed tail** and **black belly**. MALE: **Black chin; white breast;** yellow eye combs. In display, male inflates air sacs on breast. FEMALE: **Light brown chin; brown breast.**

Feeding: Eats sagebrush leaves, weed seeds, flowers, and buds.

Nesting: Nest a scraped depression lined with grasses and sage leaves, placed under sagebrush. Eggs: 6–15, yellow-olive with darker marks; I: 25–27 days; F: 7–10 days, precocial; B: 1.

Other Behavior: Famous for "strutting" behavior. A large group of males congregates on a display ground. Here individual males strut with tails fanned in a complex sequence of stepping, wing-brushing movements. They deflate their air sacs, which makes a plopping sound. Females are attracted to the group and usually mate with the dominant male. Females then raise broods alone.

Habitat: Sagebrush.

Voice: Males make plopping noise with air sacs; also give weak "wa-um-poo" sound. Females make clucking noises.

Conservation:
BBS: W ⇑ C ⇓ CBC:→ Habitat loss of sagelands to agriculture and grazing causing population decline.

121

Greater Prairie-Chicken
Lesser Prairie-Chicken
Tympanuchus cupido   Tympanuchus pallidicinctus

Greater Prairie-Chicken male

Lesser Prairie-Chicken male

Identification: Greater 17", Lesser 16" Both species have **dark barring on brown back and on whitish chest and belly;** tail is dark and rounded. Lesser Prairie-Chicken is slightly smaller and paler. Ranges do not overlap. **MALES: Fleshy yellow eye combs.** In display, Lesser shows orange-red air sacs on sides of neck; Greater shows yellow-orange air sacs. **FEMALES:** Thin yellow eye combs and no air sacs.

Greater   Lesser

Feeding: Both eat grasshoppers, seeds, and grain.

Nesting: GREATER: Grassy nest in depression. Eggs: 7–17, olive with dark marks; I: 23–24 days; F: 7–10 days, precocial; B: 1. **LESSER:** Grassy nest in depression. Eggs: 11–13, yellowish with brown marks; I: 22–24 days; F: 7–10 days, precocial; B: 1.

Other Behavior: Males display in groups with tails erect, wings drooped, then deflate air-filled sacs, making booming noise in Greater, and gobbling noise in Lesser Prairie-Chicken. Males then jump and run at each other with sacs inflated. Females mate with dominant male, raise broods alone.

Habitat: Greater lives on tallgrass prairie; Lesser on short-grass prairie.

Voice: Booming and gobbling.

Conservation: Greater: BBS: W ↑ C ↑ CBC: ↓ Lesser: POP. DECLINING. Subspecies of Greater, Attwater's Prairie-Chicken, endangered in U.S.

122

Sharp-tailed Grouse

Tympanuchus phasianellus

Male

Identification: 18″ Dark spots on light brown back and on whitish chest and belly; tail is pointed, with squared-off central feathers projecting well beyond the others. In display, male exposes purple air sacs on either side of neck. IN FLIGHT: Note white on sides of tail.

Feeding: Feeds on the ground, eating plant parts, berries, grains, insects.

Nesting: Nest a scraped depression lined with grasses, ferns, and leaves, in grass or under shrub. Eggs: 5–17, light brown with darker marks; I: 21–24 days; F: 7–10 days, precocial; B: 1.

Other Behavior: As with some other species of grouse, males display communally in groups at a traditional site called a lek. With tails fanned and wings drooped, they make cooing sound by deflating neck air sacs. They also jump and run at one another. Females come and mate with the dominant male, who usually is the one occupying the center spot in the group. Females then go off to nest and raise the young by themselves.

Habitat: Grasslands, shrublands, and partially cleared boreal forest.

Voice: Males make cooing sound.

Conservation: BBS: W ⇓ C ⇑ CBC: ⇑ Declining in much of its range due to habitat loss by conversion of grasslands to agricultural areas.

Wild Turkey
Meleagris gallopavo

Female

Identification: 36–49" Its **large size** and **familiar turkey shape** make it unmistakable. Body is dark and iridescent; **head is naked.** MALE: Larger and more iridescent than female and with tuft of hairlike feathers on breast. FEMALE: Smaller than male, has less iridescence, and usually lacks tuft on breast.

Feeding: Feeds on the ground, eating nuts, acorns, and seeds. Also eats grains, vegetation, insects, frogs, lizards.

Nesting: Nest is placed in a natural or scraped depression and lined with leaves and grasses. Eggs: 6–20, whitish buff with marks; I: 27–28 days; F: 6–10 days, precocial; B: 1.

Other Behavior: Spends the winter in same- or mixed-sex flocks. In courtship, male struts and gobbles with tail fanned. Female responds with yelping call. Male may mate with many females. Female raises young. Domestic turkey is a subspecies that had been tamed and taken from Mexico to Europe by Spanish in 16th century. English settlers brought domestic turkey back to N. America.

Habitat: Open forests, forest edges, wooded swamps.

Voice: Gobbling, yelping, and clucking notes.

Conservation: BBS: W ⇑ C ⇑ CBC: ⇑ Habitat loss and hunting had previously reduced populations. Has now been reintroduced into much of former range.

Montezuma Quail

Cyrtonyx montezumae

Male (l.), female (r.)

Identification: 9" Both sexes have a **rounded overall shape** and **bushy brown crown** that protrudes at the back of the neck. MALE: Distinctive **black-and-white pattern on head;** heavily spotted with white on sides. FEMALE: **Brownish overall** with faint cheek pattern of male. **Distinctive crown** and **short tail** help identify her.

Feeding: Feeds by scratching in ground to get at the bulbs and roots of plants such as wood sorrel, chufa, or nut grass. Also eats insects, acorns, and seeds.

Nesting: Nest consists of a shallow scrape in the ground, lined and roofed over with grass. Eggs: 6–14, creamy white; I: 25–26 days; F: 10 days, precocial; B: 1.

Other Behavior: When alarmed, sits motionless until almost stepped on. In nonbreeding season, they form coveys of about 7–8 birds from same family. They feed together and roost on the ground in a semicircle around a rock or grass clump. Nest during the summer rainy season. Unmated males call most during July and Aug.

Habitat: Grassy open woodlands on semiarid mountain slopes, in canyons.

Voice: A quavering call somewhat like Screech Owl's.

Conservation: BBS: W ⇑ C CBC: ↑ Destruction by grazing animals of bulb-bearing forbs, an important food source for quail, has hurt populations.

Northern Bobwhite

Colinus virginianus

Female (l.), male (r.)

Identification: 10" Both sexes have a **light eyebrow and chin** and a wide **dark streak through the eye.** Sides are streaked with reddish brown and tail is gray. **MALE: White eyebrow** and chin. **FEMALE: Buffy eyebrow** and chin.

Feeding: Feeds on grass seeds, grains, leaves, fruits, tender plant parts, and insects. Also comes to bird feeders for seed placed on the ground.

Nesting: Nest a scrape in the ground lined with grasses, moss, pine needles, placed usually within 50 ft. of a clearing. Eggs: 12–14, white; I: 23 days; F: 14 days, precocial; B: 1.

Other Behavior: The famous "bob-white" call is best clue to presence of this wary bird. Call is given most loudly and frequently by unmated males in spring and early summer, around the areas where mated pairs are breeding. After chicks hatch, family feeds and stays as tight flock. Parents will give alarm call, and may do distraction display when threatened by possible predator. In winter, multiple family groups form a covey of about 12–16 birds that feed and roost together in a fixed range. Each night the covey sleeps on the ground in a tight circle with tails pointed inward.

Habitat: Farmland, brushy fields, open woodland.

Voice: Wide variety of calls include "toilick" for alarm; "koilee" by covey at dawn and dusk; and "bob-white" by males.

Conservation: BBS: W ⇑ C ↓ CBC: ⇓ Does not survive harsh winters in North.

126

Scaled Quail
Callipepla squamata

Identification: 11″ **White-tipped crest** is distinctive. Gray feathers on breast and back tipped with black, making them look like scales. Sexes similar.

Feeding: Feeds on ground, eating grass and weed seeds.

Nesting: Concealed nest lined with grasses and feathers is placed in a scraped depression in grass or shrubbery. Eggs: 9–16, creamy white, plain or with light marks; I: 21–23 days; F: ?, precocial; B: 1.

Other Behavior: During breeding, unmated males call from exposed perches to attract potential mates. Females may defer egg laying until summer rainy season starts. In fall, families form into a large covey of 50 or more birds that feed and roost together. May hybridize with Gambel's Quail.

Habitat: Arid grassland and scrub.

Voice: "Pey-cos" location call given by both sexes when separated. Unmated male gives "whock" call.

Conservation: BBS: W ⇓ C ⇓ CBC: ⇓ Species was introduced into Wash. and Nev.

Gambel's Quail

Callipepla gambelii

Male

Female

Identification: 11" Black plume on forehead, reddish-brown sides; unscaled belly. MALE: Black chin; light yellow belly with black patch in center. FEMALE: Light chin; no dark patch on belly.

Feeding: Feeds on the ground on seeds, grain, green plants, and the fruit of cacti. Will come to bird feeders for seed spread on the ground. Forages primarily in morning and late afternoon.

Nesting: Nest lined with twigs, grass, and leaves, placed in a scraped depression near the base of vegetation. Sometimes nests off the ground in old roadrunner or Cactus Wren nest. Eggs: 9–14, whitish buff with darker marks; I: 21–24 days; F: 10 days, precocial; B: 1–2.

Other Behavior: Winter coveys consist of family units and some nonbreeding adults. During breeding season, coveys split up. Unmated males establish crowing posts and attract mates. After the brood is hatched the male may take over the care of the chicks so female can begin a 2nd clutch. May hybridize with Scaled Quail.

Habitat: Arid scrubby areas, also riparian woodland.

Voice: Both sexes give 4-note "chi-ca-go-go" location call. Unmated males give "kaa" call.

Conservation: BBS: W ↓ C CBC: ↑

California Quail
Callipepla californica

Female (l.), male (r.)

Identification: 10″ Both sexes have a **black plume on forehead** and a scaled appearance to belly. MALE: **Black chin;** light forehead. FEMALE: **Light chin.**

Feeding: Eats weeds, grasses, grain, insects. Will come to bird feeders for grain and seeds.

Nesting: Concealed nest lined with grasses and dead leaves, placed in a scraped depression near a log, rock, or stump, or in the low fork of a tree. Eggs: 12–16, creamy white with dark marks; I: 18–23 days; F: 10 days, precocial; B: 1–2.

Other Behavior: Roosts in trees, not on the ground. In fall birds form large coveys of 30–40 birds on average, but can be up to 600 birds. In breeding season, covey disperses and mated pairs begin nesting. Unmated males call for females. Female may renest in favorable years, in which case male takes over care of 1st brood.

Habitat: Open woodlands or shrubby areas, parks, and suburbs; usually near water.

Voice: Location call is a 3-note "chi-ca-go," lower pitched than Gambel's Quail's. Unmated males give "cow" note.

Conservation: BBS: W ↓ C CBC: ↓

129

Mountain Quail
Oreortyx pictus

Identification: 11" Distinctive **long thin double plumes on forehead.** Both sexes have a reddish-brown chin, gray breast, and chestnut belly with white barring along sides.

Feeding: Feeds on the ground, eating leaves, buds, and flowers of legumes; also underground plant bulbs, seeds, insects, and acorns.

Nesting: Concealed nest lined with grass, leaves, feathers, and pine needles, placed in a scraped depression at base of log, tree trunk, or grass tuft. Eggs: 6–15, pale creamy buff; I: 21–25 days; F: ?, precocial; B: 1–2.

Other Behavior: Spends the fall and winter in coveys of 10–30 birds. Has seasonal migrations. In spring moves from lower altitudes to higher altitudes that have a combination of open brush and tree cover. Pairs separate out from covey and nest. Unmated males give repeated whistled calls to try to attract a mate. Wary and somewhat secretive.

Habitat: Brushy mountainous areas.

Voice: Unmated male gives loud whistled call like "plu-ark."

Conservation: BBS: W ↑ C CBC: ↓

Yellow Rail
Coturnicops noveboracensis

Identification: 7" Very secretive; **heard more than seen.** Calls mostly at night during breeding season. **Tiny, brownish, chickenlike bird; wide dark streaks on back crossed by fine white lines;** buffy breast. Short bill varies from yellowish to dark. **IN FLIGHT:** Note white patch on trailing edge of wings.

Feeding: Feeds in shallow water, eating snails, insects, and some seeds and grasses.

Nesting: Canopied saucerlike nest of fine grass lined with finer material, placed on ground or in surrounding stems a few inches above water. Eggs: 7–10, yellow-buff with dark marks; I: 16–18 days; F: 35 days, precocial; B: ?

Other Behavior: This bird is so secretive its behavior is hard to observe. Its call, which is given occasionally in the middle of the day, is most often heard at the end of the day and at night. It seems to occur primarily at the beginning and middle stages of the breeding cycle.

Habitat: Summers on wet meadows, marshes; winters on grasslands, fields, coastal marshes.

Voice: Call sounds like 2 small stones clicking together in a regular rhythm, like "tik tik, tik tik tik" repeated.

Conservation: BBS: W C ⇑ CBC: ↑ Populations declining due to habitat loss and pesticides.

Black Rail
Laterallus jamaicensis

Identification: 5½" Our smallest rail and almost as secretive as the Yellow Rail. Listen for its nocturnal call. **Black; fine white spotting on wings;** brown on back of neck. More likely to scurry away through the marsh grasses than take flight.

Feeding: Feeds in shallow water and on the ground, eating insects and aquatic plant seeds.

Nesting: Cuplike nest of soft grasses with a grass canopy, placed on the ground. Eggs: 6–13, white with buffy marks; I: 16–20 days; F: ?, precocial; B: ?

Other Behavior: Rarely seen but can be heard, especially at night. Very little is known about other aspects of this species' behavior.

Habitat: Salt and freshwater marshes, wet meadows.

Voice: A repeated "kikidoo, kikidoo, kikidoo."

Conservation: CBC: ↑

Clapper Rail

Rallus longirostris

Identification: 14" Large rail with long slightly downcurved bill. Back feathers dark-centered with broad gray edges, giving back a grayish look. Breast color varies regionally from gray to reddish brown.

Feeding: Feeds in shallow water and on mudflats, eating crabs, crayfish, small fish, insects, and some plants.

Nesting: Cupped platform nest of grasses and aquatic plants, placed on the ground. Eggs: 5–12, buff with dark marks; I: 20–23 days; F: 63–70 days, precocial; B: 2.

Other Behavior: In eastern U.S., occasionally hybridizes with King Rail.

Habitat: Salt marshes.

Voice: Harsh notes varying in speed, like "chit chit chit, chit, chit — chit — chit."

Conservation: BBS: W C ↑ CBC: ↓ Federally endangered in the West.

Virginia Rail

Rallus limicola

Identification: 9″ Small rail; **long bill;** similar in coloration to much larger King Rail. **Back feathers dark-centered with reddish-brown edges; face gray** (rather than buff as in King Rail); bill can be reddish, especially at base.

Feeding: Feeds in mudflats by probing in the mud with bill searching for worms, snails, and aquatic insects.

Nesting: Loose, canopied, cuplike nest of coarse grasses, reeds, and sedges, placed on ground a few inches above mud or water. Eggs: 5–12, buff with dark marks; I: 18–20 days; F: 25 days, precocial; B: 1–2.

Other Behavior: Heard more than seen. Calls are given most at dawn and dusk, but may occur sporadically at other times of day or night. Pair does courtship feeding and mutual preening.

Habitat: Summers on freshwater and brackish marshes; winters also on salt marshes.

Voice: Call of territorial male is a metallic "kit kidit kidit kidit kidit." Also gives a "kikikikeeer" and a series of descending grunts.

Conservation: BBS: W ⇓ C ⇓ CBC: ⇑

Sora
Porzana carolina

Identification: 9" Small, brownish, chickenlike bird; **black face** and upper throat; **bright yellow bill**. Back is dark brown with fine white streaks; belly is gray with dark barring. In winter, gray edges to face and throat feathers hide the black markings in these spots.

Feeding: Feeds in the water and on the ground, eating aquatic insects and weed seeds.

Nesting: Saucerlike nest of dead cattail leaves, reeds, and sedges, attached to surrounding plant stems a few in. above water. Eggs: 6–18, buff with dark marks; I: 18–20 days; F: 21–25 days, precocial; B: 1–2.

Other Behavior: As with other rails, Sora's body is compressed laterally, which may help it move more easily throughout its reedy environment. Any sudden sound near breeding ground may start the birds calling. They tend to leave breeding ground on night of first frost. Soras migrate at night, like most rails.

Habitat: Salt and freshwater marshes, wet meadows.

Voice: A common call is a plaintive ascending "puweee, puweee." Also gives call like a descending whinny that slows down near the end.

Conservation:
BBS: W ↓ C ⇓ CBC: ↑

135

Common Moorhen
Gallinula chloropus

Winter adult

Summer adult

Immature

Identification: 14" **SUMMER:** Dark; ducklike; black head; yellow-tipped red bill; also has red forehead and white line of feathers along flanks. Often seen swimming. **WINTER:** Like summer, but with brownish yellow-tipped bill and brownish forehead. **IMM:** Brownish gray overall; whitish throat; dark bill. White line along flanks distinguishes it from similar imm. Purple Gallinule. Imm. plumage kept until midwinter. Red forehead does not fully develop until late next summer.

Feeding: Feeds by walking over aquatic vegetation or by swimming and diving. Eats seeds, grasses, small snails, and aquatic and land insects.

Nesting: Platform nest of cattail stems lined with grasses, placed on ground or suspended in vegetation 4–6 in. high. Eggs: 4–17, olive-buff with dark marks; I: 19–22 days; F: 40–50 days, precocial; B: 2–3.

Other Behavior: Courtship display may include head held low, wings raised, and white undertail exposed. Young of 1st broods may help in feeding later broods.

Habitat: Freshwater marshes, ponds, lakes.

Voice: A wide variety of sounds, many like the clucks of a chicken; others are short grating noises.

Conservation:
BBS: W ↓ C ⇓ CBC: ⇑

American Coot

Fulica americana

Adult

Immature

Identification: 15" Slate-colored; ducklike; white bill; partial ring around tip of bill. **Imm:** Grayish overall; whitish chin and throat; bill light-colored with no partial ring at tip. Imm. plumage gradually changes to adult through winter.

Feeding: Feeds on water by diving or tipping its body like a duck, eating seeds, leaves, roots, and small aquatic animals. Also feeds on land.

Nesting: Platform nest of stems lined with finer material, placed on a floating mass of vegetation attached to surrounding stems. Eggs: 8–12, pink-buff with dark marks; I: 21–25 days; F: 49–56 days, precocial; B: 1–2.

Other Behavior: Many conspicuous visual displays easily seen. Coots defend breeding and feeding territories by charging at other birds and running across water. In courtship, male may chase female with flapping wings or swim with head and neck held close to the water, wing tips raised, and tail lifted, displaying white patches. Birds may build up to 9 nests and then chose 1 for eggs. Occasionally, female coots will lay eggs in another coot's nest.

Habitat: Summers on marshy lakes; winters also along the coast.

Voice: A wide variety of calls, most of which sound like the toots of a tiny toy trumpet.

Conservation: BBS: W ↓ C ↓ CBC: ↓

Sandhill Crane

Grus canadensis

Identification: 45" Tall, gray, heronlike bird; dark red patch on forehead; black bill. Some feathers on back and wings are rusty-colored, possibly due to staining as bird preens with iron-laden mud on its bill. IMM: Grayish with more extensive rust coloring; forehead lacks dark red patch; bill orangish. Imm. plumage kept about 2 years.

Feeding: Feeds by picking or probing with bill, eating seeds, agricultural grains, and small animals.

Nesting: Moundlike nest of marsh plants, grasses, and weeds, placed on ground or in shallow water. Eggs: 1–3, olive with dark marks; I: 28–32 days; F: 90 days, precocial; B: 1.

Other Behavior: These birds form huge flocks in winter and during migration, when they feed primarily in agricultural fields and then roost at night in the center of shallow lakes or large shallow rivers. Courtship displays are easily seen during migration and involve graceful jumps off the ground in a dancing manner. Subspecies *G. c. pulla,* in Miss., is endangered.

Habitat: Summers on prairies and tundra; during winter, roosts on shallow water and feeds in agricultural fields.

Voice: A low-pitched "karooo karooo karooo."

Conservation: BBS: W ⇑ C ↑ CBC: ↑ Dependent on unprotected migration stopovers in Midwest.

Whooping Crane
Grus americana

Identification: 55" Tall, white, heronlike bird; black facial mask; dark red crown. IN FLIGHT: Note the black wing tips. IMM: White except for rust-colored head and wing tips; lacks adult facial markings. Imm. plumage kept 1 year.

Feeding: Feeds in shallow water or mudflats eating crabs, shrimp, clams, and snails, as well as amphibians, reptiles, and plant parts.

Nesting: A mound of wetland plants and grasses placed in shallow water. Eggs: 1–3, creamy buff with dark marks; I: 34–35 days; F: 100–115 days, precocial; B: 1.

Other Behavior: Family groups of several birds defend winter feeding territories. Courtship displays are typical of many cranes and include high leaps between the pair and bills pointing up and down. In order to help keep the bird from extinction, eggs laid by captive birds have been placed in Sandhill Crane nests and these parents raise the Whooping Crane young.

Habitat: Summers on freshwater marshes; winters on saltwater marshes.

Voice: A loud, repeated "kalooo kaleeooo."

Conservation: Endangered in U.S. and Can. Only about 200 birds alive. Being reintroduced into Fla.

Most people see their first shore-birds in mid-to-late summer, when they are on vacation and near the coast. At this time, as well as in spring, large numbers of shore-birds stop over to feed along sandy beaches and mudflats as they migrate south from their breeding grounds in the Arctic. A few very common species make up about 80–90% of what you see. If you start by learning to identify these species, it will then be much easier to learn the others.

Most of these common species migrate inland as well as along the coasts. So if you live inland, look for shorebirds along mudflats and shallow edges of streams, rivers, ponds, and lakes.

In fall, you will see young and adult shorebirds. Adults are often in transition between their summer and winter plumages; young are in their juvenal plumage and by late fall may be molting into their win-ter plumage. Because of this, you may see a lot of variation within the same species. For complete descriptions of these birds, refer to their main accounts on the pages mentioned.

MOST COMMON SHOREBIRDS ON MUDFLATS AND BEACHES

Western Sandpiper, p. 169

Least Sandpiper, p. 170

Smallest Sandpipers Sometimes called "peeps." Smallest shorebirds; brownish; feed along mudflats.

Sanderling Small; grayish; black legs; chases the edges of waves as it feeds. P. 167.

Semipalmated Plover Small; stub-by bill; dark brown above; single dark neck-ring. P. 145.

Dunlin Medium-sized; long bill that droops slightly at the tip; may have some black on belly from summer plumage. P. 175.

Killdeer Medium-sized; short bill; 2 dark neck-rings. P. 147.

Long-billed

Short-billed and Long-billed Dowitchers
Medium-sized; very long straight bills; feed by probing sand with rapid sewing-machine action. Pp. 179, 180.

Black-bellied Plover Medium-sized; short thick bill; often some black on belly from summer plumage; in flight, look for black armpits. P. 142.

Willet Large; long heavy bill; long grayish legs; in flight, shows black wings with bold white stripe down center. P. 155.

Whimbrel Large; long downcurved bill; 2 dark stripes on crown; dark eyeline. P. 159.

Marbled Godwit Large; long slightly upturned bill is pink at base. P. 162.

American Avocet Large; long, thin, upturned bill; black and white areas on wings and back; rusty head; white belly. P. 151.

141

Black-bellied Plover
Pluvialis squatarola

Summer

Winter

Transition to winter

Fall juvenile

Identification: 12″ SUMMER: **Whitish crown; black from face to belly; white undertail coverts.** Female has white flecks in black areas. WINTER: **Grayish overall; darker above than below; faint eyebrow. Relatively larger head and longer bill** than similar golden-plovers. IN FLIGHT: All plumages show distinctive **black armpits; wide white wing-stripe; white rump.** FALL JUV: Like winter adult, but wings and back darker and with pale whitish-yellow spots; underparts finely streaked. Can be very similar to winter golden-plovers; note bill proportions and flight marks.

Feeding: Feeds on marine worms, insects, crustaceans, and mollusks in salt marshes and broad tidal flats. Also eats grasshoppers, earthworms, and seeds.

Nesting: Nest is a scraped depression of grasses and mosses. Eggs: 4, pale greenish with marks; I: 26–27 days; F: 30–35 days, precocial; B: 1.

Other Behavior: Birds often fly and roost in flocks, but scatter when feeding.

Habitat: Summers on arctic tundra; winters on sandy beaches, mudflats, and plowed fields near coast.

Voice: Distinctive melancholy 3-note whistle, with the 2nd syllable lower in pitch, like "tleeooee."

Conservation: CWS: W→ C→ CBC: ↑

142

American Golden-Plover
Pacific Golden-Plover
Pluvialis dominicus   Pluvialis fulva

Summer American

Fall juvenile American

Winter Pacific

Identification: 10″ SUMMER: **Dark crown; black face and underparts, including undertail coverts.** In American, white neck-stripe is wide and stops at shoulder; in Pacific, it is narrower and continues along flank to undertail coverts. WINTER: **American tends to have white eyebrow and be grayish brown above; Pacific tends to have yellowish eyebrow and yellow tinge to back and wings.** Pacific wing tips project to or slightly beyond tail; American wing tips project noticeably beyond tail. IN FLIGHT: All plumages show **dark wings** (no wing-stripe); **dark rump; gray armpits.** FALL JUV: Pacific tends to be more golden on breast and back; American tends to be grayer.

Feeding: Both species feed on insects, worms, seeds.

Nesting: Both species' nest a scrape in the ground. Eggs: 4, tinged green with dark blotches; I: 26–27 days; F: 22 days, precocial; B: 1.

Other Behavior: Some of our longest-distance migrants.

American   Pacific

Habitat: Summer on arctic tundra; winter on plowed fields, short-grass fields, mudflats.

Voice: American: short "queedle." Pacific gives a 2-note whistle like "chuwi," or 3 notes like "chuwheedle."

Conservation: American: CWS: W→ C→ CBC: ↓ Pacific: CBC: ↓

wy Plover

drius alexandrinus

Summer male

Identification: 6″ In all plumages, **pale sandy above; partial neck-ring; thin, pointed, black bill; gray legs.** SUMMER: Male has dark bar across forehead, dark eye patch, and dark partial neck-ring. Female is light brown in these areas. WINTER: Both sexes like summer female. FALL JUV: Like summer female, but legs can be pale gray.

Feeding: Feeds by quickly running then picking up food, or probing on beaches and at surf line. Eats marine worms, small crustaceans, and, inland, insects.

Nesting: Nest a shallow depression on salt flat or open beach. Eggs: 2–3, buff with dark marks; I: 25–30 days; F: 31 days, precocial; B: 1–2.

Other Behavior: Breeding may be loosely colonial. In the East, there is 1 brood per year. In the West, there can be 2 broods per year. Female leaves young within 6 days to male's care, and she renests with new male. Male may also choose to renest with new female. In 1980s, population declines of 70–80% were recorded in Calif.

Habitat: Sandy beaches; alkaline lakes in West.

Voice: Low, whistled flight call like "ku-wheet."

Conservation: CBC: ⇓ Population is declining due to loss of nesting habitat and nest destruction on beaches.

Semipalmated Plover
Charadrius semipalmatus

Summer

Winter

Identification: 7″ In all plumages, **dark brown above; dark neck-ring is complete.** SUMMER: **Black bar across forehead and from eye to bill;** black neck-ring. **Bill orange with dark tip; legs orange.** WINTER: **Black areas of summer plumage are brown; bill mostly dark;** legs dull orange. FALL JUV: Like dull winter adult; back and wing feathers lightly scalloped.

Feeding: Feeds by running then stopping and picking up prey item, then running again. Also may stir up prey by vibrating 1 foot on the ground. On migration and in winter, eats mainly marine worms.

Nesting: Nest a slight depression that may contain bits of shells or grass, on sandy or gravelly area. Eggs: 4, buffy brown with dark marks; I: 23–25 days; F: 21–31 days, precocial; B: 1.

Other Behavior: These little plovers space themselves out while feeding and aggressively defend their own feeding spots. May be seen running around with Sanderlings on exposed sandy beaches. Tend to roost by themselves in small groups.

Habitat: Summers on tundra; winters on muddy shores, tidal flats, sandy beaches.

Voice: A clear rising whistle like "chee-wee"; also an accelerating chortling note when defending feeding territory.

Conservation:
CWS: W→ C→ CBC: ↑

Piping Plover
Charadrius melodus

Summer

Winter

Identification: 7″ In all plumages, **pale sandy above; neck-ring complete or incomplete; short thick bill.** SUMMER: **Bill orange with black tip; legs bright orange;** black neck-ring and bar across forehead. Female less distinctly patterned than male. WINTER: **Bill all black;** legs pale orange; neck-ring and forehead pale sandy. IN FLIGHT: Note white base of tail. FALL JUV: Similar to winter adults.

Feeding: Feeds on crustaceans, mollusks, fly larvae, and marine worms and other small marine animals and their eggs.

Nesting: Nest a hollow in sand, sometimes lined with shells and pebbles; occurs on sandy or pebble beach above high-water mark, or on lakeshore. Eggs: 3–4, gray to buff with dark dots; I: 26–28 days; F: 21–28 days, precocial; B: 1.

Other Behavior: Territorial when nesting, with nests spaced at least 200 ft. apart. Seen in small flocks or singly during migration and in winter.

Habitat: Sandy beaches, lakeshores.

Voice: A whistled "peep" or a 2-note "peep-lo."

Conservation: CWS: W C ↓ CBC: ↓ Interior population endangered in U.S. and Can. Habitat destroyed by development, vehicles, and human activity on beaches.

Killdeer
Charadrius vociferus

Identification: 10" Only North American plover with **2 neck-rings.** Light **reddish-brown rump** is easily seen when bird flies or displays. Dark brown above, white below. FALL JUV: Like adult, but with buffy edges on feathers of back and wings; these edges wear off in fall.

Feeding: Eats mostly insects.

Nesting: Nest is a scraped depression in bare ground with pebbles added. Eggs: 3–4, pale brown with darker marks; I: 24–28 days; F: 25 days, precocial; B: 1–2.

Other Behavior: Most frequently encountered by humans not at the shore, but in suburban settings. Nests on athletic fields, agricultural fields, lawns, gravel rooftops, or any area that has short sparse vegetation. Can be very noisy and give a variety of calls, such as when flying overhead, or on the ground during territorial interactions. Killdeers are famous for their predator-distracting "broken-wing display," in which they appear to be injured and run along the ground dragging their wing, leading a potential predator away from nest or chicks.

Habitat: Open ground with gravel or short grass; suburban or rural.

Voice: Many varied calls. The most common is a repeated 2-part "kill-deah."

Conservation: BBS: W ⇓ C ↓ CBC: →

147

ountain Plover

radrius montanus

Summer

Identification: 8" SUMMER: White forehead with black bar above it; large dark eye; unmarked white beneath; dark line between eye and black bill. WINTER: Like summer but lacks dark marks on forehead and before eye and has buffy breast.

Feeding: Eats insects, especially grasshoppers, beetles.

Nesting: Nest a scraped depression on bare ground, lined with grasses, rootlets, and cow manure chips. Eggs: 3–4, olive with spotted marks; I: 28–31 days; F: 33–34 days, precocial; B: 2.

Other Behavior: Found on short-grass plains and fields, not mountains. Runs away on foot when approached. Female can sometimes mate with more than 1 male. She will leave 1st clutch of eggs for male to incubate. She then mates with another male and incubates the 2nd clutch herself. In winter flocks may number in the hundreds.

Habitat: Summers on dry prairies and short-grass plains; winters on plowed agricultural fields.

Voice: Low drawn-out whistle.

Conservation: BBS: W ⇓ C ⇓ CBC:→ Endangered in Can. Prairie habitat is lost to development. New surveys show 50–90% decline in range and population.

Black Oystercatcher

Haematopus bachmani

Identification: 18" Long, thin, red bill; all-black body; pink legs. IMM: Browner plumage; orange bill darker toward tip. Imm. plumage kept 1 year.

Feeding: Very similar to American Oystercatcher, but feeds more on limpets, which it pries off surf-hammered rocks.

Nesting: Nest a hollow in beach gravel or rocky depression, sometimes lined with beach debris, above high-tide line. Eggs: 3–4, buff with brown spots; I: 26–27 days; F: 30 days, precocial; B: 1.

Other Behavior: Seen on rocky shores and jetties, often in family groups or pairs. Their dark color camouflages them against the dark rocks and seaweed. Flocks of nonbreeding immature birds may also be seen. Flight displays given in spring, with much calling.

Habitat: Rocky coastlines.

Voice: Loud piping whistle like "wheep, wheep."

Conservation:
BBS: W ⇓ C CBC: ↓ In Calif., there is an increasing shortage of breeding sites on small offshore rocks, due to growing populations of seals and sea lions.

149

Black-necked Stilt

Himantopus mexicanus

Female

Identification: 14" **Black above; white below; long pink legs.** MALE: Dark areas all black. FEMALE: Dark areas dark brown and faded by end of summer.

Feeding: Strides about and uses its long needlelike bill to pick up food on or just below the water surface, or on muddy shore.Wades to belly-deep on long legs. Eats larvae, nymphs, and adults of many aquatic insects, especially brine flies. Also eats crayfish, small fish, seeds.

Nesting: In small colonies, usually in marshy areas. Nest a depression on ground, lined with sticks, shells, and mud, on hummock or small island. Eggs: 3–4, buff with dark marks; I: 25 days; F: 28 days, precocial; B: 1.

Other Behavior: May move to new breeding areas from year to year if nesting localities dry up or become too flooded.

Habitat: Shallow water in marshes, ditches, ponds, salt ponds, or fields.

Voice: A loud "kek-kek-kek."

Conservation: BBS: W ↓ C ⇓ CBC: ⇑

American Avocet
Recurvirostra americana

Summer male (l.), female (r.)

Winter

Identification: 18" **Long, thin, upturned bill; black on wings and back; white body.** Female has shorter, more strongly upcurved bill. SUMMER: **Head and neck rich cinnamon.** WINTER· Head and neck whitish. IN FLIGHT: Striking pattern of black and white on wings and back.

Feeding: Feeds in flocks. Thrusts bill underwater and swings it from side to side, feeling for prey. Can swim in deep water. Eats crustaceans, fish, aquatic insects, seeds.

Nesting: Usually in colonies. Nest a shallow depression with minimal lining, out in open on mudflat, marsh, beach. If waters rise, may build up nest with sticks and weeds. Eggs: 4, olive with dark spots; I: 23–25 days; F: 27–35 days, precocial; B: 1.

Other Behavior: Noisy and aggressive in breeding colonies and will dive-bomb intruders. Mostly silent on migration. A bird of saline lakes. One of their main concentrations is at Great Salt Lake, where there are hundreds of thousands in summer.

Habitat: Summers on shallow inland lakes; winters on coastal flats.

Voice: A loud penetrating "kleet."

Conservation: BBS: W ⇑ C ↑ CBC: ↓

151

Greater Yellowlegs
Tringa melanoleuca

Summer

Fall juvenile

Identification: 14" Long yellow-to-orange legs; whitish marks on dark upperparts. **Distinguish from similar Lesser Yellowlegs by size** when they are together — Lesser noticeably smaller — and **by proportion of bill to head size** when they are alone. Greater's bill is about 1½ times the length of its head; Lesser's bill is about equal to length of its head. Also see Voice. SUMMER: Head and neck heavily streaked with black; sides heavily barred with black. WINTER: Grayish overall with faint streaking on head and neck; dark bill is gray at base. FALL JUV: Similar to winter adult, except breast has fine distinct black streaks; back is finely spotted.

Feeding: Feeds in water, often dashing about. Picks at or skims surface, or swings bill back and forth through water. Eats fish, insects, worms, snails, berries.

Nesting: Nest a depression in the ground. Eggs: 4, buff with marks; I: 23 days; F: 18–20 days, precocial; B: 1.

Other Behavior: Both yellowlegs regularly seen together. Usually occurs singly or in small flocks.

Habitat: Summers on subarctic forest bogs; winters on coastal marshes.

Voice: Descending series of 3–4 notes, like "whew-whew-whew."

Conservation:
CWS: W→ C→ CBC: ↑

152

Lesser Yellowlegs
Tringa flavipes

Summer

Fall juvenile

Identification: 10" Long yellow-to-orange legs; whitish marks on dark upperparts. **Distinguish from similar Greater Yellowlegs by size** when they are together — the Greater is noticeably larger — and **by proportion of bill to head size** when they are alone. Lesser's bill is about equal to the length of its head; Greater's bill is about 1½ times the length of its head. Also see Voice. SUMMER: **Head and neck finely streaked with black; sides lightly barred with black. WINTER: Upperparts grayish with faint streaking on head and neck; bill all black.** FALL JUV: Similar to winter adult, except breast has indistinct brownish streaks; back finely spotted.

Feeding: Feeds in shallow water, methodically walking and probing; rarely as animated as the Greater Yellowlegs. Eats fish, insects, worms, snails, berries.

Nesting: Nest is a grass-lined depression in the ground. Eggs: 4, yellow-buff, marked; I: 22–23 days; F: 18–20 days, precocial; B: 1.

Other Behavior: May defend winter feeding territories.

Habitat: Summers on subarctic forest bogs; winters on coastal marshes.

Voice: Usually a 2-note "tu tu"; less musical than Greater Yellowlegs' call.

Conservation:
CWS: W→ C→ CBC: ↑

153

Solitary Sandpiper
Tringa solitaria

Summer

Identification: 8″ Often found alone or in small groups at freshwater ponds and puddles. **SUMMER: Streaked brown head and neck; dark wings with whitish dots; greenish legs; bold white eye-ring;** repeatedly bobs head. The similar Lesser Yellowlegs has yellow legs and a finer eye-ring. **WINTER: Similar to summer, but head and neck appear unstreaked gray-brown. IN FLIGHT: Wings all dark above and below; tail barred on sides.**

Feeding: Feeds in shallow water, picking at surface or probing in the water or mud. May also walk through water shaking forward foot to stir up insects from bottom. Eats aquatic insects, grasshoppers, small crustaceans, frogs.

Nesting: Adds a little material to deserted nests of other birds such as Common Grackle, American Robin, or Rusty Blackbird. Nest located in coniferous tree up to 36 ft. high. Eggs: 4, greenish buff with dark marks; I: 23–24 days; F: ?, precocial; B: 1.

Other Behavior: Often found in small muddy puddles, partially dried up in late summer.

Habitat: Summers on boreal bogs; winters on small ponds.

Voice: A high-pitched 3-note "wheet, wheet, wheet."

Conservation:
CWS: W→ C→ CBC: ↓

Willet
Catoptrophorus semipalmatus

Winter

Summer

Winter

Identification: 15″ SUMMER: Long, straight, rather heavy bill; long grayish legs; brown streaking on head and neck; brown barring on breast. WINTER: Body plain gray-brown above; whitish below. IN FLIGHT: Distinctive bold white wing-stripe on black wing.

Feeding: Feeds on mud- and sandflats by probing with its bill. Eats insects, crustaceans, mollusks, grasses, seeds.

Nesting: Nest a hollow lined with dry grasses and sedges, on open area up to several hundred yards from water. Often concealed by grasses. Eggs: 4, olive with dark marks; I: 22–29 days; F: ?, precocial; B: 1.

Other Behavior: On breeding grounds, Willets are quite noisy. They flash white wing marks during aerial displays. On the ground and in flight, give the "pill-will-willet" song. Will perch on trees and fence posts to watch intruder and give alarm calls. Range in East is expanding.

Habitat: Summers on coastal marshes in East and prairie marshes in West; winters on coastal marshes, beaches, and mudflats.

Voice: Named after song given on breeding ground, "pill-will-willet." Alarm notes sound like "kip-kip-kip."

Conservation: CWS: W→ C→ CBC: ↓

Wandering Tattler

Heteroscelus incanus

Summer

Winter

Identification: 11" Bobs tail when walking. SUMMER: **Gray above; underparts covered with fine dark barring.** WINTER: All gray except for white belly. IN FLIGHT: **Plain dark gray above with no markings on tail or wings.**

Feeding: Feeds on the rocky beds of mountain streams, and on rocky coastlines, eating caddisfly larvae, insects, mollusks, crustaceans, and marine worms.

Nesting: Nest a depression lined with twigs, rootlets, and leaves, on dry streambed. Eggs: 4, greenish white with dark marks; I: 23–25 days; F: ?, precocial; B: 1.

Other Behavior: Relatively solitary birds. Roost in groups. Even though may feed near one another, when flushed they fly off alone. Named for scolding or tattling alarm call.

Habitat: Summers along mountain streams; winters along rocky shores.

Voice: Alarm call is a series of clear notes on 1 pitch, like "pew-tu-tu-tu-tu."

Conservation: CWS: W→ C CBC: ↓

Spotted Sandpiper

Actitis macularia

Summer

Winter

Identification: 8″ Distinctive flight and tail bobbing help identify this bird. SUMMER: **Large dark spots on white underparts; repeatedly bobs tail while walking;** bill pinkish orange with darker tip. Female more boldly patterned than male. WINTER: **Grayish above; pure white below; bill is dark. IN FLIGHT: Flies with stiff wings beating in a shallow arc.**

Feeding: Feeds along water edges, eating flies, worms, small crustaceans, fish, beetles.

Nesting: Nest a shallow depression lined with a few grasses. Eggs: 4, buff with brown spots; I: 21 days; F: 21 days, precocial; B: 1–5.

Other Behavior: Most common on inland lakes and streams, where it breeds in summer; less common on seashore. In a majority of cases Spotted Sandpipers are polyandrous, the female having 2 or more males as mates. She courts the male, lays a clutch of eggs for him to incubate and raise, and immediately leaves him to court another male. Up to 4 or 5 males have been reported for 1 female.

Habitat: Summers along rivers, lakes, and seashore; winters along edges of fresh or salt water.

Voice: In alarm or aggression gives series of short whistles like "weet weet weet." During courtship gives "peetaweet peetaweet."

Conservation:
CWS: W→ C→ CBC: ↑

Upland Sandpiper

Bartramia longicauda

Identification: 12″ Proportionally **small head** and **large dark eye; short yellow bill and yellow legs; long neck; long tail** projects well beyond wing tips when bird is standing. **IN FLIGHT:** Underwings heavily barred with brown and white; wings often held above back for short period after landing.

Feeding: Feeds in grasslands. Eats worms, grasshoppers, beetles, and other insects.

Nesting: Sometimes in loose colonies. Nest a depression lined with grasses, on prairie, meadow, or field. Eggs: 4, creamy buff; I: 21–27 days; F: ?, precocial; B: ?

Other Behavior: On breeding grounds does aerial and ground displays. Upon landing, often holds wings raised. Perches on fence posts. May act tame.

Habitat: Prairies and meadows.

Voice: In flight, calls "pulip, pulip." On breeding ground gives a reedy wolf whistle.

Conservation: CWS: W ↓ C ↓

Whimbrel

Numenius phaeopus

Identification: 17" Large brown shorebird; **long downcurved bill; 2 dark stripes on crown;** dark streak through eye. **IN FLIGHT:** Underwings brown and belly pale.

Feeding: Feeds on wetlands, grasslands, shores. Probes or picks at insects, marine worms, crustaceans, mollusks. Also eats fiddler crabs and, in Arctic, berries.

Nesting: Nest a depression in tundra, heath, or bog. Eggs: 4, greenish olive with marks; I: 22–24 days; F: 35–42 days, precocial; B: 1.

Other Behavior: In large flocks on migration and at evening roosts. Birds defend individual feeding territories at low tide and then roost together in flocks at high tide. May fly long distances from feeding to roosting areas.

Habitat: Summers on tundra; winters along fresh or salt water and on agricultural fields.

Voice: Loud, repeated, whistlelike "whi whi whi whi whi" and many other calls.

Conservation: CWS: W→ C→ CBC: ↓

Long-billed Curlew
Numenius americanus

Identification: 23" **Extremely long downcurved bill,** equal in length to more than half the length of the body; **crown finely streaked with brown;** neck and underparts washed with cinnamon. Female has much longer bill than male. **IN FLIGHT:** Cinnamon underwings. **FALL JUV:** Similar to adults, but with shorter bill for first few months; at this time its bill is not much longer than that of a Whimbrel.

Feeding: Probes into mud for crabs and other invertebrates. Also eats grasshoppers, beetles, insects, and eggs of other birds.

Nesting: Nest a slight hollow lined with weeds, grasses, and cow manure chips, on prairie, meadowland, or short-grass area. Eggs: 4, white to buff or olive with brown marks; I: 27–30 days; F: 32–45 days, precocial; B: 1.

Other Behavior: On breeding territories does roller-coaster display flights. Feeds in flocks and flies in line formations.

Habitat: Summers on grasslands; winters on coastal grasslands, fields, mudflats.

Voice: A loud rising "cur-lew."

Conservation: CWS: W ↓ C ↓ CBC: →

Hudsonian Godwit

Limosa haemastica

Transition to winter plumage

Summer

Fall juvenile

Identification: 15″ SUMMER: **Large** shorebird; **long slightly upturned bill pink at base;** body brown above, reddish brown below with variable amounts of dark barring. Female larger, longer-billed, and paler underneath than male. WINTER: **Bill as in summer;** body gray above, white below. IN FLIGHT: In all plumages, **black tail; white rump; black wing linings; white wing-stripe.** FALL JUV: Dark brown back and wings; lighter edges to feathers; light grayish brown on chest.

Feeding: Feeds by probing shallow waters, beaches, and mudflats. Eats crustaceans, mollusks, marine worms, and insects.

Nesting: Nest a saucerlike depression lined with dead leaves, on moist bog, marsh, or dry hummock, often near birches. Eggs: 4, brownish olive with marks; I: 22–23 days; F: 25–30 days, precocial; B: 1.

Other Behavior: In spectacular fall migration, most fly from Hudson Bay to Patagonia and Tierra del Fuego. Flights are over 3,000 miles, often nonstop. Winters at southern tip of S. America. In spring, migrates through center of N. America.

Habitat: Summers on tundra near tree line; winters on mudflats and flooded fields.

Voice: On breeding ground, call is loud "quee-quip."

Conservation: CWS: W→ C→ During spring migration, key staging areas exist in Tex. and La. and in Can.

Marbled Godwit

Limosa fedoa

Summer

Winter

Identification: 18" Large shorebird; **long slightly upturned bill is pink at base; back and wings are cinnamon marked with black.** SUMMER: Underparts heavily barred. WINTER: Underparts buffy with no barring. IN FLIGHT: **Underwings cinnamon. FALL JUV: Similar to adult.**

Feeding: Probes with its bill on tidal flats, eating worms, mollusks, and crustaceans. Also eats grasshoppers and seeds and tubers of pondweeds and sedges.

Nesting: Semicolonial. Nest a hollow, with minimal lining, on prairie wetland. Eggs: 4, green-brown with dark marks; I: 21–23 days; F: 21 days, precocial; B: 1.

Other Behavior: During breeding, males do circling flight displays. Usually found in small groups.

Habitat: Summers on moist grass-lands; winters along coast.

Voice: During breeding, calls "god-wit."

Conservation: CWS: W→ C ↓ CBC: ↓

Ruddy Turnstone
Arenaria interpres

Summer

Winter

Identification: 8″ **Black bib** and **orange legs** in all adult plumages. SUMMER: **White head; bright chestnut on back and wings.** Female tends to have more brown wash on head and nape and more streaking on crown. WINTER: **Back, wings, and head brown;** 2 white patches enclosed by bib. IN FLIGHT: Conspicuous white stripes on wings and back.

Feeding: Feeds by turning over stones, shells, earth, seaweeds, and other objects with its strong bill. Also digs with bill in sand. Eats sand fleas, mollusks, crustaceans, insects, worms.

Nesting: Nest a shallow depression lined with mosses, grasses, leaves, seaweed, next to rock or vegetation. Eggs: 3–4, greenish olive with dark marks; I: 22–24 days; F: 19–21 days, precocial; B: 1.

Other Behavior: Feeds singly, in small groups, or with flocks of other shorebirds. May feed on eggs of colonial seabirds in West and frequents garbage dumps in the North. Eastern population depends heavily on Delaware Bay for food during spring migration.

Habitat: Summers on high arctic tundra; winters on sandy and rocky beaches.

Voice: A common call is a grating "tuk-e-tuk." Also gives low staccato sound, or a low "tuk" note.

Conservation:
CWS: W→ C→ CBC: ↑

163

Black Turnstone
Arenaria melanocephala

Summer

Winter

Identification: 9″ A black shorebird with a white belly. Note that **dark breast meets white belly in a straight line,** rather than in 2 lobes as in the Ruddy Turnstone. SUMMER: Distinctive **white spot between eye and bill.** WINTER: **No white spot on face.** IN FLIGHT: Conspicuous white stripes on wings and back.

Feeding: Feeds along rocky shores, eating crustaceans, mollusks, barnacles, worms. Turns over clumps of seaweed with its bill in search for food.

Nesting: Nest a hollowed-out depression lined with bits of grass, in dead grass near water. Eggs: 4, olive-yellow with brown splotches; I: 21 days; F: ?, precocial; B: 1.

Other Behavior: Noisy and aggressive on nesting grounds, where it does zigzag chases and display-flight dives. Gives alarm calls at intruder's approach. Roosts in mixed flocks with other shorebirds, like Ruddy Turnstones, Surfbirds, and Rock Sandpipers.

Habitat: Rocky coastal areas and occasionally sandy beaches and mudflats.

Voice: A trilled "skirrr," higher-pitched than Ruddy Turnstone's.

Conservation:
CWS: W→ C CBC: ↓

Surfbird
Aphriza virgata

Summer

Winter

Identification: 10" The **short blunt-tipped bill** (much like that of a plover) and **short yellow legs** are distinctive in all plumages. Larger than other rock-loving species with which it is found. SUMMER: **Head and neck evenly streaked with gray; breast and sides marked with dark chevrons; reddish-brown patches on sides of back.** WINTER: **Gray overall except for white belly with dark spots.** IN FLIGHT: White tail with broad black band at tip; white stripes on wings but not on back.

Habitat: Summers on rocky mountain tundra; winters along rocky coasts.

Voice: A shrill whistled "kee-ah-wee."

Conservation: CWS: W→ C CBC: ↓

Feeding: Runs over mountain rocks or rocky shores and picks up insects, small crustaceans, barnacles, and mollusks.

Nesting: Nests in mountains, above timberline. Nest a natural depression lined with dead leaves and lichens, on dry, open ridge. Eggs: 4, buff with marks; I: ?; F: ?, precocial; B: 1.

Other Behavior: To protect nest, will fly up at the face of intruders such as caribou.

Red Knot

Calidris canutus

Summer

Winter

Identification: 11" SUMMER: **Reddish-brown face and underparts; gray, black, and rufous back; short straight bill** (about same length as head); legs dark gray. WINTER: Plain **gray back; gray breast; white belly;** legs greenish.

Feeding: Feeds on beaches and in muddy areas, eating mollusks, worms, fish, the eggs of king crabs, and seeds.

Nesting: Nest a hollow lined with leaves and lichens, on high rocky tundra. Eggs: 4, buff-olive, spotted with brown; I: 21–22 days; F: 18 days, precocial; B: 1.

Other Behavior: Feeds and roosts in tight flocks of hundreds of birds. May associate with other shorebirds like Ruddy Turnstones, Dunlins, and Black-bellied Plovers. Like Hudsonian Godwits and several other shorebirds, this species makes tremendous overwater flights of more than 2,000 miles from Hudson Bay to S. America during fall migration. Spring migration is primarily along the East Coast, where a key stopover point for feeding is the Delaware Bay.

Habitat: Summers on tundra; winters on coastal beaches and mudflats.

Voice: A low harsh "knut" while feeding; a soft "kuret" while flying.

Conservation: CWS: W→ C→ CBC: ⇑

166

Sanderling
Calidris alba

Summer

Winter

Fall juvenile

Identification: 8 " Most often seen in winter plumage **chasing the edges of waves** on sandy beaches. SUMMER: **Upperparts reddish to orange-brown with darker brown streaking; belly white; legs black.** WINTER: **Pale gray above; white below; black legs;** black shoulder may be visible. Straight comparatively short bill. IN FLIGHT: All plumages have bold white wing-stripe. FALL JUV: Like winter adult but darker above, with brown and black mixed with the gray.

Feeding: On beaches and mudflats. Probes with its bill. Eats minute crustaceans, mollusks, marine worms, and insects.

Nesting: Nest a scraped depression on dry tundra. Eggs: 4, olive-green with dark marks; I: 24–31 days; F: 17 days, precocial; B: 1–2.

Other Behavior: These little sandpipers are always scurrying along at the surf line, like windup toys. They run back and forth, following advancing and receding waves. On breeding grounds, female may be polyandrous, laying several clutches of eggs that are each attended by a different male.

Habitat: Summers on arctic tundra; winters along sandy coasts.

Voice: A quiet "kip" in flight.

Conservation: CWS: W→ C→ CBC:↓ Drastic population declines; up to 80% declines in last 10 years in East.

167

Semimalmated Sandpiper

Calidris pusilla

Summer

Winter

Fall juvenile

Identification: 6¼" All plumages have **dark legs; short, relatively straight, blunt-tipped bill; grayish-brown appearance.** SUMMER: **Grayish brown on back,** with some black but little or no reddish brown; **whitish breast;** little or no streaking on flanks. WINTER: **Uniform grayish brown above; light streaking on breast.** FALL JUV: Grayish brown above, with black tips and pale edgings to back feathers. Finely streaked darker crown makes eyebrow look light. Variable, with some birds quite reddish brown on back.

Feeding: Feeds on sandy or muddy flats with its head down and snatching up food. Eats crustaceans, mollusks, marine worms, and aquatic insects.

Nesting: Nest a depression on flat ground, often near a birch tree. Eggs: 4, buff to yellow with dark marks; I: 18–22 days; F: 19 days, precocial; B: 1.

Other Behavior: Gregarious. Can be found in huge numbers in favored feeding places along migration routes in East. Rare during migration in West.

Habitat: Summers on tundra; winters on tidal flats.

Voice: Typical flight call a short low-pitched "cherk."

Conservation: CWS: W ↑ C→ CBC: ⇓ Populations recently declining. Two key spots for their survival during migration are Delaware Bay in spring and Bay of Fundy in fall.

Western Sandpiper
Calidris mauri

Summer

Winter

Fall juvenile

Identification: 6½" All plumages have **dark legs; relatively long sharp-pointed bill, usually drooping slightly at the tip. SUMMER: Contrasting reddish-brown markings on shoulder; reddish brown also on crown and ear patch.** Black chevron marks from breast continue down along flanks. **WINTER:** Uniform grayish brown above; light streaking on breast. Best distinguished from very similar Semipalmated Sandpiper by bill and voice. **FALL JUV:** Typically shows contrasting rusty-edged feathers on sides of grayish back.

Feeding: Often feeds in deeper water or farther out on mudflats than Semipalmated or Least Sandpipers. Eats crustaceans, mollusks, worms, and aquatic insects.

Nesting: Nest a depression on moist tundra or mossy slopes. Nest may be concealed under shrubs. Eggs: 4, buff, marked with brown; I: 20–22 days; F: 19 days, precocial; B: 1.

Other Behavior: Gregarious and can occur in flocks of thousands, especially in West. Sometimes aggressively defends feeding territory; other times feeds peaceably.

Habitat: Summers on tundra; winters on coastal beaches and mudflats.

Voice: A high-pitched "dzheet."

Conservation:
CWS: W→ C   CBC: ↓

Least Sandpiper

Calidris minutilla

Summer

Winter

Fall juvenile

Identification: 6″ In all plumages, **yellowish or greenish legs; short, thin, pointed bill; smallest of "peeps."** Crouched appearance when feeding. SUMMER: **Dark brown above; brown wash on breast, with dark streaks ending abruptly on upper breast;** feathers along sides of back have black centers. WINTER: **More evenly grayish on upperparts, but still darker than other winter peeps, especially on breast.** FALL JUV: Similar to summer adult, but breast only faintly streaked and washed with buff; richly colored above; distinct white stripes on back.

Feeding: Often found feeding in muddy, grassy areas closer to shore than other peeps. Eats insects, mollusks, crustaceans, and marine worms.

Nesting: Nest a shallow depression on bog or upland. Eggs: 4, pinkish buff with dark marks; I: 19–23 days; F: ?, precocial; B: 1.

Other Behavior: Roosts near feeding areas, alone or in small groups, among marsh vegetation or on upper beach in wrack line.

Habitat: Summers on tundra and bogs near tree line; winters along coastal and inland marshes.

Voice: Flight note a high-pitched "kreeet."

Conservation: CWS: W→ C→ CBC: ↓

White-rumped Sandpiper

Calidris fuscicollis

Summer

Winter

Fall juvenile

Identification: 7½" In all plumages, **wings extend beyond tail** when bird is standing (also true of Baird's Sandpiper); **white rump seen in flight** or when bird preens; noticeably larger than other "peeps" except Baird's. **SUMMER: Reddish brown on crown and sides of back** (similar to summer Western Sandpiper); **streaks on breast extend down along flanks as small chevrons.** **WINTER:** Evenly grayish brown above and on breast; white eyebrow. **FALL JUV:** Breast buffy with fine streaks; usually no streaks along sides; upperparts similar to summer adult's, but more richly colored.

Feeding: Feeds by probing in mud or shallow water. Eats marine worms, insects, snails.

Nesting: Nest of grass, moss, and leaves on hummock. Eggs: 4, light green with dark marks; I: 22 days; F: 16–17 days, precocial; B: 1.

Other Behavior: Found in single-species flocks, or mixed in with other shorebirds. On breeding grounds males do display flights. The male is polygynous.

Habitat: Summers on tundra near coast; winters on muddy areas near coast.

Voice: A high thin "jeeet."

Conservation:
CWS: W→ C→ CBC: ⇓

171

Baird's Sandpiper

Calidris bairdii

Summer

Fall juvenile

Identification: 7″ In all plumages, **wings extend well beyond tail** when bird is standing (also true of White-rumped Sandpiper); **dark rump.** SUMMER: **Buffy wash on face and breast; fine streaking on breast that does not extend along sides;** back looks splotchy with dark-centered feathers. WINTER: This plumage is acquired on wintering ground in S. Am. and only briefly seen in spring as birds start to enter N. Am. Similar to summer plumage, but duller, paler, and not so buffy. FALL JUV: More evenly brown plumage; light-edged feathers on back give it a scalloped effect.

Feeding: Rapidly moves along and picks up food on inland wetlands or grasslands. Eats insects.

Nesting: Nest a shallow depression on tundra. Eggs: 2–4, pink to olive-buff with markings; I: 19–21 days; F: 16–20 days, precocial; B: 1.

Other Behavior: Seen in small groups or singly. Adults migrate inland through the interior; juveniles migrate through interior and along both coasts.

Habitat: Summers on dry tundra; winters on inland and coastal lakes and marshes, mudflats, and grasslands.

Voice: A low trilling "preet," or a grating "krrt."

Conservation:
CWS: W→ C→ CBC: ↓

Pectoral Sandpiper
Calidris melanotos

Adults

Fall juvenile

Identification: 9″ Most often seen at grassy edges of salt or freshwater marshes, rather than with other shorebirds on mudflats. In all plumages, **dense brown streaking on breast stops abruptly at white belly;** legs yellowish; bill droops slightly at tip. Male is distinctly larger and darker-breasted than female. Summer and winter plumages similar. FALL JUV: Similar to adults, but finer streaking on buffy breast; broader white edges on back feathers form 2 white V's.

Feeding: Eats insects, grass seeds, worms, fiddler crabs.

Nesting: Concealed, well-built cup of grasses and leaves lined with finer material, on upland tundra or grassland. Eggs: 4, pale buff-olive with brown splotches; I: 21–23 days; F: 18–21 days, precocial; B: 1.

Other Behavior: Promiscuous breeding system. Males mate several times. Females visit other males. Male has an air sac beneath the breast, which emphasizes the demarcation line of streaking. Male pumps the sac in and out in flight display.

Habitat: Summers on wet tundra; winters along grassy marshes.

Voice: Flight call is a low "churk." In courtship flight male gives "oo-ah" hooting sound 2–3 times per second.

Conservation:
CWS: W→ C→ CBC: ↓

173

Rock Sandpiper
Calidris ptilocnemis

Summer

Winter

Identification: 9" Legs greenish yellow; long thin **bill, slightly drooping** at tip. SUMMER: **Black area on lower breast; crown and back feathers black with reddish-brown edges;** base of bill usually yellowish. WINTER: **Clear gray head and neck; gray back and wings; breast with gray spots continuing along flanks and onto white belly.** Young usually molt into adult winter plumage before migrating south. IN FLIGHT: Dark above with white wing-stripe and white on sides of rump.

Feeding: Forages on rocky shores and jetties. Picks food off the algae and barnacle beds. Eats crustaceans, mollusks, algae, seeds.

Nesting: Nest a scraped depression on tundra. Eggs: 4, olive with brown spots; I: 20 days; F: ?, precocial; B: 1.

Other Behavior: Its coloration helps it cryptically blend into the rocky terrain it inhabits. Roosts on the rocks just above the high-tide spray. Often found with Surfbirds and Black Turnstones. Winter flocks return to same sites each year.

Habitat: Summers on tundra; winters on rocky coastal areas.

Voice: A short "tweet" note.

Conservation:
CWS: W→ C CBC: ⇓

174

Dunlin
Calidris alpina

Summer

Winter

Transition to winter

Fall juvenile

Identification: 8″ **Long bill, drooping at the tip; black legs.** SUMMER: Whitish face and underparts, with **large black patch on belly;** back reddish brown; crown variably streaked reddish brown. **WINTER: Plain, with head, neck, and breast gray-brown; wings and back gray; belly white.** FALL JUV: Buffy breast and head; reddish-brown back; lines of dark spots extend from lower breast onto belly and flanks. This plumage rarely seen since juveniles molt into winter plumage on breeding ground before migrating south.

Feeding: Feeds mostly on mudflats or, at times, on beaches. Probes with its bill for crustaceans, mollusks, marine worms, and insects.

Nesting: Nest placed on a hummock. Eggs: 4, green to olive-buff with spots; I: 19–22 days; F: 18–25 days, precocial; B: 1.

Other Behavior: Roosts on beaches or upland fields. Can be found in huge flocks that put on impressive aerial maneuvers when flushed, or when pursued by a predator.

Habitat: Summers on tundra; winters on beaches, coastal mudflats.

Voice: Flight call a harsh "kreee."

Conservation:
CWS: W→ C CBC: ↓

Stilt Sandpiper

Calidris himantopus

Summer

Winter

Identification: 8½" Legs long and greenish; bill long, thin, and slightly drooped at tip. SUMMER: Dark with heavy barring on breast and belly; whitish eyebrow; reddish-brown ear patch. WINTER: Grayish overall with white belly and white eyebrow. IN FLIGHT: All plumages have white rump; no wing-stripe. FALL JUV: Upperparts black and brown; belly white; buffy edges on feathers create a strongly scalloped effect; whitish eyebrow.

Feeding: Feeds in compact flocks. Probes with its bill and may plunge head underwater. Eats small mollusks, mosquito larvae, worms, and parts of aquatic plants.

Nesting: Nest a scrape on relatively dry sedge meadows. Eggs: 4, pale green to olive with dots; I: 19–21 days; F: 17–18 days, precocial; B: 1.

Other Behavior: Rapid feeding motion is like that of dowitchers, with which it often occurs, but it brings its bill completely out of water more often than those species. Also found feeding in single-species groups. Migrates through the Great Plains; rare sightings in fall on West Coast are mostly juveniles.

Habitat: Summers on tundra; winters on ponds and marshes near coast.

Voice: Flight call is a rattling trilled "kirr."

Conservation: CWS: W→ C→ CBC: ⇑

Buff-breasted Sandpiper

Tryngites subruficollis

Adult

Fall juvenile

Identification: 8″ **Buffy face, breast, and belly,** with some dark spotting along sides of breast; bill short; legs yellow. Summer and winter plumages alike. Male considerably larger than female. **IN FLIGHT:** Bright white underwings. **FALL JUV:** Similar to adult, but back feathers edged with white instead of buff.

Feeding: Feeds on insects, spiders, seeds of aquatic plants.

Nesting: Nest a shallow cavity on dry tundra. Eggs: 4, white to buff or olive with spots; I: ?; F: ?, precocial; B: 1.

Other Behavior: Promiscuous mating system in which males display in groups. Females arrive and mate with them, then nest elsewhere and raise the broods alone. Migrates mostly through central N. America; rare occurrences on the coasts are mostly juveniles during fall migration.

Habitat: Summers on dry arctic tundra; winters on short-grass areas and dry lake margins.

Voice: Flight call is a low "pr-r-reet."

Conservation:
CWS: W ↓ C ↓
Nearly hunted to extinction in late 1800s.

Ruff
Philomachus pugnax

Summer male

Fall juvenile

Identification: 9–11" This Eurasian species is a rare migrant along the coasts and casual in the rest of N. Am. Extremely variable in plumage, but can be recognized by its distinctive shape. **Small head; long neck; large plump body; bill relatively short and slightly downcurved.** SUMMER: Males vary from white to rufous to black; always have distinctive erectile ear tufts and neck feathers. Female (reeve) dark with light belly; black blotches on breast and flanks. WINTER: Gray-brown above; whitish below; some grayish-brown mottling on breast. Female like male but smaller. FALL JUV: Dark back feathers fringed with buff; head and breast unstreaked and buffy.

Feeding: Eats aquatic insects, mollusks, and crustaceans.

Nesting: Grass-lined hollow on tundra marsh. Eggs: 4, greenish; I: 20–23 days; F: 25–27 days, precocial; B: 1.

Other Behavior: Males do courtship on communal display grounds called leks. Darker males hold territories in center of lek; paler males move around the edges. Females visit and mate with 1 or several males.

Habitat: Summers in Eurasia; during migration seen on grasslands, fresh- or saltwater pools, mudflats.

Voice: Usually quiet.

Conservation: CBC: ↓

Short-billed Dowitcher

Limnodromus griseus

Summer *griseus*

Summer *hendersoni*

Winter

Fall juvenile

Identification: 11–11½" **Medium-sized; long straight bill; greenish legs.** Three subspecies. **SUMMER:** *L. g. griseus* (seen in Northeast, S. to N.J.) has an orange-blotched chest with dense black spotting and a white belly; *L. g. hendersoni* (seen in Midwest and Southeast S. of N.J.) has a reddish-brown chest and belly and minimal dark spotting; *L. g. caurinus* (seen west of the Rockies) is usually heavily spotted underneath, with white limited to the lower belly. **WINTER:** Gray-brown above; whitish below. Short-billed and Long-billed Dowitchers **best distinguished by voice.** **FALL JUV:** Back feathers broadly edged and internally marked with reddish buff; breast buffy and speckled with darker marks.

Feeding: Feeds by rapidly probing in sewing-machine-like motion. Eats marine worms, mollusks, some insects.

Nesting: Hollow in moss or wet meadow. Eggs: 4, buff-green with marks; I: 21 days; F: ?, precocial; B: 1.

Other Behavior: Roosts in large groups.

Habitat: Summers on bogs at northern limit of coniferous forests; winters on coastal mudflats.

Voice: Flight call is a medium-pitched repeated "tututu."

Conservation:
CWS: W→ C→ CBC: ⇑

Long-billed Dowitcher
Limnodromus scolopaceus

Summer

Winter

Fall juvenile

Identification: 11–11½" Medium-sized shorebird; long straight bill; greenish legs. SUMMER: Underparts entirely reddish brown with heavy barring on breast and flanks; no white belly. WINTER: Gray-brown above; whitish below. Long-billed and Short-billed Dowitchers best distinguished by voice. IN FLIGHT: In all plumages, both Long-billed and Short-billed show a distinctive white wedge on lower back and a barred tail. FALL JUV: Back feathers, narrowly edged with dark reddish brown, lack internal markings of Short-billed Dowitcher; breast mostly gray with little speckling.

Feeding: Feeds using up-and-down probing motion with bill, like a sewing machine. Eats insects, mollusks, crustaceans, marine worms.

Nesting: Nest a scraped depression in a wet meadow. Eggs: 4, brown to olive with marks; I: 20 days; F: ?, precocial; B: ?1.

Other Behavior: Most common in standing freshwater situations, rather than on extensive tidal flats.

Habitat: Summers just north of tree line; winters on freshwater ponds and marshes.

Voice: Flight call is a high-pitched thin "keeek," sometimes given in a series.

Conservation: CWS: W→ C→ CBC: ⇑

Common Snipe

Gallinago gallinago

Identification: 11" A bird of wet meadows and boggy areas. **Extremely long straight bill; plump body; short legs.** Black and white stripes on head; **conspicuous white stripes on dark back.** IN FLIGHT: Flies in a zigzag manner; wings are pointed.

Feeding: Feeds in wet areas by plunging its bill into soft ground. Eats larvae of craneflies and other insects, earthworms, crayfish, mollusks, frogs, seeds.

Nesting: Nest of grasses, leaves, and moss, placed in a scraped depression in a bog. Eggs: 4, olive-buff with spots; I: 18–20 days; F: 14–20 days, precocial; B: 1.

Other Behavior: Both sexes do unusual aerial display during breeding (female does it mostly at beginning of breeding season). Bird rises 300–360 ft. in air, then dives down. Air vibrating through the 2 outer tail feathers makes bleating or whinnying sound. This is done most over nesting area in early morning or early evening.

Habitat: Wet meadows, marshes, bogs.

Voice: When flushed, gives nasal "scaip" note. Sings "wheet-wheet" notes from perches on breeding ground.

Conservation: CWS: W→ C ↓ CBC: ↓

Wilson's Phalarope

Phalaropus tricolor

Summer female

Summer male

Adult, 1st winter

Identification: 9″ The phalarope most often seen inland. **Bill is very long and very thin.** SUMMER: **Broad dark streak goes through eye and continues down neck;** light reddish-brown wash on breast. The more colorful female has a gray crown; male has a blackish crown. WINTER: Gray and unstreaked above; white below; **thin grayish line through eye;** legs greenish black. IN FLIGHT: No wing-stripes; whitish rump. JUV: Back feathers strongly edged with buff; pale thin eye-stripe; legs yellow. Juv. plumage kept for only brief period.

Feeding: Wades along muddy shores and shallow water, whirling around while stabbing the water's surface. Eats brine shrimp, mosquito larvae, insects.

Nesting: Semicolonial. Nest a grass-lined hollow, concealed in grass or marsh. Eggs: 4, buff with blotches; I: 20 days; F: 20 days, precocial; B: 1–2.

Other Behavior: Females are larger than males and occasionally mate with more than 1 male. Male builds the nest, incubates the eggs, and raises the young.

Habitat: Summers on marshy areas of meadows or lakes; winters along shallow edges of saline lakes.

Voice: A soft grunting "aangh" note.

Conservation: CWS: W ↑ C→ CBC: ↓ Being affected by loss of breeding and feeding areas. Range expanding in West.

Red-necked Phalarope

Phalaropus lobatus

Summer female

Summer male

Winter

Identification: 7" Migrates primarily at sea but occasionally shows up inland, especially in fall. **Small phalarope with a short very thin bill. Summer: Bright reddish-brown patch on side of dark gray neck;** on female this patch continues across breast. **Winter: Dark patch through eye; back is gray and black with a suggestion of white streaks; white forehead and crown. In Flight:** White wing-stripe. **Fall Juv:** Wide dark patch behind eye; dark back with 2 buffy streaks on either side.

Feeding: Feeds by picking prey from the water's surface, often while rapidly twirling about. Eats insects, mollusks, crustaceans.

Nesting: Grass-lined scrape in moist tundra. Eggs: 4, olive with brown dots; I: 19 days; F: 20 days, precocial; B: 1–2.

Other Behavior: Females can be polyandrous. Massive fall staging areas in West, especially at Great Salt Lake, Utah (600,000 birds) and Mono Lake, Calif. (80,000 birds).

Habitat: Summers on marshy tundra ponds; winters primarily at sea.

Voice: A low-pitched "twick."

Conservation: CWS: W→ C→ CBC: ⇓ Eastern Canadian staging populations have shown significant recent shifts or possible declines.

Red Phalarope

Phalaropus fulicaria

Summer female

Summer male

Winter

Identification: 8″ Migrates almost exclusively at sea. **Chunky phalarope with a short, thick, blunt-tipped bill. SUMMER: Bill is yellow with dark tip;** deep reddish-brown underparts; white patch over eye. In more colorful female, white patch is well defined and encompasses eye; in male, it is less defined and is mostly behind the eye. **WINTER: Wide dark patch through eye; gray unstreaked back; white forehead and crown. IN FLIGHT:** White wing-stripe. **FALL JUV:** Similar to summer male, but pinkish buff on breast and dark bill.

Feeding: Spins around on water and eats aquatic insects, larval fish, crustaceans.

Nesting: Nest a grassy scrape, often domed over with grasses. Eggs: 4, gray to olive with dark spots; I: 19 days; F: 16–21 days, precocial; B: 1–2.

Other Behavior: Males incubate and raise young. Females can be polyandrous. Like Red-necked Phalarope, this species may be blown toward shore by storms during its offshore migrations.

Habitat: Summers on tundra ponds near arctic coast; winters at sea.

Voice: A high-pitched shrill "wit."

Conservation: CWS: W→ C→ CBC: ⇑

184

Pomarine Jaeger

Stercorarius pomarinus

Light-morph immature

Light-morph adult

Identification: 22″ Light and dark morphs, and intermediate forms, occur. Light morphs greatly outnumber dark morphs. IN FLIGHT: **Large-bodied; thick-necked; wings wide at base; wingbeats deep, slow, and steady. Central tail feathers long, twisted, and spoon-shaped** (can be missing or broken); **flash of white at base of primaries on underwing.** Light morph has variable **mottled barring on flanks under wings; chestband, when present, mottled.** Dark morph all dark except for white on primaries. JUV/IMM: Central tail feathers, no matter how short, are rounded at tip. Imm. plumage kept 3–4 years.

Feeding: During breeding eats lemmings and voles, also other birds and their eggs; during winter, captures fish off ocean surface, also robs other birds of food.

Nesting: Nest is unlined depression in ground. Eggs: 1–2, brown with darker markings; I: 26 days; F: 31–37 days, precocial; B: 1.

Other Behavior: During migration, seen singly or in small flocks.

Habitat: Summers on tundra; winters at sea.

Voice: Generally quiet off breeding ground, but may be heard calling during migration.

Conservation: CBC: ⇑

Parasitic Jaeger

Stercorarius parasiticus

Light-morph adult

Dark-morph adult

Identification: 18″ Light and dark morphs, and intermediate forms, occur. Either morph can be common. **IN FLIGHT:** Compared to Pomarine Jaeger, **neck and body slightly thinner, wings narrower at base; central tail feathers long and pointed** (can be missing or broken); **white at base of primaries on underwing.** Alternates quick wingbeats with short glides. In light morph, flanks under wings clear white; chestband (when present) **smooth gray. Dark morph all dark except for white on primaries.** JUV/IMM: Tail feathers, no matter how short, are pointed. Imm. plumage kept 3–4 years.

Feeding: Breeding birds eat small mammals, birds, insects, berries; winter birds steal fish from other birds, scavenge, and prey on other birds, such as terns.

Nesting: Nest a shallow scrape lined with sparse vegetation. Eggs: 1–3, brown or greenish with darker marks; I: 25–28 days; F: 25–30 days, precocial; B: 1.

Other Behavior: May nest in loose colonies or alone. Most frequently seen jaeger from shore in West.

Habitat: Summers on tundra; winters at sea.

Voice: Generally quiet off breeding ground, but may make sounds at sea.

Conservation: CBC: ↑

Long-tailed Jaeger
Stercorarius longicaudus

Light-morph adult

Identification: 22" Light morph most common; dark morph extremely rare. Smallest of the N. American jaegers (although tail feathers make it long overall). **In Flight: Slim-bodied; wings narrow at base; wingbeats graceful, buoyant, ternlike. Very long central tail feathers pointed** (can be missing or broken); no white at base of primaries on underwing. **Light morph white on chest with no chestband; gray back and wings, with primaries and trailing edge darker.** **Juv/Imm:** Central tail feathers, no matter how short, rounded at tip. Imm. plumage kept 3–4 years.

Feeding: Eats mice and lemmings, also insects, fish, and eggs and chicks of other birds.

Nesting: Nests singly or in loose colonies. Nest a shallow depression in ground lined with some vegetation. Eggs: 1–2, brown or greenish with darker marks; I: 23 days; F: 21 days, precocial; B: 1.

Other Behavior: During migration, seen farther offshore than other jaegers; may pursue Arctic Terns.

Habitat: Summers on tundra; winters at sea.

Voice: Generally quiet off breeding ground.

Conservation: TREND UNKNOWN.

Gulls are generally seen along the coasts and near other water, such as large rivers and lakes. There are two aspects to learning gulls: identifying adults and identifying immatures.

Identifying Adult Gulls

You can recognize a gull as an adult by its lack of brown plumage and its whitish tail with no dark bars (except Heermann's Gull, which has a black tail); immature gulls usually have some dark areas on their tail and usually some brown in their body and/or wing plumage (especially in earlier years). Adult gulls have both a summer and a winter plumage. Gulls whose heads are white in summer usually have a little brown streaking on their heads in winter; gulls whose heads are black in summer have a partial grayish hood or a dark spot behind the eye in winter.

Start learning to identify adult gulls by looking for the most common species. The Learning Pages show these species in both summer and winter plumage. For complete information, see their individual accounts. To identify gulls, look at overall size; whether the head is white or patterned; color and shape of the bill, and the marks on

it, if any; the color of the back and wings; and the patterns on the outer wings when in flight.

Identifying Immature Gulls

Immature gulls can be more difficult to identify, for several reasons. One is that gulls take from 2 to 4 years to reach adult plumage and, in each of those years, they generally have a winter and a summer plumage. Thus, after its initial juvenal plumage, a 2-year gull can have up to 4 additional plumages (1st winter, 1st summer, adult winter, adult summer); a 4-year gull has up to 8 different plumages in addition to its juvenal plumage. (If 1st summer and 1st winter plumages are essentially the same, they are jointly called 1st-year plumage.) There is not room to cover all of these immature plumages in a field guide.

In this guide, we describe adult and 1st-year plumages in detail. There are two reasons for this: there are more 1st-year gulls than any other age class of immatures, due to mortality of immatures in later years; and 1st-year plumages are better defined than those of later years, when individual variations in coloration and timing of molt begin to occur.

COMMON WESTERN GULLS

Heermann's Gull
Medium-sized; dark gray body; dark gray wings; black tail; red bill.
P. 192.

Summer

Winter

Summer

Ring-billed Gull   Large, but noticeably smaller than Herring Gull; black ring near tip of yellow bill; pale gray back; wing tips more extensively black below than Herring Gull's; yellow legs. P. 194.

Winter

California Gull   Large; black-and-red spot near tip of lower mandible; dark eye; greenish-yellow legs; wings dark bluish gray with more black on tips than wings of Herring or Ring-billed Gulls. P. 195.

Summer

Winter

Summer (winter similar)

Western Gull   Large; dark gray back and wings; massive yellow bill with red spot at tip; pink legs. P. 198.

Herring Gull   Large; gray back and wings; black wing tips; pink legs. P. 196.

Winter

Summer

Franklin's Gull

Larus pipixcan

Summer

Immature, 1st winter

Winter

Immature, 1st summer

Identification: 14″ SUMMER: Black hood; dark red, short, straight bill. White crescents above and below eye are thick and usually meet behind eye (true for all ages). WINTER: Like summer, but head whitish with dark half-hood; bill black. IN FLIGHT: Dark gray upperwings separated from rounded black wing tip by white band; underwings white except at tip; tail with grayish center. IMM—1ST WINTER: Black bill; dark half-hood; gray back; white breast. Eye crescents as in adult. IN FLIGHT: Brown wings with black tips; narrow black tail band does not cross outer feathers. 1ST SUMMER: Wings now gray with black tips; tail with faint band or none. Three-year gull.

Feeding: Eats aerial insects, worms in agricultural fields.

Nesting: Colonial. Nest of grasses on ground or floated in shallow water. Eggs: 2–3, greenish brown with marks; I: 18–20 days; F: 35–40 days, precocial; B: 1.

Other Behavior: A gull of the prairies during breeding.

Habitat: Summers on northern prairie lakes; mostly coastal in winter.

Voice: Common call a "weea weea weea."

Conservation: BBS: W ⇑ C ⇓ CBC: ↑

Bonaparte's Gull

Larus philadelphia

Summer

Immature, 1st winter

Winter

Immature, 1st winter

Identification: 13″ SUMMER: **Black hood; orange-red legs; thin white eye crescents; black bill.** WINTER: Like summer, but with **black ear patch and pinkish-red legs.** IN FLIGHT: **Outer wing has white wedge on leading edge and narrow black trailing edge. Buoyant, ternlike flight.** IMM—1ST WINTER: Black ear patch; bill black, sometimes reddish at base. 1ST SUMMER: Similar to 1st winter, but with incomplete black hood. IN FLIGHT: From below, as in adult. From above, dark shoulder bar and dark trailing edge on inner wing. Two-year gull.

Feeding: Feeds on fish, dipping to water's surface in flight; eats worms and aerial and ground insects when inland.

Nesting: Nest of sticks and twigs lined with grass and moss, placed on horizontal branch of spruce or fir tree 5–20 ft. high. Eggs: 3, olive-brown with darker marks; I: 24 days; F: about 30 days, precocial; B: 1.

Other Behavior: After breeding, large flocks gather on large lakes and saltwater bays. Often feeds with terns.

Habitat: Summers in northern coniferous forests; winters on coasts and inland waterways.

Voice: Common call is a repeated nasal "cherr."

Conservation:
BBS: W ⇓ C CBC: ⇑

Heermann's Gull

Larus heermanni

Summer

Immature, 1st year

Winter

Immature, 1st year

Identification: 18" SUMMER: **White head; red bill; dark gray belly, back, and wings;** black tail with thin white band at tip. WINTER: Like summer, but with **gray-streaked head.** IN FLIGHT: **Dark gray wings (above and below) and tail unique among adult gulls.** IMM—1ST YEAR: Uniformly black-brown body; bill pale with dark tip; all-dark tail; black legs and feet (at all ages). Three-year gull.

Feeding: Feeds on fish, crustaceans, and mollusks; also may steal food from other birds.

Nesting: Nest of sticks and grasses occasionally lined with feathers, placed on the ground or between boulders. Eggs: 2–3, gray with darker marks; I: ?; F: ?, precocial; B: 1.

Other Behavior: Heermann's Gulls can be quite aggressive to other gulls and seabirds, chasing them as they try to steal their food, and thus resembling jaegers. Breeds only in western Mex.; migrates north to Calif., Ore., and Wash. in summer through fall.

Habitat: Coastal.

Voice: "Kawak" and a high-pitched "weeee."

Conservation: CBC: ↓

Mew Gull
Larus brachyrhynchos

Summer

Immature, 1st year

Winter

Immature, 1st year

Identification: 16″ SUMMER: **Short, pointed, all-yellow bill; dark eye;** forehead very rounded. WINTER: Like summer, but with **brown spotting on head and nape.** IN FLIGHT: **Black wing tips have large white spots** on outer 2 feathers. IMM—1ST YEAR: Pale dark-tipped bill; grayish-brown back. IN FLIGHT: Brown wings and belly; dark tail band blends into light brown markings on tail. Three-year gull.

Feeding: Hovers over water to catch fish and sand eels, and searches mudflats and plowed fields for insects, worms, and other small animals.

Nesting: Colonial or solitary nester. Shallow nest of seaweed and grasses, placed on the ground. Eggs: 2–3, olive with dark marks; I: 23–28 days; F: about 35 days, precocial; B: 1.

Other Behavior: Winter birds may form temporary small feeding territories and defend them with the same displays used during breeding. Generally roosts in large numbers on sandbanks, islands, or beaches.

Habitat: Summers on lakes; winters along coast.

Voice: High-pitched "kyah kyah" and a lower "meew meew."

Conservation:
BBS: W ⇓ C CBC: ↓

Ring-billed Gull

Larus delawarensis

Summer

Immature, 1st year

Winter

Immature, 1st year

Identification: 19" SUMMER: Pale gray mantle; dark ring just before tip of thin yellow bill; yellow legs; yellow eye. WINTER: Like summer, but **light brown spotting on crown and nape.** IN FLIGHT: **Light gray back and wings; black wing tips have small white dots and are more extensively black below than Herring Gull's.** IMM—1ST YEAR: Pale dark-tipped bill; gray back; brown wings; light brown mottling on breast and belly; pink legs. IN FLIGHT: Clearly defined tail band contrasts with white tail base. Three-year gull.

Feeding: Gulls outside a fast-food restaurant are almost always Ring-billed Gulls; they seem to have found a niche. They also eat worms from plowed fields, eggs from nesting seabirds, and flying dispersing ants.

Nesting: Usually colonial nester. Nest of grasses, pebbles, sticks, placed on ground. Eggs: 3, light brown with dark marks; I: 21 days; F: ?, precocial; B: 1.

Other Behavior: Coming into conflict with humans, especially near airports, where they can get in the way of planes.

Habitat: Coasts, lakes, dumps, fields, fast-food locations.

Voice: "Hyah hyah" and other calls.

Conservation: BBS: W ⇑ C ⇑ CBC: ⇑ Since 1970, populations have increased around Great Lakes and in urban areas.

California Gull

Larus californicus

Summer

Immature, 1st year

Winter

Immature, 1st year

Identification: 19" **SUMMER:** Greenish-yellow legs; black-and-red spot near tip of lower mandible; dark eye; gray back slightly darker than in Herring and Ring-billed Gulls. **WINTER:** Like summer, but with brown-streaked head and shoulders. **IN FLIGHT:** Wings dark bluish gray with more black on outer wing than in Ring-billed Gull; white trailing edge more apparent than on Ring-billed or Herring Gull. **IMM—1ST YEAR:** Dark brown head and body; barring on wings and back; pink bill with well-defined dark tip; pink legs. **IN FLIGHT:** Tail is all blackish brown; rump is whitish with bold dark barring. Four-year gull.

Feeding: Feeds on insects and rodents; may also go to dumps, and follow fishing boats for scraps.

Nesting: Colonial nester. Nest of weeds, grasses, trash bits, placed on the ground. Eggs: 3, olive with dark marks; I: 23–27 days; F: ?, precocial; B: 1.

Other Behavior: Large concentration of up to 150,000 California Gulls around Great Salt Lake in summer.

Habitat: Summers on lakes; winters along coast.

Voice: Soft "kow kow kow."

Conservation:
BBS: W ↓ C ⇑ CBC: ⇑

Herring Gull
Larus argentatus

Summer

Immature, 1st year

Winter

Immature, 1st year

Identification: 25" **SUMMER:** Pale gray back; pinkish legs; yellow bill with red spot near tip of lower mandible; yellow eye. **WINTER:** Like summer, but with **brown-streaked head and neck. IN FLIGHT:** Wing tips less extensively black than in Ring-billed and California Gulls and with small white dots. **IMM—1ST YEAR:** Uniformly mottled brown head and body; bill black with pale base (at first just lower mandible). **IN FLIGHT:** Wide all-dark tail; brown rump; black wing tips and prominent pale windows on inner primaries. Four-year gull.

Feeding: Eats mussels, clams, fish, garbage, rodents, insects, young of other gulls; steals from other birds.

Nesting: Nests colonially. Nest a scrape in ground lined with grasses and seaweed. Eggs: 3, brownish with dark marks; I: 26 days; F: about 35 days, precocial; B: 1.

Other Behavior: During long-call, head is dipped down and then raised up; an aggressive display. During choking-call, body is tipped forward and bird may scrape feet backward; a courtship or territorial display.

Habitat: Coasts, dumps, lakes, rivers, fields.

Voice: Long-call is like "ow ow ow keekeekee kyow kyow kyow"; choking-call is like "huoh huoh huoh"; alarm call is "ga ga ga ga."

Conservation:
BBS: W ⇑ C ⇑ CBC: ↑

Thayer's Gull
Larus thayeri

Summer

Immature, 1st year

Winter

Immature, 1st year

Identification: 24" SUMMER: **Dark pink legs; yellow bill with red spot near tip of lower mandible; dark eye.** WINTER: Like summer, but with **brown spotting on head and shoulders.** IN FLIGHT: From below, **wing all light except for black dots on trailing edge of tip;** from above, **wings gray with 3 thin black stripes along tip.** IMM—1ST YEAR: Variable body usually light; wing tips brown (not black as in Herring Gull); primaries have a pale buffy fringe; bill black. IN FLIGHT: Tail with wide brown band (not barred as in Iceland Gull). From above, wing tips only slightly darker than rest of wing; from below, outer wings appear translucent. Four-year gull.

Feeding: Opportunistic. Eats small rodents, insects, fish, garbage, eggs and young of other gulls.

Nesting: Nests colonially. Nest a scrape in the ground, placed on cliffs. Eggs: 3, olive-brown with darker marks; I: 25–27 days; F: about 35 days, precocial; B: 1.

Other Behavior: May be a subspecies of Iceland Gull.

Habitat: Coastal and sometimes inland during migration and winter.

Voice: Many calls, similar to those of Herring Gull.

Conservation: TREND UNKNOWN.

Western Gull

Larus occidentalis

Summer

Immature, 1st year

Summer

Immature, 1st year

Identification: 26" SUMMER: The only common **dark-backed white-bodied** gull in the West. **Massive bill** yellow with red spot near lower tip; **legs pink.** WINTER: Like summer, but **head lightly streaked with brown. IN FLIGHT: Upperwings dark gray with slightly darker tips.** IMM—1ST YEAR: Mottled grayish brown overall; bill black in winter, then with pale base in summer. IN FLIGHT: Pale rump contrasts with darker back; no obvious wing windows. Four-year gull. ►Southern subspecies, *L. o. wymani,* is darker with black back. Yellow-footed Gull, *L. livens,* is similar, but with yellow legs; breeds in Mex., but regularly seen only at Salton Sea.

Feeding: At sea, eats fish and shrimp; also eats eggs of other nesting seabirds and garbage.

Nesting: Colonial. Nest of grasses, on ground or rocky ledge. Eggs: 3, olive with dark marks; I: 25–29 days; F: 40–50 days, precocial; B: 1.

Other Behavior: Hybridizes with Glaucous-winged Gull in north; hybrids fairly common in Calif. in winter.

Habitat: Coastal.

Voice: Low-pitched "cuk cuk cuk."

Conservation:
BBS: W ↓ C CBC: →

Glaucous-winged Gull
Larus glaucescens

Summer

Immature, 1st year

Winter

Immature, 1st year

Identification: 23″ SUMMER: **Massive yellow bill with red spot; pink legs; dark eyes.** WINTER: Like summer, but **head moderately streaked with brown.** IN FLIGHT: **Upperwings pale gray overall; usually just single large white dot in outermost primary feather; underwings white.** IMM—1ST YEAR: Large; bill black in winter, then with pale base in summer. IN FLIGHT: Pale brown upperwings with wing tips the same color or lighter than rest of wing. Four-year gull. ►Commonly hybridizes with Western Gull, resulting in extensive black or dark gray on upper wing tips; wings mostly white below.

Habitat: Coastal.

Voice: "Kow kow" and others.

Conservation:
BBS: W ⇑ C CBC: ⇑

Feeding: Eats carrion, fish, and garbage, and steals food from other birds.

Nesting: Colonial nester. Nest a mound of seaweed, other vegetation, and feathers, placed on ground or ledge. Eggs: 2–3, olive with darker marks; I: 26–28 days; F: 35–55 days, precocial; B: 1.

Other Behavior: Nests in huge seabird colonies on islands off the coast.

199

Glaucous Gull
Larus hyperboreus

Summer

Immature, 1st year

Winter

Immature, 1st year

Identification: 28" SUMMER: **Large; pale gray back and wings with white wing tips;** heavy relatively long bill; pink legs; yellow eye. **WINTER:** Like summer, but with **pale brown streaking on head and upper breast. IN FLIGHT: Broad pale gray wings with extensive white on wing tips** (no darker gray or black on wings). IMM—1ST WINTER: Pale buff to almost all white; bill pinkish with sharply defined dark tip. 1ST SUMMER: Even paler. Four-year gull.

Feeding: During breeding season, eats lemmings and voles, as well as young and eggs of other seabirds and ducks. Also eats small fish, mollusks, crustaceans, and carrion, and feeds at dumps.

Nesting: Often colonial nester. Nest a mound of seaweed and other vegetation, placed on ground or cliff ledge. Eggs: 2–3, olive with darker marks; I: 27–28 days; F: 45–50 days, precocial; B: 1.

Other Behavior: Glaucous Gulls often rob other birds of food, attacking ducks or other diving birds just as they surface after catching prey. They also eat other adult seabirds.

Habitat: Coasts, large inland lakes, landfills.

Voice: Generally quiet, but has a variety of low hoarse calls.

Conservation: CBC: ⇑

Black-legged Kittiwake

Rissa tridactyla

Summer

Immature, 1st year

Winter

Immature, 1st year

Identification: 16" SUMMER: **Small, unmarked, yellow bill; black legs.** WINTER: Like summer, but with **dark gray smudge behind eye; gray nape.** IN FLIGHT: Gray wings with **triangular all-black wing tip.** IMM—1ST WINTER: Black bill; white body with wide black collar and small ear patch; white tail has thin black terminal band. 1ST SUMMER: Bill paler; lighter collar; tail band and M pattern on upperwings faint. IN FLIGHT: Dark lines on upperwings form large M. Two-year gull.

Feeding: Eats primarily fish picked from the surface of the ocean.

Nesting: Colonial nester. Nest of mud, seaweed, and grass, placed on small ledge of cliff or on building. Eggs: 1–3, yellowish with dark marks; I: 25–32 days; F: 33–55 days, precocial; B: 1.

Other Behavior: Gathers into large flocks during migration in spring and fall. Usually feeds in smaller flocks during winter. Flocks follow fishing ships at sea to feed on refuse.

Habitat: Summers on coastal cliffs; winters at sea.

Voice: "Kekekek" and "kittewake."

Conservation: CBC: ⇓

Sabine's Gull
Xema sabini

Summer

Summer

Juvenile

Identification: 13" SUMMER: **Head black; bill black with yellow tip.** WINTER: Like summer, but **head whitish with dark nape.** IN FLIGHT: From above, **wing colors form 3 large triangles — black, gray, and white.** JUV: Retains juvenal (rather than 1st winter) plumage through fall. Brown crown, nape, and upperparts; upperparts with darker scalloping. IN FLIGHT: Above, like adult, but with brown instead of gray on back and shoulders; thin black tail band. 1ST SUMMER: Like adult summer, but with some white mottling on black hood. Two-year gull.

Feeding: During breeding, feeds mostly on land, eating insects, worms, and other invertebrates. At other times, eats fish from water's surface or makes shallow dives.

Nesting: Colonial. Nest a shallow depression rimmed with a little vegetation, placed on the ground. Eggs: 1–3, olive with dark markings; I: 23–25 days; F: ?, precocial; B: 1.

Other Behavior: Unlike other gulls, has complete molt in spring, partial molt in fall. May nest with Arctic Terns.

Habitat: Summers on arctic lakes; migrates at sea; winters in S. America.

Voice: Harsh grating call.

Conservation: TREND UNKNOWN.

Caspian Tern
Sterna caspia

Winter

Summer

Winter

Winter

Identification: 21" Only large tern regularly seen inland. **Summer: Large; crested; black cap; massive blood-red bill** (sometimes slightly darker at tip). **Winter:** Like summer, but **cap splotchy, gray, and extends over forehead to bill. In Flight: Broad wings; slow powerful flight;** from below, **extensive dark on wing tip. Juv:** Like winter adult, but bill orange; upperparts lightly marked with dark bars and V's.

Feeding: Catches fish by diving completely underwater from air; also may pick fish off the surface of the water.

Nesting: Nests singly or in colonies. Nest a depression in ground lined with grasses and seaweed, located on sandy beaches. Eggs: 2–3, pinkish with darker markings; I: 20–22 days; F: 28–35 days, precocial; B: 1.

Other Behavior: May steal fish from other seabirds. When fishing, generally flies low over water, but when traveling back to nest, will fly high and even soar in circles to gain altitude.

Habitat: Coasts and inland along rivers and lakes.

Voice: A harsh "cahar" and "kwok."

Conservation:
BBS: W ⇑ C ⇑ CBC: ↑

Royal Tern

Sterna maxima

Summer

Summer

Winter

Identification: 20" Seen only on coast. SUMMER: Large; **all-orange bill; crested black cap.** WINTER: Like summer, but **forehead white; crown pale gray to white; nape black.** IN FLIGHT: From below, note **dark on outermost primary and trailing edge of wing tip.** JUV: Bill yellowish. IN FLIGHT: From above, dark primaries and bold dark bars on inner portion of wings.

Feeding: Dives into water from 40–50 ft. high to catch fish.

Nesting: Colonial nester. Nest a shallow scrape in sand, lined with bits of grass. Eggs: 1–2, buffy with darker dots; I: 20–22 days; F: 28–35 days, precocial; B: 1.

Other Behavior: Often migrates in large flocks with other tern species. Nesting colonies can reach 10,000 birds along Gulf Coast.

Habitat: Coast.

Voice: Calls include a whistled "tooree" and a harsh "keeer."

Conservation: BBS: W C ⇓ CBC: ↓

Elegant Tern
Sterna elegans

Summer

Summer

Winter

Identification: 16" Seen only on coast. **SUMMER: Large** (but smaller than Royal Tern); **thin, slightly drooping, orange bill; black cap; long crest. WINTER:** Like summer, but **forehead white; crown pale gray; black nape extends forward through eye** (in similar Royal Terns in the West, black on nape does not reach the eye). **IN FLIGHT:** From below, note **dark on outermost primary and trailing edge of wing tip. JUV:** Bill yellow and shorter than in Royal Tern. **IN FLIGHT:** From above, dark primaries and bold dark bars on inner portion of wings.

Feeding: Dives for small fish from air.

Nesting: Colonial nester. Nest a shallow scrape in sand. Eggs: 1–2, pinkish; I: 20 days; F: ?, precocial; B: 1.

Other Behavior: Breeds primarily in Mex., where protection has encouraged increases in population; winters from Peru to Chile.

Habitat: Coastal.

Voice: A medium-pitched grating "kareek kareek."

Conservation:
TREND UNKNOWN. Postbreeding range slowly expanding up Calif. to Wash. coast. Breeds mostly in Mex. First started breeding in U.S. at San Diego Bay in 1959.

Common Tern

Sterna hirundo

Summer

Juvenile

Summer

Immature

Identification: 15″ SUMMER: **Medium-sized; pale gray underparts contrast with white undertail coverts; orange-red bill, usually black-tipped; white black-edged tail; tips of folded wings project just past tail.** Black cap kept well into fall; molt occurs mostly after migration. WINTER: Like summer but **forecrown white; nape and bill black; underparts white; dark shoulder bar.** IN FLIGHT: Below, **gray body; fairly wide black trailing edge on wing tip.** Above, **outer primaries darker than rest of wing.** Dark shoulder bar in winter. JUV/IMM: Forehead light brown wearing to white; dark nape; dark shoulder bar; back brownish wearing to gray; underwings as in adult; bill red-based at first, then mostly black; legs red.

Feeding: Feeds on small fish by diving into water.

Nesting: Colonial. Nest scrape in ground. Eggs: 3, buffy with spots; I: 21–27 days; F: 28 days, precocial; B: 1.

Other Behavior: Courting male flies with fish in beak.

Habitat: Lakes, coast.

Voice: Short "kip" and harsh "keear."

Conservation:
BBS: W ⇑ C ⇑ CBC: ↓ Populations have decreased almost 75% since 1920s due to breeding habitat loss, competition with gulls for nesting sites, and predation by gulls and Great Horned Owls.

Arctic Tern

Sterna paradisaea

Summer

Summer

Summer

Juvenile/immature

Identification: 16" **SUMMER: Medium-sized; short all-red bill; white black-edged tail extends well beyond tip of folded wing;** black cap and nape; **very short legs. WINTER:** Adult winter plumage not seen in U.S. and Canada. **IN FLIGHT:** From below, note **distinctive very narrow black trailing edge on wing tip; long forked tail; pale gray underparts. JUV/IMM:** Light forehead; dark nape; faint shoulder bar; distinctive underwings as in adult; black bill; reddish legs; white trailing edge of inner wing.

Feeding: Often hovers over water, then dives to pick fish off the surface; seldom plunge-dives as many other terns do.

Nesting: Colonial. Nest a scrape in ground, sometimes lined with grass bits, located on a beach or ledge. Eggs: 2–3, olive with darker marks; I: 23–27 days; F: 28 days, precocial; B: 1.

Other Behavior: A long-distance migrant, spending the breeding season in the Arctic and wintering as far south as Antarctica — a round trip of about 22,000 miles.

Habitat: Summers on lakes, rivers, coast; winters at sea.

Voice: A harsh "kee-yeer."

Conservation:
BBS: W ⇑ C
Population drastically reduced by plume trade in late 1800s. With protection, it is slowly recovering.

Aleutian Tern

Sterna aleutica

Summer

Summer

Identification: 14" SUMMER: **Black cap; white forehead;** black bill and legs. Generally not in our range when in winter plumage. IN FLIGHT: From below, **gray chest and belly; all-white tail; dark bar along trailing edge of inner wing.** JUV: Feathers on upperparts dark with buffy fringes; head and breastband washed with buff; otherwise, white below; tail dark-tipped.

Feeding: Catches fish by diving into water from air.

Nesting: Colonial. Nest a slight depression in ground. Eggs: 2, yellowish with darker marks; I: 21 days; F: about 21–28 days, precocial; B: 1.

Other Behavior: Often nests in colonies with Arctic Terns and may benefit from Arctic's readiness to attack intruders. Somewhat sparsely distributed and nowhere common.

Habitat: Summers on coastal islands; winters at sea, but locations still largely unknown.

Voice: Distinctive whistled call like "whee whee whee."

Conservation: TREND UNKNOWN.

Forster's Tern
Sterna forsteri

Summer

Winter

Summer

Juvenile/immature

Identification: 15″ SUMMER: Medium-sized; orange-red bill with black tip; underparts white; gray white-edged tail extends well beyond tips of folded wings; black cap and nape. Molts in August into winter plumage. WINTER: Like summer, but with **black patch from eye to ear; white forehead; pale to dark gray nape; no dark shoulder bar; black bill. IN FLIGHT:** Below, white belly; fairly wide dark gray trailing edge on wing tip. Above, primaries and secondaries silvery white; in early summer, tips of primaries darken. In winter, wings all pale with no shoulder bar. JUV/IMM: Black patch from eye to ear. Crown and back light brown wearing to white and gray; above, wings dusky with no obvious shoulder bar.

Feeding: Eats aerial insects; plunge-dives for fish.

Nesting: Colonial. Nest a scrape in ground. Eggs: 3–4, olive with marks; I: 22–23 days; F: ?, precocial; B: 1.

Other Behavior: Winters in U.S.

Habitat: Lakes, marshes, coast.

Voice: A short "keer" and "zreep" and "kip."

Conservation: BBS: W ⇑ C ⇑ CBC: ⇑ Breeding grounds very susceptible to human disturbance. Has recently expanded range north along Atlantic Coast.

Least Tern

Sterna antillarum

Summer

Summer

Summer

Identification: 9″ SUMMER: **Very small; black cap; white forehead; yellow bill** with tiny black tip. WINTER: Like summer, but more **extended white on forehead; bill black.** IN FLIGHT: **Narrow wings; rapid wingbeats;** distinctive **black leading edge of outer wing;** short shallow-forked tail. FALL JUV: Whitish crown and forehead; black line through eye and often around nape; black bill; dark V's on feathers of upperparts. IN FLIGHT: Wings show dark leading edge and dark tips.

Feeding: Catches small fish by plunge diving into water or skimming over the surface.

Nesting: Colonial or solitary. Nest a shallow scrape in the sand. Eggs: 2, olive with darker marks; I: 20–22 days; F: 28 days, precocial; B: 1.

Other Behavior: As with all tern nesting colonies, it is best not to disturb them. When the adults fly up in alarm, it is a chance for gulls and other birds to fly in and eat eggs and young. May nest on gravel roofs of large buildings in Fla. in response to beach disturbance.

Habitat: Coast and along major rivers.

Voice: A repeated "kip kip kip" and a harsh "zreeet."

Conservation:
BBS: W C ⇓ CBC: ↓
In late 1800s, plume trade killed up to 100,000 birds each year. West Coast subspecies *C. a. "browni"* and interior pop. endangered in U.S.

Black Tern

Chlidonias niger

Summer

Summer

Winter

Identification: 10" SUMMER: **Small; head and body are black.** IN FLIGHT: Wings and tail uniformly dark gray. WINTER: **White underparts; dark gray upperparts; partial blackish cap; black patches** (or "half collar") **on either side of breast.** IN FLIGHT: Dark gray above, white below. FALL JUV: Similar to winter adult, but with a grayish cap and a brownish back.

Feeding: Eats insects from air and by fluttering down to pick them off vegetation. Often feeds over meadows and agricultural lands. Feeds on fish when along coast and out at sea.

Nesting: Colonial. Nest a loose construction of reeds, placed at water's edge or floating on surface. Eggs: 3, olive with dark marks; I: 21–22 days; F: 21–28 days, precocial; B: 1.

Other Behavior: Birds nest in vegetation of marshes and become very excited if you approach the nest. Seeing their fluttering over the area and hearing their "kreeek" calls should warn you to back up and cause no further disturbance to the nest. See Conservation.

Habitat: Summers on wet meadows, marshes, ponds; winters on coast and at sea.

Voice: Short "krik" or longer "kreeek."

Conservation:
BBS: W ⇓ C ⇓ CBC: ↓ Population declining, possibly due to loss of freshwater marsh nesting sites, pesticide use, and disturbance by humans.

Black Skimmer

Rynchops niger

Identification: 18″ Strikingly **black above and white below; large, red, black-tipped bill** with lower portion longer. In winter, plumage duller with faint white collar. **Imm:** Similar to adult, but upperparts mottled brown.

Feeding: Unique and entertaining feeding method of rapidly flying over water and skimming the surface with its longer lower mandible until it hits a fish, and then snapping it up.

Nesting: Colonial. Nest a hollow in the sand. Eggs: 4–5, whitish with dark marks; I: 21–23; F: 23–25, precocial; B: 1.

Other Behavior: When the bird is skimming over water, note that it must fly with its wings held high in order to stay clear of the water; at other times, flies with deeper wingbeats. Often nests in colonies with terns. Occasionally roosts on gravel roofs in Fla.

Habitat: Coast.

Voice: Variety of short low-pitched calls.

Conservation: CBC: ⇓

Common Murre
Thick-billed Murre
Uria aalge   Uria lomvia

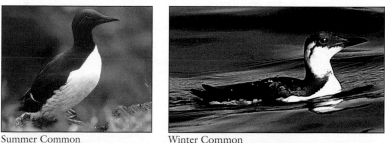

Summer Common

Winter Common

Summer Thick-billed

Winter Thick-billed

Identification: Common 17", Thick-billed 18" SUMMER: Both species have **dark head, neck, and upperparts; white underparts; long black bill. COMMON: Slender, pointed, all-black bill; line between white and black on throat smoothly rounded; brownish cast to head and back. THICK-BILLED: White line along gape of thick relatively short bill; line between white and black on throat comes to a point; head and back black. WINTER—COMMON:** Cheek and throat white; dark streak through cheek. **THICK-BILLED:** Cheek and throat white.

Feeding: Feed on fish by diving underwater from the surface. Usually dive 10–25 ft. down, but have been caught in crab traps at 300 ft.

Nesting: Colonial nesters. For both species, no nest built except for a few pebbles brought to the nest site; eggs laid directly on ledge of cliff. Eggs: 1, blue-green with darker marks; I: 32–33 days; F: 21 days, precocial; B: 1.

Other Behavior: Young leave nest before they can fully fly, gliding down from nesting cliffs to the sea.

Common   Thick-billed

Habitat: Summer on coastal cliffs; winter at sea.

Voice: Make sounds like their name, like "murrr"; also low growling sounds.

Conservation:
Common:
BBS: W ⇓ C   CBC: ⇓
Thick-billed:
CBC: ⇑
Both species susceptible to gill nets and oil spills.

213

Pigeon Guillemot
Cepphus columba

Summer

Winter

Identification: 13" SUMMER: Conspicuous white patch on wing has black triangle (sometimes 2) in lower half; otherwise, bird black. WINTER: Head, neck, and underparts white; back mottled gray and white; summer wing markings still conspicuous. IN FLIGHT: White patches on upperwing; dusky lining to underwing. IMM: Like winter adult, but black on white wing patch may be reduced. Imm. plumage kept until following summer.

Feeding: Catches fish and some shrimp with underwater dives. Tends to feed in deeper water a little offshore.

Nesting: Nest a scrape, made in a protected rock crevice, under boulders, or in burrows; can excavate burrow with beak and claws; also nests on buildings such as old canneries. Eggs: 1–2, light blue-green with darker marks; I: 29–32 days; F: 35 days, precocial; B: 1.

Other Behavior: Birds depart from the vicinity of nesting sites in Calif. (except those on Monterey Peninsula) and are thought to disperse to the north, perhaps Puget Sound. When underwater, they use their wings to propel them through the water.

Habitat: Summers on coast; winters also out at sea.

Voice: A "tsik" call and a longer "peeeeo."

Conservation:
BBS: W ⇓ C CBC: ↓

214

Marbled Murrelet
Kittlitz's Murrelet

Brachyramphus marmoratus   Brachyramphus brevirostris

Summer Marbled

Winter Marbled

Winter Kittlitz's

Identification: Marbled 9½", Kittlitz's 9"
SUMMER—MARBLED: Dark brown above;
mottled brown and white below; may appear
to have darker cap; black tail. KITTLITZ'S:
Finely mottled buff and white, except for
white belly; tail black with white outer
feathers; very short bill. WINTER—MARBLED:
White lines on sides of black back; black cap
extends below eye; tail as described.
KITTLITZ'S: White lines on sides of black back;
black cap well above eye; tail as described.

Feeding: Both species eat fish and some crustaceans.
Feeding is done mostly near shore in shallow water.

Nesting: Marbled's nest in tree, up to 150 ft. high,
constructed of moss. Eggs: 1, light olive with dark
marks; I: 30 days; F: 28 days, precocial; B: 1. Kittlitz's
nest a shallow depression in ground, under rocks or on
talus slopes. Eggs: 1, olive with darker marks; I: 30
days; F: 20–21 days, precocial; B: 1.

Other Behavior: Average distance from nest to sea:
Marbled about 5 miles; Kittlitz's about 10 miles.

Marbled   Kittlitz's

Habitat: Summer
on coast and
inland; Kittlitz's
winters out at sea,
Marbled on coast.

Voice: Twittering
high-pitched calls.

Conservation:
Marbled:
BBS: W ⇓ C CBC: ↑
Kittlitz's:
TREND UNKNOWN.
Pop. probably
declining, due to
loss of old-growth
forest habitat.

Xantus' Murrelet
Craveri's Murrelet

Synthliboramphus hypoleucus   Synthliboramphus craveri

Xantus'

Craveri's

Identification: Xantus' 10", Craveri's 10" These species are similar in size and coloration and the differences are subtle. Best clue is underwings, seen as they are about to take flight. **XANTUS':** **Black above; breast all white;** bill short and relatively thick; black cap extends to middle of bill. **IN FLIGHT: Note white wing linings.** **CRAVERI'S: Brownish black above; partial black collar on sides of breast;** bill longer and relatively thin; black cap extends to below bill. **IN FLIGHT: Note grayish wing linings.**

Xantus'   Craveri's

Feeding: Both feed mostly on fish, especially anchovies and larvae of other fish.

Nesting: Xantus' nest in crevice or found burrow, with no lining. Eggs: 2, greenish with dark marks; I: 32 days; F: ?, precocial; B: 1. Craveri's nest in crevice or burrow. Eggs: 2, buff with darker marks; I: 31–33 days; F: ?, precocial; B: 1.

Other Behavior: Adults approach nests at dusk and leave before dawn. Young are not fed by parents at nest; they leave nest 1–2 days after hatching and go to the sea.

Habitat: Summer on coast and coastal islands; winter at sea.

Voice: Trills and whistles.

Conservation: Xantus': TREND UNKNOWN. Craveri's: TREND UNKNOWN. Xantus' susceptible to egg predation by deer mice.

Ancient Murrelet

Synthliboramphus antiquus

Identification: 10" Gray back; black head and throat; white on underparts extends up onto cheek; short pale yellow bill. **Imm:** Similar to adult, but with white chin.

Feeding: Feeds on crustaceans in plankton.

Nesting: Nest is a dug burrow about 4 ft. long lined with some vegetation, usually placed under rock or tree root. Eggs: 2, buff with darker marks; I: 34–42 days; F: ?, precocial; B: 1.

Other Behavior: Adults approach nests at dusk and leave before dawn. Young leave nest at night 1–2 days after hatching and climb down to sea. Their nighttime departure may help protect them from predation by gulls. In some areas, Ancient Murrelets are an important part of the Peregrine Falcon's diet during breeding.

Habitat: Summers on coast and coastal islands; winters at sea.

Voice: Trills and whistles.

Conservation: CBC: ↑ Introduced rats on islands where Ancient Murrelet breeds may prey on eggs.

Cassin's Auklet

Ptychoramphus aleuticus

Identification: 9″ Small; all gray; darker above than below; white crescents above and below eye; pale mark at base of lower bill.

Feeding: Eats mostly crustaceans and some small fish. Has food storage pouch in mouth that enables it to collect food for young during day and then fly back to feed young at night.

Nesting: Colonial. Nest excavated in soft earth at base of tree or rock. Eggs: 1, whitish; I: 37–42 days; F: 41 days, precocial; B: 1.

Other Behavior: Burrows are dug only at night and may take 3 months to complete. Visits burrow after dark to avoid predation by gulls. When feeding at sea, may have trouble getting airborne from calm sea surface when full with krill.

Habitat: Summers along coast; winters farther out to sea.

Voice: Shrill whistles.

Conservation: TREND UNKNOWN.

Parakeet Auklet
Rhinoceros Auklet

Ptychoramphus psittacula   Cerorhinca monocerata

Winter Parakeet

Summer Rhinoceros

Winter Rhinoceros

Identification: Parakeet 10", Rhinoceros 15"
SUMMER—PARAKEET: **Short, red, upturned bill; single white plume off back of each eye;** bright white belly. RHINOCEROS: **Larger; large, straight, orange bill with horn at base; 2 white plumes on each side of face;** whitish belly.
WINTER—PARAKEET: Similar to summer, but **bill duller; chin and throat white.** RHINOCEROS: Similar to summer, but **lacks horn on bill; white plumes on face faint or absent.**

Feeding: Parakeet eats mostly crustaceans found in plankton. Rhinoceros eats mostly small fish and some squid.

Nesting: Parakeet nest in a shallow depression in crevices of boulder slope. Eggs: 1, bluish white; I: 35–36 days; F: 34–37 days, precocial; B: 1. Rhinoceros nest in excavated burrow 8–10 ft. long, sometimes with side passages. Eggs: 1, whitish and sometimes marked; I: 39–52 days; F: 48–56 days, precocial; B: 1.

Other Behavior: Rhinoceros Auklet can dig burrow in 1–2 weeks; is also known to nest in human-made nesting boxes.

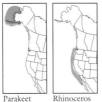

Parakeet   Rhinoceros

Habitat: Coastal.

Voice: Parakeet gives ascending trills; Rhinoceros gives repeated high-pitched groans. Other calls as well.

Conservation:
Parakeet:
TREND UNKNOWN.
Rhinoceros:
BBS: W ⇑ C CBC: ⇑
In Alaska, Arctic Foxes raid nests.

219

Tufted Puffin
Horned Puffin

Fratercula cirrhata   Fratercula corniculata

Summer Tufted

Winter Tufted

Summer Horned

Identification: Tufted 15", Horned 15"
SUMMER—TUFTED: **Massive orange bill with greenish base; long golden tufts behind eyes; white face; dark belly.** HORNED: **Massive bill, yellow at base, orange at tip; white face with no tufts off eyes;** white breast and belly.
WINTER—TUFTED: **All dark with orange bill; no tufts.** HORNED: Similar to summer, but with **grayish face.**

Feeding: Both species feed on fish, squid, and crustaceans caught while diving underwater.

Nesting: Colonial nesters. Tufted nests are burrows up to 9 ft. long, excavated by the birds. Eggs: 1, whitish with light marks; I: 43–53 days; F: 43–47 days, precocial; B: 1. Horned nests are burrows up to 3 ft. long, either found or excavated by the birds. Eggs: 1, whitish with light marks; I: 40–42 days; F: 38–40 days, precocial; B: 1.

Other Behavior: During breeding, both species often seen in large flocks on the water near their nesting sites. At other seasons, tend to be solitary. Tufted Puffin may run along water surface when trying to take flight.

Tufted   Horned

Habitat: Summer along coast; winter at sea.

Voice: Variety of growling notes and purring sounds.

Conservation:
Tufted:
TREND UNKNOWN.
Horned:
TREND UNKNOWN.

Rock Dove (Pigeon)
Columba livia

Typical version

Variations

Identification: 13" The familiar Pigeon. Due to breeding by humans, colors can range from all white to all black, with just about anything in between. Most often **dark gray head; iridescent neck; light gray back; 2 dark wing bars. IN FLIGHT: Note squared tail with dark band at tip; white rump.**

Feeding: Feeds on the ground, eating grain, seeds, crumbs, and other garbage in cities. At bird feeders, eats scattered seed and cracked corn.

Nesting: Saucerlike nest of roots, stems, and leaves, placed on building ledge, rafters, beams under bridge, or inside barn. Eggs: 1–2, white; I: 18 days; F: 25–29 days, altricial; B: 2–5.

Other Behavior: Pigeons have many courtship displays. Breeding birds do wing-clapping flight, in which they clap wings as they take flight, then glide with wings held in a V. In bowing display, male spreads tail and fluffs neck feathers while bowing and circling in front of female; between bows, male runs for short distance, dragging tail on ground. First introduced into N. America in 1606. Now widespread.

Habitat: Cities, parks, bridges, steep cliffs.

Voice: At nest site, call by male or female is "k't'coo"; during courtship display male gives "oorook'tookoo." Wing-clapping sound made during display flights.

Conservation: BBS: W ↑ C ↓

221

Band-tailed Pigeon

Columba fasciata

Identification: 14" Dark gray wings and back; purplish head and breast; **white band on nape with iridescence below it; bill yellow with black tip;** yellow feet. **IN FLIGHT:** To distinguish from Pigeon, note **dark rump; wide light gray band at tip of tail;** and uniformity of birds in a flock (Pigeons vary). **IMM:** All gray; bill and feet may vary from yellow to gray. Imm. plumage kept into winter.

Feeding: Feeds on the ground and in shrubs, eating nuts, berries, seeds, waste grain, and, especially in the fall and winter, acorns. As with all pigeons, young are fed crop milk, a nutritious liquid secreted from parents' crop.

Nesting: Flimsy platform of sticks and twigs lined with pine needles, placed in a fork or horizontal branch of a tree (above a slope). Eggs: 1–2, white; I: 18–20 days; F: 25–27 days, altricial; B: 2–3.

Other Behavior: Coos in upright posture with neck inflated and tail spread. In flight display, male glides in circle with wings and tail spread.

Habitat: Dry pine forests inland; oak forests along coast; may be seen in parks and gardens.

Voice: Low-pitched "oohooo."

Conservation: BBS: W ⇓ C CBC: ↑ Historically in U.S. almost reduced to extinction through hunting; now recovered.

Spotted Dove
Streptopelia chinensis

Identification: 12" Light gray head; pinkish-brown body; conspicuous black collar with white dots. IN FLIGHT: Long rounded tail; central tail feathers dark brown; outer tail feathers black with white tips.

Feeding: Feeds on seed and grain. May come to seed on ground under feeders.

Nesting: Flat nest, placed in tree or bush or on building. Eggs: 2, white; I: ?; F: ?, altricial; B: 1 or more.

Other Behavior: During bowing display, the plumage on sides and back of neck is erected, forming a broad collar. Introduced from Asia to Los Angeles in the early 1900s.

Habitat: Suburban gardens and parks.

Voice: "Coo croo coo."

Conservation: BBS: W ⇓ C CBC: ⇓

White-winged Dove

Zenaida asiatica

Identification: 11" Light gray-brown; heavyset; **conspicuous white line along edge of closed wing;** small black dash below cheek; red eye surrounded by blue skin. **IN FLIGHT: Conspicuous white patches across center of wings;** tail rounded with white on either side.

Feeding: Feeds on ground or by clinging to plants from which it is eating. Eats weed, flower, and other plant seeds, acorns, cactus fruit, and waste grain such as sorghum. May come to seed on ground under feeders.

Nesting: Sometimes colonial. Saucerlike nest of sticks, twigs, grass, weed stems, placed at fork of horizontal branch or on top of deserted nest in tree 4–25 ft. high. Eggs: 1–4, creamy white; I: 13–14 days; F: 13–16 days, altricial; B: 2–3.

Other Behavior: Often roosts and nests colonially, especially in mesquite thickets. Flies singly, in pairs, or in small groups, and congregates in large numbers at good feeding areas. When nest-calling near female, male spreads tail and wings. Nesting habitat destroyed in S. Tex. in early 1900s. Now expanding northward in suburban areas.

Habitat: Throughout dry areas of Southwest, including suburbs.

Voice: A distinctive "who cooks for you?" Much like a softer version of the Barred Owl's.

Conservation: BBS: W ↑ C ↑ CBC: ⇑

Mourning Dove
Zenaida macroura

Male

Identification: 12" Sleek; gray-brown; **long pointed tail; black dots on wings.** Male has light gray crown and iridescent sides of neck; female is evenly brown on head and neck. **IN FLIGHT: Long pointed tail; shorter outer tail feathers broadly tipped with white.**

Feeding: Common at bird feeders, where it feeds on scattered seed, or takes seed from trays or hoppers. Eats weed, grass, and grain seeds, and some insects.

Nesting: Loose, flat nest of twigs, grass, weeds, and pine needles, placed in a vertical fork or horizontal branch of a tree 3–30 ft. high or, rarely, on the ground. Eggs: 2, white; I: 14–15 days; F: 12–14 days, altricial; B: 2–3.

Other Behavior: Unmated males do aerial display in which they clap wings as they rise up, then descend in long spiral glide with wings held slightly lower than body. From perches, courting male does conspicuous cooing in which he puffs out his throat and bobs tail. When cooing on ground in front of female, male repeatedly bows head and gives long coo.

Habitat: Can be found in almost any open habitat, including suburban areas.

Voice: Unmated males give a commonly heard "ooahoo oo oo oo." Breeding males and females can give a short "ooahoo" near the nest.

Conservation: BBS: W ↓ C ↓ CBC: ⇑

225

Inca Dove
Columbina inca

Identification: 8″ Small; dark-tipped feathers create **scalloped effect all over body; tail almost as long as rest of body. IN FLIGHT:** Reddish-brown wing tips; **long tail with white along sides and corners.**

Feeding: Feeds on the ground, eating weed seeds and grain. Sometimes feeds alongside poultry. May come to bird feeders and eat seed scattered on ground.

Nesting: Saucerlike nest of twigs, sticks, grass, leaves, and rootlets lined with grass, placed on horizontal limb of bush or tree, or sometimes in hanging planter. May reuse nest of other bird such as Mourning Dove. Eggs: 2, white; I: 14 days; F: 14–16 days, altricial; B: 2–5.

Other Behavior: Does bowing display with tail held vertical and fanned, showing markings. In summer, nonbreeding adults and immatures form loose flocks, which may congregate in large numbers in good feeding areas. Roost communally in flocks with birds perched close together, sometimes even roosting on top of other flock members.

Habitat: Cactus and mesquite country; suburbs, parks, and gardens.

Voice: A continually repeated "werl-pool."

Conservation: BBS: W ⇑ C ↑ CBC: ↑ Range expanding eastward along Gulf of Mexico.

Common Ground-Dove

Columbina passerina

Male

Identification: 7″ Very small; gray; scalloped effect on head and breast only; black-tipped reddish bill; **short tail** often raised. **MALE:** Pinkish gray. **FEMALE:** Gray. **IN FLIGHT: Reddish-brown wing tips; short dark tail with white spots at the corners.**

Feeding: Feeds on the ground, eating weed, grass, and waste grain seeds, crumbs, insects, and small berries. May come to seed on ground under feeders.

Nesting: Saucerlike nest of sticks, rootlets, and grass, placed on the ground, on the beach, in woods, in cultivated field, or occasionally in low bush. Eggs: 2–3, white; I: 12–14 days; F: 11 days, altricial; B: 2–4.

Other Behavior: Male bows with lowered head when cooing at female. Spends most of the time on the ground, usually in pairs or small groups. Unafraid of humans.

Habitat: Open areas at the edge of vegetation, including suburbs.

Voice: An ascending "coo ah, coo ah."

Conservation: BBS: W ↓ C ⇓ CBC: ⇓

Black-billed Cuckoo
Coccyzus erythropthalmus

Adult   Immature

Identification: 12″ **Black downcurved bill; red eye-ring; long tail** with pairs of narrowly white-tipped feathers progressing down the dark underside of the tail. **In Flight: Wings and upperparts dark brown; tail feathers narrowly tipped with white. Imm:** Similar to adult, but with buffy eye-ring and less prominent white tips on tail feathers. Imm. plumage kept into winter.

Habitat: Woods edges, thickets, hedgerows.

Feeding: Eats insects, especially caterpillars; also spiders, frogs, lizards, small mollusks, fishes, and berries.

Voice: A soft repeated "cucucu, cucucucu."

Nesting: Platform nest of twigs and grasses, lined with ferns, rootlets, catkins, placed near the trunk of a tree 2–20 ft. high. Eggs: 2–5, bluish green; I: 10–14 days; F: 9–14 days, altricial; B: 1.

Conservation: BBS: W ⇓ C ↓

Other Behavior: On rare occasions, lays eggs in nests of other birds, such as Yellow-billed Cuckoo, Gray Catbird, Wood Thrush, Yellow Warbler, and Chipping Sparrow. This activity occurs during times of food abundance, such as when there is an outbreak of caterpillars.

Yellow-billed Cuckoo
Coccyzus americanus

Adult

Adult

Identification: 12" **Downcurved bill black above, yellow below; long tail** with 3 pairs of large white ovals on its dark underside. **IN FLIGHT: Wings reddish brown on outer half; tail feathers broadly tipped with white. IMM:** Similar to adult, but with less prominent white ovals on underside of tail; bill may be all dark or partly yellow; similar to imm. Black-billed Cuckoo. Imm. plumage kept into winter.

Feeding: Eats mostly hairy caterpillars, such as tent caterpillars; also eats cicadas, beetles, grasshoppers, crickets, and other insects, berries, frogs, and lizards.

Nesting: Platform nest of twigs, lined with leaves, grasses, mosses, rootlets, placed on the horizontal limb of a tree or bush 3–20 ft. high. Eggs: 1–5, pale bluish green; I: 9–14 days; F: 7–9 days, altricial; B: 1–2.

Other Behavior: Heard more than seen. Quite shy. Stays in dense canopy of trees or tangles of undergrowth. On rare occasions, lays eggs in nest of Black-billed Cuckoo.

Habitat: Open woods, thickets, riparian habitats.

Voice: Sounds like "kukukukakaka kalp kalp kalp," slowing near the end.

Conservation:
BBS: W ↓ C ↓ CBC: →

Greater Roadrunner

Geococcyx californianus

Identification: 22″ Long legs; long tail; **streaked brown;** blue-and-red streak behind eye; **usually on the ground;** when stopped, often raises crest and tail. IMM: Lacks colorful streak behind the eye.

Feeding: Feeds on the ground, eating insects, small rodents, the eggs and young of other birds, small snakes including rattlesnakes, spiders, lizards, and fruit.

Nesting: Platform nest of sticks lined with roots, feathers, grasses, snakeskins, mesquite pods, and dried horse or cattle manure, placed in low cactus, tree, or bush 3–15 ft. high. Eggs: 4–6, yellowish white; I: 20 days; F: 17–19 days, altricial; B: 1–2.

Other Behavior: Can run up to 15 miles per hour in pursuit of lizards or insects. Pair lives on its territory year round.

Habitat: On ground in woodlands, brushlands, grasslands; often arid areas.

Voice: A series of low dovelike coos, descending in pitch.

Conservation: BBS: W ↓ C ↓ CBC: ↑

Barn Owl
Tyto alba

Identification: 18" Pale; slim **long-legged** owl; **large, white, heart-shaped facial disk;** dark eyes; breast white to buffy and sparsely spotted.

Feeding: Locates prey almost entirely by sound. Typically flies 10 ft. over marshes, meadows, and woodlands hunting mice and rats, which it grabs in its talons. Also eats insects, bats, and reptiles.

Nesting: Nests in barns and other old buildings, tree hollows, church steeples, old burrows of woodchucks or badgers, and in holes in banks and cliffs, which it may enlarge. Will use human-made nest boxes. No nest material is added. Eggs: 4–7, white; I: 32–34 days; F: 45–58 days, altricial; B: 1–2.

Other Behavior: Barn Owl has the most acutely developed sense of hearing of all the owls. It can pinpoint prey with 100% accuracy in total darkness. It can hear a mouse's footsteps on packed earth 30 yd. away. Because of this, it can be extremely beneficial to farmers who want to get rid of mice around barns. In winter it roosts in conifers, abandoned buildings, and other dark places.

Habitat: Open farmlands, grasslands, deserts, and suburbs.

Voice: Mostly harsh hissing or screeching sounds; some metallic clicks.

Conservation:
BBS: W ⇓ C CBC: ↑

231

Flammulated Owl

Otus flammeolus

Identification: 7″ Only small owl with dark eyes; **small ear tufts** can be lowered or raised; reddish-brown lines on either side of back meet at rump to form a V. Red morph shows reddish-brown feathers on the facial disks, especially around the eyes. Gray morph generally more common in north; red morph generally more common in south.

Feeding: Agile nighttime hunter of flying insects; 90% of food is insects. Also eats spiders, scorpions, mice.

Nesting: Sometimes loosely colonial. Nests in old tree cavity or abandoned woodpecker hole, usually in oak, pine, or aspen; will also use human-made nest box. Does not add nest material. Eggs: 2–5, white; I: 25 days; F: ?, altricial; B: 1.

Other Behavior: Very inconspicuous. Usually found in montane areas at altitudes of 3,000–10,000 ft., in dense thickets close to open areas. Roosts in pines and oaks. Highly migratory.

Habitat: Pine (especially Ponderosa) and oak forests.

Voice: A low-pitched single or double hoot, given every few seconds; also makes clucks and mewing sounds.

Conservation:
TREND UNKNOWN.

Eastern Screech-Owl
Western Screech-Owl
Otus asio   Otus kennicottii

Eastern

Western

Identification: 9″ **Small owls** with **yellow eyes** and **ear tufts** (which can be lowered and hidden). Almost identical in appearance, although **Eastern has a pale bill,** while **Western has a dark bill; best distinguished by calls** (see Voice). Both species have red and gray morphs; however, the Western red morph is rare and limited to the Northwest Coast.

Feeding: Eastern eats mice, insects, amphibians, birds. Western eats arthropods, reptiles, amphibians.

Nesting: Eastern nests in tree cavity, old woodpecker hole, or birdhouse; no nest material added. Eggs: 3–5, white; I: 21–28 days; F: 30–32 days, altricial; B: 1. Western nests in tree cavity, saguaro cactus, old magpie nest, old woodpecker hole, or nest box; no nest material added. Eggs: 2–5, white; I: 21–30 days; F: 28 days, altricial; B: 1.

Other Behavior: As with all owls, males have lower voice than females, and are smaller in size. Male feeds female while she is incubating. They roost, as well as nest, in natural cavity or nest box; a pair may use the same site for 7 or more years.

Eastern   Western

Habitat: Woods, swamps, parks, suburbs, deserts.

Voice: Eastern: eerie rising and falling whinny; long trill on 1 note. Western: series of short low-pitched whistles, speeding up at end.

Conservation: Eastern: BBS: W C ⇓ CBC: ⇑ Western: BBS: W ⇓ C CBC: ⇑

233

Whiskered Screech-Owl

Otus trichopsis

Identification: 7″ A **small owl** with **yellow eyes** and **ear tufts** (which can be lowered and hidden). Nearly identical to gray morph Western Screech-Owl and best distinguished by calls. See Voice.

Feeding: Eats primarily large insects, such as crickets, moths, and beetles.

Nesting: Nests in natural cavity in tree, or old woodpecker hole, frequently in white oak tree. Eggs: 3–4, white. Nesting biology not well studied, but probably similar in timing of stages to other screech-owls.

Other Behavior: Usually found in deciduous forests between 4,000 and 7,000 ft. in altitude. Roosts in oaks, junipers, walnuts, sycamores. Because of plumage pattern, very cryptic when perched close to tree trunk. During courtship, male and female call back and forth in a duet.

Habitat: Oak and oak-conifer woods.

Voice: Four to six low-pitched whistles, given evenly spaced; also a series of short hoots, irregularly spaced, like Morse code.

Conservation: TREND UNKNOWN.

Great Horned Owl
Bubo virginianus

Identification: 22″ **Very large; widely spaced ear tufts;** yellow eyes; **white throat** that sometimes continues in a thin V down the chest.

Feeding: This large fearsome hunter will capture a wide variety of prey, ranging from insects to prey the size of a Great Blue Heron. Eats squirrels, mice, rabbits, snakes, skunks, weasels, porcupines, domestic cats, crows, Ospreys, as well as other owls and hawks, including Barred Owl and Red-tailed Hawk.

Nesting: Uses old nest of hawk, heron, squirrel, or tree hollow or cliff ledge; adds feathers from its breast to nest. Frequently uses Red-tailed Hawk nest since both live in same habitat. Eggs: 1–4, white; I: 28–30 days; F: 35 days, altricial; B: 1.

Other Behavior: Crows frequently mob this owl, and their drawn-out caws are often a clue to the owl's presence. The owl is more inconvenienced than disturbed by this and often just temporarily shifts its location. Great Horned, and all other owls, cough up pellets of undigested bones, fur, and feathers. Great Horned Owl's pellets are 3–4 in. long, and accumulate on the ground under its roosting spot. Has most widespread range of all N. American owls.

Habitat: Extremely varied; woods, deserts, suburbs.

Voice: Four to six deep resonant hoots, given in various rhythms by different individuals; often like "hoohoohoo hoohoo hoo." Female hoots higher-pitched.

Conservation: BBS: W ⇑ C ↑ CBC: ↑

235

Snowy Owl
Nyctea scandiaca

Adult

Immature

Identification: 24″ **Large white owl;** yellow eyes; **variable amounts of black spots and barring.** Immatures darker than adults; females darker than males. Thus, immature females are the darkest, with almost equal amounts of white and black on body and wings; adult males are almost pure white.

Feeding: Frequently hunts during the day. Eats mainly rodents, Arctic and Snowshoe Hares, fish, birds (including waterfowl), and carrion. When breeding, eats mostly lemmings.

Nesting: Nest on tundra, in shallow depression on top of mound, or on gravel bank, is lined with scattered feathers and bits of moss. Eggs: 3–10, white, clutch size is larger when prey are abundant; I: 32–39 days; F: 14–28 days, altricial; B: 1.

Other Behavior: Southward migration in winter is irruptive. Some years many more owls are seen than in others. This may or may not be correlated with lemming population cycle. Most of the birds that move south into U.S. in winter are immatures.

Habitat: Open tundra, or similar habitats south of the tundra, such as airports, beaches, marshes.

Voice: Barking noises on breeding grounds; quiet during winter.

Conservation: CBC: ↓

236

Northern Hawk Owl
Surnia ulula

Identification: 16" Medium-sized owl; long tail; grayish facial disks with wide black borders. Has no ear tufts; eyes are yellow; grayish underparts are heavily barred with brown. Birds that come south in winter are often seen perched along roadsides or fields when hunting.

Feeding: Hunts by swooping down on prey, then returning to perch. Will use favorite perch regularly, often for a period of years. Can also rapidly maneuver through woods, like Cooper's Hawk. Eats voles, mice, and lemmings in summer; in winter, eats more birds, including grouse and ptarmigan, also rabbits.

Nesting: Nests in hollowed end of broken-off dead tree; also uses old woodpecker hole or tree cavity. Eggs: 3–9, white; I: 25–30 days; F: 25–35 days, altricial; B: 1.

Other Behavior: Unafraid of humans. Much more of a daytime hunter than other owls. Has excellent daytime sight, and vision plays a more important role in its hunting than hearing, which is not as acute as that of other owls.

Habitat: Northern conifer woods and bogs, swamps, and woods; roadsides and fields.

Voice: Variety of calls, including whistled trills, rattles, screams, and a "kikikiki."

Conservation: CBC: ↓

Northern Pygmy-Owl

Glaucidium gnoma

Front view

Back of head

Identification: 7″ Small owl; long dark tail with light bars; 2 black marks on back of head (they seem to mimic eyes); spots on crown; yellow eyes; no ear tufts. ➤Its close relative, the Ferruginous Pygmy-Owl, *G. brasilianum*, is now rare north of Mex.; it is similarly shaped and marked, but has a brown tail with black barring and streaks on crown.

Feeding: This swift fierce little owl will attack and kill prey much larger than itself. Eats many birds, also ground squirrels, rodents. Diurnal hunter, hunting most at dawn and dusk.

Nesting: Nests in tree cavity, old flicker or woodpecker hole. Eggs: 3–6, white; I: 28 days; F: 27–28 days, altricial; B: 1.

Other Behavior: Frequently mobbed by groups of small birds. Flight is noisy for an owl, with audible whirring of wings. Since this owl is mostly a diurnal flier, silent flight is not that important. Most other owls are nocturnal hunters and have furry indentations on the leading edges of their flight feathers, which cushion the passing air in flight and mute the sound.

Habitat: Open woods and forest edges in mountains and foothills.

Voice: Most common call an evenly repeated whistled "toot" or "toot-toot."

Conservation: BBS: W ⇑ C CBC: ↑

238

Elf Owl

Micrathene whitneyi

Identification: 6″ **Our smallest owl; yellow eyes; short tail; no ear tufts.** Distinguished from Northern Saw-whet Owl by smaller size and lack of streaks on underparts.

Feeding: Eats insects, scorpions, spiders, centipedes, mice, and shrews. Hunts nocturnally.

Nesting: Nests in old woodpecker hole in hardwood tree or saguaro cactus; no nest material added. Eggs: 2–5, white; I: 24 days; F: 28–33 days, altricial; B: 1.

Other Behavior: Uses separate cavity for roosting and breeding. Roosts during day in tree cavity or in dense thickets, where its coloration makes it very difficult to detect. When female is incubating, male may roost with other males.

Habitat: Deserts with saguaro cacti, wooded streams, pine-oak woods.

Voice: High-pitched barks and chirps and a variety of other calls.

Conservation: TREND UNKNOWN. Almost gone from Calif. Reintroduction attempted; success uncertain. More common in rest of range.

Burrowing Owl
Speotyto cunicularia

Identification: 9″ Small; long legs; white throat; boldly spotted except for barred belly; yellow eyes; no ear tufts; **usually perched on ground.** Bows when approached.

Feeding: Eats insects, scorpions, crayfish, mice, ground squirrels, young prairie dogs, rabbits, amphibians, snakes, and, rarely, birds.

Nesting: Nests in small colonies, in deserted burrow of prairie dog, tortoise, armadillo, woodchuck, skunk, or other mammal. May dig own burrow, or enlarge another's; nest lined with horse or cow dung, grasses, weeds. Eggs: 6–11, white; I: 21–28 days; F: 28 days, altricial; B: 1.

Other Behavior: These endearing owls can often be seen standing on the raised mound at the entrance to their burrow, in habitats such as airport fields, highway shoulders, golf courses, and vacant lots, as well as their more traditional location, within prairie dog towns. They do not share a burrow with a prairie dog, but live in a deserted burrow. Rattlesnakes may live in prairie dog towns, and prey on owls and dogs. The owls are able to imitate the rattling sound of the rattlesnake as a defense against would-be predators.

Habitat: Open plains, grasslands, desert scrub.

Voice: A "coo-coo" given by male during courtship; a long chattering given during alarm.

Conservation: BBS: W ⇑ C ⇓ CBC: ↑ Declining in Calif.; increasing in Fla.

Spotted Owl
Barred Owl
Strix occidentalis   Strix varia

Spotted

Barred

Identification: Spotted 18", Barred 20" Besides the Barn Owl, our only **large owls** with **dark eyes.** SPOTTED: White spots on chest and belly (sometimes looks like barring on belly). BARRED: **Barring on chest; streaking on belly.**

Feeding: Spotted eats mice, rabbits, squirrels. Barred eats mice, rabbits, amphibians, reptiles, insects.

Nesting: Spotted nests in cave, tree cavity, or abandoned nest of hawk or crow. Eggs: 2–4, white; I: 28–32 days; F: 35 days, altricial; B: 1. Barred nests in tree cavity, or abandoned hawk or crow nest. Eggs: 2–4, white; I: 28–32 days; F: 40–45 days, altricial; B: 1.

Other Behavior: By 1990 pop. of subspecies N. Spotted Owl, *S.o. caurina*, was about 3,000–4,000 rangewide, and habitat had been reduced by 90%. Territorial female pop. declined by 7.5% yearly 1985–1991. Habitat loss and fragmentation, due to logging, may favor Great Horned Owl, which preys on young Spotted Owls. Also threatened by range expansion of the Barred Owl, which is moving into Pacific Northwest. Recovery plans include habitat protection, logging bans, population monitoring.

Spotted   Barred

Habitat: Spotted: old-growth forests. Barred: woods, wooded swamps.

Voice: Spotted: "hoohoo hoo." Barred: "Who cooks for you?"

Conservation:
Spotted:
BBS: W ↓ C CBC: ↑
Barred:
BBS: W C ⇑ CBC: ↑
N. Spotted Owl endangered in U.S. and Can.

Great Gray Owl

Strix nebulosa

Identification: 29" Our **largest owl; large facial disks** filled with concentric rings; **comparatively small yellow eyes;** 2 white marks below chin, like a **white bow tie;** tail relatively long; no ear tufts.

Feeding: Mostly voles, mice; also gophers, weasels, less usually birds and squirrels. In addition to pouncing on prey with talons, will occasionally plunge headfirst into snow in pursuit of vole. Daytime as well as nighttime hunter.

Nesting: Nests in abandoned hawk, crow, or raven nest, or on top of tree stump. Eggs: 1–5, white; I: 30 days; F: 20–28 days, altricial; B: 1.

Other Behavior: Rare and irregular winter visitor to areas outside its permanent range. Usually shows up in large, open, moist areas surrounded by woods, where it can be seen hunting for voles during the day.

Habitat: Northern coniferous and deciduous forests.

Voice: Slow series of deep hoots, evenly spaced.

Conservation: CBC: ↑

Long-eared Owl
Asio otus

Identification: 15″ Slim owl; long close-set ear tufts; rufous facial disk; long wings that extend beyond tip of tail; yellow eyes; no white throat.

Feeding: Eats mostly voles, mice; also amphibians, reptiles, and insects.

Nesting: Sometimes loosely colonial. Nests in abandoned nest of crow, hawk, magpie, squirrel, or heron, or tree cavity. May add to nest with strips of bark or leaves, and feathers from female's breast. Eggs: 3–8, white; I: 21–28 days; F: 23–26 days, altricial; B: 1.

Other Behavior: At times, forms communal winter roosts of up to 50 or more birds, usually in dense conifers. It is important that bird watchers not disturb these through too much visiting. Has large vocal repertoire (although often silent), including catlike noises and canarylike twitterings when flying into nighttime roost before dawn. Feather tufts on head are not ears; they help the owl appear camouflaged when it elongates its body, looking like the ragged stub of a broken tree branch.

Habitat: Woods near open fields and marshes.

Voice: Single or double "hoo," given at a slow pace; barking sounds; high twittering calls; and a long tremulous "hoooo."

Conservation: CBC: ↓

Short-eared Owl

Asio flammeus

Identification: 15″ Medium-sized; often seen hunting at dusk over fields and marshes; dark areas surround yellow eyes, like sunglasses; boldly streaked chest; light belly. Although it has short ear tufts, these are rarely seen. IN FLIGHT: Often seen flying low over ground while hunting. Note irregular floppy flight; pale buffy patches on upperwings; and dark wrist patches on underwings.

Feeding: Feeds mostly on voles. When it has young to feed, it will also hunt songbirds and some gamebirds. Hunts mainly at dawn and dusk.

Nesting: Nests on the ground, in a depression concealed by surrounding reeds and grasses, lined with dried grasses and feathers from female's breast. Eggs: 4–14, white; I: 21–28 days; F: 31–36 days, altricial; B: 1.

Other Behavior: Irruptive species that varies in abundance from year to year. Will wander to locate good prey areas, then settle and breed. Has larger clutch sizes when there is ample prey. Forms winter communal roosts.

Habitat: Open fields, marshes, dunes, and grasslands.

Voice: Low-pitched "hoo" in a long series, given while perched or flying; also various snarls, squeals, and barking calls.

Conservation: BBS: W ⇓ C ↑ CBC: ↓ Declining through much of range, due to habitat loss.

Boreal Owl
Northern Saw-whet Owl
Aegolius funereus   Aegolius acadicus

Boreal

Saw-whet

Identification: Boreal 10″, Saw-whet 8″
BOREAL: **Small;** yellow eyes; no ear tufts; **facial disk light gray bordered by black; forehead black, covered with white spots;** bill pale. SAW-WHET: **Small;** yellow eyes; no ear tufts; **facial disk reddish brown with no dark border; forehead brown with fine white streaks;** bill is dark.

Feeding: Boreal eats voles, lemmings, mice. Saw-whet eats mice, voles, chipmunks, shrews, bats, insects.

Nesting: Boreal nests in tree cavity or old woodpecker hole; may also use nest box. Eggs: 3–10, white; I: 25–30 days; F: 28–32 days, altricial; B: 1. Saw-whet nests in tree cavity or old woodpecker hole; may use nest box. Eggs: 4–7, white; I: 25–30 days; F: 28–35 days, altricial; B: 1.

Other Behavior: Saw-whet is sometimes incredibly tame. Solely nocturnal. Roosts in dense evergreens in winter. Boreal Owl is irruptive, often coinciding with irruptions of Great Gray Owl and Northern Hawk Owl. Not easily discovered, because it is strictly nocturnal and roosts during the day in dense conifers.

Boreal   Saw-whet

Habitat: Coniferous or mixed woods.

Voice: Boreal: 5–10 rapid whistled "hoo"s, rising at end. Saw-whet in spring gives low tooting whistle, 2 per second for long periods; in fall, a descending whistle.

Conservation:
Boreal:
CBC: ↓
Saw-whet:
BBS: W ↓ C CBC ↑

Lesser Nighthawk
Common Nighthawk
Chordeiles acutipennis   Chordeiles minor

Lesser

Common

Common

Common

Identification: Lesser 9", Common 10" Fly at dusk or dawn, sometimes during day. LESSER—IN FLIGHT: **Long, thin, rounded wings with conspicuous whitish bar across tips;** bar closer to tip than in Common. Flight tends to be low (10–20 ft. above ground), with rapid wingbeats. COMMON—IN FLIGHT: **Long, thin, pointed wings with conspicuous whitish bar across tips.** Flight tends to be high (over 40 ft.), with slower, deliberate wingbeats. In both species, male has white band near tail tip; female does not.

Feeding: Both scoop flying insects into their large mouths while flying. Common may feed near city lights.

Nesting: Lesser nests on ground in arid lowlands, sides of canyons. Eggs: 2, grayish with dots; I: 18–19 days; F: 21 days, precocial, B: 1. Common nests on gravelly soil in fields or on gravel rooftops. Eggs: 2, olive with dark marks; I: 19–20 days; F: 21 days, precocial; B: 1.

Other Behavior: Common male makes booming dives in courtship displays. Sound is caused by air rushing through primary feathers.

Lesser   Common

Habitat: Lesser inhabits desert, grasslands, fields. Common lives in forests, plains, urban areas.

Voice: Lesser gives a soft trill. Common gives a nasal "peent."

Conservation:
Lesser:
BBS: W ⇑ C ⇑ CBC: ↑
Common:
BBS: W ↓ C ↓ CBC: ↓

246

Common Poorwill
Whip-poor-will
Phalaenoptilus nuttallii   Caprimulgus vociferus

Common

Whip-poor-will

Identification: Common 8", Whip-poor-will 10"
**Both mostly heard calling in evening. See
Voice for main identification clues. COMMON—IN
FLIGHT: Small; short rounded wings; short
tail.** Sometimes seen at night along roads hunting
insects. **WHIP-POOR-WILL—IN FLIGHT: Larger;
dusky; rounded wings; relatively long tail.**

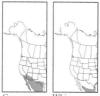

Common   Whip.

Feeding: Eat aerial insects, mostly night-flying moths;
also beetles, grasshoppers.

Nesting: Common's nest a scraped depression or none,
on gravelly ground or flat rock. Eggs: 2, whitish with
dark marks; I: ?; F: ?, altricial; B: 1. Whip-poor-will nests
on woodland floor. Eggs: 2, white with spots of gray or
brown; I: 19–20 days; F: 20 days, precocial; B: 1–2.

Other Behavior: Both nocturnal; rest during day. When
temperatures are cold, Common can lower body
temperature and enter state of torpor to conserve
energy.

Habitat: Open
woods, canyons,
dry, brushy areas.

Voice: Common:
"poorwill" or
"poorwillip," with
accent on "will."
Whip-poor-will:
"whip poorwill,"
with emphasis on
last syllable.

Conservation:
Common:
BBS: W ⇓ C ⇑ CBC: ↓
Whip-poor-will:
BBS: W   C ↑ CBC: ↓

247

Black Swift

Cypseloides niger

Identification: 7" IN FLIGHT: Long, thin, pointed wings; relatively long notched tail. All black.

Feeding: Feeds on the wing, eating flying insects.

Nesting: Nests in small colonies, on ledge, sea cliff, or mountain crevice, often behind waterfall. Saucerlike nest of mosses, algae, ferns, lined with rootlets. Eggs: 1, white; I: 24–27 days; F: 45–49 days, altricial; B: 1.

Other Behavior: Can wander widely through mountains in its search for insects, sometimes ascending to great heights.

Habitat: Near cliffs in mountainous regions; occasionally coastal.

Voice: Generally quiet when flying.

Conservation: BBS: W ⇓ C

Chimney Swift
Chaetura pelagica

Identification: 5½" IN FLIGHT: Very rapid wingbeats with stiffly held wings, followed by gliding. Long, thin, pointed wings; short square tail; dark gray-brown above, paler below on throat and chest.

Feeding: Feeds while flying, catching insects in its mouth.

Nesting: Nests in chimneys or around the eaves of old barns or buildings. While in flight, breaks dead twigs off trees with its feet, then carries them back to nest in its bill. Cements twigs onto vertical surface with sticky "saliva," to form nest cup. Eggs: 4–5, white; I: 19 days; F: 14–18 days, altricial; B: 1.

Other Behavior: The most common courtship flight display involves two birds flying together, one slightly above the other. The hind one abruptly lifts its wings into a V and glides; then the one in front does the same. Done between members of a pair throughout the breeding cycle. During migration, large flocks roost communally in chimneys or steeples. Will swirl around above the roost for over 45 minutes before entering at dusk.

Habitat: Rural or urban areas where there are chimneys; more rarely in hollow trees.

Voice: A rapidly repeated "chitter-chitter-chitter" and a quick series of separate "chip" calls.

Conservation:
BBS: W   C ↓

Vaux's Swift
Chaetura vauxi

Identification: 4½" IN FLIGHT: Long, thin, pointed wings; short square tail; dark gray-brown above, paler below on throat and chest. Distinguished from very similar Chimney Swift by range, smaller size, higher calls, paler throat and rump, flying with less gliding, and nesting in hollow trees rather than chimneys.

Feeding: Flies high or low, catching insects. Likes to feed over lakes.

Nesting: Uses a sticky saliva-like substance to glue twigs and pine needles to wall of hollowed-out tree or, sometimes, a chimney. Eggs: 3–7, white; I: 18–20 days; F: 20–21 days, altricial; B: 1.

Other Behavior: Communally roosts in large numbers on migration, in chimney or tall hollowed-out tree. Nesting activity is concentrated in old-growth forests where there are suitable holes in rotted snags; this makes the bird susceptible to excessive logging.

Habitat: Woodlands near water.

Voice: A rapidly repeated, very high-pitched "chitter-chitter-chitter" and a quick series of separate "chip" calls.

Conservation:
BBS: W ⇑ C CBC: ⇑

White-throated Swift

Aeronautes saxatalis

Identification: 6½" IN FLIGHT: Long, thin, pointed wings; relatively long notched tail; black-and-white body — white on throat, central belly, and sides of rump. Appears extremely slender in all aspects.

Feeding: Catches insects while flying.

Nesting: Nest consists of feathers glued together with bird's special sticky "saliva" and attached to vertical surface of crevice, high rocky cliff, or building. Eggs: 3–6, white; I: ?; F: ?, altricial; B: ?

Other Behavior: Nesting location on high cliffs makes nest inaccessible to predators and humans. Nests in small colonies. Same location used for many years.

Habitat: Cliffs and canyons.

Voice: Descending twitter.

Conservation:
BBS: W ⇓ C ↓ CBC: ↑

Broad-billed Hummingbird
Cynanthus latirostris

Male

Female

Identification: 4″ Limited to Southwest. **Slightly downcurved bill is red at base, black at tip;** forked tail bluish black. **MALE:** All **iridescent green,** except for **blue throat,** whitish undertail coverts, and white dot behind eye. **FEMALE:** Iridescent green except for **grayish throat and central belly** and white undertail coverts.

Feeding: Eats nectar, insects. Comes to hummingbird feeders.

Nesting: Cuplike nest of grass stalks and plant material lined with plant down and covered with bark bits, small leaves; held together with spider silk. Not covered with lichens. Eggs: 2, white; I: ?; F: ?, altricial; B: 2.

Other Behavior: Broad-billed Hummingbirds nest in arid areas at the base of mountain canyons or along small streambeds. Nest often placed out over creek or stream in shrub, vine, or small tree. Like all hummingbirds, they lick rather than suck nectar. They can dip their tongue into a flower at the rate of 13 licks per second.

Habitat: Canyons, wooded streams, wooded desert washes.

Voice: Call a repeated chattering "jijijijit."

Conservation:
BBS: W ⇑ C CBC: ↑

Violet-crowned Hummingbird

Amazilia violiceps

Identification: 4" Limited to S.E. Ariz. and S.W. N.Mex. **Violet-blue head; bright red bill with black tip; bright white underparts.** Sexes alike.

Feeding: Feeds on nectar and insects. Comes to hummingbird feeders.

Nesting: Nest of lichens and plant down, held together with spider's silk, placed usually on branch of sycamore tree 20–40 ft. above the ground. Eggs: 2, white; I: ?; F: ?, altricial; B: 2 or possibly more.

Other Behavior: Very little has been studied about this species. Like most hummingbirds, it has fantastic flight abilities and can fly forward, backward, and even upside down.

Habitat: Canyons with sycamore trees.

Voice: Call is "tsik," either singly or strung together into a chatter.

Conservation:
TREND UNKNOWN.

Blue-throated Hummingbird
Lampornis clemenciae

Male

Female

Identification: 5″ Limited to Southwest. **Large; long broad tail with outer feathers broadly tipped with white; white eye-stripe. MALE: Upperparts iridescent green; throat blue;** belly gray. **FEMALE: Upperparts green; throat and belly gray.**

Feeding: Nectar, insects, spiders. Often seen snapping up gnats in air for extended periods. Comes to hummingbird feeders.

Nesting: Nest of moss, grass stems, bits of leaves, lined with down; decorated outside with lichens and held together with spider's silk. Built in small tree or shrub, on stem of flowering plant or fern, along stream, on wire, or under eaves of house. Eggs: 2, white; I: 17–18 days; F: 24–29 days, altricial; B: 1–3.

Other Behavior: The largest (by weight) N. American hummingbird. Male is larger than female; in most N. American hummingbirds, female is larger than male. Hummingbirds are mostly attracted to flowers by sight, not smell. This is evidenced by the fact that they explore anything that is red, to see if it offers nectar.

Habitat: Wooded mountain or canyon streams.

Voice: Loud high "seeyeek," given when perched or in flight, and singly or in a rapid series.

Conservation: TREND UNKNOWN.

Magnificent Hummingbird

Eugenes fulgens

Male

Female

Identification: 5 " Limited to Southwest. **Large. MALE: All dark; green back;** emerald-green throat; iridescent purple crown; **black belly;** black bill; white spot behind eye. **FEMALE: Iridescent green back and sides; grayish underparts; light spotting on throat;** white line behind eye; **square tail with small white tips.**

Feeding: Hovers and takes flower nectar, also insects and small spiders from the leaves of trees. Comes to hummingbird feeders.

Nesting: Nest of mosses and plant fibers, coated with lichens and lined with down; held together with spider's silk; placed straddling branch of tree along mountain stream. Eggs: 2, white; I: 16 days; F: ?, altricial; B: 1 or possibly more.

Other Behavior: During breeding, males and females have different territories. Aggressive to other hummingbirds around food sources. Dominates areas with flowering agave, penstemon, honeysuckle, salvias.

Habitat: Wooded canyons, open pine woods.

Voice: Call a short "chit."

Conservation: TREND UNKNOWN.

255

Lucifer Hummingbird

Calothorax lucifer

Male

Female

Identification: 3½" Limited to Big Bend, Tex., S.E. Ariz. and S.W. N.Mex. **Small; relatively long tail; markedly downcurved bill.** MALE: **Tail deeply forked; purple gorget extends along sides;** grayish belly and buffy flanks. FEMALE: **Green above; buff below; downcurved bill.**

Feeding: Eats lots of insects, also flower nectar, spiders.

Nesting: Nest of plant fibers, bud scales, lined with down, covered with lichens, held together with spider's silk. Eggs: 2, white; I: 15–16 days; F: 21–24 days, altricial; B: 1 or possibly more.

Other Behavior: Long downcurved bill is adapted to getting insects, as well as nectar, from flowers. Associated with agave plants in lower slopes of arid mountains. During breeding season, males defend small territories, which include several agave plants. Females often build nests on agave stalks. After breeding, the birds move to higher elevations.

Habitat: Desert slopes and gullies; flowering agaves.

Voice: High-pitched "chip."

Conservation: TREND UNKNOWN.

Ruby-throated Hummingbird
Archilochus colubris

Male

Female

Identification: 3½" The only hummingbird in most of eastern N. America. **MALE: Upperparts green; throat iridescent red** (may appear black); **black patch from bill to below eye;** breast and central belly whitish. **FEMALE: Upperparts green; underparts whitish and unmarked.**

Feeding: Eats flower nectar, insects, spiders, sap from sapsucker-drilled holes. Comes to hummingbird feeders.

Nesting: Nest of plant down, bud scales, covered with lichens, bound with spider's silk, and placed on a small horizontal limb, 10–20 ft. high. Eggs: 2, white; I: 16 days; F: 30 days, altricial; B: 1–2.

Other Behavior: In spring, male defends territory of about ¼ acre. In dive displays, he flies in a U shape, rising 10–40 ft. on each side. In courtship or aggressive situations, male and female display by shuttling back and forth on horizontal plane and with tail spread. After mating, female builds nest and raises young alone. On migration, males and females will temporarily defend food source, such as your hummingbird feeder. Ruby-throats migrate 600 mi. across Gulf of Mexico, storing enough fat to make crossing. A male Ruby-throat weighs about the same as 2½ paper clips.

Habitat: Woods edges, streams, parks, gardens.

Voice: Varied chips and twitterings.

Conservation:
BBS: W ↑ C ↑ CBC: ↓

Black-chinned Hummingbird

Archilochus alexandri

Male

Female

Identification: 3½" MALE: **Black chin bordered by violet** (violet may appear black); **white collar;** chest and central belly white; back and sides green. FEMALE: **Green above; white below; throat clear to evenly and lightly streaked; repeatedly spreads and flips tail while feeding. See Voice.**

Feeding: Hovers and takes nectar from flowers. Eats small insects, spiders.

Nesting: Female constructs nest of plant down, gathered from willows or undersides of sycamore leaves; also uses feathers and tree flowers. Nest is bound with spider's silk; outside not coated with lichens; placed in tree or shrub 5–10 ft. high. Successive nests can be built on top of one another. Eggs: 1–3, white; I: 13–16 days; F: 21 days, altricial; B: 1–2.

Other Behavior: Has most extensive breeding range of any western hummingbird. Male and female defend separate territories, mate on neutral ground. Female rears young. Later in season, when breeding areas are too dry, they move into foothills or lower mountains where there are lush flowers.

Habitat: Dry lowlands and foothills.

Voice: Call a distinctive descending "tyew."

Conservation: BBS: W ↓ C ↑ CBC: ↓ Planting nectar-rich flowers can provide additional feeding habitat.

Anna's Hummingbird
Calypte anna

Male

Female

Identification: 4″ Limited to West Coast. **MALE:** Bright **rose iridescence on throat and crown;** green back and sides; white chest and central belly. **FEMALE: Green upperparts; red spotting on the throat** that may form a small patch.

Feeding: Nectar, insects; visits hummingbird feeders.

Nesting: Female builds nest of downy plant fibers, decorated with lichens, held together with spider's silk; placed in variety of locations, often near houses. Eggs: 2, white; I: 14–19 days; F: 18–23 days, altricial; B: 1–2.

Other Behavior: Early breeder; can lay eggs in Dec., during which time it feeds on early-blooming goose-berry (*Ribes spp.*). Male defends ¼ acre territory and does spectacular dive display, rising to 120 ft., diving down at speeds reaching 65 mph, then veering up at bottom while giving a loud "speeek" sound. After mating, female raises young alone. In the morning, she feeds them nectar, for quick energy to warm them while she forages. In afternoon, she feeds them insects. During nonbreeding season, Anna's do not migrate, but shift their range to local areas with more food.

Habitat: Open woods, shrubs, gardens, parks.

Voice: Complex song is a series of squeaky phrases; call is "chip."

Conservation: BBS: W ↓ C CBC: ⇑ Planting gardens with nectar-rich flowers, shrubs, and trees can help replace lost feeding and breeding habitats.

Costa's Hummingbird
Calypte costae

Male

Female

Identification: 3″ Limited to southwest desert areas. MALE: **Purple iridescence on throat and crown and extending down sides;** back and sides green; chest and central belly white. FEMALE: Green above and white below. Not easily distinguished from Black-chinned female, but call note is different. See Voice.

Feeding: Nectar, spiders, insects; visits feeders.

Nesting: Composed of dead leaves, downy material, feathers, fine bits of bark and lichens, held together with spider's silk; placed on trees, shrubs, cacti, sage, yucca stalks. Eggs: 2, white; I: 16 days; F: 20–23 days, altricial; B: 1.

Other Behavior: Prefers dry environments. Forms territory of 2–4 acres where there is low vegetation with a few taller stalks, such as yuccas and flowering plants. Male does oval-shaped dive display, giving drawn-out sound at bottom of flight path. Female nests near male territory and raises young alone. Up to 6 nests have been found within 200 ft. of one another. In nonbreeding season, found in same habitats as Anna's Hummingbird, which dominates it.

Habitat: Desert areas.

Voice: Call is a short "tsik."

Conservation:
BBS: W ⇑ C CBC: ↑

Calliope Hummingbird
Stellula calliope

Male

Female

Identification: 3″ **Smallest bird in N. America.** MALE: Only hummingbird with **separate streaks of purple iridescence on throat;** green above and on sides; white on breast and central belly. FEMALE: **Green above, with some reddish brown on tail; some buffy wash across breast; light buffy sides;** short bill; **short rounded tail.**

Feeding: Eats nectar, insects, spiders; visits hummingbird feeders.

Nesting: Nest of bark shreds, willow-seed filaments, moss, lichens, pine needles, bound with spider's silk and nestled among pine cones or on branch with overhanging limb of dense greenery. Eggs: 2, white; I: 15 days; F: 18–23 days, altricial; B: 1.

Other Behavior: Males do dive displays, diving from as high as 90 ft., and hover displays, to other hummers and other birds. Female evaluates male on basis of quality of food in his territory. She rears young alone. On cold nights, males go into state of torpor, in which they can lower their body temperature by 50 degrees F. Incubating females, however, stay warm by sinking low into downy nest material.

Habitat: Mountain meadows and open forests.

Voice: Call a "chip."

Conservation: BBS: W ⇑ C

Broad-tailed Hummingbird
Selasphorus platycercus

Male

Female

Identification: 4" MALE: Wings create a high-pitched buzz that advertises its presence. Upperparts green; throat iridescent rose-red (may appear black); breast and central belly whitish. FEMALE: Upperparts green; underparts whitish and unmarked; pale buffy flanks; rufous at base of outer tail feathers.

Feeding: Feeds on flower nectar, insects, spiders, tree sap; visits hummingbird feeders.

Nesting: Nest of downy materials, such as willow or cottonwood seeds, covered with bits of bark, fine rootlets, lichens, and held together with spider's silk; placed on horizontal limb 5–15 ft. high. Eggs: 2, white; I: 16–17 days; F: 18–23 days, altricial; B: 1–2.

Other Behavior: More frequently heard than seen, due to continuous buzz during flight, which is produced by air moving through the 9th and 10th primary feathers of the wings. It occurs only in the male and is an important part of his aggressive behavior in territorial defense against other Broad-tailed Hummingbirds.

Habitat: Open mountain woodlands and meadows.

Voice: Variety of chips and twitters.

Conservation:
BBS: W ↑ C CBC: ↓

Rufous Hummingbird

Selasphorus rufus

Male

Female

Identification: 3½" MALE: **All orange-brown, except for red iridescent throat and white collar. FEMALE: Green upperparts; orange-brown tail and sides; white throat and central belly; iridescent dots on throat.** Cannot be distinguished from female Allen's Hummingbird in the field.

Feeding: Nectar, insects, spiders, sap from holes drilled by sapsuckers; visits hummingbird feeders.

Nesting: Nest of downy plant fibers and moss, covered with lichens, held together with spider's silk; placed on downward-sloping limb of tree or shrub. Eggs: 2, white; I: 12–14 days; F: 20 days, altricial; B: 1–2.

Other Behavior: During migration, defends temporary feeding territories, and is the most aggressive of all hummers, readily displacing Anna's, Broad-tailed, Calliope, and Black-chinned Hummingbirds from flower areas. Has longest migration route of any N. American hummer; along coast in spring, and down Rocky Mountains after breeding. All hummingbirds are important pollinators of flowers, especially red tubular flowers that are generally not pollinated by insects.

Habitat: Woods edges, thickets, parks, gardens, mountain meadows.

Voice: Series of "chup" calls; male can create wing whistle, especially during displays.

Conservation:
BBS: W ⇓ C CBC: ↑

263

Allen's Hummingbird

Selasphorus sasin

Male

Female

Identification: 3½" MALE: Orange-brown on tail and sides; green on back and crown; red iridescent throat; white collar. FEMALE: Green upperparts; orange-brown tail and sides; white throat and central belly; iridescent dots on throat. Cannot be distinguished from female Rufous Hummingbird in the field.

Feeding: Nectar, insects; visits hummingbird feeders.

Nesting: Nest of moss, dried weed stems, willow down, animal hair, feathers, tied together with spider's silk; placed straddling a branch of bush or vine. May rebuild over old nest. Eggs: 2, white; I: 15–17 days; F: 22–25 days, altricial; B: 1–2.

Other Behavior: Male does spectacular U-shaped dive display, rising up 25 ft. on each side. After several swings, he spirals 75–100 ft. high, then dives, making a rough whistling sound at bottom. Done toward females and territorial intruders. Females raise young alone, nesting well away from males' territories. In some cases, female lays eggs while nest is just a shallow cup, then continues to add material to nest until young fledge. Migrates north along coast as early as Jan.

Habitat: Woods, thickets, gardens, parks.

Voice: A series of "chup" calls; male can create wing whistle, especially during displays.

Conservation: BBS: W ↓ C CBC: ⇑

264

Elegant Trogon

Trogon elegans

Male

Female

Identification: 12" Limited to S.E. Ariz.
Colorful long-tailed bird with a **broad yellow
bill. MALE: Metallic green** on head, chest, and
back; **white breastband; red belly. FEMALE:
Brown** head, chest, and back; **whitish upper
belly; red lower belly.**

Feeding: Feeds on many kinds of insects, such as moths,
beetles, grasshoppers, caterpillars; also eats fruits. Flies
out from perch and hovers, picking insects off leaves.

Nesting: Nest of straw, grasses, feathers, moss, and trash,
placed in old woodpecker hole or tree cavity, often in
large sycamore by stream. Eggs: 3–4, white; I: ?; F: ?,
altricial; B: 1 or possibly more.

Other Behavior: Male and female call while perched and
with head thrown back. In female, the pitch of the voice
is higher and not as hoarse. A rare bird in U.S., so
caution must be exercised by bird watchers not to
disturb it, especially during breeding.

Habitat: Wooded
canyons.

Voice: Series of
croaks, like "croah
crowee croway."

Conservation:
TREND UNKNOWN.

Belted Kingfisher

Ceryle alcyon

Female

Male

Identification: 13″ Our only kingfisher outside Tex. **Large bill; blue-gray head, back, and wings; white collar. MALE: All-white belly. FEMALE: Reddish-brown belly band.**

Feeding: Hovers, then plunges into water, or dives from perch. Eats fish, amphibians, reptiles, and insects.

Nesting: Nest tunnel is excavated in a vertical bank. Entrance hole of 3–4 in. diameter is 1½ ft. down from top of bank. Tunnel is 3–15 ft. in length, with a spherical chamber at end where eggs are laid. Can be far from water. Eggs: 5–7, white; I: 22–26 days; F: 18–28 days, altricial; B: 1.

Other Behavior: Tunnel excavation is done with the bill. Birds alternate turns excavating, each one kicking out the earth excavated by the other when it enters tunnel, creating a spray of dirt coming out of the hole. Can dig about a foot of tunnel in a day. Kingfishers defend individual feeding territory during the nonbreeding season; size of territory averages about 500 yd. of stream length.

Habitat: Near water, such as rivers, lakes, coastal bays.

Voice: A continuous woody rattle; often given in flight. Very vocal.

Conservation:
BBS: W ↓ C ↓ CBC: ↑

Green Kingfisher

Chloroceryle americana

Male

Identification: 8" Limited to S. and central Tex.
A **small** kingfisher with **proportionately large
bill; dark green above; white collar. MALE:
Reddish-brown breast. FEMALE: No reddish
brown on breast; band of dark spots across
breast.**

Feeding: From perch, dives into water after fish,
amphibians, crustaceans, and insects.

Nesting: Male and female excavate tunnel 2–3 ft. long
with nest chamber at end; in sandy bank, usually half-
hidden behind vegetation. Eggs: 3–6, white; I: 19–21
days; F: 22–27 days, altricial; B: 1 or possibly more.

Other Behavior: Solitary or in pairs. Very territorial.
Hunts from low perches, generally over shallow water.

Habitat: Near lakes
and clear streams.

Voice: Call a sharp
"tick," often given
in a series.

Conservation:
CBC: ↓

Lewis' Woodpecker

Melanerpes lewis

Identification: 11″ Dark; greenish-black upperparts; grayish collar and breast; pinkish belly; red facial mask. **IN FLIGHT:** Note steady crowlike wingbeats, rather than bursts of wingbeats like most other woodpeckers.

Feeding: Feeds mostly on insects, including crickets, ants, grasshoppers, flies, beetles; also eats acorns and other nuts, and fruit, including fruit in orchards. Eats seeds and fruit at feeders.

Nesting: Excavated nest in tall tree, often dead, or one blackened by fire, or utility pole. Entry hole is 2–2½ in. in diameter. Eggs: 5–9, white; I: 14 days; F: 28–34 days, altricial; B: 1 or possibly more.

Other Behavior: Catches insects in the air, by gliding out from perch; also picks insects off leaves, or from the ground. Stores acorns and nuts by removing shell and breaking nut into pieces, which it then wedges into crevices. Northern part of population moves to south part of range in nonbreeding season.

Habitat: Dry open woods, orchards, farmlands, foothills.

Voice: A repeated "churr." Drumming is faint.

Conservation: BBS: W ⇓ C CBC: ↓ Drought and too much grazing may adversely affect its habitat along streams and rivers in arid country.

Red-headed Woodpecker
Melanerpes erythrocephalus

Identification: 8" Only woodpecker with an all-red head; body and wings boldly patterned with black and white. IN FLIGHT: Note white rump and white inner trailing half of wings. FALL JUV: Pattern similar to adult, but with brown head and back. Gradually molts into adult plumage in fall and winter.

Feeding: Feeds on acorns, beechnuts, and other nuts, insects, bird eggs and nestlings, sap from sapsucker holes, fruit, and berries.

Nesting: Both sexes excavate hole in live or dead tree or utility pole. Uses birdhouses. Eggs: 4–5, white; I: 12–13 days; F: 30 days, altricial; B: 1–2.

Other Behavior: Catches insects in midair, as well as foraging on leaves and on the ground. Caches pieces of nuts and acorns, also insects, in small cavities for use during nonbreeding season. Will even conceal the cache by closing it off with slivers of wet wood. Defends caches from other woodpeckers, jays, and crows. Northern populations are migratory and concentrate in woods with abundant acorns.

Habitat: Farmlands, open woodlands, suburbs, orchards.

Voice: Common call a loud "kweeer." Drums softly in short bursts.

Conservation: BBS: W C ↓ CBC: ↓ Declining due to woodlands being cut down and competition with starlings for nest sites.

269

Acorn Woodpecker
Melanerpes formicivorus

Male

Female

Identification: 8" **Clear black back; red on crown; white eye surrounded by black;** white forehead and cheek; and yellowish throat. **MALE:** Red crown touches white forehead. **FEMALE:** Red on back half of crown separated from white forehead by black. **IN FLIGHT:** Note **white rump and white patch near tip of wing.**

Feeding: Eats insects, tree sap, and fruit. Caches acorns and other nuts in holes drilled in trees, utility poles, even buildings; 1 communal group can store 50,000 nuts in a season. Will come to suet and seed at feeders.

Nesting: In colonies. Excavates nesting cavity in dead or live tree, usually an oak, 6–25 ft. above ground. Entrance hole is 1½ in. in diameter. Eggs: 4–6, white; I: 14 days; F: 30–32 days, altricial; B: 2–3.

Other Behavior: Lives in communal groups and breeds cooperatively in parts of range. Groups are composed of up to 4 breeding males, 1–2 breeding females, and up to 10 offspring of preceding years. All group members help with excavating nest and with feeding and brooding young. Some birds in Ariz. do not nest communally or store acorns.

Habitat: Oak and pine woods, parks, suburbs.

Voice: Repeated "chacup chacup chacup."

Conservation:
BBS: W ↑ C CBC: ↓
Preserving dead snags on trees is important for all woodpeckers — providing food, nest sites, and, for this species, a place to store acorns.

Gila Woodpecker

Melanerpes uropygialis

Male

Female

Identification: 8″ Head and belly tan; wings, back, and tail black barred with white. MALE: Red patch on crown. FEMALE: No red.

Feeding: Eats insects, acorns, cactus fruit, berries, corn, bird eggs. Comes to bird feeders for seed, scraps, and fruit.

Nesting: Excavates cavity in tree, such as willow or cottonwood. In Ariz., also nests in saguaro cactus that is at least 15 ft. tall. Eggs: 3–5, white; I: 14 days; F: ?, altricial; B: 2–3.

Other Behavior: Vocal and active. Receives competition for nest sites in saguaro cactus from European Starling, especially near areas that have lawns and agriculture, where the starling can feed. Other species such as owls, kestrels, and flycatchers use old nest holes of Gila.

Habitat: Deserts, dry streams, and suburbs in dry regions.

Voice: A "churr" call and a repeated "kikikiki."

Conservation:
BBS: W ↑ C CBC: ↑
Along lower Colorado River, habitat loss and starling competition threaten this species.

271

Golden-fronted Woodpecker

Melanerpes aurifrons

Male

Female

Identification: 9" Head and belly tan; yellow on forehead and nape; wings, back, and tail black barred with white. MALE: Small red patch on crown. FEMALE: No red.

Feeding: Eats a variety of insects, such as beetles, grasshoppers, ants; also grubs, berries, and fruit. Eats sunflower seed at feeders.

Nesting: Excavates a nest cavity in live trunk of large tree, usually mesquite, pecan, or oak, or in a dead limb; also uses fence posts and utility poles. May use nest box. Eggs: 4–5, white; I: 12–14 days; F: 25–30 days, altricial; B: 2–3.

Other Behavior: Noisy and conspicuous. Uses same cavity to nest in, year after year.

Habitat: Woodlands, parks, gardens.

Voice: Harsh "churr." Drums.

Conservation: BBS: W C ↓ CBC: ↑

Yellow-bellied Sapsucker

Sphyrapicus varius

Male

Female

Identification: 8″ **Black-and-white-streaked face; red patch on forehead;** elongated white patch on shoulder of black wings; central belly yellowish. **MALE:** Red chin. **FEMALE:** White chin. **IN FLIGHT:** Note white rump and white shoulder patches. **FALL JUV:** Brownish overall, but with white wing patch like adult's. Gradually molts into adult plumage by spring.

Habitat: Woods and orchards.

Feeding: Drinks sap from trees and catches insects on the wing or on the ground. Also eats fruit, berries.

Nesting: Nests in a hole in live tree, often an aspen that is diseased by a tinder fungus that decays the heartwood but not the sapwood. Sapsucker easily excavates the softened heartwood but leaves tough sapwood, which remains as outer shell protecting the nest. Eggs: 5–6, white; I: 12–13 days; F: 25–29 days, altricial; B: 1.

Voice: A "churr" call; a "weep weep" call. Drumming is short burst followed by irregular beats, like "tatatat tatat tatat."

Conservation:
BBS: W ⇓ C ⇑

Other Behavior: Drills horizontal rows of holes in trunks of many species of trees; when it finds abundant sap flow, it drills vertical rows of holes to take advantage of it. It then returns repeatedly to drink sap from holes. Other birds may also come to sap, such as titmice, nuthatches, and hummingbirds.

Red-naped Sapsucker

Sphyrapicus nuchalis

Male

Female

Identification: 8″ Black-and-white-streaked face; red patch on forehead and a separate patch on nape; elongated white patch on shoulder of black wings; central belly yellowish. MALE: Red chin. FEMALE: White chin, edged with red at base. IN FLIGHT: Note white rump and white shoulder patches.

Feeding: Drills horizontal and vertical rows in tree trunks and drinks sap from them. Uses aspen, birch, or conifer. Also eats insects.

Nesting: Excavates nest in dead tree, or living tree with rotting heartwood caused by fungus. Makes new nest each year, but often in same tree for 5–6 years. Eggs: 3–6, white; I: 12–13 days; F: 25–29 days, altricial; B: 1.

Other Behavior: Male and female drum on trees as part of courtship and territorial activities. Hybridizes with Yellow-bellied and Red-breasted Sapsuckers where ranges overlap. Hummingbirds also drink the sap from holes drilled by sapsuckers.

Habitat: Woods and orchards.

Voice: A series of "churr" calls; a "weep weep" call. Drumming is short burst followed by irregular beats, like "tatatat tatat tatat."

Conservation:
BBS: W ↑ C ⇑

274

Red-breasted Sapsucker

Sphyrapicus ruber

Identification: 8″ **Red head and breast; whitish mark over bill** (may extend onto cheek); elongated white patch on shoulder of black wings; central belly yellowish; flanks streaked. **IN FLIGHT:** Note white rump and white shoulder patches.

Feeding: Drinks sap from holes drilled in trees. Also eats insects.

Nesting: Excavates nest hole in tree whose heartwood is weakened by fungus. Entrance hole usually 1¼–1½ in. in diameter. Eggs: 3–6, white; I: 12–13 days; F: 25–29 days, altricial; B: 1.

Other Behavior: Hybridizes with Red-naped Sapsucker where ranges overlap. Rufous Hummingbird drinks from sapsucker holes and may depend on this sap for early spring food when it migrates north.

Habitat: Moist woodlands.

Voice: A series of "cheerr" calls; a "weep weep" call. Drumming is short burst followed by irregular beats, like "tatatat tatat tatat."

Conservation:
BBS: W ↓ C

Williamson's Sapsucker
Sphyrapicus thyroideus

Male

Female

Identification: 9" MALE: Mostly **black, with bold white patch on wing; yellow belly; red chin.** FEMALE: **Brownish head; barred black and white on back, wings, and flanks.** No white patch on her wings. IN FLIGHT: Note white rump in male and female and white wing patches on male.

Feeding: Drinks sap from holes drilled in tree. Also eats insects, especially ants, and berries.

Nesting: Excavates nest in deciduous or coniferous tree. Eggs: 3–7, white; I: 14 days; F: 21–28 days, altricial; B:1.

Other Behavior: Makes new nest each year, usually in the same tree, sometimes for many years.

Habitat: Coniferous forests, especially Ponderosa Pine.

Voice: A series of "cheerr" calls. Drumming is short burst followed by irregular beats, like "tatatat tatat tatat." Generally rather quiet.

Conservation: BBS: W ⇑ C CBC: ↑

Ladder-backed Woodpecker

Picoides scalaris

Male

Female

Identification: 7" Black-and-white-barred back; buffy-white face and underparts; black eye-stripe and black line off the base of the bill connect behind the cheek. MALE: Red from nape to forehead, wearing away over summer to black on forehead. FEMALE: No red.

Feeding: Eats fruit of cactus, and insects such as beetle larvae.

Nesting: Excavates nesting cavity in dead stub or dying branch of willow or mesquite, or in live saguaro cactus. Also excavates in agave, yucca, fence post, or utility pole. Eggs: 3–6, white; I: 13 days; F: ?, altricial; B: 1 or possibly more.

Other Behavior: During courtship, in spring, male and female do drumming on dry resonant tree limbs.

Habitat: Arid and semiarid brushlands, creeks, farms, and suburbs.

Voice: Call is a sharp "peek." Loud short bursts of drumming.

Conservation:
BBS: W ↓ C ⇓ CBC: ↓

Nuttall's Woodpecker

Picoides nuttallii

Male

Female

Identification: 7″ Black-and-white-barred back; white face and underparts; black eye-stripe is much wider than the black line off the base of the bill; the two connect behind the cheek. MALE: Red on the nape. FEMALE: No red.

Feeding: Eats many wood-boring insects, also some fruit, berries.

Nesting: Excavates nesting cavity in dead wood of willow, cottonwood, alder, oak. Eggs: 3–6, white; I: 14 days; F: 29 days, altricial; B: 1.

Other Behavior: Searches for insects by creeping diagonally over bark of tree trunk, like a nuthatch. Prefers moister habitats than Ladder-backed Woodpecker, such as narrow canyons with streamside sycamores and alders.

Habitat: Shrublands, streamsides, and oak woods.

Voice: A 2-syllable "pitik" and a high-pitched whinny. Drumming is 1–2 seconds of rapid even taps.

Conservation: BBS: W ↑ C CBC: ↑

Downy Woodpecker
Hairy Woodpecker
Picoides pubescens   Picoides villosus

Female Downy

Male Downy

Female Hairy

Identification: Downy 6", Hairy 9" **Both species have a white back and white underparts;** white-spotted black wings; black-and-white-streaked faces. Males have red on nape; females have no red. **DOWNY: Bill is about half the length of the head;** white outer tail feathers with a few black bars. **HAIRY: Bill is almost as long as the head;** outer tail feathers all white.

Feeding: Both feed on a variety of insects, especially wood-boring insects. At feeders, suet, sunflower seeds.

Nesting: Downy excavates nest cavity in dead wood. Eggs: 4–5, white; I: 12 days; F: 21 days, altricial; B: 1–2. Hairy excavates nest cavity in live wood. Eggs: 4–6, white; I: 11–12 days; F: 28–30 days, altricial; B: 1. Both species only rarely accept a nest box.

Other Behavior: Both species do drumming — loud, continuous, very rapid pecking on resonant surfaces, such as dead tree stubs. This functions to announce territory and attract a mate during the breeding season. Sounds of pecking for food or nest-hole excavation are different; they are light taps in irregular rhythms.

Downy   Hairy

Habitat: Woods, farmland, suburbs.

Voice: Both have "teek" contact call. Downy: whinny call and a "queek queek" given during courtship. Hairy: "wickiwicki–wicki" during courtship.

Conservation:
Downy:
BBS: W ↓ C ↑ CBC: ↑
Hairy:
BBS: W ↑ C ↑ CBC: ↑

Strickland's Woodpecker
Picoides stricklandi

Male

Female

Identification: 8" Limited to S.E. Ariz. and S.W. N.Mex. **Clear dark brown back; whitish breast heavily spotted with brown;** brown patch behind eye. **MALE:** Small red patch on nape. **FEMALE:** No red.

Feeding: Eats insects, fruit, acorns.

Nesting: Excavates nest cavity in trunk or stub of deciduous tree, 20–50 ft. high. Eggs: 3–4, white; I: 14 days; F: ?, altricial; B: 1 or possibly more.

Other Behavior: Forages primarily on oaks, in foothills and mountain slopes, especially at 4,000–7,000 ft. elevation.

Habitat: Oak and pine woodlands, canyons.

Voice: "Teeek" contact call. Drums in 1–2 second bursts.

Conservation: BBS: W ⇓ C

White-headed Woodpecker
Picoides albolarvatus

Male

Female

Identification: 8" White head and throat; otherwise all black. **MALE:** Red patch at back of crown. **FEMALE:** No red. **IN FLIGHT:** Note black rump and white patches near wing tips.

Feeding: Large portion of diet is Ponderosa Pine seeds; also pries bark off trees to get at insects.

Nesting: Excavates in live tree or dead stub of pine. Eggs: 3–7, white; I: 14 days; F: 26 days, altricial; B: 1.

Other Behavior: Can land on trunks or branches upside down or sideways. Usually found in montane coniferous forests at 4,000–9,000 ft. elevation. In winter may go to lower elevations.

Habitat: Coniferous woods in mountains.

Voice: "Teedeek" or "teedeedeek." Drums often, with 1–2 second volleys.

Conservation: BBS: W ⇑ C CBC: ↑

Three-toed Woodpecker
Black-backed Woodpecker
Picoides tridactylus   Picoides arcticus

Female Three-toed

Male Black-backed

Identification: Three-toed 8 ", Black-backed 9 "
Both species have **black head with a fine white eye-stripe; wider white line off the base of the bill; barred flanks.** Males have yellow patch on crown; females have no yellow. THREE-TOED: **Black-and-white-barred back.** BLACK-BACKED: **Clear, glossy, black back.**

Feeding: Three-toed eats mostly insects, also berries, sap, nuts. Often forages on fire-killed trees. Black-backed eats larvae of wood-boring beetles and other insects, fruit, nuts.

Nesting: Three-toed is loosely colonial where food is abundant. Excavates nest cavity in dead, or sometimes live, tree, 2–15 ft. high; will also use utility pole. Eggs: 2–6, white; I: 12–14 days; F: 22–26 days, altricial; B: 1. Black-backed excavates nest cavity in live tree with rotting heartwood, 5–12 ft. high; may peel off bark around nest hole. Eggs: 2–6, white; I: 14 days; F: 25 days, altricial; B: 1.

Other Behavior: Both forage by scaling large patches of bark off dead trees. Black-backed more irruptive.

Three-toed   Black-backed

Habitat: Boreal coniferous forest.

Voice: Three-toed gives a "teek" contact call and short volleys of drumming. Black-backed gives a "kik" contact call and long volleys of drumming.

Conservation:
Three-toed:
BBS: W ⇩ C CBC: ↑
Black-backed:
BBS: W ⇧ C CBC: ↑

Northern Flicker

Colaptes auratus

Male "Yellow-shafted"

Male "Red-shafted"

Female "Yellow-shafted"

Identification: 13″ Brown-and-black-barred back and wings; whitish or buffy breast with black spots; wide black necklace. IN FLIGHT: Conspicuous white rump. "YELLOW-SHAFTED" MORPH: Red patch on nape; gray crown; yellow undertail and underwings. MALE: Black line off base of bill. FEMALE: No line off base of bill. "RED-SHAFTED" MORPH: Lacks red patch on nape; brown crown; reddish undertail and underwings. MALE: Red line off base of bill. FEMALE: No line off base of bill.

Feeding: Feeds on ground, probing for ants, which are 45% of its diet; also catches insects in air and eats fruit, berries, seeds. Comes to bird feeders.

Nesting: Excavates nest cavity in tree, post, cactus. Uses nest box. Eggs: 7–9, white; I: 11–12 days; F: 14–21 days, altricial; B: 1–2.

Other Behavior: Head bobbing, accompanied by the "woikawoikawoika" call, is done by mated pairs as part of courtship. When done between birds of the same sex, it is usually competition for a mate or territory.

Habitat: Parks, suburbs, farmlands, woodlands.

Voice: Loud "kekekekeke" for territory advertisement; a "woika-woikawoika" during courtship. Soft muffled volleys of drumming.

Conservation: BBS: W ↓ C ⇓ CBC: ↓

Gilded Flicker
Colaptes chrysoides

Male (l.), female (r.)

Identification: 13″ Brown-and-black-barred back and wings; whitish breast with black spots; wide black necklace. Only flicker with brown crown and golden undertail and underwings. MALE: Red line off base of bill. FEMALE: No line off base of bill. IN FLIGHT: Conspicuous white rump; colorful golden underwings.

Feeding: Feeds on ground, probing for ants, which are 45% of its diet; also catches insects in air and eats fruit, berries, seeds.

Nesting: Excavates nest cavity in cactus or tree. Uses nest box. Eggs: 7–9, white; I: 11–12 days; F: 14–21 days, altricial; B: 1–2.

Other Behavior: This species is limited in range to southern California and the Southwest, where it inhabits dry areas and uses saguaro cactus for its home site and shelter.

Habitat: Dry foothills and lowlands.

Voice: Loud "kekekekeke" for territory advertisement; a "woika-woikawoika" during courtship. Soft muffled volleys of drumming.

Conservation: BBS: W ↑ C

Pileated Woodpecker

Dryocopus pileatus

Male

Female

Identification: 18″ Crow-sized; mostly black with a bright red crest. **MALE:** Has red patch on black line off base of bill. **FEMALE:** All-black line off base of bill. **IN FLIGHT:** Note large size and striking white on linings of underwings.

Feeding: Eats large numbers of carpenter ants, especially in winter. Also eats beetles and other insects, seeds, fruit. Comes to bird feeders for suet mixes.

Nesting: Nest cavity is excavated in dead wood, 15–70 ft. high. The entrance hole is about 3½ in. in diameter, with a cavity depth of 10–24 in. Eggs: 3–5, white; I: 15–16 days; F: 28 or more days, altricial; B: 1.

Other Behavior: Territory size can be 150–200 acres. Signs of a Pileated's presence are chiseled-out, squarish, 3–6 in. holes in trees. These are feeding holes, where the bird has searched for, or obtained, carpenter ants that live in tunnels deep in the wood. Sometimes the Pileated will excavate a long gash in a tree to obtain ants. Drumming is done by unmated males to advertise for a female, or it can be done between mated pairs as part of courtship.

Habitat: Mature forests, suburbs.

Voice: Ten to fifteen "cuk" calls given between mates; "woika-woika" calls given during courtship or territorial interactions. Low-pitched drumming that trails off in speed and volume at the end.

Conservation: BBS: W ⇑ C ↓ CBC: ↑

285

Flycatchers are a large family of birds that all share the habit of sitting on exposed perches and making short flights out to catch passing insects. A few North American flycatchers are brightly colored, but most are shades of gray, white, and olive-green.

One of the best ways to start identifying flycatchers is to learn to identify the distinctive groups within the family, such as phoebes, kingbirds, crested flycatchers, etc. The Learning Pages outline the characteristics of each group, list the species in that group, and illustrate the most common representative of the group. Knowing this information will give you an excellent basis for learning the more difficult and/or less common species.

The few species not covered by these groups are distinctive and, in many cases, brightly colored. They include Northern Beardless-Tyrannulet (p. 288), Vermilion Flycatcher (p. 302), Sulphur-bellied Flycatcher (p. 307), and Rose-throated Becard (p. 313).

FLYCATCHER GROUPS

Pewees

Contopus spp. Medium-sized brownish-gray flycatchers that perch upright and have a small peak at the top of the head; may have faint wing bars.

Western Wood-Pewee, p. 291

Phoebes

Sayornis spp. Medium-sized flycatchers that perch upright and have a habit of continuously bobbing the tail; wing bars faint or lacking. Often build nests on bridges or buildings.

Black Phoebe, p. 299

Other species:

Olive-sided Flycatcher, p. 289
Greater Pewee, p. 290

Other species:

Eastern Phoebe, p. 300
Say's Phoebe, p. 301

Kingbirds

Tyrannus spp. Large flycatchers that perch at a diagonal. They have large bills, dark upperparts, and white or yellow bellies. They are often aggressive to other birds.

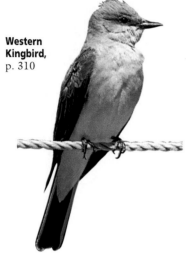

Western Kingbird, p. 310

Other species:

Tropical Kingbird, p. 308
Cassin's Kingbird, p. 308
Thick-billed Kingbird, p. 309
Eastern Kingbird, p. 311
Scissor-tailed Flycatcher, p. 312

Crested Flycatchers

Myiarchus spp. Large flycatchers with a prominent rounded crest; many are brownish above, gray and yellow below, and have reddish brown on tail.

Ash-throated Flycatcher, p. 304

Other species:

Dusky-capped Flycatcher, p. 303
Great Crested Flycatcher, p. 305
Brown-crested Flycatcher, p. 306

Pacific-slope Flycatcher, p. 297

Empidonaxes

Empidonax spp. Small flycatchers with light eye-rings and wing bars; generally olive above and lighter below. Perch upright. Many species look so similar that even experts have trouble identifying them by sight and rely on song. Often referred to as "Empids."

Other species:

Yellow-bellied Flycatcher, p. 292
Alder Flycatcher, p. 293
Willow Flycatcher, p. 293
Least Flycatcher, p. 294
Hammond's Flycatcher, p. 295
Dusky Flycatcher, p. 295
Gray Flycatcher, p. 296
Cordilleran Flycatcher, p. 297
Buff-breasted Flycatcher, p. 298

Northern Beardless-Tyrannulet

Camptostoma imberbe

Identification: 4½" Limited to S.E. Ariz. and S. Tex. **Very small; bushy crest; 2 buffy wing bars;** grayish olive above; gray below; pale lower bill.

Feeding: Gleans insects from twigs, and eats small berries; sometimes hawks insects from air.

Nesting: Nest a globular collection of plant fibers, attached to pendant branches. Eggs: 2–3, white; I: ?; F: ?, altricial; B: 1 or possibly more.

Other Behavior: Nest often built in clump of mistletoe that is growing in a tree. The entrance is on the side.

Habitat: Subtropical woodlands, thickets, and riverside trees.

Voice: Song a loud descending series of "peer" notes; call is a loud "pee-yeerp."

Conservation:
BBS: W ↑ C

Olive-sided Flycatcher

Contopus borealis

Identification: 7½" **Prominent peak at back of head; dark grayish olive overall** except for a **strip of white from chin to belly;** white patches on either side of lower back unique, but may be hidden by wings.

Feeding: Flies out from prominent perch to catch insects in the air.

Nesting: Nest of twigs and rootlets, lined with pine needles and moss, placed on a horizontal limb of deciduous or evergreen tree. Eggs: 3–4, whitish with darker marks; I: 14–17 days; F: 15–19, altricial; B: 1.

Other Behavior: More than most other flycatchers, this species has the habit of perching on high dead branches.

Habitat: Northern and mountainous coniferous forests.

Voice: An energetic "quick, three beers," with the 1st word quiet and 2nd accented. Also a repeated "pep-pep-pep."

Conservation: BBS: W ⇓ C ⇓

Greater Pewee
Contopus pertinax

Identification: 7½" Limited to S.E. Ariz. and S.W. N.Mex. **Prominent peak at back of head, sometimes raised into a crest; dark upper bill, orange lower bill;** appears grayish overall; pale throat; **gray breast;** belly sometimes slightly yellowish; long tail.

Feeding: Flies out from perch to catch insects in the air.

Nesting: Compact nest of grasses, weed stems, and dried leaves lined with fine grasses, placed on horizontal branch. Eggs: 3–4, white with few or no markings; I: ?; F: ?, altricial; B: 1–2.

Other Behavior: After the young leave the nest, they move with parents to lower altitudes, often in canyons. Aggressive protector of nesting area from predators; other small bird species sometimes nest nearby or in same tree, possibly to take advantage of its vigilance.

Habitat: Oak and pine woods in mountains.

Voice: A slow "ho-say-ma-ri-a" with accent on 2nd syllable. Thus, nicknamed José Maria.

Conservation: BBS: W ⇑ C CBC: ↑

Western Wood-Pewee

Contopus sordidulus

Identification: 6″ Prominent peak at back of head; grayish olive above; **2 wing bars; whitish throat; grayish chest; whitish or yellowish belly.** ADULT: **Black upper bill, usually some orange at base of lower bill;** wing bars whitish. Distinguished from Eastern Wood-Pewee by range and song. IMM: Bill can be all dark; wing bars cinnamon or buffy. Imm. plumage kept into winter.

Feeding: Flies out from perch to catch aerial insects.

Nesting: Compact nest of plant fibers and downy materials, covered with silvery leaves or lichens, built over a horizontal limb or fork 8–40 ft. high. Eggs: 2–4, creamy white with darker marks at one end; I: 12–13 days; F: 14–18 days, altricial; B: 1.

Other Behavior: Male sings continuously through breeding season. In early part of breeding season, may occasionally fly to treetops to give a loud version of song. Dawn-song, a rapidly repeated version of song, lasting up to a half hour, can be given early in the morning. Male may chase female as part of courtship; otherwise, very few displays seem to be associated with pairing. Territory is about 2–6 acres.

Habitat: Open woods, streamside trees.

Voice: Song is "fee-rrr-reet." Call is a burry descending "feeer."

Conservation: BBS: W ↓ C ⇑ CBC: ↓

Yellow-bellied Flycatcher

Empidonax flaviventris

Identification: 5½" A relatively large-headed short-tailed *Empidonax;* most common in E. Can. **Back green; throat yellow;** breast yellow with olive wash on sides; thin even-width eye-ring; conspicuous wing bars on dark wings. **See Voice.**

Feeding: Flies out from perch to catch aerial insects.

Nesting: Deep cup of mosses lined with finer material, placed on the ground under partial protection of tree roots, or among sphagnum moss. Eggs: 3–4, white with light markings; I: 12–13 days; F: 13–14 days, altricial; B: 1 or more.

Other Behavior: Our only flycatcher to regularly build its nest on the ground. Birds are quiet around nest, and male approaches only when feeding young. Female allows very close approach to nest and then flies off silently. Inconspicuous during migration, perching low in woods and thickets.

Habitat: Dense coniferous woods.

Voice: Song is a soft evenly stressed "cheluk," with the 2nd syllable lower-pitched; call is a whistled ascending "purweee" or just "preee."

Conservation:
BBS: W ⇑ C

Alder Flycatcher
Willow Flycatcher

Empidonax alnorum   Empidonax traillii

Alder   Willow

Identification: 6″ Relatively heavy-billed broad-tailed members of *Empidonax* genus that look identical and can be distinguished only by voice. During breeding, the Alder is most common in Can., the Willow is most common in U.S. south of Can. **Back olive-brown; throat white; breast pale olive; belly pale yellow;** eye-ring faint or lacking (sometimes bolder on Alder); wing bars dull white and do not stand out. **See Voice.**

Feeding: Fly out from low perch to catch insects.

Nesting: For both species, nest is firm thick-walled cup of plant fibers lined with plant down and cottony fibers, placed in shrub 2–6 ft. high. Eggs: 3–4, whitish with darker marks; I: 12–13 days; F: 12–14 days, altricial; B: 1 or possibly more.

Other Behavior: During migration, either species can be found in a wide variety of habitats.

Conservation:
Alder: BBS: w ↑ c ⇓
Willow: BBS: w ⇓ c ⇑

Alder   Willow

Habitat: Alder: alder thickets at edge of lakes or swamps. Willow: shrubby swamps.

Voice: Alder song a burry "rreebeet" or "rreebeea," accent on 2nd syllable; call is "peep." Willow song is "fitzbew," accent on 1st syllable; call is "wit."

Least Flycatcher

Empidonax minimus

Identification: 5″ The **smallest** *Empidonax;* has a relatively small bill; commonly seen throughout the East during migration. **Back brown-olive; throat whitish; breast washed with gray; belly pale yellow; eye-ring bold;** wing bars conspicuous. **See Voice.**

Feeding: Flies out from perch to catch aerial insects.

Nesting: Nest a compact cup of grasses, bark strips, and plant down, placed in the crotch of a limb. Eggs: 3–4, whitish; I: 14 days; F: 12–16 days, altricial; B: 1–2.

Other Behavior: Males chase females during courtship, frequently calling "chibek." Intruding males are chased out of the relatively small territory of 2–4 acres. Male may feed female on nest during incubation. Young are fed by parents for about 3 weeks after leaving the nest.

Habitat: Open woods, orchards, suburbs.

Voice: Song, given by both male and female, is an often-repeated "chibek," with accent on 2nd syllable; call a short "whit."

Conservation:
BBS: W ⇑ C ↓ CBC: ↑

Hammond's Flycatcher
Dusky Flycatcher

Empidonax hammondii   Empidonax oberholseri

Hammond's

Dusky

Identification: 5½" Two very similar western *Empidonax*es; best distinguished by calls. See Voice. **Back olive-gray; throat pale gray; breast brownish gray and darker on sides; belly pale yellow; eye-ring bold and widest behind eye (less conspicuous in Dusky);** wing bars muted. HAMMOND'S: **Tiny dark bill.** Molts before migrating south; more brightly colored in fall than Dusky. DUSKY: **Long tail.** Molts after migration; colors faded in fall.

Feeding: Fly from perch to catch aerial insects.

Nesting: Nest a tight cup of bark strips, grasses, and plant down lined with hair, moss, and feathers. Hammond's nest usually on horizontal branch 25–40 ft. high; Dusky nest usually in crotch of small tree or shrub 4–7 ft. high. Eggs: 3–4, whitish; I: 12–15 days; F: 17–18 days, altricial; B: 1 or more.

Other Behavior: Hammond's tends to forage high in trees and repeatedly flicks its tail and wings while doing so; Dusky tends to forage low over shrubs and flicks its wings and tail less often.

Hammond's   Dusky

Habitat: Dusky: dry open forests. Hammond's: wet mountain forests.

Voice: Hammond's song "chibek brrk breet"; call "peet." Dusky's song "chip greep swee," last note high; call "whit."

Conservation:
Hammond's:
BBS: W ↓ C CBC: ↑
Dusky:
BBS: W ↑ C ↓ CBC: ↑

Gray Flycatcher

Empidonax wrightii

Identification: 5½" A long-billed long-tailed *Empidonax*, most common in the Great Basin. Has distinctive habit of **repeatedly bobbing its tail,** much like a phoebe. **Palest member of genus; back, head, and throat grayish;** belly pale yellow; eye-ring pale; wing bars muted.

Feeding: Flies out from perch to catch aerial insects; also flies down to ground for insects.

Nesting: Nest of bark strips lined with animal hair and feathers, placed in the crotch of a shrub a few feet high. Eggs: 3–4, whitish; I: 14 days; F: 16 days, altricial; B: 1–2.

Other Behavior: May nest in loose colonies where there is favorable habitat.

Habitat: Arid areas of sagebrush or pinyon pines and junipers.

Voice: Song is "chawip teeah"; call is "whit."

Conservation: BBS: W ⇑ C CBC: ⇑

Pacific-slope Flycatcher
Cordilleran Flycatcher
Empidonax difficilis   Empidonax occidentalis

Pacific-slope

Cordilleran

Identification: 5½" These two *Empidonax*es are distinguishable in the field only by the call notes of the males; songs and female call notes (high-pitched "seeet") are identical. Back olive-green; **throat yellow;** breast washed with olive; belly yellow; **eye-ring usually extending at the back to a point;** wing bars noticeable. **See Voice.**

Pacific   Cordilleran

Feeding: Fly from perch to catch aerial insects; eat some berries and seeds.

Nesting: Nest a mounded cup of green and dried leaves, bark strips, fresh and dried moss, lined with finer hair and feathers, and placed on protected portion of a bank or in trees or outbuildings. Eggs: 3–4, whitish with darker marks; I: 14–15 days; F: 14–18 days, altricial; B: 1–2.

Other Behavior: Nest may be reused in successive years, by adding to the top, much the way phoebes do. Nest often contains bits of human-made materials, such as paper or string.

Conservation:
Pacific-slope: BBS: w ⇑ c ⇑
Cordilleran: BBS: w ⇑ c ⇑

Habitat: Open woods, damp wooded canyons.

Voice: Song for both is 3 high-pitched repeated phrases. Male Pacific call a single upslurred "sweeet"; male Cordilleran call a 2-part upslurred "swee-deet."

Buff-breasted Flycatcher

Empidonax fulvifrons

Identification: 5" Limited to S.E. Ariz. A **small distinctively buffy** *Empidonax*. Back, head, and breast buffy; throat white; belly whitish; eye-ring widened at the back; wing bars noticeable.

Feeding: Flies from perch to catch aerial insects; also forages among shrubs and along ground.

Nesting: Nest a deep tightly made cup of leaves and weed stems held together by spider or caterpillar silk and lined with finer grasses, hair, feathers; placed on a branch next to tree trunk. Eggs: 3–5, whitish; I: 14–15 days; F: 14–16 days, altricial; B: 1 or more.

Other Behavior: May be found nesting in loose colonies where habitat is favorable.

Habitat: Open mountain woodland with brushy understory.

Voice: Song "chicky chew"; call "whit."

Conservation: TREND UNKNOWN.

Black Phoebe

Sayornis nigricans

Identification: 7" **All black except for white belly; repeatedly bobs tail.**

Feeding: Flies out from perch, often over water or on rocks in water, to catch aerial insects.

Nesting: Nest a cup made of mud mixed with hair and grasses, lined with finer materials, and stuck to vertical surface with some overhanging protection, such as cliff, wooden or concrete wall, or bridge. Eggs: 4–5, white; I: 15–18 days; F: 14–21 days, altricial; B: 2 or more.

Other Behavior: Nest site used in successive seasons and, like Eastern Phoebe's nest, may be placed near human activity without any noticeable concern from the birds.

Habitat: Wooded streams and canyons, farms and suburbs near water.

Voice: Song an ascending then descending "peeyee yeewee"; call a short "chirp."

Conservation: BBS: W ⇑ C ⇓ CBC: ⇑

299

Eastern Phoebe

Sayornis phoebe

Identification: 7" **Gray-brown above and whitish below; bill all dark; repeatedly bobs tail.** After molt in late summer, belly may be yellowish.

Feeding: Flies out from perch to catch aerial insects; also picks insects off ground.

Nesting: Nest a mounded cup of mud and moss, lined with fine grasses, placed on a ledge of building or bridge. Eggs: 4–5, white; I: 16 days; F: 18 days, altricial; B: 2–3.

Other Behavior: Males defend territories of several acres through chases and song. When female arrives, most singing stops, except for early in the morning when the pair get together briefly. Female builds nest and does all incubation. When she leaves nest to feed, male may come near nest; at other times the female will chase him away from the vicinity of the nest. Both parents feed the young. Once the young leave the nest, the female may start renovating nest for next brood, and male may renew singing for a short time. Twenty-five percent, or more, of phoebe nests are parasitized by cowbirds. This is the only flycatcher that winters in southeastern U.S.

Habitat: Woods, farmlands, suburbs; nests on bridges, outbuildings.

Voice: Song sounds like a hoarse rendition of name, like "feebee"; call is "chirp."

Conservation:
BBS: W ⇓ C ↑ CBC: ↓

Say's Phoebe
Sayornis saya

Identification: 8″ Brownish gray above; grayish throat and breast; cinnamon belly; repeatedly bobs blackish tail.

Feeding: Flies from perch to catch aerial insects; also hovers above grass to find insects.

Nesting: Nest a mounded cup of grasses, moss, cocoons, lined with hair or wool, placed most often in natural sheltered nook or in building or under bridge. Eggs: 4–5, white; I: 14 days; F: 14–16 days, altricial; B: 2–3.

Other Behavior: Nest reused in successive years. Unlike other phoebes, this species rarely uses mud in the construction of its nest.

Habitat: Arid open areas with sparse vegetation.

Voice: Song is repeated "pitseedar"; call a high-pitched downslurred "peeer."

Conservation: BBS: W ↑ C ↑ CBC: ↑

301

Vermilion Flycatcher

Pyrocephalus rubinus

Male

Female

Identification: 6" **MALE:** Scarlet crown and underparts; black back, wings, and tail. **FEMALE:** Gray-brown above; whitish breast lightly streaked with gray; **belly salmon-pink.** **IMM—MALE:** Crown and breast with varying amounts of red; belly salmon-pink; brown back, wings, and tail. **FEMALE:** Like adult female, but with light yellow belly. Imm. plumage kept 1 year.

Feeding: Flies from perch to catch aerial insects.

Nesting: Nest a shallow cup of twigs, weed stalks, grasses, bark, lined with downy materials, placed on horizontal branch of tree 8–55 ft. high. Eggs: 2–3, white with darker marks; I: 12 days; F: 14–16 days, altricial; B: 2.

Other Behavior: Watch for courtship display. With red belly and crest fluffed, male sings and rises with fluttery flight to 50 ft., then continues with level flight and drops down.

Habitat: Wooded or brushy areas near water.

Voice: Repeated "pit pitasee, pit pit pitasee," sometimes given in flight. Call a short "pitz."

Conservation:
BBS: W ⇑ C ⇓ CBC: ⇓

Dusky-capped Flycatcher

Myiarchus tuberculifer

Identification: 7″ Limited to S.E. Ariz. and S.W. N.Mex. **Small; crested;** brownish-olive back; gray breast; **lemon-yellow belly. No reddish brown on dark tail. See Voice.**

Feeding: Flies out from perch to catch aerial insects.

Nesting: Nest in natural cavity or old woodpecker hole lined with fine grass, hair, and fur. Eggs: 4–5, whitish with dark marks; I: 14 days; F: 14–16 days, altricial; B: 1 or more.

Other Behavior: A secretive bird, more often heard than seen. Dependent on tree holes for nests; not known to use nest boxes.

Habitat: Wooded streams and canyons.

Voice: Song a repeated "weet pweeyur"; calls include "pweeyur" and a "prree prree prreeet."

Conservation:
BBS: W ↑ C

Ash-throated Flycatcher

Myiarchus cinerascens

Identification: 8″ Crested; grayish-brown upperparts; pale gray breast; pale yellow belly. Very similar to Brown-crested Flycatcher, but smaller, with a shorter thinner bill and paler underparts. **See Voice.**

Feeding: Flies from perch to catch aerial insects.

Nesting: Nest a natural cavity, old woodpecker nest, or nest box lined with weed stems, rootlets, chips of manure, hair, and fur, and occasionally snakeskins. Eggs: 4–5, whitish with darker marks; I: 15 days; F: 14–16 days, altricial; B: 1.

Other Behavior: Will accept nest box with entrance hole 1½–2 in. in diameter. May nest in seemingly strange spots, such as mailbox, drainpipe, or fence post.

Habitat: Varied: open woods, wooded streams, arid brush.

Voice: Common calls include "prrrt" and burry "kabrik" and "kaweer."

Conservation: BBS: W ↑ C ↑ CBC: ↓

Great Crested Flycatcher

Myiarchus crinitus

Identification: 8″ **Crested; bright yellow belly; strongly reddish-brown tail.** Additional distinctions from other crested flycatchers: lower mandible yellow at base, and throat darker gray. The only crested flycatcher in the East, except for S. Tex. **See Voice.**

Feeding: Flies from perch to catch aerial insects; usually feeds high in treetops. Eats some berries.

Nesting: Nest in natural cavity, old woodpecker hole, or nest box lined with grass, fur, bits of paper, occasionally bits of snakeskin. Eggs: 5–6, whitish with darker marks; I: 12–15 days; F: 14–21 days, altricial; B: 1.

Other Behavior: Crest erected in alarm or curiosity. Aggressive displays involve showing the reddish-brown feathers of the wings and tail by fully spreading them. Will nest in nest box with a 1½–2½ in. diameter entrance hole, but often has to compete with starlings and flickers.

Habitat: Woods and wooded urban areas.

Voice: A loud strongly ascending "wheeep," and a burry "prreet."

Conservation:
BBS: W ⇑ C ↓ CBC: ↓

Brown-crested Flycatcher

Myiarchus tyrannulus

Identification: 8½" **Crested; relatively large bill;** upperparts gray-brown; throat gray; belly lemon-yellow; tail feathers edged with reddish brown down to tip. Voice helpful in distinguishing from other crested flycatchers. **See Voice.**

Feeding: Flies out from perch to catch aerial insects.

Nesting: Nest in natural wood cavity or old woodpecker hole lined with hair, fur, and other soft materials. Eggs: 3–5, whitish with darker marks; I: 13–15 days; F: 12–20 days, altricial; B: 1 or more.

Other Behavior: In Ariz., often nests in abandoned woodpecker holes in saguaro cactus — holes made by Gila Woodpeckers or Northern Flickers. Many species of birds in desert areas depend on these holes for nesting,. and in some cases roosting, including Elf Owl, screech-owls, American Kestrel, Cactus Wren, Purple Martin, and Ash-throated Flycatcher.

Habitat: Arid or semiarid brush with saguaro cactus, streamsides, subtropical woodlands.

Voice: Song a repeated "weer per berg"; calls include a "whit" and "pureer."

Conservation: BBS: W ⇑ C ⇑ CBC: ↓

Sulphur-bellied Flycatcher

Myiodynastes luteiventris

Identification: 8" Limited to S.E. Ariz. **Heavily streaked body; reddish-brown tail; light yellow belly.**

Feeding: Flies out from perch to catch aerial insects, or gleans them from tree leaves. Also eats some berries and seeds.

Nesting: Nest in a natural cavity, often in a sycamore tree, filled with leaves, trash, and debris to nearly the top, where fresh leaves and plant stems are arranged in a circular cup. Eggs: 3–4, whitish with many darker spots; I: 15–16 days; F: 16–18 days, altricial; B: 1 or more.

Other Behavior: Part of courtship involves male and female shaking heads, snapping bills, and duetting. This may be followed by the pair's flying and perching close together.

Habitat: Wooded canyons.

Voice: Most common call a high squeaky "kit kit squeezya" or "squeegee," like a rubber ducky.

Conservation: BBS: W ⇑ C

Tropical Kingbird
Cassin's Kingbird

Tyrannus melancholicus   Tyrannus vociferans

Tropical

Cassin's

Identification: 9" TROPICAL: Local and limited to S.E. Ariz. **Large bill; light gray head with slightly darker ear patch; breast washed olive; deeply notched brownish tail. CASSIN'S: Bill relatively short; head, throat, and upper breast dark gray; tail squarish with no white on outer edges and tipped with buff;** belly dull yellow.

Feeding: Both fly out from perches to catch aerial insects; also eat some berries. May skim over water surface to drink water.

Nesting: Tropical — Nest of moss, bark strips, and plant down, placed on branch of tree 8–22 ft. high. Eggs: 3–4, whitish with darker marks; I: 15–16 days; F: 17–19 days, altricial; B: 1. Cassin's — Bulky nest of twigs, plant stems, rootlets, lined with finer materials, placed on a horizontal limb 20–45 ft. high. Eggs: 3–4, white with darker marks; I: 12–14 days; F: 16–17 days, altricial; B: 1–2.

Other Behavior: Tropical Kingbird's courtship includes birds calling loudly while flapping their wings and pointing their bills downward. Both species aggressive to larger birds that come near the nest.

Tropical   Cassin's

Habitat: Tropical: open woodlands. Cassin's: sparse woods, dry scrub.

Voice: Tropical's call is metallic twittering. Cassin's common call is "chikweeer," accent on 2nd syllable; also "kideedeedee."

Conservation:
Tropical:
CBC: ↓
Cassin's:
BBS: W ⇓ C ⇑ CBC: ↑

308

Thick-billed Kingbird

Tyrannus crassirostris

Identification: 9″ Limited to S.E. Ariz. and S.W. N.Mex. **Thick-necked; heavy-billed;** brown upperparts; whitish underparts; pale yellow wash across belly (brighter in fall). **Imm:** Dark head and wings; gray back; bright yellow belly. Imm. plumage kept into winter.

Feeding: Eats insects caught in the air and off the ground.

Nesting: Nest a thin loosely built platform of twigs and grasses, placed up to 60 ft. high in a tree. Eggs: 3–4, white with dark marks; I: ?; F: ?, altricial; B: 1 or possibly more.

Other Behavior: At the beginning of the nesting season, sings a song at dawn that consists of extended 2-second phrases.

Habitat: Wooded streamsides.

Voice: A short "pureet" and a loud "weeerr."

Conservation:
BBS: W ⇑ C

Western Kingbird

Tyrannus verticalis

Identification: 9″ Most widespread kingbird in West. Relatively **short bill; head, throat, and upper breast light gray;** belly bright yellow; **square-tipped tail black** with **thin white edges,** which are distinctive but sometimes hard to see.

Feeding: Eats mostly insects caught in midair; also some berries.

Nesting: Bulky nest of twigs, plant stems, rootlets, lined with finer materials, sometimes trash, placed in trees 8–40 ft. high. Eggs: 3–5, white with darker marks; I: 13–15 days; F: 16–18 days, altricial; B: 1 or possibly more.

Other Behavior: Has orange-red crown that is normally concealed, but exposed during aggressive encounters. Like other kingbirds, it is aggressive to large birds near the nest.

Habitat: Open areas with some trees or shrubs.

Voice: Call is "kit," sometimes extended to "kit kit kittledot."

Conservation:
BBS: w ↑ c ↑ CBC: ↓

Eastern Kingbird

Tyrannus tyrannus

Identification: 9″ **Black upperparts; white underparts;** conspicuous **white tip to black tail.**

Feeding: Sits on perches and flies out after insects, catching them in the air or off the ground.

Nesting: Somewhat disheveled nest of soft materials, such as weeds, moss, bark strips, feathers, cloth, and string, placed near the tip of a horizontal branch 10–20 ft. high. Eggs: 3–4, white with dark marks; I: 14–16 days; F: 14–17 days, altricial; B: 1.

Other Behavior: Male patrols territory of about an acre, in morning and afternoon, giving "zeer" and "kitter" calls. When the female first arrives on the territory, the male may chase her; after that, whenever they meet, they do a fluttering flight and give "kitter" call. Other kingbirds are allowed in the territory, if they do not get too close to the nest or try to mate with the female. Larger birds are chased out of the area, with the kingbirds diving onto their back and chasing them much farther than the territorial boundaries; a special aerial tumbling flight may occur after this. During incubation, the female may be aggressive toward the male in the vicinity of the nest. Once the young hatch, both parents feed them.

Habitat: Open areas with some trees.

Voice: Calls include "kitterkitterkitter," "kt'zee kt'zee," and "zeer."

Conservation:
BBS: W ↑ C ↑ CBC: ↓

Scissor-tailed Flycatcher

Tyrannus forficatus

Identification: 14″ **Very long split tail;** pale gray body; **pinkish wash on flanks. IN FLIGHT:** Underwings bright pinkish orange. **IMM:** Tail long, but shorter than adult's; body paler with little or no pink on belly. Imm. plumage kept into winter.

Feeding: Flies from perch to catch insects on the ground or in the air.

Nesting: Nest a loose collection of soft natural and human-made materials, placed on horizontal limb or telephone pole. Eggs: 4–5, white with dark marks; I: 12–15 days; F: 14–16 days, altricial; B: 1.

Other Behavior: Courtship involves male doing spectacular flight to about 100 ft.; he then drops down in a series of shallow arcs, then may fly higher and somersault in midair before finally landing. Flights are accompanied by bill snapping and "kakweee" calls. From a few to 250 birds may roost together in trees at night; during breeding, female stays on eggs or with nestlings and does not go to roost.

Habitat: Open areas with scattered trees.

Voice: Call a "kit" and, during display flight, a "kakweee kakweee."

Conservation:
BBS: W ⇓ C ↑ CBC: ↓

Rose-throated Becard

Pachyramphus aglaiae

Male

Identification: 6½" Limited to S. Ariz. and S. Tex. **Stocky, thick-necked, and short-tailed. MALE: Dark gray above, light below; rosy patch on throat. FEMALE: Gray cap; brown wings and tail;** light buffy underparts. **IMM:** Like adult female; imm. male has some rosy feathers on throat.

Feeding: Flies out from perch to catch insects in air or off leaves; eats some seeds.

Nesting: Long pendant nest of woven plant fibers, suspended from the end of a tree branch 30–50 ft. high. Eggs: 4–6, white with darker marks; I: ?; F: ?, altricial; B: 1.

Other Behavior: Often perches hidden in foliage; best located by call.

Habitat: Large trees along rivers or streams.

Voice: Rapid chattering followed by a descending "seeeoh."

Conservation: TREND UNKNOWN.

Northern Shrike
Loggerhead Shrike

Lanius excubitor   *Lanius ludovicianus*

Northern adult

Northern immature

Loggerhead

Identification: Northern 10" Loggerhead 9"
Northern Shrike breeds in Far North, generally
only seen in winter; Loggerhead widespread in
lower 48 states. **NORTHERN: Rounded forehead;
long strongly hooked bill; thin black mask;**
pale gray back blends with whitish breast. **IMM:**
Mask may be faint; grayish-brown head and back;
barring on breast and belly. Imm. plumage kept
until spring. **LOGGERHEAD: Flattened forehead;
relatively short, slightly hooked bill; thick
black mask;** dark gray back contrasts with whitish
breast. **IN FLIGHT:** White patches on wings and
tail corners in both species.

Feeding: Both swoop on prey from perches. Prey on
insects, small birds, and small animals.

Nesting: Nest of twigs, bark strips, placed in shrub or
tree. Northern—Eggs: 2–9, gray with dark marks; I:
15–16 days; F: 20 days, altricial; B: ? Loggerhead—
Eggs: 4–7, gray with dark marks; I: 10–17 days; F:
17–21 days, altricial; B: 2.

Other Behavior: Both store prey by impaling on thorns.

Northern   Loggerhead

Habitat: Open
country with some
shrubs and trees.

Voice: Song for
both a series of
whistles and calls;
call a "chak chak."

Conservation:
Northern:
CBC: ↑
Loggerhead:
BBS: W ⇓ C ⇓ CBC: ↓
Loggerhead
endangered in Can.
and on San
Clemente Is., Calif.

Bell's Vireo
Vireo bellii

Identification: 4¾" Indistinct whitish eye-ring and lores ("spectacles"); 2 wing bars, the upper 1 faint or lacking; some birds may have a whitish eyebrow. **In East, birds are greenish above and yellowish below; in West, birds are grayish above and whitish below.** Plumage of this species varies in presence or absence of eye-ring, wing bars, spectacles, and eyebrow. Generally indistinct and hard to identify when not singing; song is distinctive among vireos.

Feeding: Very active. Forages low to ground in dense underbrush, shrubs. Eats insects, spiders, and fruits.

Nesting: Nest of bark, plant fibers, and cocoons lined with hair and fine grasses, suspended from fork of tree branch 1–10 ft. above ground. Eggs: 3–5, white with brown spots; I: 14 days; F: 11–12 days, altricial; B: 2.

Other Behavior: The Calif. subspecies is endangered due to loss of riparian habitat and the invasion of remaining habitat fragments by Brown-headed Cowbirds, which parasitize this vireo's nests. Restoration of habitat and local cowbird control may facilitate some recovery.

Habitat: Riparian brush, mesquite, thorny thickets.

Voice: Song a rapid series of harsh notes increasing in loudness, sometimes ending with an up or down inflection.

Conservation:
BBS: W ↑ C ⇓ CBC: ↑ Calif. subspecies, Least Bell's Vireo (*V. b. pusillus*), is endangered in U.S.

315

Black-capped Vireo

Vireo atricapillus

Identification: 4½" Small; dark cap and cheek; bold white eye-ring and lores ("spectacles"); 2 yellowish wing bars. **MALE:** Glossy black cap. **FEMALE:** Dark gray cap.

Feeding: Forages for food among low dwarf oaks and other thickets. Eats insects, spiders, and fruit.

Nesting: Nest of grasses, dried leaves, bark strips, catkins, and spider's cocoons, bound with spider's silk, lined with pine needles and fine grasses, suspended from fork of tree or shrub branch 1–15 ft. above the ground. Eggs: 3–5, white; I: 14–17 days; F: 10–12 days, altricial; B: 2.

Other Behavior: Very active. Most often seen in low brush. Populations are perilously declining due to habitat loss from housing development, brush clearance for range management, and sheep and goat grazing. There is also extremely heavy cowbird parasitism on this species. Despite some management attempts for recovery, the future survival of this species is in doubt.

Habitat: Shrubby hillside thickets, oak scrublands.

Voice: Song a rapid series of harsh 2–3 note phrases; call "chitit."

Conservation:
TREND UNKNOWN. Endangered in U.S. Ninety percent of U.S population is under immediate threat from land development.

Gray Vireo

Vireo vicinior

Identification: 5½" Grayish above; light gray below; wings and tail dark; 2 faint wing bars and faint eye-ring; relatively long tail.

Feeding: Takes food from the ground and gleans low foliage, eating insects and caterpillars.

Nesting: Nest of leaves, grasses, plant fibers, spiderweb, lined with fine grasses, suspended from fork of tree or shrub branch 2–8 ft. above the ground. Eggs: 3–5, rosy with brown spots; I: 13–14 days; F: 13–14 days, altricial; B: 2.

Other Behavior: The Gray Vireo is often seen restlessly flitting through low foliage, rapidly flicking its tail as it forages for food. Like many of the vireos, this species is a frequent victim of cowbird parasitism. Sometimes it builds a 2nd floor of nesting material, covering and killing the cowbird eggs that have been laid among its own eggs. It then lays a new clutch of its own eggs. Interestingly, despite cowbird parasitism, its population seems to be growing.

Habitat: Dry shrubby areas, chaparral, sparse woodlands.

Voice: Song a short rapid series of musical notes, like "chuweechuwee-chuweechuwee," with long pauses between series.

Conservation: BBS: W ⇑ C

Solitary Vireo
Vireo solitarius

West Coast form

Identification: 5½" **Gray head; bold white eye-ring and lores ("spectacles"); 2 bold white wing bars.** Eastern birds have an olive back and yellowish flanks; Rocky Mountain and Great Basin birds (*V. s. plumbeus*) basically all gray and white; West Coast birds have grayish-green back.

Feeding: Forages for food in tree foliage, eating insects, spiders, and some fruit. Occasionally hawks for insects from perch.

Nesting: Nest of forbs, grasses, strips of inner bark, spiderweb, and rootlets lined with vine tendrils, pine needles, and decorated with lichens, suspended from fork of horizontal tree branch 3–30 ft. above ground. Eggs: 3–5, white with brown spots; I: 11–12 days; F: 14 days, altricial; B: 1–2.

Other Behavior: Moves about more sluggishly than the smaller vireos. Stays in treetops. Frequently parasitized by the Brown-headed Cowbird, which lays its eggs among the vireo's eggs.

Habitat: Mixed coniferous and deciduous woods.

Voice: Song is a short series of high-pitched whistled notes with long pauses between each series; call note a harsh "churr."

Conservation:
BBS: W ↑ C ⇑ CBC: ↑

Hutton's Vireo
Vireo huttoni

Identification: 4½" Small; white eye-ring broken at top; whitish lores; 2 bold white wing bars; short stout bill. Looks very similar to Ruby-crowned Kinglet; distinguished by thicker bill.

Feeding: Gleans food from tree foliage, eating insects, spiders, and some seeds.

Nesting: Nest of lichens, mosses, plant down, and feathers, bound with spiderweb, lined with fine grasses, and suspended from fork of tree branch 6–25 ft. above the ground. Eggs: 3–5, white with brown spots; I: 14 days; F: 14 days, altricial; B: ?

Other Behavior: Joins mixed-species flocks in winter that include the smaller Ruby-crowned Kinglet.

Habitat: Moist woods, especially live oaks.

Voice: A series of 2-note, buzzy, whistled phrases with short pauses between, like "zooee, zeeah, zeeay."

Conservation: BBS: W ↑ C CBC: ⇑

Warbling Vireo

Vireo gilvus

Western form

Identification: 5½" **Whitish eyebrow; faint eyeline and pale lores; whitish underneath** with variable amounts of yellow; yellow, if present, is brightest on flanks. Western birds slightly greener and yellower; eastern birds grayer.

Feeding: Gleans prey from tree foliage by both searching through and hovering above it. Eats insects and some berries.

Nesting: Nest of leaves, bark strips, grasses, and plant down, bound with spiderweb, lined with plant stems and horsehair, suspended in horizontal branch of tree 4–90 ft. above ground. Eggs: 3–5, white with brown spots; I: 12–14 days; F: 12–16 days, altricial; B: ?

Other Behavior: Best detected by its long, flowing, warbling song, which it sings throughout the day. Commonly parasitized by the Brown-headed Cowbird.

Habitat: Deciduous woods and streamside shrubs; aspen groves.

Voice: Song is an extended rambling series of slurred whistles.

Conservation: BBS: W ↑ C ↑ CBC: →

Philadelphia Vireo
Vireo philadelphicus

Identification: 5" White eyebrow; dark eyeline and dark lores; variably yellowish underneath, with brightest yellow on the center of the throat and upper breast.

Feeding: Feeds at end of tree branches and in dense foliage, hovering before or hanging from twigs and branches. Eats insects, spiders, and fruit.

Nesting: Nest of lichens, birch bark, grasses, plant down, bound with spiderweb, lined with fine grasses and pine needles, suspended from horizontal branch of tree 10–90 ft. above the ground. Eggs: 3–5, white with brown spots; I: 14 days; F: 12–14 days, altricial; B: ?

Other Behavior: Its song resembles that of the Red-eyed Vireo but usually is higher, thinner, with the phrases slower.

Habitat: Open woods and streamside shrubs.

Voice: Song is short, high-pitched, whistled phrases with pauses between, like "teeyay, teeyee, teeyit."

Conservation:
BBS: W ↑ C CBC: →

Red-eyed Vireo

Vireo olivaceus

Identification: 6" Two eyebrows — a white one and a black one above it; dark eyeline; gray cap. Red eye visible from close up. **IMM:** Like adult, but with brown eyes; eyes change to red in spring. ▶The closely related Yellow-green Vireo, *V. flavoviridis*, has similar gray cap and eye patterns, but is otherwise yellowish overall. It lives in Mex. and only occasionally is seen in S. Tex. or coastal Calif.

Feeding: Forages in foliage of treetops, eating mostly insects. Also eats wild fruits and berries.

Nesting: Nest of fine grasses, rootlets, paper, grapevine bark, spiderweb, decorated with lichens, placed in horizontal tree or shrub branch 2–60 ft. above the ground. Eggs: 3–5, white with dark marks; I: 11–14 days; F: 10–12 days, altricial; B: 1–2.

Other Behavior: Female does all nest building and incubation. During incubation, the male sings faster, 50–60 phrases per minute. When he stops, the female comes off the nest and he feeds her, or they feed together. She then resumes incubating. This species is one of those most frequently parasitized by cowbirds.

Habitat: Deciduous woods, rural to suburban.

Voice: Short, medium-pitched, whistled phrases with space in between, like "eeyay, oolee, eeyup"; calls "nyaah" and "tjjjj."

Conservation: BBS: W ↓ C ↓ CBC: ↓

Gray Jay

Perisoreus canadensis

Identification: 12″ **White forehead; dark gray cap; short bill.** Varies geographically in darkness of gray upperparts and brightness of white underparts.

Feeding: Feeds on wide variety of items, including small rodents, invertebrates, the young and eggs of birds, berries, fruit, and human food scraps. Attracted to campsites, where it is unafraid of humans, takes handouts, and boldly steals food, even snatching it off plates.

Nesting: Nest of twigs, bark, mosses, lined with feathers and fur, placed on horizontal branch of tree, usually conifer, 6–28 ft. from ground. Eggs: 2–5, pale green or white with dark blotches; I: 16–18 days; F: 15 days, altricial; B: 1.

Other Behavior: Has special mucus-secreting glands inside bill, which allow it to use sticky saliva to form berries into balls. It stores these for future use by sticking them to tree branches or lichen clumps. Moves to lower elevations in winter. When food is scarce, large groups may move to areas outside their normal range.

Habitat: Mostly northern coniferous forests.

Voice: Often quiet; alarm call is a harsh "churrr"; many other calls given.

Conservation: BBS: W ↑ C ⇓ CBC: ⇑

323

Steller's Jay
Cyanocitta stelleri

Identification: 13″ **Prominent crest; brownish-black head, breast, and back** grading to a **deep blue on wings, belly, rump, and tail.** Varies geographically in prominence and color of small streaks on forehead and marks around eye.

Feeding: Eats acorns and other nuts and seeds, insects, berries and fruit, small birds, frogs. Takes table scraps from humans at campsites.

Nesting: Bulky nest of twigs, leaves, mud, lined with rootlets, grass, placed 9–90 ft. high in tree, shrub, or occasionally in tree hollow or building. Eggs: 2–6, blue or pale green marked with brown; I: 16 days; F: 18 days, altricial; B: 1.

Other Behavior: Young stay with parents into winter months. May assemble in larger numbers at good feeding spots. Occasionally hybridizes with Blue Jay. In winter, may move to lower elevations.

Habitat: Mostly mountain coniferous forests.

Voice: Most common call is a repeated "shaack shaack shaack."

Conservation:
BBS: W ↑ C CBC: ↑

Blue Jay
Cyanocitta cristata

Identification: 12″ Crested; black collar and necklace; wings and tail spotted with white; blue above, grayish below.

Feeding: Eats acorns and other nuts; also fruit, insects, bird eggs and nestlings. Comes to bird feeders for sunflower seed and cracked corn, which it may cache.

Nesting: Nest of twigs, bark, leaves, and human-made objects, lined with fine rootlets, placed in a tree. May build preliminary nest of a loose platform of twigs that is not completed or used for breeding. Eggs: 4–5, greenish blue, spotted with brown; I: 17 days; F: 17–19 days, altricial; B: 1–2.

Other Behavior: In fall, forms large roaming feeding flocks that divide into smaller groups by midwinter. In spring, courtship flocks fly about in the mornings in a follow-the-leader fashion and give a variety of calls. These flocks are believed to be composed of 1 female and a number of males; the female is always in the lead as the birds take flight. After the flock lands, the males display with bobbing, raising and lowering their whole body repeatedly, while giving the "toolool" call. During breeding, the birds are quiet and inconspicuous. Blue Jays will mob and dive at hawks, giving "jaay" calls.

Habitat: Woods and suburbs.

Voice: A harsh "jaay, jaay," given in alarm and within flock; a liquid "toolool"; and a grating ratchetlike call. Also imitates hawk calls.

Conservation:
BBS: W ⇑ C ↓ CBC: ↑

Santa Cruz Island Scrub-Jay
Western Scrub-Jay
Aphelocoma insularis   *Aphelocoma californica*

Santa Cruz Island

Western

Identification: 12″ Both species have **blue head, wings, and tail; no crest; throat streaked gray and white bordered by a bluish necklace; thin white eyebrow; grayish back.** SANTA CRUZ ISLAND: Lives only on Santa Cruz Island, Calif. **Deep blue on head, wings, and tail; large thick bill.** WESTERN: **Sky blue on head, wings, and tail; shorter thinner bill.**

Feeding: Eat insects, acorns, pine seeds, invertebrates, eggs and nestlings of birds, frogs, berries, fruit. Caches food. Western Scrub-Jay may steal seeds from Clark's Nutcrackers; comes to bird feeders.

Nesting: Nest of twigs, grass, lined with fibers, rootlets, placed in shrub or bush. Eggs: 2–6, pale green or gray with marks of reddish brown; I: 16–19 days; F: 18 days, altricial; B: 1–2.

Other Behavior: Found in pairs that live throughout the year on a fixed territory. Can become tame at picnic areas, parks, and feeders.

Western

Habitat: Variety of habitats, including brushy, open country, desert scrub, orchards, canyons.

Voice: Calls are varied and include a chattering "kaykaykaykay."

Conservation: Santa Cruz Island: TREND UNKNOWN. Western: BBS: W ↑ C ⇑

Mexican Jay
Aphelocoma ultramarina

Identification: 12″ No crest; uniformly blue above; gray below; no other markings.

Feeding: Eats acorns, invertebrates, seeds, fruit.

Nesting: Nest of twigs lined with rootlets and grass, placed in tree 6–45 ft. above ground. Eggs: 4–5, green or blue-green with dark speckles; I: 17–18 days; F: 24–26 days, altricial; B: 1–2.

Other Behavior: Western race of Ariz. and N.Mex. lives in flocks of 6–20 birds all year, consisting of 2 breeding pairs and offspring from previous years, which help raise nestlings. Tex. race is solitary breeder.

Habitat: Mixed forests of pine and oaks; often in canyons along streams.

Voice: A repeated "weenk weenk," plus many other calls.

Conservation: BBS: W ↑ C CBC: ↑

Pinyon Jay

Gymnorhinus cyanocephalus

Identification: 10" **Blue overall; long wedge-shaped bill; short tail;** faint white streaks on throat. Often seen in large wandering flocks. **Imm:** Paler overall, with grayish-blue underparts. Imm. plumage kept 1 year.

Feeding: Eats primarily seeds of conifers, especially pinyon pines. Caches seeds near nesting areas. Also eats insects, fruit, bird eggs.

Nesting: Breeds colonially, occasionally with 1–3 nests in tree. Nest a deep cup of sticks, weeds, grasses, lined with wool, hair, placed in tree 3–75 ft. above ground. Eggs: 3–6, pale blue or green with dark speckles; I: 16 days; F: 21–25 days, altricial; B: 1–2.

Other Behavior: Lives in large flocks of about 250 or more birds that forage together, roaming over about 13 square miles. Roosts communally when not breeding. Roost located up to 3 miles away from feeding area. Pairs remain together year round. Rarely breeds before 3 years of age.

Habitat: Semiarid foothills with pinyon pine and juniper.

Voice: A rapid series of "kway" sounds and a descending "craaah." Many other calls.

Conservation: BBS: W ↓ C ⇑ CBC: ↑

Clark's Nutcracker
Nucifraga columbiana

Identification: 13" **Gray with black wings;** black central tail feathers. **IN FLIGHT:** White on inner trailing edge of wings and on outer tail feathers is conspicuous.

Feeding: Main food is pinyon or whitebark pine nuts, which it caches. Opens nuts with bill, or by wedging in a crevice, or holding with foot and cracking them open. Scavenges at campsites and picnic areas; eats suet at feeders. Also eats insects, bird eggs and nestlings, fruit.

Nesting: Nest of twigs and bark lined with fibrous bark, pulp, hair, placed 9–150 ft. high in tree. Eggs: 2–6, pale green with brown spots; I: 16–18 days; F: 22–28 days, altricial; B: 1.

Other Behavior: On ground, often walks rather than hopping like other jays. Pair may cache 22,000–33,000 nuts and seeds on south-facing hills each fall, and retrieve them by memory the next spring as they feed their young. Irruptive movements occur about every 15 years, when pines fail to produce many seeds. May venture all the way to Pacific Coast at these times.

Habitat: Coniferous forests in mountains.

Voice: A harsh nasal "kraaaa."

Conservation:
BBS: W ⇑ C CBC: ⇑

Black-billed Magpie

Pica pica

Identification: 20″ **Body boldly marked with black and white; long tail; black bill.** Wings and tail are iridescent, and sometimes appear greenish. **IN FLIGHT:** Bold white wing patches.

Feeding: Feeds mostly on ground. Mainly eats insects; also berries, fruit, bird eggs and nestlings, carrion at roadsides. Scavenges at picnic sites. At feeders, eats a variety of foods, including sunflower seeds and cracked corn.

Nesting: Solitary or in loose colony. Large domed nest of thorny twigs has side entrance and inner cup of mud lined with soft material, placed near crown of tree or in shrub. Eggs: 2–9, blue-green with brown speckles; I: 14–23 days; F: 10 days, altricial; B: 1.

Other Behavior: Communal roosts may be used throughout the year. Can mob other birds such as gulls or kites, to make them drop their food, which magpies then take. The 1930s saw efforts to exterminate this imagined threat to crops and livestock; thankfully, this is no longer the case.

Habitat: Open areas with trees and shrubs; farmlands, gardens, parks.

Voice: Alarm call a rapid series of "chak" notes; also gives an ascending "maaag."

Conservation: BBS: W ↓ C ⇓ CBC: ↓

Yellow-billed Magpie

Pica nuttalli

Identification: 19″ Limited to central Calif. **Body boldly marked with black and white; long tail; yellow bill.** Wings and tail are iridescent, and sometimes appear greenish. **IN FLIGHT:** Bold white wing patches.

Feeding: Feeds primarily on ground; eats insects, but also fruit, nuts, bird eggs and nestlings, carrion. At feeders, eats a variety of foods, including sunflower seed and cracked corn.

Nesting: Nests in loose colonies with 1 nest in a tree. Prefers trees near water. Large domed nest consists of sticks with inner bowl of mud lined with finer material, placed 45–60 ft. high. Eggs: 5–8, olive with brown marks; I: 18 days; F: 49 days, altricial; B: 1.

Other Behavior: More sociable and tolerant of humans than Black-billed Magpie. Has communal feeding areas that several colonies may share. In 1930s, there were organized efforts to exterminate this imagined threat to crops and livestock; this is no longer the case.

Habitat: Farmlands, protected valleys with streams.

Voice: High-pitched "chek" and other calls.

Conservation: BBS: W ↓ C CBC: ⇑

American Crow
Northwestern Crow

Corvus brachyrhynchos   Corvus caurinus

American

Northwestern

Identification: American 18", Northwestern 17"
Large; all black; tip of tail square or slightly
rounded. **Best distinguished by range and calls.
See Voice.**

Feeding: American Crow eats insects, nuts, seeds, corn,
fruit, bird eggs and nestlings, carrion. Comes to bird
feeders. Northwestern Crow eats fish, shellfish, crabs,
carrion, offal, insects, human food scraps, nuts, seabird
eggs.

Nesting: Nest of twigs, sticks, lined with bark, grass,
moss, placed high in trees. Eggs: 4–5, bluish green to
greenish buff, speckled with brown; I: 18 days; F:
28–35 days, altricial; B: 1–2.

Other Behavior: Both cache food and have communal
roosts. In addition, both have helpers at the nest —
offspring from previous years that help with territory
defense and feeding of the young. Northwestern Crows
breed in small colonies or pairs.

American   N.W.

Habitat: American:
varied habitats.
Northwestern:
along coast.

Voice: American call
a long, descending
"caaaw."
Northwestern call a
lower, hoarser
"caar." Both have
other calls.

Conservation:
American:
BBS: W ↓ C ↑ CBC: ↑
Northwestern:
BBS: W ↑ C CBC: ⇑

Common Raven
Chihuahuan Raven
Corvus corax Corvus cryptoleucus

Common

Chihuahuan

Identification: Common 24", Chihuahuan 19"
Both are large, all black, with massive bill;
when flying, tip of tail is **wedge-shaped,** rather
than square or slightly rounded as in crows. Also
note range, habitat, and voice. **COMMON: Very
large; long shaggy feathers on the chin and
throat; often soars like a hawk. CHIHUAHUAN:
Smaller; less shaggy throat; less massive bill.**

Feeding: Both eat carrion, shellfish, rodents, insects,
seeds, fruit, food scraps, bird eggs and nestlings. Both
cache food.

Nesting: Nest is bulky mass of twigs, branches, earth,
lined with roots, moss, hair, placed on mostly cliffs, but
also trees and buildings. Eggs: 3–8, blue to greenish
with brown marks; I: 21 days; F: 35–42 days, altricial;
B: 1.

Other Behavior: Males have elaborate courtship flight
maneuvers, including steep dives, tumbles, and barrel
rolls. Both have large communal roosts in fall and
winter, generally consisting of nonbreeding birds.
Breeding pairs tend to stay on their territories year
round. Featured in many Native American myths.

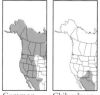

Common   Chihuahuan

Habitat: Common:
mountains, forests,
canyons, deserts;
coast. Chihuahuan:
arid areas.

Voice: Common
call a very low
"gronk";
Chihuahuan call a
higher-pitched
"kraak."

Conservation:
Common:
BBS: W ⇑ C ⇑ CBC: ⇑
Chihuahuan:
BBS: W ↓ C ⇓ CBC: ⇓

Sky Lark
Alauda arvensis

Identification: 7″ Stocky; brown-streaked; small crest (often raised); white outer tail feathers. IN FLIGHT: Note white on tail and white trailing edge of inner upperwing.

Feeding: Feeds on ground, eating weed seeds and grain, as well as insects, spiders, and earthworms.

Nesting: Nest a shallow hollow in ground lined with grasses and rootlets. Eggs: 3–4, grayish with darker spots; I: 11–12 days; F: 9–10 days, altricial; B: 1 or possibly more.

Other Behavior: Male does courtship flight, rising hundreds of feet high and singing at top before diving down. Male also raises crest and tail, and droops wings, as he moves about prospective mate. Inconspicuous most of year.

Habitat: Open ground with low vegetation.

Voice: Song is varied musical trills given in flight; call a short "chirup."

Conservation: Introduced to N. America on Vancouver Island, B.C., in 1903 and is now established there and on mainland.

Horned Lark
Eremophila alpestris

Identification: 8″ **Distinctive black facial marks** — black forehead with black "horns" (more prominent on males); black line from bill to eye and down cheek; and black bib. Other areas on **face, throat, and belly vary from whitish to deep yellow** based on subspecies. IN FLIGHT: Note **light underwings; black tail with white outer feathers.**

Feeding: Feeds on ground, eating weed seeds and grain, insects, spiders.

Nesting: Nest a depression in ground lined with grasses, placed near a grass clump or clod of manure. Eggs: 3–5, gray, sometimes spotted with brown; I: 11 days; F: 9–12 days, altricial; B: 1–3.

Other Behavior: Male does spectacular courtship flight up to 800 ft. high, circling and singing at the top, then dives down quietly. Male also raises "horns" and walks stiffly in front of female during courtship. Female starts 2nd brood about a week after young leave nest. Forms large flocks during migration and in winter. Has expanded range in East.

Habitat: Open ground with low vegetation.

Voice: Song a light twittering, given during display flight; call "tsee-titi" or "zeet."

Conservation:
BBS: W ↓ C ↓ CBC: ↓

335

Purple Martin

Progne subis

Male (l.), female (r.)

Immature male,
1st summer

Identification: 8″ MALE: **All dark purple** with black wings and tail. Purple areas are shiny. FEMALE: Gray chest; **whitish belly; dull purple back;** black wings and tail. IMM: Female is like adult female. Male, in first fall, is also like adult female. The next spring and summer, he resembles adult female, but has more shiny purple on back and is slightly darker on the belly. Imm. plumage kept 1 year.

Feeding: Feeds on the wing, eating insects.

Nesting: Colonial nester in East, primarily in man-made birdhouses consisting of many individual compartments. In West, tends to nest singly, in natural cavities in trees and in holes in saguaro cactus. Nest composed of mud, sticks, twigs, feathers, bark, paper; fresh green leaves added during incubation. Eggs: 5–6, white; I: 15–16 days; F: 27–35 days, altricial; B: 1.

Other Behavior: Native Americans were the first to put out hollow gourds for breeding martins. Now, thousands of people put out martin nest boxes. After nesting, young and adults gather in premigratory roosts of many thousands.

Habitat: Open areas, often near water.

Voice: Song is pairs of notes followed by guttural warble, given during pair interactions. "Cher cher" call given near nest.

Conservation: BBS: W ⇑ C ↑ CBC: ↑

336

Tree Swallow
Tachycineta bicolor

Adult

Immature female

Identification: 6″ Upperparts iridescent blue; underparts bright white; dark on head encloses eye. In fall, iridescent upperparts may appear greenish. Adult females may have a brownish forehead. **Imm:** Male like adult male. Female has mostly brown upperparts, mixed with varying amounts of iridescent blue; over 2 years, this plumage gradually becomes like adult's.

Feeding: Eats insects while flying. Before migration, will land in bayberry shrubs and eat berries.

Nesting: Often in loose colony. Grass nest lined with feathers, placed in tree cavity, old woodpecker hole, or nest box. Eggs: 5–6, white; I: 14–15 days; F: 21 days, altricial; B: 1–2.

Other Behavior: The Tree Swallow is the only N. American passerine with an imm.-plumaged female in the 1st (and sometimes 2nd) year. This imm. plumage allows them to approach breeding adults and their nests without being chased away. This, in turn, lets them monitor breeding pairs and be ready to replace any adult female that dies during the nesting season.

Habitat: Open areas near woods and water.

Voice: Song, given by male, is 3 descending notes, followed by warble. "Cheedeep" call is given during alarm.

Conservation: BBS: W ↑ C ↑ CBC: ↓ Competes for nest sites with starlings, House Sparrows, House Wrens, and bluebirds.

Violet-green Swallow
Tachycineta thalassina

Male

Identification: 5" Upperparts iridescent green; underparts bright white; white extends above eye; white also extends onto either side of **rump** (looking like a white rump patch in flight). Females may appear more bronze-green; males more purple-green.

Feeding: Feeds in small groups or loose flocks. Eats insects, which it catches in the air. Sometimes forages on the ground, on accumulations of insects like mayflies.

Nesting: Nest of straw, grasses, string, and hair, lined with feathers, placed in natural cavity, old woodpecker hole, or nest box. Eggs: 4–6, white; I: 13–14 days; F: 21 days, altricial; B: 1–2.

Other Behavior: Where nest sites are numerous, may nest in groups. Outside the breeding season, forms large flocks.

Habitat: Open mountain woodlands, suburbs.

Voice: "Chee chee" call, most common near nest, is given during alarm and aggressive interactions.

Conservation: BBS: W ↑ C ⇑ CBC: ↑ House Sparrow is competitor for nest sites.

Northern Rough-winged Swallow
Stelgidopteryx serripennis

Identification: 5″ **Upperparts grayish brown; chin, breast, and flanks grayish;** belly white. Slower deeper wingbeat than similar Bank Swallow.

Feeding: Eats insects while flying.

Nesting: Alone or in small scattered groups. Sometimes a few pairs will nest on the periphery of Bank Swallow colonies. Nest of grass, leaves, twigs, moss, straw, placed in cavity or crevice, such as cave, old tunnel of Bank Swallows, drainpipe; rarely uses tree hole. Eggs: 4–8, white; I: 16–18 days; F: 18–21 days, altricial; B: 1.

Other Behavior: After the breeding season, forms large flocks that roost together in marshes, mangrove islands, sugar cane fields.

Habitat: Open areas, especially near water and cutaway banks.

Voice: A harsh "brrrt" given during alarm and aggressive encounters.

Conservation: BBS: W ↓ C ↓ CBC: ⇓

Bank Swallow

Riparia riparia

Identification: 5″ Upperparts dark brown, underparts white except for brown breastband. Rapid shallow wingbeat.

Feeding: Eats a wide variety of insects.

Nesting: Highly colonial. Nest of grasses, weeds, lined with feathers, placed in a tunnel in vertical sandy river bank, coastal cliff, gravel quarry; nests may be as close as 1 ft. apart. Bird excavates nest tunnel; it is about 20–40 in. long, slopes upward, and ends in a wider chamber, where nest is placed. Eggs: 3–6, white; I: 12–26 days; F: 22 days, altricial; B: 1–2.

Other Behavior: Older birds return to nest sites well before 1st-year birds, and they choose nest sites higher on the bank. Bank Swallows are not as site-tenacious as some other swallows with more stable nest sites. After breeding, hundreds or thousands may form flocks that feed and roost together. Nests are often placed in stream banks and gravel quarries where development and quarry operations destroy them.

Habitat: Open areas near water with cutaway banks.

Voice: Contact call between pair is a harsh "tchrrt tchrrt"; a long twittering may be given during courtship; also a rapid buzzy chatter.

Conservation: BBS: W ↓ C ↓ CBC: ↓

Cliff Swallow

Hirundo pyrrhonota

Identification: 6″ Buffy rump; whitish forehead; dark reddish-brown throat. Also, belly is white; back has white streaking; **tip of tail is square.**

Feeding: Feeds in close-knit flocks. Eats mainly insects; rarely berries.

Nesting: Colonial, sometimes in enormous colonies. Nest a spherical cavity with narrow entrance tunnel, built of mud pellets mixed with a little grass, and lined with grass and feathers. Nests are sometimes built on cliffs, but usually under bridges, in culverts, and on buildings. Eggs: 2–5, white with brown blotches; I: 12–15 days; F: 24 days, altricial; B: 1–3.

Other Behavior: Birds within a colony breed synchronously. May reuse old nesting sites, but can switch sites from year to year, possibly to avoid nest parasites, such as fleas and lice, present in old nests. At colony, birds try to steal grass and mud from each other's nests. Females may lay their eggs in other female's nest, or even carry them there from their own nest. Males may copulate with females who are not their mates.

Habitat: Open areas near cliffs, bridges, outbuildings.

Voice: An extended, harsh twittering, given by male; a "churr" call, given between a pair; and a nasal "nyew" call, given during alarm.

Conservation: BBS: W ↑ C ↑ CBC: ↓ Has begun to adapt to nesting on built structures, to its advantage.

Cave Swallow
Hirundo fulva

Identification: 6″ Buffy rump; reddish-brown forehead; buffy throat. Also, belly is white; back has white streaking; **tip of tail is square.**

Feeding: Feeds in small flocks, sometimes in mixed flocks with Cliff and Barn Swallows.

Nesting: In colonies. Nest is open half-bowl made of mud pellets or guano lined with fibers, grass, feathers, placed in cave, culvert, bridge, wall, or building. Old nests may be repaired and reused. Eggs: 3–5, white with reddish-brown speckles; I: 15–16 days; F: 22–26 days, altricial; B: 1–3.

Other Behavior: Less synchronous breeder than Cliff Swallow. First bred in the U.S. in 1914; at first in caves, more recently in highway culverts and buildings. Sometimes nests in association with Barn Swallows. May hybridize with Barn Swallows.

Habitat: Open areas near caves, culverts, and bridges.

Voice: An extended song of squeaks, followed by a warble; a "choo," given during alarm; a "chuweet," given within flock.

Conservation: BBS: W C ⇑ Use of culverts for nesting has allowed for range expansion.

Barn Swallow

Hirundo rustica

Identification: 7″ Long forked tail; upperparts blue-black; breast buffy; chin and throat reddish brown.

Feeding: Eats insects. Feeds in pairs while egg-laying, in loose flocks at other times. Feeds in flight, and can skim over water to pick up floating insects.

Nesting: Singly or in colonies. Nest a deep bowl of mud pellets and grass lined with feathers, placed on beam or some projection in barn, under bridge, in culvert, mine shaft, cave. Eggs: 2–7, white with reddish-brown speckles; I: 14–16 days; F: 18–23 days, altricial; B: 1–3.

Other Behavior: Both male and female build nest, usually in the morning, and can make up to 1,000 trips to collect mud. Usually monogamous, but rarely males will pair with 2 females. In colonies males may copulate with females other than their mate. Paired male aggressively defends small area around nest, and guards his mate from intruding males that might attempt to copulate with her.

Habitat: Open country near barns or open outbuildings, bridges, culverts.

Voice: Both sexes give song of continuous twitter interspersed by grating sounds; during feeding or alarm, call "chitchit."

Conservation: BBS: W ↓ C ↑ CBC: ↑

343

Black-capped Chickadee
Mexican Chickadee

Parus atricapillus   Parus sclateri

Black-capped

Mexican

Identification: Black-capped 5¼", Mexican 5" Mexican Chickadee is limited to S.W. N.Mex. and S.E. Ariz.; its range does not overlap that of Black-capped Chickadee. Both species have **black cap and bib; white cheeks. BLACK-CAPPED: Shorter bib; buffy flanks. MEXICAN: Much longer bib; gray flanks.**

Black-cap.   Mexican

Feeding: Both acrobatically forage in trees, eating insects, seeds, and berries. Black-capped very common at bird feeders, where it favors sunflower seed.

Nesting: Mexican's nest is cup of loose fur, placed in tree cavity, 5–45 ft. above ground, frequently in dead willow. Eggs: 5–8, white with red-brown speckles; I: ?; F: ?, altricial: B: ? Black-capped excavates nest hole in rotted wood or uses birdhouse or natural cavity. Nest materials are mosses, wood chips, hair. Eggs: 6–8, white with red-brown speckles; I: 12 days; F: 16 days, altricial; B: 1–2.

Other Behavior: Black-capped forms winter flock of 6–10 birds that have a fixed dominance hierarchy and defend a winter territory of about 20 acres. In spring, males sing, flock breaks up, and pairs breed.

Habitat: Black-capped: woods. Mexican: mountain forests.

Voice: Black-capped's song 2 whistled notes, 1st slightly higher than 2nd, like "feebee." Mexican's song a warbled whistle.

Conservation: Black-capped: BBS: W ↓ C ↑ CBC: ⇑ Mexican: TREND UNKNOWN.

Mountain Chickadee

Parus gambeli

Identification: 6″ Black cap and bib; white cheek; thin white line over eye; gray flanks. Eyebrow is black feathers with white tips which wear off during summer as bird enters and leaves nest hole; by late summer, eyebrow is faint or absent. After late summer molt, it is again obvious.

Feeding: Acrobatically forages for insects and seeds. Comes to bird feeders for sunflower seeds, suet.

Nesting: Nest of wood chips, hair, feathers, placed in natural or excavated cavity or birdhouse. Eggs: 7–9, white; I: 14 days; F: 17–20 days, altricial; B: 1–2.

Other Behavior: Forms winter flocks. In spring, male sings and defends breeding territory, does courtship feeding of female.

Habitat: Open coniferous forests in mountains.

Voice: Song is 3–4 whistled notes, such as "feebee feebee" or "fee bee bay." Calls include a raspy "chickadee-deedee."

Conservation:
BBS: W ↓ C CBC: ↑

345

Boreal Chickadee

Parus hudsonicus

Identification: 5¼" **Brown cap; black bib; limited white on cheek; flanks strongly reddish brown.** In general, appears plumper, and brown rather than gray as in other chickadees; worn, late summer plumage quite dull.

Feeding: Acrobatically clings to branches, searching for insects. Also eats seeds. Comes to bird feeders for sunflower seed and suet.

Nesting: Nest of mosses, lichens, plant down, hair, fur, placed in a natural or excavated tree cavity, or abandoned woodpecker hole. May also use nest box. Eggs: 4–9, white with brown speckles; I: 11–16 days; F: 18 days, altricial; B: 1.

Other Behavior: Rather shy. Common in spruce-fir forests. Forms winter flocks. Sometimes wanders south of range in winter.

Habitat: Northern coniferous woods; spruce bogs.

Voice: Calls and song wheezy and more drawn out than those of Black-capped Chickadee.

Conservation:
BBS: W ⇑ C CBC:→

Chestnut-backed Chickadee

Parus rufescens

Identification: 5" Most brightly colored chickadee. **Dark gray cap; black bib; white cheek; rich reddish-brown back;** flanks reddish brown. Birds that live on central Calif. coast have gray flanks.

Feeding: Acrobatically clings to branches, searching for insects and seeds. Comes to bird feeders for sunflower seeds and suet.

Nesting: Nest of moss, hair, feathers, and other downy material, placed in natural or excavated tree cavity, or birdhouse. Eggs: 6–7, white with light reddish speckles; I: 11–12 days; F: 13–17 days, altricial; B: 1–2.

Other Behavior: Forms winter flocks that roam a fixed area. Chickadee flocks are joined temporarily by other bird species such as kinglets, nuthatches, creepers, and titmice, and they all move through the woods, foraging together. In spring, pair defends breeding territory of about 10 acres and male does courtship feeding of female. Female does all incubation.

Habitat: Coniferous or mixed woods.

Voice: Calls are a hoarse "chick-zee-zee" and a "chek chek." Has no whistled song.

Conservation:
BBS: W ↓ C CBC: ↑

Bridled Titmouse

Parus wollweberi

Identification: 4½" Common on its limited range in the Southwest. **Small and gray; crested; distinctive black-and-white facial pattern.**

Feeding: Forages on the branches of oak and other trees, looking for insects, insect eggs, and larvae. Comes to feeders.

Nesting: Nest of grasses and leaves lined with plant down, placed in natural cavity or birdhouse. Eggs: 5–7, white; I: ?; F: ?, altricial; B: ?

Other Behavior: Rather elusive. In nonbreeding season forms flocks of up to 25. Other species may join these flocks. Breeding biology needs more study.

Habitat: Woodlands, especially along streams.

Voice: High-pitched versions of other titmouse calls, such as "jwee jwee" and "peer peer peer."

Conservation: BBS: W ⇓ C CBC: ⇑

Plain Titmouse

Parus inornatus

Identification: 5½" **Small; all plain gray; small crest.** Differentiated from black-crested morph of Tufted Titmouse, which it approaches in range, by having gray forehead and no black on crest.

Feeding: Acrobatically hangs from the limbs of trees, or forages on the ground, eating mostly seeds, nuts, and acorns. Also eats insects. Comes to feeders.

Nesting: Nests in natural cavities, abandoned woodpecker holes, and birdhouses. Nest composed of mosses, grasses, feathers, fur. Eggs: 6–8, sometimes with small brown dots; I: 14–16 days; F: 16–21 days, altricial; B: 1–2.

Other Behavior: In late winter, males begin to sing and defend small breeding territories of 2–5 acres. As part of courtship, male does mate-feeding. He gets food and presents it to the female, who quivers her wings and gives a high-pitched call while receiving it.

Habitat: Sparse pinyon-juniper and oak woodlands.

Voice: Song is whistled "teewee teewee teewee"; call is "tsikadee-dee."

Conservation: BBS: W ⇓ C CBC: ↑

Tufted Titmouse
Parus bicolor

Gray-crested morph

Black-crested morph

Identification: 5" **Small gray bird; black on forehead or crest;** flanks usually buffy. Black-crested morph has whitish forehead and lives in S., C., and W. Tex.; gray-crested morph has black forehead and lives in rest of range.

Feeding: Eats insects, seeds, berries. Common at bird feeders, where it prefers sunflower seed and suet.

Nesting: Nest of mosses, hair, grasses, leaves, cotton, bark strips, placed in natural cavity or birdhouse. Eggs: 4–8, white with small brown speckles; I: 13–14 days; F: 17–18 days, altricial; B: 1–2.

Other Behavior: In late winter or early spring, family flocks break up and the male starts singing and defending breeding territory of 2–5 acres. Rival males come together at territorial boundaries and sing back and forth. As part of courtship, the male feeds the female while she quivers her wings and gives high-pitched notes. This mate-feeding continues through nest-building and incubation phases. The female does almost all of the nest building and often collects large amounts of moss or bark.

Habitat: Woods and suburbs.

Voice: Song is a downslurred whistle, like "peter peter peter." Calls include a scolding "jweejweejwee" and "tseejwee"; a contact note of "tseet"; and a series of extremely high-pitched whistles.

Conservation: BBS: W ↑ C ↑ CBC: ↑

Verdin
Auriparus flaviceps

Identification: 4¼" **Tiny and gray; yellow head.** Small reddish-brown patch on shoulder may be visible. **Juv:** Dull gray-brown overall; its shorter tail and longer, straight bill help distinguish it from the similar-looking Bushtit.

Feeding: Feeds by gleaning insects from trees and shrubs. Also eats seeds and berries.

Nesting: Conspicuous spherical nest of thorny twigs, grasses, and spider's silk lined with feathers and plant down, placed at end of low branch in shrub, cactus, or tree, especially mesquite. Eggs: 3–6, pale greenish white with dark marks; I: 10 days; F: 21 days, altricial; B: 2.

Other Behavior: Several nests are built by male, then female chooses one for breeding. Smaller nests are built for winter roosting.

Habitat: Brushy desert and semi-desert areas.

Voice: Song is 3 notes with 2nd higher, like "tee tsee tee"; calls include loud "chip" and "tzee."

Conservation: BBS: W ↓ C ⇓ CBC: ↑

Bushtit

Psaltriparus minimus

Coastal

Interior

Identification: 3½" Tiny and gray; tiny beak (top of upper mandible strongly curved); **long tail.** Coastal birds are light with gray-brown cap; interior birds are dark with a brownish cheek; southwest males or juveniles may have black cheek patch. In all morphs, males have dark eyes, females light yellow eyes.

Feeding: Acrobatically feeds, gleaning aphids, bugs, beetles, and other insects from outer branches of trees or shrubs. Also eats seeds and fruits. Comes to feeders.

Nesting: Gourd-shaped nest of mosses, rootlets, lichens, and leaves lined with plant down, hair, and feathers is attached by spider's silk to twigs of tree or bush 4–25 ft. above ground. Eggs: 5–7, white; I: 12 days; F: 14–15 days, altricial; B: 1–2.

Other Behavior: In winter, moves about in animated flocks of 6–30 or more birds that give an ongoing chatter of soft contact calls. At night flocks roost huddled together, possibly for warmth.

Habitat: Open woods, chaparral, suburbs, parks, gardens.

Voice: Song is a high-pitched trill; calls include short "tseep" and "tsip," possibly given as contact notes when the flock moves about.

Conservation: BBS: W ↓ C ⇑ CBC: ⇑

352

Red-breasted Nuthatch
Sitta canadensis

Male

Identification: 4½" White eyebrow separates dark cap from black eyeline; rusty underparts. MALE: Black cap with richly colored underparts. FEMALE: Gray cap with more lightly colored underparts.

Feeding: Creeps headfirst down trunks of trees searching for insects. Eats the seeds of conifers. Will come to bird feeders for sunflower seed and suet.

Nesting: Nest of rootlets, grasses, mosses, and shredded bark, placed in excavated hole, birdhouse, or abandoned woodpecker hole 5–120 ft. above ground. Smears pitch around the entrance of nest cavity to deter predators. Eggs: 5–7, white or slightly pink with brown speckles; I: 12 days; F: 16–21 days, altricial; B: 1–2.

Other Behavior: Has periodic irruptions south in winter in years when there is a failure of cone crop in northern regions. Birds must therefore move south to find food and often become more abundant at bird feeders in those years. Has breeding territory of 20–30 acres. Uses birdhouses and tree cavities to roost in, as well as for breeding.

Habitat: Coniferous woods.

Voice: Common call is a nasal "nyeep nyeep," also a short "tsip."

Conservation:
BBS: W ⇑ C ⇑ CBC: ⇑

353

White-breasted Nuthatch
Sitta carolinensis

Male

Female

Identification: 6″ **Dark crown and nape; white face; gray back.** Varying amounts of reddish brown on rump and flanks. Sexes differ in color of crown and back, except in Southeast, where they cannot be reliably distinguished by plumage. MALE: **Glossy black crown and nape; blue-gray back.** FEMALE: **Gray or dull black crown and nape; gray back.**

Feeding: Creeps headfirst down tree trunks. Eats nuts, acorns, and insects. Comes to bird feeders for suet and sunflower seed.

Nesting: Nest of twigs, bark shreds, fur, and hair, placed in natural cavity, birdhouse, or abandoned woodpecker hole 15–50 ft. above ground. Eggs: 3–10, white with dark marks; I: 12 days; F: 14 days, altricial; B: 1–2.

Other Behavior: Nuthatches are best known for their habit of storing food in bark crevices and their ability to move headfirst down trees, enabling them to find food that "right-side up" birds, like woodpeckers, might miss. Courtship begins in late winter with the male singing. He does mate-feeding — presenting female with food — through the incubation phase.

Habitat: Deciduous and mixed woods.

Voice: Song is "werwerwerwer"; calls include contact notes of "ip" and "ank ank," the latter given in a rapid series during aggressive encounters.

Conservation: BBS: W ⇑ C ↑ CBC: ↑

Pygmy Nuthatch
Sitta pygmaea

Identification: 4¼" Tiny; grayish-brown cap bordered by darker eyeline; gray back; buffy belly. Dull white spot on nape may be seen at close range.

Feeding: Climbs over branches and down trunks of trees in search of insects and pine seeds. Comes to feeders.

Nesting: Nest of plant down, bark, pinecone scales, and hair, placed in excavated cavity or abandoned woodpecker hole 6–60 ft. above ground. May also use nest box. Eggs: 4–9, white with dark marks; I: 15–16 days; F: 20–22 days, altricial; B: 1.

Other Behavior: Nuthatches roam in loose flocks of 4–15 birds during winter as they search for food. They roost communally in a single cavity. Breed communally, in group of 2–5 birds, consisting of mated pair and unmated male relative "helpers."

Habitat: Pine forests, especially Ponderosa Pine.

Voice: A high-pitched "peedee" given irregularly or in a rapid series.

Conservation:
BBS: W ⇑ C CBC: ↑

Brown Creeper
Certhia americana

Identification: 5½" Small brown bird that hitches up tree trunks; brown-streaked above; whitish below; relatively long downcurved bill; long pointed tail feathers.

Feeding: Has distinctive habit of feeding by creeping up tree trunk then dropping down to base of next tree and starting up again. Probes bark for insects and larvae. Sometimes visits bird feeders for chopped nuts and suet.

Nesting: Hammocklike crescent-shaped nest of bark, twigs, mosses, lined with feathers, placed behind loose piece of bark of dead tree, or in natural cavity 5–15 ft. above the ground. Eggs: 5–6, white with dark spots; I: 14–16 days; F: 13–15 days, altricial; B: ?

Other Behavior: Usually located first by its distinctive song or high-pitched call. Looks very camouflaged against tree trunks. When alarmed, will flatten itself and remain motionless against trunk, becoming even more inconspicuous.

Habitat: Woods.

Voice: Song is a series of high-pitched whistles like "see wee see tu wee." Call is a high "tseee."

Conservation: BBS: W ↓ C CBC: ↑

Cactus Wren
Campylorhynchus brunneicapillus

Identification: 8″ **Our largest wren. Dark crown, wide white eyebrow; heavily spotted breast; barred wings.** Long tail prominently barred black and white underneath.

Feeding: Forages on ground. Eats insects, spiders, small lizards, berries, and seeds. May visit bird feeders for bread, seeds, and pieces of fruit.

Nesting: Large football-shaped nest of plant stems and grasses has side entrance leading through small passage to inner chamber lined with fur, feathers. Nest is placed in cholla or prickly pear cactus, tree yucca, or other thorny plant. Eggs: 3–7, pinkish white with dark marks; I: 16 days; F: 19–23 days, altricial; B: 2–3.

Other Behavior: Female selects nest site. When female is almost through incubating, male builds another nest to use for 2nd brood or as a roost. Old nests are used as winter roosts.

Habitat: Deserts and semideserts with cactus, such as prickly pear, cholla.

Voice: Song is a low-pitched "cha cha cha cha" or "choo choo choo choo."

Conservation:
BBS: W ↑ C ⇓ CBC: ↓ Coastal Calif. pop. in jeopardy due to clearing for grazing land, vineyards, and development.

Rock Wren
Salpinctes obsoletus

Identification: 5½" Upperparts grayish brown with fine white spotting; breast and belly pale. IN FLIGHT: Note cinnamon rump; buffy corners of tail.

Feeding: Forages on the ground, eating insects and spiders.

Nesting: Nest of rootlets, grasses, and plant stems lined with wool, spider's silk, and feathers, placed in crevice of rocky slope or abandoned gopher burrows. Entrance to nest is paved with small pebbles and pieces of rock. Eggs: 4–6, white with brown marks; I: 12–14 days; F: 14–16 days, altricial; B: 1–2.

Other Behavior: Often bobs its head, especially when frightened. When nest sites are reused in subsequent years, more pebbles are added to entrance. In one case, there were more than 750 pebbles and bits of stone in front of the nest.

Habitat: Sparsely vegetated rocky areas, including talus slopes and road cutaways.

Voice: Song is repeated 2-part phrase, like "tawee tawee tawee tawee"; calls include a sharp "tikeer" and a high trill.

Conservation: BBS: W ↓ C ⇓ CBC: ↑

Canyon Wren

Catherpes mexicanus

Identification: 5½" **Bill very long; throat and breast white; belly rich brown; crown dark gray; rest of upperparts brown,** all with fine whitish spotting.

Feeding: Creeps mouselike over rocky areas, and probes for insects and spiders.

Nesting: Nest of twigs and mosses lined with spider's silk, feathers, fur, and plant down, placed in crevice of canyon, rock wall, or building. Eggs: 5–6, white with light marks; I: ?; F: ?, altricial; B: ?

Other Behavior: Little is known about its breeding biology. Needs more study.

Habitat: Canyon walls, cliffs, mesas, boulders, stone homes.

Voice: Spectacular song is a loud series of downslurred whistles, like "tew tew tew tew tew tew," often amplified by its habitat; call is a harsh "jeet."

Conservation:
BBS: W ⇓ C ⇓ CBC: ↑

359

Carolina Wren

Thryothorus ludovicianus

Identification: 6″ Warm brown above; rich buff below; prominent white eyebrow; no streaking on back or white barring on tail edges.

Feeding: Forages on the ground and on the bark and foliage of trees, eating insects, tree frogs, and some vegetable matter. May come to bird feeders.

Nesting: Nest of twigs, mosses, rootlets, bark, and sometimes snakeskin lined with fine materials, placed in natural cavity or a host of other places, including birdhouse, pail, brushpile, mailbox. Eggs: 4–8, creamy or pink-white with brown marks; I: 12–14 days; F: 12–14 days, altricial; B: 2–3.

Other Behavior: Expands population northward in years with mild winters. Males can sing up to 40 versions of song and sing throughout the year. Expanding range in Northeast.

Habitat: Forest understory, vines, and woodlands in rural or suburban areas.

Voice: A loud, repeated, 3-part phrase, like "tea kettle, tea kettle, tea kettle"; calls include a piping alarm note, a raspy buzz, and a harsh descending "teeer."

Conservation: BBS: W C ↑ CBC: ↑

Bewick's Wren
Thryomanes bewickii

Identification: 5½" A sleek wren with a **white eyebrow; long tail marked with black and white underneath. Underparts pale gray;** upperparts grayer in West, browner in East. Tail often flicked from side to side, showing white outer tips.

Feeding: Feeds on the ground and in trees and bushes, eating insects and spiders.

Nesting: Nest of twigs, hair, leaves, and grasses lined with feathers and grasses, placed in a variety of cavities. Eggs: 4–11, white with dark spots; I: 14 days; F: 14 days, altricial; B: ?

Other Behavior: Carries tail cocked upward. Explores every crevice. Has been known to nest in wide variety of places, such as mailbox, fence post, tin can, clothing hung in outbuilding, crevice in wall. May also use nest box.

Habitat: Thickets, brush, and open woodlands in rural or suburban areas.

Voice: Song a complex jumble of thin notes and trills (similar to that of Song Sparrow); call a "chip."

Conservation: BBS: W ↓ C ↓ CBC: ↑ The Appalachian Bewick's Wren, a subspecies, has declined extensively.

361

House Wren
Troglodytes aedon

Identification: 5″ Plump little bird with short tail often cocked; upperparts unstreaked and grayish brown; faint buffy eyebrow; underparts grayish white with some buffy barring on flanks. Our dullest-colored wren, with no prominent field marks.

Feeding: Forages on the ground and in foliage for insects.

Nesting: Nest of twigs lined with grass, rootlets, feathers, and hair, placed in a wide variety of cavities, including birdhouse or tree hole 4–30 ft. above ground. Eggs: 5–6, white with brown marks; I: 12–15 days; F: 16–17 days, altricial; B: 1–2.

Other Behavior: In spring, male establishes a small breeding territory by singing from exposed perches and putting stick foundations in prospective nest holes. When female enters his territory, his song becomes very high and squeaky and he vibrates his wings. After pairing with him, the female chooses one of the nests, adds a lining of soft material, and lays eggs. Male brings food to female while she incubates. House Wrens can be aggressive to other hole-nesting species and even destroy their eggs and young.

Habitat: Woods edges in rural or suburban areas; also mountain forests and clearings, and aspen groves.

Voice: Song a descending warble lasting 2–3 seconds; calls include a series of short buzzes and a rattlelike "churr."

Conservation:
BBS: W ⇑ C ↑ CBC: ↓

Winter Wren

Troglodytes troglodytes

Identification: 4" Very small; extremely short tail; chocolate brown above; buffy brown below; dark barring on belly and undertail coverts.

Feeding: Forages on the ground near rotting logs and brush and in tree foliage, eating insects and spiders.

Nesting: Nests near water. Nest of mosses, grasses, and twigs lined with hair and feathers, placed under roots, in rock crevice, in stump, stream bank, or other natural cavity. Eggs: 4–7, white with brown spots; I: 14–16 days; F: 19 days, altricial; B: ?

Other Behavior: Rather secretive. Bobs head. Known to be polygynous.

Habitat: Summers along rocky woodland streams, especially in coniferous forests; winters in woods, wood piles, and tangles.

Voice: Song is a beautiful long series of tinkling twitters and trills; call is "chip-chip."

Conservation:
BBS: W ↑ C ⇑ CBC: ↑

Sedge Wren

Cistothorus platensis

Identification: 4½" Small; upperparts brown; fine white streaks on crown and upper back; underparts buffy; indistinct buffy eyebrow.

Feeding: Forages in foliage, eating insects and spiders.

Nesting: Spherical nest of dried and green grasses, reeds, and sedges lined with down, feathers, and catkins woven into grass and sedges 1–3 ft. above the ground or shallow water. Eggs: 4–8, white; I: 12–15 days; F: 12–14 days, altricial; B: 2.

Other Behavior: Formerly known as Short-billed Marsh Wren. May not return to former breeding site, since it shifts breeding areas from year to year.

Habitat: Summers in wet grasslands, often with sedges; winters also in coastal marshes.

Voice: Song is a few short staccato notes followed by a long chatter, like "chip chip chip churrrrr."

Conservation: BBS: W ⇓ C ↑ CBC: ↑

Marsh Wren

Cistothorus palustris

Identification: 5" Warm brown above; usually shows white streaks on upper back; dark brown unstreaked crown; white eyebrow; white throat and breast; pale belly. Secretive.

Feeding: Forages on the ground and in dense foliage. Eats aquatic insects and sometimes bird eggs.

Nesting: Spherical nest of soaked reeds, grass, and cattails lined with plant down and feathers is lashed to marsh grasses 1–3 ft. above the ground. Eggs: 3–8, cinnamon brown with dark spots; I: 13–15 days; F: 14–16 days, altricial; B: 1–2.

Other Behavior: In spring, the male frequently does a flight display over his small territory. He flies up, then flutters gradually down, giving his dry rattling song. He also builds about 5 or 6 "courting nests," consisting of an outer shell of woven cattails. After the female arrives and pairs with the male, she selects 1 of these nests and adds a lining, or she may build a new nest herself. She then lays and incubates the eggs. Marsh wrens are often polygynous, with 2 or 3 females paired with 1 male. Polygyny can be advantageous to females when male territories are especially rich in food, making it easier to raise young.

Habitat: Marshy areas, especially with tall cattails and rushes.

Voice: Song is a dry rattling warble; call a single "chek," sometimes rapidly repeated in a chatter.

Conservation:
BBS: W ⇑ C ↑ CBC: ⇑

American Dipper

Cinclus mexicanus

Identification: 8″ Stout; short tail (often cocked); **all dark gray; lives along rushing streams.**

Feeding: Dips head into water, or walks underwater on the bottom of rushing streams. Eats aquatic larvae.

Nesting: Arched-over nest of mosses and grasses lined with moss, placed on cliff face in damp location. Often found on rock in midstream, underneath bridge over water, or behind a waterfall. Eggs: 3–6, white; I: 14–17 days; F:18–25 days, altricial; B: 2.

Other Behavior: Special adaptations enable the dipper to go underwater: scales that cover its nostrils; dense plumage that resists saturation; and an extra-large oil gland with which it waterproofs its plumage.

Habitat: Rushing mountain streams and high-elevation lakes.

Voice: Song is a loud musical series of whistles with repeated phrases; call is a "bzeet."

Conservation:
BBS: W ⇓ C CBC: ↑

Golden-crowned Kinglet

Regulus satrapa

Female

Identification: 3½" Very small; black cap with yellow or orange patch in center; white eyebrow; 2 white wing bars. **MALE:** Yellow crown with orange center. **FEMALE:** Yellow crown.

Feeding: Gleans food from the bark of trees, eating insects, spiders, fruit, and seeds. Drinks tree sap.

Nesting: Globular nest of moss, lichens, and spiderweb lined with inner bark, rootlets, and feathers, hung from branches 4–60 ft. above ground. Eggs: 8–11, creamy white with dark marks; I: 14–15 days; F: 14–19 days, altricial; B: 2.

Other Behavior: Kinglets have a habit of nervously flicking their wings when hopping about from limb to limb. Often found in mixed-species flocks with chickadees, nuthatches, woodpeckers, Brown Creepers, and Ruby-crowned Kinglets.

Habitat: Summers in coniferous woods; winters also in mixed and deciduous forests.

Voice: Song several high notes ending in a chatter; call is very high and like "tsee tsee tsee."

Conservation:
BBS: W ⇓ C CBC: ⇑

Ruby-crowned Kinglet
Regulus calendula

Male

Identification: 4¼" **Very small; grayish green above; white eye-ring; no white eyebrow; 2 white wing bars.** MALE: Red patch on crown, usually concealed. FEMALE: No patch on crown.

Feeding: Feeds at the tips of branches by hovering and gleaning from leaves. Eats insects, spiders, and some fruit and seeds. Drinks tree sap.

Nesting: Nest of mosses, twigs, and lichens lined with fur and other fine materials, hung from branch 2–100 ft. above the ground. Eggs: 5–11, creamy white with brown marks; I: 12 days; F: 12 days, altricial; B: ?

Other Behavior: Flicks wings and chatters as it moves about. Found in winter in mixed-species flocks with chickadees, titmice, woodpeckers, warblers, Golden-crowned Kinglets.

Habitat: Summers in coniferous woods; winters in woods and brushy edges.

Voice: Song a series of descending high notes followed by 3-part phrases, like the words "see see see you you you look-at-me, look-at-me, look-at-me."

Conservation:
BBS: W ↑ C ⇑ CBC: ↑

368

Blue-gray Gnatcatcher
Polioptila caerulea

Male

Male

Identification: 4½" **Slim; upperparts bluish gray; long tail black above, mostly white below, white eye-ring.** Tail often cocked or flicked from side to side, like a miniature mockingbird. **MALE:** Black eyebrow during breeding. **FEMALE:** No black eyebrow. ➤The Black-capped Gnatcatcher, *P. nigriceps,* is a Mexican species that is rarely seen in S.E. Ariz. It is similar in most respects to the Blue-gray Gnatcatcher, except that its call is a descending "mew," it has a noticeably longer bill, and, in breeding plumage, the male has an entirely black cap.

Feeding: Actively searches trees and crevices for insects, their eggs and larvae, and spiders.

Nesting: Tiny cup nest of plant fibers, down, and spiderweb lined with finer materials and covered with bits of lichen, saddled on horizontal branch or in fork of tree 2–80 ft. above the ground. Eggs: 3–6, pale blue with dark spots; I: 13 days; F: 10–12 days, altricial; B: 1–2.

Other Behavior: Darts out to catch flies and gnats in midair.

Habitat: Woods, swamps, and shrubby areas.

Voice: Song is a series of buzzy grasshopper-like notes; call is a thin peevish "zeeeee."

Conservation:
BBS: W ⇑ C ↓ CBC: ↑

Black-tailed Gnatcatcher
California Gnatcatcher

Polioptila melanura   Polioptila californica

Black-tailed male

California male

Black-tailed

California

Identification: 4½" BLACK-TAILED: **Upperparts bluish gray; underparts whitish; tail long and mostly black beneath except for thin white edges and broad white tips to outermost feathers.** Male has black cap during breeding. CALIFORNIA: **Upperparts dark gray; underparts grayish; tail long, has thin white edges, and appears all black beneath.** Male has black cap during breeding.

Black-tailed   California

Feeding: Hovers and gleans food from foliage. Eats insects, spiders, and some seeds.

Nesting: Nest of plant down, leaves, and fibers lined with fine materials, placed in the branches of shrubs 1–4 ft. above the ground. Eggs: 3–5, pale greenish blue with dark marks; I: 14–15 days; F: 9–15 days, altricial; B: ?

Other Behavior: Both move about very actively, constantly flicking tail up and down, or from side to side. California Gnatcatcher population is jeopardized by continuing development of coastal sage areas.

Habitat: Black-tailed lives in desert regions and dry creeks. California lives in coastal brushlands.

Voice: Black-tailed call a raspy "cheee." California call a descending "mew."

Conservation: Black-tailed: BBS: W ↓ C CBC: ⇑ Calif. Gnatcatcher endangered in U.S.

Northern Wheatear

Oenanthe oenanthe

Male

Female

Identification: 6″ **White rump; dark wings; black band at tail tip.** Eastern birds are more cinnamon below; western birds are more whitish below. **SUMMER—MALE: Black mask; black wings. FEMALE: No black mask; brown wings. WINTER: Male similar to female except for black lores** (in female, lores are brown) **and black wings; female is same as in summer.**

Feeding: Feeds on ground, eating insects, snails, earthworms.

Nesting: Nest of rootlets, mosses, and grasses lined with rootlets, grasses, wool, hair, and feathers, placed in a cavity or under a group of rocks or other sheltered location. Eggs: 3–8, light blue with reddish marks; I: 14 days; F: 15–16 days, altricial; B: ?

Other Behavior: Actively flits about as it feeds, often fanning tail and constantly bobbing. During courtship, male also fans tail and exposes white rump during flight displays and while hopping about the female on the ground. Western birds migrate to Siberia and eastern birds migrate through Europe and into Africa, but a few migrants are regularly seen along the Atlantic Coast.

Habitat: Summers in rocky tundra; winters in plowed fields and sparsely vegetated fields.

Voice: Alarm call is "chak"; song is a series of musical notes interspersed with the "chak" call and mimicry of other birds.

Conservation: TREND UNKNOWN.

Eastern Bluebird
Sialia sialis

Male

Female

Identification: 6½" MALE: **Brilliant blue head, back, wings, and tail; brick-red throat and breast.** FEMALE: **Rich buffy throat and breast; grayish-blue head and back; light blue wings and tail; white eye-ring.** Color on upperparts of female varies from almost as deep blue as on male to grayish brown.

Feeding: Feeds from perches, dropping down to the ground to catch insects. May come to bird feeders for peanut butter mixes, berries, mealworms, raisins.

Nesting: Nest of grasses, plant stems, pine needles, lined with hair, feathers, and fine grasses, placed in birdhouse, natural tree cavity, or abandoned woodpecker hole 3–20 ft. above the ground. Eggs: 3–6, pale blue; I: 12–18 days; F: 16–21 days, altricial; B: 2–3.

Other Behavior: Bluebird populations severely declined up until the 1970s due to loss of nesting cavities and nest competition from House Sparrows and European Starlings. In 1978, the North American Bluebird Society was formed. This society, along with many others, has placed bluebird nesting boxes all across the country. This is helping bluebird populations recover.

Habitat: Farmland and rural yards; open woodlands.

Voice: Song a series of downslurred whistles, like "cheer cheerful charmer"; call a mellow "turwee."

Conservation:
BBS: W ↓ C ⇑ CBC: ⇑

Western Bluebird

Sialia mexicana

Male

Female

Identification: 6½" MALE: Deep purplish blue on head, throat, wings, and tail; brick-red on breast; usually shows chestnut patch on back. FEMALE: Gray throat; buffy breast; grayish-blue head and back; light blue wings and tail; white eye-ring.

Feeding: Feeds from perches, dropping down to the ground to catch insects. Also catches insects in the air and, while hovering, may drop to ground to catch prey. May visit bird feeders for berries, raisins, peanut butter mixes, and mealworms.

Nesting: Nest of weed stems, grasses, and twigs lined with hair, fine grasses, and often feathers, placed in natural tree cavity, abandoned woodpecker hole, or birdhouse 2–50 ft. above ground. Eggs: 5–8, pale blue; I: 13–17 days; F: 19–22 days, altricial; B: 2–3.

Other Behavior: Populations severely dropped from 1900 to 1940s due to loss of habitat and competition for nests from House Sparrows. Bluebird trails, consisting of many nest boxes, were begun in the 1970s due to conservation efforts of national and local bluebird societies. Western Bluebirds have been helped by these efforts, but more needs to be done.

Habitat: Forest edges, open woods, lowlands in winter.

Voice: Song is a varied mixture of "cheer," "chup," and "churchur"; call is "chweer."

Conservation: BBS: W ↓ C CBC: ↑

373

Mountain Bluebird

Sialia currucoides

Male

Female

Identification: 6½" Sleeker than other bluebirds, with longer wings, tail, and legs. MALE: **Sky blue above; lighter blue below.** FEMALE: **Uniform pale grayish-brown body; wings and tail sky blue** (color seen best when bird flies); white eye-ring.

Feeding: Often feeds by hovering and dropping down to catch insects. May also hawk insects out of the air, or drop down to ground from perches. May visit bird feeders.

Nesting: Nest of grasses, shreds of sage or aspen bark, twigs, and pine needles lined with feathers and hair, placed in birdhouse, natural tree cavity, or building. Sometimes inhabits old Cliff Swallow nest. Eggs: 4–8, pale blue; I: 12–16 days; F: 19–23 days, altricial; B: 2.

Other Behavior: Its longer wings help it hover while looking for food, since it lives in habitats that have few perches. Mountain Bluebird conservation efforts started from 1955 to the 1970s, when U.S. and Canadian bluebird organizations began promoting use of bluebird nest boxes. Some of these trails of nest boxes extend for several thousand miles in Can., and one runs across the entire state of Mont.

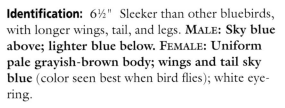

Habitat: Summers in mountain meadows, open rangeland, open coniferous woods, sagebrush; winters in lowlands, including desert.

Voice: Song is short sequences of a variety of "chur's" and rattles; call is "churchur."

Conservation:
BBS: W ⇑ C ⇓ CBC: ↑

Townsend's Solitaire

Myadestes townsendi

Identification: 9″ Slender-looking; all gray; white eye-ring; short bill; long tail. IN FLIGHT: Buffy patches on wings; outer tail feathers white. JUV: Similar to adult, but with heavy buff spotting on breast and back.

Feeding: Darts from perch, catching and eating insects. Also eats spiders, worms, and various berries, especially juniper.

Nesting: Nest of twigs, sticks, and grasses lined with fine grasses, placed on or near the ground and protected by overhanging rocks, tree roots, branches, and other kinds of natural shelter. Eggs: 3–5, dull white or pale pinkish blue with dark marks; I: ?; F: ?, altricial; B: ?

Other Behavior: Migrates from northernmost summer range. It can be an erratic wanderer, and birds occasionally show up on the northeast Atlantic Coast. Can be territorial in winter around sources of abundant berries.

Habitat: Summers in coniferous mountain woods; winters at lower elevations in wooded valleys, pinyon-juniper areas.

Voice: Song is a series of flutelike whistles; call is a high-pitched "eeek."

Conservation: BBS: W ↑ C ↑

Veery
Catharus fuscescens

Identification: 7½" Uniformly reddish brown above; blurry spotting and buffy wash on upper breast; gray flanks; no conspicuous eye-ring. •Eastern subspecies (*C. f. fuscescens*) is cinnamon above; western subspecies (*C. f. salicicolus*) is darker brown above and has more spotting on breast.

Feeding: Gleans food from the forest floor and the bark of trees, often overturning leaves on the ground with bill in search of food. Eats insects, larvae, spiders, snails, earthworms, and wild fruit.

Nesting: Nest of weed stems, twigs, and mosses lined with grasses, inner bark, and rootlets, on top of foundation of dead leaves. Placed on or very near the ground. Eggs: 3–5, light blue; I: 10–12 days; F: 10 days, altricial; B: 1–2.

Other Behavior: The male Veery often sings his beautiful song from a perch at dusk. Although commonly heard, this bird frequently stays hidden in dense woods, making it a challenge to observe. Much more needs to be learned about its behavior.

Habitat: Moist deciduous woods, especially along streams.

Voice: Song is a descending spiral of flutelike notes, like "tureeooreeoo-reeooreeoo"; call is a loud descending "veeer," also a querulous snarl.

Conservation: BBS: W ↓ C ⇓ CBC: ↓

Gray-cheeked Thrush

Catharus minimus

Identification: 8″ Grayish brown above; bold spotting on all of breast; gray cheek; indistinct eye-ring; no buff on face. See Voice for further help in distinguishing from other thrushes.

Feeding: Feeds mostly on the ground, eating insects, spiders, crayfish, caterpillars, earthworms, and various wild berries.

Nesting: Nest of twigs, moss, grass, some mud, and decayed leaves lined with rootlets, fine grasses, and sometimes lichen, placed in tree 1–20 ft. above the ground. Eggs: 3–5, pale blue with faint marks; I: 13–14 days; F: 11–13 days, altricial; B: 1–2.

Other Behavior: Rather shy. During migration may be seen in a variety of habitats.

Habitat: Coniferous woods at tree line, tall shrubby areas.

Voice: Song a series of descending reedy whistles; call a downslurred whistle, like "weeah."

Conservation: CBC: ↓

Swainson's Thrush

Catharus ustulatus

Identification: 7½" **Conspicuous buffy eye-ring; buffy lores and breast;** spotting on all of breast. Upperparts uniformly grayish brown in East, dark reddish brown in West. See Voice for further help in distinguishing from other thrushes.

Feeding: Feeds on the ground and in foliage, eating all kinds of insects, spiders, cherries, and berries.

Nesting: Nest of twigs, barks, mosses, grasses, and plant fibers lined with skeletonized leaves, lichens, and fine materials, placed on horizontal branch of tree 2–20 ft. above the ground. Eggs: 3–5, light blue with brown spots; I: 11–14 days; F: 10–14 days, altricial; B: ?

Other Behavior: Sings a lot. On migration is often found with flocks of warblers, feeding in the tree canopy.

Habitat: Coniferous and mixed woods, shrub thickets along streams.

Voice: Song is a series of rising whistles; calls a short "whit" and a Spring Peeper–like "heep."

Conservation:
BBS: W ↑ C ⇊ CBC: ↓

Hermit Thrush
Catharus guttatus

Identification: 7½" Brown head, back, and wings; reddish-brown tail; spotting on all of breast; thin whitish eye-ring. See Voice for further help in distinguishing from other thrushes.

Feeding: Feeds mostly on the ground, eating insects, spiders, earthworms, snails, and wild fruits and berries.

Nesting: Nest of mosses, grasses, and rotted wood lined with rootlets, bark strips, and other fine materials, built on the ground or 2–8 ft. above it in a bush or tree. Eggs: 3–6, light blue or blue-green; I: 12–13 days; F: 12 days, altricial; B: 2.

Other Behavior: After alighting on a perch, this thrush has a habit of slightly raising and lowering its tail, an action often accompanied by a "chuck" note. Also frequently flicks wings. Sings on migration.

Habitat: Coniferous and mixed woods; shrub thickets.

Voice: One long whistle followed by 3–4 higher and differently pitched whistles; calls a soft "chuck" and a whining "tweee."

Conservation: BBS: W ↑ C ↑ CBC: ↑

American Robin
Turdus migratorius

Male

Identification: 10″ Dark gray above; brick-red below; yellow bill; white undertail coverts; white eye crescents. MALE: Black head and dark red breast. FEMALE: Dark gray head and pale reddish breast. JUV: Similar to adult, but heavily spotted on breast.

Feeding: Hops about on lawns, meadows, and golf courses looking for earthworms. Also eats insects, fruit, berries. Occasionally comes to feeders for fruit.

Nesting: Nest of grasses and middle layer of mud, lined with fine grasses, placed on horizontal limb of shrub, tree, or on building ledge 5–20 ft. above the ground. Eggs: 3–7, light blue; I: 12–14 days; F: 14–16 days, altricial; B: 2–3.

Other Behavior: The song of male birds usually functions to advertise territory or attract a mate, but with robins it is not strongly associated with either. Robins sing most just before the young hatch. During nest building the female may have mud across her breast due to pressing it against the muddy lining as she forms the inner cup. After the breeding season, robins flock together and go to large communal roosts at night; this continues from fall through winter.

Habitat: In many environments, from woods to open lawns and plains to timberline.

Voice: Song a ringing whistle, like "cheeryup cheerily"; calls a "teeek" or "tuk tuk tuk" and a "tseeep" given in overhead flight.

Conservation: BBS: W ↑ C ⇑ CBC: ↑

Varied Thrush
Ixoreus naevius

Male

Female

Identification: 9½" Dark above; reddish orange below; orange line behind eyes; 2 orange wing bars. MALE: Blue-gray upperparts; broad black breast band. FEMALE: Dark gray upperparts; faint or no breast band.

Feeding: Feeds mostly on the ground, eating insects, spiders, earthworms, snails, weed seeds, acorns, and various wild berries. Uncommon at feeders, but may eat raisins, fruit, or suet.

Nesting: Nest of twigs, mosses, bark strips, and occasionally mud, lined with rootlets, grasses, and dead leaves, placed on the horizontal branches of tree 9–25 ft. above the ground. Eggs: 2–5, light blue with brown spots; I: 14 days; F: ?, altricial; B: ?

Other Behavior: In winter may rarely wander as far as East Coast. Breeding biology needs more study.

Habitat: Moist coniferous woods.

Voice: Song is a series of clear ethereal trills on different pitches; call a quiet "tuck."

Conservation:
BBS: W ↑ C CBC: ↓

Wrentit
Chamaea fasciata

Identification: 6″ Plain grayish-brown bird;
long tail (often cocked); **pale eye; faint
streaking on breast.** Birds more reddish in
North, more grayish in South.

Feeding: Gleans food from trees and shrubs. Eats
insects, caterpillars, and small fruits and berries.

Nesting: Nest of spiderweb, bark, and grasses lined with
fine fibers and hair, placed in the twigs of a shrub or
bush 1–15 ft. above the ground. Eggs: 3–5, pale green-
blue; I: 15–16 days; F: 15–16 days, altricial; B: ?

Other Behavior: Usually remains concealed in thick
underbrush, but its constant singing reveals its presence.
Its song has a "bouncing ball" quality. The pair remains
year round on small territory of several acres.

Habitat: Chaparral,
tangled brush, or
dense shrubs.

Voice: Song is short
whistled notes
speeding up and
ending in a
descending trill;
female version lacks
trill; call is "churr."

Conservation:
BBS: W ↓ C CBC: ↑

Gray Catbird

Dumetella carolinensis

Identification: 9" **All gray with a black cap;** inconspicuous reddish-brown patch under base of tail.

Feeding: Feeds on the ground and in foliage, eating various insects, as well as spiders, wild grapes, and berries.

Nesting: Nest of twigs, leaves, grasses, and grapevine bark lined with rootlets, pine needles, and horsehair, placed in shrub, vine, or small tree 2–10 ft. above the ground. Eggs: 2–6, dark blue-green; I: 12–14 days; F: 10–13 days, altricial; B: 1–2.

Other Behavior: When the male catbird arrives on the breeding ground, he soon begins to sing within his chosen territory. When the female arrives, the male does several courtship displays, including fluffing out the body feathers, high squeaky singing, and prolonged chases of the female within the territory. Both sexes give the "meeow" call in situations of alarm.

Habitat: Shrubs, tangled thickets, woods edges; rural to suburban.

Voice: Song mimics other birds', each version given only once; calls include catlike "meeow" and "kwut."

Conservation:
BBS: W ↑ C ↓ CBC: ↓

Northern Mockingbird

Mimus polyglottos

Identification: 11" Gray above; whitish below; white outer feathers on long tail; small white patch on lower edge of folded wing. IN FLIGHT: Bold white patches on wings.

Feeding: Feeds on the ground and in foliage, eating various insects, spiders, snails, crayfish, lizards, small snakes, and wild fruits and berries. May occasionally come to bird feeders for raisins, other fruit, bread, and suet.

Nesting: Nest of twigs, plant stems, mosses, cloth, string, and dry leaves lined with rootlets and grasses, placed in shrub, vine tangle, cactus, or tree 3–10 ft. above the ground. Eggs: 2–6, blue-green with brown marks; I: 12–13 days; F: 10–13 days, altricial; B: 1–3.

Other Behavior: Mockingbirds form territories of about 1–2 acres, 2 times a year. In spring, the male sings and defends a breeding territory against other mockingbirds, cats, snakes, people, large birds, and any other potential predator. In fall, both male and female sing and defend a feeding territory centered around a good source of berries. They will chase out other mockingbirds, robins, jays, and starlings. Mockingbirds often sing at night.

Habitat: Open areas with shrubs, gardens, parks.

Voice: Song mimics other birds', each version repeated 3 or more times; calls include a raspy "chjjj" and a loud "chewk."

Conservation: BBS: W ↓ C ↓ CBC: ↓

Sage Thrasher

Oreoscoptes montanus

Identification: 8½" **For a thrasher, relatively short tail; relatively short straight bill; gray upperparts; heavily streaked breast and flanks; outer tips of tail white; 2 white wing bars.** In late summer, wing bars and much of streaking on breast can be worn away.

Feeding: Feeds by running around on the ground, picking up and eating various insects and spiders. Often comes to cultivated gardens of grapes and berries in summer and fall, to eat the fruit.

Nesting: Bulky nest of twigs, grasses, leaf shreds, and bark lined with rootlets, horsehair, and fur, placed on the ground or in low bush, especially sage, up to 3 ft. above ground. Eggs: 1–7, deep green-blue with brown spots; I: 13–17 days; F: 11–14 days, altricial; B: ?

Other Behavior: Sage Thrashers spend most of their time on the ground, but it is common to see and hear males singing from prominent elevated perches. One of the few birds found in the Great Basin sage deserts and valleys, but here typical and common.

Habitat: Summers in sage; winters in desert scrub.

Voice: Song is warbled notes, sometimes repeated; call is "chuck."

Conservation:
BBS: W ↑ C ⇑ CBC: →

Brown Thrasher

Toxostoma rufum

Identification: 11" Long downcurved bill;
reddish-brown upperparts; heavily streaked
breast and belly; long tail; pale eye. Only
thrasher throughout most of East.

Feeding: Feeds on the ground, using its bill to toss aside
leaves in search of food. Occasionally jumps into the air
to catch its prey. Eats insects, lizards, snakes, tree frogs,
and various wild berries.

Nesting: Nest of twigs, grass, dead leaves, grapevine,
and paper lined with grasses and rootlets, placed on the
ground or in bush, vine tangle, or tree up to 15 ft.
above the ground. Eggs: 2–6, light blue with fine dark
marks; I: 12–14 days; F: 9–12 days, altricial; B: 2.

Other Behavior: In their attempt to attract females, male
Brown Thrashers often sing loudly from prominent
perches when they first arrive on their breeding grounds
in spring. Brown Thrashers, along with Northern
Mockingbirds and Gray Catbirds, share the feature of
endlessly improvising their song, mimicking the songs
and calls of other birds. A good way to tell these birds
apart is to remember that, in general, catbirds repeat
phrases once, Brown Thrashers twice, and mockingbirds
3 or more times.

Habitat: Thickets
and shrubs in open
areas or at woods
edges.

Voice: Song a loud
series of twice-
repeated phrases,
mimicking other
birds; call a loud
"smack."

Conservation:
BBS: W ⇓ C ↓ CBC: ⇓

Bendire's Thrasher
Curve-billed Thrasher
Toxostoma bendirei   Toxostoma curvirostre

Bendire's   Curve-billed

Identification: Bendire's 10", Curve-billed 10½"
Of these 2 similar thrasher species, Curve-billed is
more common, conspicuous, and widespread.
BENDIRE'S: **Fine dark spotting on upper breast;
bill medium length for a thrasher and with a
straighter lower mandible than Curve-billed;
yellowish eye.** See Voice. CURVE-BILLED: **Large,
blurry, rounded spotting on upper breast; long
noticeably downcurved bill; orangish eye.** See
Voice.

Feeding: Both forage on the ground for insects. Curve-
billed also eats seeds, berries, and often comes to bird
feeders for fruit, and to birdbaths.

Nesting: Both have nest of twigs, grasses, and leaves
lined with horsehair, grass, and rootlets, placed in cholla
cactus, thorny bush, or small tree 2–15 ft. above the
ground. Bendire's — Eggs: 3–5, light gray-green with
brown marks; I: ?; F: ?, altricial; B: 2–3. Curve-billed—
Eggs: 1–5, light green-blue with brown spots; I: 12–15
days; F: 12–18 days, altricial; B: 2–3.

Other Behavior: Curve-billed's sharp "whit-weet" call
(2nd syllable higher) is commonly heard in Southwest.

Bendire's   Curve-billed

Habitat: Bendire's:
thickets. Curve-
billed: semidesert
scrub and suburban
parks and yards.

Voice: Bendire's
song a long warble;
call is "chuck."
Curve-billed song
is whistled phrases;
call is "whit-weet."

Conservation:
Bendire's:
BBS: W ⇓ C CBC: ⇓
Curve-billed:
BBS: W ↓ C ⇓ CBC: ↓

387

California Thrasher
Crissal Thrasher
Toxostoma redivivum   Toxostoma crissale

California

Crissal

Identification: California 12", Crissal 11½"
These 2 similar thrashers have different ranges
except for a limited area in S. Calif. **Both are
dark brown above; long strongly downcurved
bills.** CALIFORNIA: **Buffy belly and undertail
coverts; dark eye.** CRISSAL: **Gray belly and dark
chestnut undertail coverts; pale eye.**

California   Crissal

Feeding: Both forage on the ground. Eat insects,
spiders, small lizards, and wild fruits and berries.
California often comes to bird feeders and birdbaths.

Nesting: Both have nest of twigs, forbs, and grasses
lined with feathers, inner bark strips, and rootlets,
placed in dense bush or small tree 2–9 ft. above the
ground. California—Eggs: 2–4, light blue with light
brown spots; I: 14 days; F: 12–14 days, altricial; B: 2.
Crissal—Eggs: 1–4, blue-green; I: 14 days; F: 11–13
days, altricial; B: 2.

Other Behavior: Both of these thrashers run in
underbrush with their tails elevated. Although mostly
terrestrial, both males sing from prominent perches in
the breeding season. Females stay concealed in cover.

Habitat: California
in chaparral. Crissal
in thickets along
dry watercourses.

Voice: Song of both
is repeated phrases
mimicking other
birds. California
call is "chuck";
Crissal call a whis-
tled "chideeri."

Conservation:
California:
BBS: W ⇓ C CBC: ↑
Crissal:
BBS: W ⇑ C CBC: ↑

388

Le Conte's Thrasher

Toxostoma lecontei

Identification: 10½" Pale gray above; long strongly downcurved bill; gray belly; buffy undertail coverts; dark eye.

Feeding: Digs in the ground for insects. Also eats other arthropods and small animals.

Nesting: Nest of thorny twigs and sticks lined with fibers, rootlets, paper, leaves, and fibers with inner lining of plant down, placed in dense cactus, bush, or small tree 1–8 ft. above the ground. Eggs: 2–4, green-blue with light brown spots; I: 15 days; F: 13–17 days, altricial; B: 2–3.

Other Behavior: Secretive and hard to find; active at dawn and dusk. Often runs swiftly with tail cocked, in the open desert or on sandy washes. Mated pair remains in permanent home range.

Habitat: Arid areas with little vegetation.

Voice: Song is a series of twice-repeated phrases mimicking other birds; call is an ascending "taweek."

Conservation:
BBS: W ↓ C CBC: ↑

389

American Pipit
Sprague's Pipit
Anthus rubescens   Anthus spragueii

Summer American   Winter American

Sprague's

Identification: 6½" AMERICAN—SUMMER: **Bobs tail as it feeds.** Grayish brown above; buffy breast and belly; buffy eyebrow above dark cheek; legs usually black or dark brown. WINTER: Like summer, but **brownish above and buff below; breast heavily streaked.** SPRAGUE'S: **Does not bob noticeably short tail while feeding.** Brown above with scaled look on back; buffy face; lightly streaked breast with whitish belly; legs yellow to pale brown. IN FLIGHT: Both show white outer tail feathers.

Feeding: Both feed on the ground, eating insects and the seeds of grasses and weeds. American also eats crustaceans and mollusks from tidal flats.

Nesting: Nest of grasses, twigs, lined with fine materials, placed on the ground. American—Eggs: 3–7, gray-white with dark marks; I: 14 days; F: 13–15 days, altricial; B: 1. Sprague's—Eggs: 3–7, gray-white with dark marks; I: ?; F: 10–11 days, altricial; B: ?

Other Behavior: American is seen in pairs or small flocks. Sprague's is more secretive and most often seen alone.

American   Sprague's

Habitat: American: tundra, open fields. Sprague's: short-grass fields.

Voice: American song is a repeated "chiwee"; call a short "peet-peet." Sprague's song descending notes; call "sweep sweep."

Conservation: American: CBC: ⇓ Sprague's: BBS: W ⇓ C ↓ CBC: ↑

Bohemian Waxwing
Cedar Waxwing
Bombycilla garrulus   Bombycilla cedrorum

Bohemian   Cedar

Identification: Bohemian 8", Cedar 7" Both are sleek crested birds; black eye-stripe; yellow tip to tail. BOHEMIAN: Grayish above; gray belly and reddish-brown undertail coverts; red, yellow, and white spots on wing. CEDAR: Brownish above; yellow belly and white undertail coverts; only red spots on wings. JUV: Both species similar to adult, but with blurry streaking on breast.

Feeding: Both eat insects and a large variety of wild fruits and berries.

Nesting: Nest of grasses, twigs, and mosses lined with rootlets and fine materials, placed in fork or branch of tree 4–50 ft. above ground. Bohemian—Eggs: 2–6, pale blue with dark marks; I: 14 days; F: 13–15 days, altricial; B: 1. Cedar—Eggs: 2–6, pale with dark marks; I: 12–16 days; F: 14–18 days, altricial; B: 1–2.

Other Behavior: Both of these waxwings are almost always found in large flocks that visit scattered locations and feast on berries and small fruits. Even during nesting season, they will leave their territory and join a flock to feed. Bohemian irrupts to South some winters.

Bohemian   Cedar

Habitat: Bohemian: coniferous woods. Cedar: open rural or suburban areas.

Voice: Bohemian call is a repeated, high-pitched, buzzy trill. Cedar call is a very high-pitched thin "seee."

Conservation: Bohemian: BBS: W ⇑ C CBC: ↓ Cedar: BBS: W ↑ C ⇑ CBC: ⇑

Phainopepla
Phainopepla nitens

Male

Female

Identification: 7½" Note crest, red eye, and long tail. MALE: Glossy black. FEMALE: Gray. IN FLIGHT: White patches on outer wings.

Feeding: Flies out into the air to catch insects. Eats lots of berries.

Nesting: Nest of twigs, grasses, flowers, leaves, bound with spiderweb, lined with hair and down, placed in fork of tree. Often nest is concealed in clump of mistletoe. Eggs: 2–4, grayish white with dark spots; I: 14–16 days; F: 19–20 days, altricial; B: 1–3.

Other Behavior: Lives mostly along watercourses in mesquite country. One of its main sources of food is mistletoe berries. Mistletoe is a parasitic plant that often grows on mesquite trees. In Calif., Phainopeplas breed in Sonoran Desert, March–April, then migrate to wetter areas for a 2nd breeding.

Habitat: Desert washes, oak woods.

Voice: Song is a short warble; call is a low "wurp." Generally fairly quiet.

Conservation: BBS: W ↑ C CBC: ⇑

European Starling
Sturnus vulgaris

Summer

Winter

Identification: 8" Short-tailed stocky "blackbird." SUMMER: **Glossy purple-black overall; long yellow bill.** Juveniles, which are commonly seen in large flocks during summer, are uniformly grayish brown and have dark bills. WINTER: **Black body speckled overall with white and gold; black bill.**

Feeding: Forages on ground for insects, spiders, earthworms, garbage, salamanders, snails, weed seeds, and berries. Comes to feeders for seed and suet.

Nesting: Nest of twigs, grasses, feathers, tree flowers, and cloth, placed in natural tree cavity, abandoned woodpecker hole, birdhouse, or any other cavity 2–60 ft. above ground. Eggs: 2–8, light blue with dark marks; I: 12–14 days; F: 18–21 days, altricial; B: 1–3.

Other Behavior: In 1890, starlings were introduced into New York City from Europe. Since then they have spread all across North America. Starlings aggressively compete with native species of birds for nesting cavities. To reduce competition from starlings for birdhouses, make sure the entrance hole is 1½ inches or less in diameter, since this is too small for starlings to enter.

Habitat: Urban and suburban areas.

Voice: Song is a running stream of squeals, squawks, and imitations of other birds; flight call a short "chjjj."

Conservation:
BBS: W ↓ C ↑ CBC: ⇑

393

Warblers are small songbirds that eat insects. They are a challenge to identify because they move very quickly and are often obscured by tree or shrub foliage. Many warblers are primarily seen during spring and fall migration, en route between their northern breeding grounds and wintering grounds in the Caribbean, Central and South America, and southern U.S.

Good places to find migrating warblers are coastal thickets, edges of lakes, river valleys, and parks.

Identifying Warblers

In spring, warblers are relatively easy to identify, because males sing and have brightly colored patterns and females generally have similar,

though more subtle, patterns.

In fall, identifying warblers can be more difficult. While the fall plumage of most adults is very similar to the spring plumage, in some cases it is significantly different.

In addition, the patterns of many immature warblers are quite dull. This is especially true of immature females, which can be very obscurely patterned and may look similar to the immature females of other warbler species.

For help in identifying fall warblers, start by familiarizing yourself with the warblers shown on these Learning Pages. They are the ones you will most commonly see. Complete descriptions of them are in their main accounts.

Common Widespread Breeding Warblers

Two warblers are commonly seen in summer, for they breed throughout most of North America and nest in areas people frequent.

Male

Common Yellowthroat
Nests in marshes, thickets, or brushy areas. Also common in fall migration. Some overwinter in West. P. 420.

Male

Yellow Warbler
Nests in shrubby areas, especially wet habitats. P. 401.

Female

Female

FALL WARBLERS

Yellow-rumped Warbler: The Most Abundant Fall Migrant

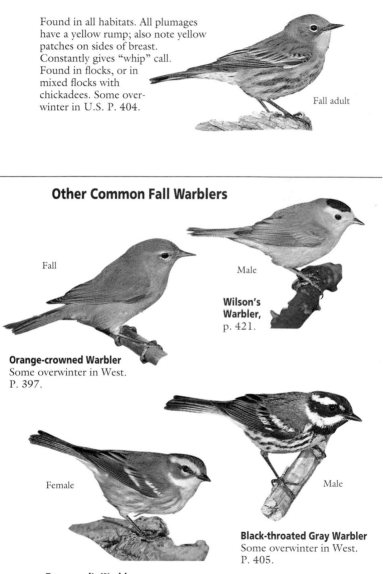

Found in all habitats. All plumages have a yellow rump; also note yellow patches on sides of breast. Constantly gives "whip" call. Found in flocks, or in mixed flocks with chickadees. Some overwinter in U.S. P. 404.

Fall adult

Other Common Fall Warblers

Fall

Male

Wilson's Warbler, p. 421.

Orange-crowned Warbler
Some overwinter in West. P. 397.

Female

Male

Black-throated Gray Warbler
Some overwinter in West. P. 405.

Townsend's Warbler
Some overwinter in West. P. 406.

Tennessee Warbler
Vermivora peregrina

Spring male

Fall adult

Immature

Identification: 4¾" SPRING—MALE: Greenish above with gray crown; white eyebrow; dark eyeline; white undertail coverts; relatively shorter tail and long straight bill. FEMALE: Similar, but head olive-gray; throat, breast, and eyebrow lightly washed with yellow. FALL—ADULT AND IMM: Olive-green above; yellow eyebrow; variable amounts of yellow on breast and belly; usually hint of a wing bar. Distinguished from Orange-crowned Warbler by white undertail coverts, more distinct eyeline and eyebrow, and no breast streaks.

Feeding: Eats insects, spiders, fruit.

Nesting: Grassy cup nest on ground, concealed by vegetation, often in damp area. Eggs: 4–7, white with reddish-brown marks; I: 11–12 days; F: ?, altricial; B: 1.

Other Behavior: Male's loud song, given from high prominent perch, makes him conspicuous during breeding season. Female is very secretive. Population increases during major outbreaks of Spruce Budworm caterpillars.

Habitat: Deciduous, mixed, or coniferous woods, forest clearings.

Voice: Song is 2–3 phrases of loud repeated notes, the last phrase fastest, like "tsit tsit tsit tsit, tsut tsut tsut tsut, tee tee tee tee tee." Call is a sweet "chip."

Conservation:
BBS: W ↑ C ⇓ CBC: ↑

Orange-crowned Warbler
Vermivora celata

Adult (western)

Fall (western)

Identification: 5" Very drab. Best identified by its lack of field marks. **Dull olive-green upperparts; pale olive-yellow below; yellow undertail coverts; faint blurred streaks on sides of breast.** IMM: Grayish wash overall; pale yellow undertail coverts. •West Coast birds are more yellow overall; eastern birds are grayer. More common in the West. Orange crown patch is seldom visible in the field.

Feeding: Eats insects, berries. Can be seen foraging low in weeds. In winter comes to bird feeding stations for nuts, suet.

Nesting: Cuplike nest of bark strips and grasses, placed on ground or in shrub. Eggs: 3–6, creamy white with reddish-brown markings; I: 12–14 days; F: 8–10 days, altricial; B: 1.

Other Behavior: The scientific name of this species, *celata*, means concealed. It refers to the orange crown patch, which is almost always hidden under the olive head feathers, except when the bird's crest is raised. Some females and imm. lack this patch.

Habitat: Dense thickets, forest edges, brushy fields.

Voice: Song is a high-pitched chipping trill, trailing off at end. Call is a metallic "chet."

Conservation: BBS: W ↓ C CBC: ↓

397

Nashville Warbler

Vermivora ruficapilla

Male

Immature

Identification: 5″ Wags tail. MALE: **Gray head with semivisible rufous crown patch; bold white eye-ring; yellow throat; yellow breast and undertail coverts are separated by patch of white on lower belly;** olive-green upperparts. Duller overall in fall. FEMALE AND IMM: **Buffy eye-ring and duller overall,** especially imm. female, which has grayish-olive head with no rufous; whitish throat. •Told from Connecticut Warbler by smaller size, dark legs, and yellow throat.

Feeding: Eats insects, including tent caterpillars, gypsy moths, and grasshoppers.

Nesting: Cuplike nest of pine needles, mosses, fur, hair, placed on ground, often at base of shrub. Eggs: 4–5, white with brown dots; I: 11–12 days; F: 11 days, altricial; B: 1.

Other Behavior: Rufous crown patch is partly concealed by other feathers. Can be exposed when bird raises crest, such as when alarmed or displaying to another bird.

Habitat: Open second-growth woods, thickets, woodland edges.

Voice: Song is a repeated 1st phrase followed by a shorter lower trill, like "see-it see-it see-it, titititi." Call is a metallic "chink."

Conservation: BBS: W ↑ C ⇑ CBC: ↑

Virginia's Warbler
Vermivora virginiae

Male

Female

Identification: 4¾" **MALE:** Bold white eye-ring; yellow rump and undertail coverts; whitish underparts, except for yellow patch on breast; gray upperparts; concealed reddish crown patch. **FEMALE AND IMM:** Female and imm. male are duller with less yellow on breast. Imm. female has brownish wash on upperparts with little or no yellow on breast.

Feeding: Eats insects, including caterpillars. Forages on ground or flies into air to catch insects.

Nesting: Nest of moss and grass, placed on ground at base of bush or in grasses. Eggs: 3–5, white with brown speckles; I: ?; F: ?, altricial; B: 2.

Other Behavior: Found in small groups in winter. Breeding biology needs more study. Tends to twitch tail frequently.

Habitat: Dry woodlands, chaparral, scrub oak brushlands, canyons and ravines at 6,000–9,000 ft. elevation.

Voice: Song is series of 1- or 2-syllable notes on same pitch or rising at end. Call is a metallic "chink."

Conservation:
BBS: W ⇑ C

399

Lucy's Warbler
Vermivora luciae

Identification: 4½" Very small; gray above; whitish below; **rufous crown and rump.**

Feeding: Eats insects it finds on mesquite, shrubs, and desert vegetation.

Nesting: Nest is cup of bark and weeds lined with hair, placed in natural cavity, old woodpecker hole, or abandoned Verdin nest. Eggs: 3–7, white with brown dots; I: ?; F: ?, altricial; B: ?

Other Behavior: This species and the Prothonotary Warbler are the only cavity-nesting warblers in N. America. It is an early spring migrant that is active and frequently flicks tail. Breeding biology needs more study.

Habitat: Woodland and riparian areas in arid Southwest.

Voice: Song is a series of staccato trilled notes that slow at end. Call is a high metallic "pink."

Conservation:
BBS: W ↓ C

Yellow Warbler

Dendroica petechia

Male

Female

Identification: 5″ In all plumages, has yellow tail spots. MALE: All yellow with reddish streaks on breast. FEMALE AND IMM: Duller yellow, with breast streaks fainter or absent. Imm. females do not have breast stripes and are buffy olive with much less yellow in plumage.

•There are a number of subspecies of this warbler. Alaskan birds are smaller and dull olive-green; Southwestern birds are paler; birds in Florida Keys are bright gold.

Feeding: Eats caterpillars, cankerworms, gypsy moths, beetles, aphids, and other insects.

Nesting: Nest of milkweed stem fibers, grasses, down from willow seeds, and spider's silk, placed in upright fork of shrub or small tree 3–12 ft. high. Eggs: 4–6, white with blotches at end; I: 10 days; F: 9–11 days, altricial; B: 1.

Other Behavior: Begins southward movement in July.

Habitat: Shrubby areas, especially near water with willows and alder; yards, gardens.

Voice: Song sounds like "sweet sweet sweet I'm so sweet," with last note accented. Also has unaccented song version. Call is a musical "chip."

Conservation: BBS: W ↑ C ↓ CBC: →

Magnolia Warbler

Dendroica magnolia

Spring male

Spring female

Immature

Identification: 5ʺ In all plumages has large white spots midway on tail. SPRING—MALE: Yellow underparts, with heavy black streaks radiating down breast; black face with broad white eyebrow; 2 wing bars join to form a white patch; yellow rump; white undertail coverts. FEMALE: Similar, with finer streaking on breast; 2 white wing bars; grayer eyebrow and face. FALL—ADULT AND IMM: Narrow gray band across upper breast; white undertail coverts; thin eye-ring; olive back.

Feeding: Eats insects and spiders, foraging at low to middle levels in trees and understory.

Nesting: Nest of twigs and grasses, placed on conifer limb. Eggs: 3–5, white with brown spots; I: 11–13 days; F: 8–10 days, altricial; B: 1.

Other Behavior: Often fans tail, revealing white spots, as it moves about branches foraging.

Habitat: Woodlands and coniferous forests, especially thickets of spruce, hemlock, balsam fir. Most abundant in earlier-growth habitats.

Voice: Song is a series of short musical notes, like "weety, weety, weety, wee." Call is a longish "clenk."

Conservation: BBS: W ⇑ C ⇓ CBC: ↓

Cape May Warbler

Dendroica tigrina

Spring male

Spring female

Immature female

Identification: 5″ Birds in all plumages have yellow or olive-yellow rumps and are streaked below. SPRING—MALE: Chestnut-orange ear patch surrounded by yellow; black streaks on yellow underparts; white wing patch; short tail. FEMALE: Yellow patch on neck below ear patch; 2 narrow white wing bars; paler yellow below with faint streaks. FALL—MALE: Duller than spring male, but still has white wing patch; at least some chestnut on ear patch. FEMALE: Duller than spring female with still a tinge of yellow on neck and underparts. IMM—MALE: Ear patch lacks chestnut; wing patch smaller than spring male's. FEMALE: Very drab, often lacking any yellow except on rump.

Feeding: Eats insects. Hovers at tips of branches.

Nesting: Bulky cup of moss, twigs, placed in spruce or fir. Eggs: 4–9, cream, marked; I: ?; F: ?, altricial; B: ?

Other Behavior: Population increases when there is Spruce Budworm outbreak.

Habitat: Spruce forests; in migration, woodlands.

Voice: Song is a very high-pitched "seet, seet, seet, seet." Call is a very high "tsee."

Conservation:
BBS: W ⇑ C CBC: ↑

Yellow-rumped Warbler

Dendroica coronata

Male "Audubon's"

Fall adult "Audubon's"

Identification: 5½" Formerly considered 2 species, the northern and eastern "Myrtle Warbler" and western "Audubon's Warbler." Now considered 1 species. **Birds in all plumages have a yellow rump and a yellow patch on side, in front of each wing.** SPRING—MALE: "Myrtle Warbler" has yellow crown patch, white throat; "Audubon's Warbler" similar, with yellow throat. SPRING FEMALE, FALL ADULTS, AND IMM: Same basic pattern as breeding males, but duller, with more brown in plumage. Some imm. females may lack yellow crown and side patch.

Feeding: Eats insects, and berries, especially in winter. Comes to bird feeders for suet and fruit.

Nesting: Cup of twigs, grasses, rootlets, placed 5–50 ft. up in conifer. Eggs: 4–5, cream with brown marks; I: 12–13 days; F: 12–14 days, altricial; B: 2.

Other Behavior: Most abundant warbler across U.S. Commonly seen on fall migration, sometimes in flocks. Regularly winters in U.S.

Habitat: Coniferous or mixed forests. In winter, brushy thickets of bayberry and wax myrtle.

Voice: "Myrtle's" song is musical trill, often in 2-note phrases. Call is sharp "check." "Audubon's" song is slow warble. Call is like "whip."

Conservation: BBS: W ↓ C ↑ CBC: ↑

Black-throated Gray Warbler

Dendroica nigrescens

Male

Identification: 5″ In all plumages, has black-and-white head pattern with black mask through the eye; 1 white stripe behind eye; another white stripe below cheek; small yellow dot in front of eye. **MALE:** Black throat. **FEMALE:** Similar, but duller overall, with some white on throat. **IMM:** Resemble adults. Imm. female grayer and browner; may have all-white throat; indistinct streaks on side.

Feeding: Actively forages for insects in trees and bushes.

Nesting: Nest of grasses and plant material is lined with feathers, hair, placed in deciduous or coniferous tree or bush. Eggs: 3–5, cream with brown marks; I: ?; F: ?, altricial; B: ?

Other Behavior: More study of breeding biology is needed.

Habitat: Dry oak or pinyon-juniper woodland, manzanita thickets, and chaparral.

Voice: Song is a series of buzzy notes with last note higher, like "weezy weezy weezy weezy wheet." Call a nonmusical "tup."

Conservation: BBS: W ↑ C CBC: ↑

Townsend's Warbler

Dendroica townsendi

Male

Female

Immature female

Identification: 5″ MALE: **Black ear patch bordered by broad yellow eyebrow and a yellow stripe below; black throat; yellow lower breast;** white underbelly; white wing bars; white on 2 outer tail feathers; black streaking on flanks. FEMALE: **Ear patch duller; throat mostly yellow, with dark streaking on lower throat and flanks.** IMM—MALE: Similar to adult female. FEMALE: Considerably duller. Told from imm. female Black-throated Green Warbler by yellowish breast, faint black smudge on breast sides, and lack of yellow on vent.

Feeding: Feeds high in treetops on insects, spiders. Occasionally visits feeders for suet, nuts, fruit.

Nesting: Cup of grasses, twigs, lichens, feathers, placed in top of tall conifer. Eggs: 3–5, white with brown marks; I: 12 days; F: 8–10 days, altricial; B: ?

Other Behavior: May join mixed-species winter flocks.

Habitat: Mature coniferous woods, especially fir and pine-oak forests.

Voice: Song is 5–6 buzzy high-pitched "zee" notes with 2–3 higher buzzy notes at end. Call is a nonmusical "tick."

Conservation: BBS: W ↑ C CBC: ⇑

406

Hermit Warbler

Dendroica occidentalis

Male

Female

Identification: 5½" **MALE: All-yellow face and forehead; black throat; gray back heavily streaked with black; white underparts. FEMALE: Much less black in throat;** hint of olive wash at edges of ear patch. **IMM—MALE:** Similar to adult female. **FEMALE: No black on throat; ear patch edged with dark olive; white underparts with no streaking; olive on upperparts.** •Can hybridize with Townsend's Warbler. The hybrids show the head pattern of Hermit Warbler, with yellow breast and dark streaks on sides like Townsend's.

Feeding: Eats insects and spiders.

Nesting: Nest of pine needles, plant fibers, and spider's silk is saddled to limb of conifer 20–100 ft. high. Eggs: 3–5, white with dark spots; I: 12 days; F: 8–10 days, altricial; B: ?

Other Behavior: Found high in the crowns of coniferous trees. Is most conspicuous during breeding, when male sings in May and June.

Habitat: Mature coniferous forests, especially with Douglas Fir and spruce.

Voice: Song is a series of high-pitched "see" notes with 2–3 slower notes at end. Call is a nonmusical "tick."

Conservation: BBS: W ↑ C CBC: ↑

Black-throated Green Warbler

Dendroica virens

Male

Female

Immature female

Identification: 5" MALE: Olive-green above; black throat and upper breast; yellow face; olive line through eye; olive ear patch surrounded by yellow. FEMALE: Similar, but has pale yellow throat with much less black on it. IMM—MALE: In nonbreeding, practically identical to adult female. FEMALE: Paler, with pale throat and breast and faint dusky streaks on sides. • In all plumages, has yellow wash on vent area.

Feeding: Eats insects and berries. Forages at medium to high levels in trees.

Nesting: Cup of grass and bark shreds is lined with feathers, hair, placed high in conifer. Eggs: 4–5, whitish with marks; I: 12 days; F: 8–10 days, altricial; B: 1.

Other Behavior: Different warbler species have varying numbers of songs, and these are sung in different contexts. The male Black-throated Green Warbler has 2 song types, 1 with an accented and 1 with an unaccented ending. Accented-ending song is given when near females, low in vegetation, or foraging. Unaccented-ending song is given from exposed perches when advertising territory or when close to other males.

Habitat: Open coniferous and mixed deciduous forests, second growth.

Voice: Song has several variants: accented "zee zee zee zoo zee"; or unaccented "zoo zee zoo zoo zee." Call is a non-musical "tick."

Conservation: BBS: W C ⇓ CBC: ↑

408

Grace's Warbler

Dendroica graciae

Male

Identification: 5" **MALE:** Yellow throat and breast; yellow eyebrow, which becomes white behind the eye; gray above with black streaks; white below with streaks on sides. **FEMALE AND IMM:** Duller than adult male, especially imm. female, which is browner and usually indistinctly streaked above.

Feeding: Forages high in trees. Creeps along branches or flycatches. Eats insects, spiders.

Nesting: Nest of grasses, oak catkins, and spiderweb lined with rootlets, feathers, placed in clump of pine needles at branch tip. Eggs: 3–4, white with brown marks; I: ?; F: ?, altricial; B: 2.

Other Behavior: Strongly associated with pines. Nests and forages chiefly in pines. More study of breeding biology needed.

Habitat: Montane pine-oak forests, usually above 6,000 ft.

Voice: Song is variable whistled notes that rise in trill at end. Call note is a sweet "chip."

Conservation: BBS: W ↓ C

Palm Warbler

Dendroica palmarum

Spring adult (eastern)

Fall

Spring adult (western)

Identification: 5½" In all plumages: constantly bobs tail; yellow undertail coverts; often forages on ground. SPRING ADULT: Sexes similar. Chestnut crown; yellow eyebrow and throat; underparts streaked with chestnut; rump olive-yellow. Eastern birds have yellowish underparts; western birds have grayish-white underparts. FALL ADULT AND IMM: Similar, but duller and browner overall, including crown.

Feeding: Eats insects, which it picks off the ground. Hops rather than walks.

Nesting: Nests in spruce bogs or dry plains of pines. Grassy cup lined with feathers, fine grasses, placed on ground near spruce trunk or low in shrub or low branches of conifer. Eggs: 4–5, creamy with wreath of brown marks; I: 12 days; F: 12 days, altricial; B: 1–2.

Other Behavior: One of the commonest warblers in S. Fla. throughout winter. Birds that breed in the East winter on the Gulf Coast from W. Fla. to N.E. Mex. Birds that breed in the West winter in S. Fla., the W. Indies, and occasionally on Atlantic Coast to Va.

Habitat: Spruce bogs. On migration and in winter, grassy fields, brushy areas, beaches, lawns.

Voice: Song is a buzzy trill that may rise. Call is a musical sharp "sup."

Conservation: BBS: W ⇓ C CBC: ⇓

Bay-breasted Warbler

Dendroica castanea

Spring male

Fall adult

Identification: 5½" **All plumages have dark gray legs.** Spring Male: **Chestnut** (i.e., bay) **crown, throat, upper breast, and sides;** black face; pinky-buff patch on side of neck; 2 white wing bars. Female: **Paler, with less chestnut on head and sides.** Fall Adult and Imm: Yellowish olive above with some streaking; underparts buffy white, with trace of chestnut or warm buff on flanks; buff undertail coverts. Imm. female lacks chestnut or buff on flanks. •The similar imm. Blackpoll Warbler has straw-colored feet and legs (which often have dark sides) and white undertail coverts; it is yellowish green below, with faint streaks on sides. The similar imm. Pine Warbler has an unstreaked back and is more gray-brown.

Feeding: Feeds on insects, which it gleans from leaves.

Nesting: Grass and twig nest in conifer. Eggs: 4–7, white with marks; I: 12–13 days; F: 11–12 days, altricial; B: 1.

Other Behavior: Fall migration is earlier than Blackpoll's.

Habitat: Coniferous forests.

Voice: Song is a series of high-pitched doubled notes, like "seetzy, seetzy, seetzy." Call is a high-pitched "see."

Conservation:
BBS: W C ↓ CBC: ↓

Blackpoll Warbler

Dendroica striata

Fall adult

Spring male

Spring female

Identification: 5½" **All plumages tend to have yellowish or yellowish-pink legs; yellow soles of feet; white wing bars; some streaking on sides.** SPRING—MALE: **Chickadee-like face pattern of black cap and white cheeks;** white below; black streaks on sides and back. FEMALE: **Olive-gray streaked cap and upperparts;** underparts whitish or yellowish, with fine streaking on sides. FALL ADULT AND IMM: Olive-green above; sides of legs may be dark brown; throat and breast greenish yellow; fine streaking on sides; belly and long undertail coverts white. Distinguished from fall Pine and Bay-breasted Warblers by leg color (usually), white undertail coverts, and lower belly contrasting with greenish-yellow breast; faint streaks on sides; pale eyebrow.

Feeding: Eats insects, spiders, a few seeds and berries.

Nesting: Grassy nest in spruce. Eggs: 4–5, white with brown dots; I: 11 days; F: 11–12 days, altricial; B: 1–2.

Other Behavior: Abundant fall migrant.

Habitat: Spruce-fir forests. In migration, other woodlands.

Voice: Song is series of extremely high "seet" notes, loudest in middle. Call is loud "chip."

Conservation:
BBS: W ⇓ C

412

Black-and-white Warbler
Mniotilta varia

Male

Female

Identification: 5¼" Creeps down tree trunks like a nuthatch. MALE: Black and white striped crown, upperparts, and underparts; black throat and ear patch much reduced or lost in winter. FEMALE: Similar, but has gray ear patch; white throat; grayish streaking on underparts. IMM—MALE: Similar to adult female, but has blacker streaking on sides and undertail coverts. FEMALE: Ear patch, flanks, and undertail coverts are buffy.

Feeding: Relatively long bill enables it to get insects from under the bark of tree trunks and limbs.

Nesting: Grassy cup with leaves, moss, placed on ground, concealed near base of tree or under fallen branch. Eggs: 4–5, creamy, circled with brown marks; I: 10–13 days; F: 8–12 days, altricial; B: 1–2.

Other Behavior: One of the earliest migrants in spring, often before trees have leafed out.

Habitat: Deciduous and mixed woodlands, especially damp woods.

Voice: Song is high-pitched "wee-see wee-see wee-see." Calls are a soft "tseet" and a sharp "pit."

Conservation:
BBS: W ⇑ C ↓ CBC: ↑

American Redstart

Setophaga ruticilla

Male

Female

Identification: 5¼" Constantly flits about with tail fanned, exposing bright orange tail patches on male and yellow tail patches on female and imm. MALE: Black upperparts and chest; orange patches on wings and sides. FEMALE AND IMM: Olive-gray upperparts; yellow patches on wings and sides. Imm. female lacks, or shows much reduced, wing patches. Imm. male, in spring, shows some black body or head feathers; salmon on wing, tail, and side patches.

Feeding: Frequently flycatches, also gleans. Eats insects, occasionally seeds and berries on migration.

Nesting: Cup of grasses, bark, and spider's silk, placed in crotch of small tree or shrub. Eggs: 2–5, whitish with brown marks; I: 12 days; F: 8–9 days, altricial; B: ?

Other Behavior: Very active. Adult males breed in more preferred habitat than 1st-year males.

Habitat: Deciduous and mixed woodlands, thickets.

Voice: Song is a quite variable series of high notes, ending with a downslurred note. Call is a sweet "chip."

Conservation: BBS: W ⇓ C ↓ CBC: ↑

Ovenbird

Seiurus aurocapillus

Identification: 6″ Orange crown bordered by 2 dark brown stripes; white eye-ring; olive brown back; white below, with heavy dark stripes composed of elongated spots on breast and flanks.

Feeding: Eats insects, worms, spiders. Pokes under leaves.

Nesting: Nest of grasses and rootlets, placed on ground, is always roofed over with branches, leaves. The entrance is a small slit. Eggs: 3–6, white with brown and gray marks; I: 11–14 days; F: 8–11 days, altricial; B: 1–2.

Other Behavior: Heard more than seen. Song often has a ventriloquial quality. The Ovenbird's name comes from the fact that its domed-over nest looks like a Dutch oven. Walks on ground and fallen branches, frequently "teeters."

Habitat: Mature deciduous or mixed forests.

Voice: Song is a ringing series of notes that increase in loudness, like "teacher teacher teacher." Call is a sharp "chip."

Conservation:
BBS: W ↓ C ⇓ CBC: ↓

415

Northern Waterthrush

Seiurus noveboracensis

Eastern

Western

Identification: 5¾" Eyebrow, of even width or tapering behind eye, is yellowish buff (eastern birds) or whitish (western birds); uniformly colored underparts are pale yellowish buff in eastern birds and whitish in western birds; heavily streaked with brown from chin to breast and along flanks; flesh-colored legs.

Feeding: Searches under leaves and on fallen logs. Wades in water. Eats insects, mollusks, crustaceans, small minnows, smaller prey than Louisiana Waterthrush.

Nesting: Nest of mosses, leaves, and grasses is concealed in roots of upturned tree or under the overhang of a bank near standing water. Eggs: 3–6, white with variable brown or purplish marks; I: 12 days; F: 10 days, altricial; B: ?

Other Behavior: Bobs tail while walking.

Habitat: Wooded ponds, swamps, willow thickets, lake shores, beside still water or slow-moving rivers.

Voice: Song is a loud series of notes with a downslurred ending. Call is a metallic "chink."

Conservation: BBS: W ↑ C ⇑ CBC: ↓

Connecticut Warbler

Oporornis agilis

Male

Identification: 5¾" In all plumages: complete bold white or whitish eye-ring; brown or gray hood; yellow underparts; short-tailed appearance created by long undertail coverts reaching more than halfway to tip of tail; long legs. MALE: Gray hood. FEMALE AND IMM: Paler underparts; browner hood; paler throat.

Feeding: Feeds on the ground or on fallen logs, searching for insects, spiders.

Nesting: Nest of leaves, grasses, plant fibers, placed on the ground, usually at the base of a shrub or sapling. Eggs: 3–5, white with brown marks; I: ?; F: ?, altricial; B: ?

Other Behavior: Generally more rare than Mourning or MacGillivray's Warbler. Skulks in undergrowth. Bobs head while walking with elevated tail. Breeding biology needs more study.

Habitat: Spruce and tamarack bogs, open poplar woods, willow scrub, young Jack Pine stands.

Voice: Song is loud repetitive notes, like "wee cher cher wee cher cher." Call is metallic "chink."

Conservation:
BBS: W ↑ C ⇑

417

Mourning Warbler
Oporornis philadelphia

Male

Female

Immature

Identification: 5¼" MALE: Gray hood; lacks eye-ring; black mottled patch on upper breast. FEMALE: Paler gray hood; very faint, broken, whitish eye-ring, which may occasionally be complete; pale throat; no black on breast. IMM: Has thin broken eye-ring; yellowish throat breaks through lower part of hood and connects to yellow underparts; hood browner, less evident than that of imm. MacGillivray's Warbler; imm. male may have some black feathers on sides of upper breast.

Feeding: Feeds on the ground or gleans from understory. Eats insects and spiders.

Nesting: Bulky cuplike nest of dead leaves and grasses, placed on ground at base of shrub, or low in tangle. Eggs: 3–5, white with variable brown marks; I: 12 days; F: 7–9 days, altricial; B: 1.

Other Behavior: Hops on ground, while Connecticut Warbler walks. Generally skulks in dense undergrowth.

Habitat: Dense undergrowth of moist woods, brushy areas, swamps, and bogs.

Voice: Song is loud series of 2-note phrases with the 2nd part lower-pitched. Call is a loud "check."

Conservation:
BBS: W ⇑ C ↑

MacGillivray's Warbler

Oporornis tolmiei

Male

Female

Identification: 5¼" **All plumages have broken white eye ring that looks like a broad white crescent above and below eye;** lack yellow throat; have appearance of breastband. **MALE:** Bluish-gray hood; dark lores; black mottled area on upper breast. **FEMALE:** Similar, but duller; gray throat; lacks black on upper breast. **IMM:** Grayish-olive or olive-brown head that blends into color of back; light gray throat creates hooded effect and contrasts with yellowish underparts. Similar imm. Mourning Warbler has yellowish throat.

Feeding: Eats insects and other invertebrates. Forages low in undergrowth.

Nesting: Nest is cup of weeds and grasses, placed low in shrub or bush. Eggs: 3–6, white with brown marks; I: 11 days; F: 8–9 days, altricial; B: 1.

Other Behavior: Pumps tail in flight. Hops, does not walk. Skulks in dense understory.

Habitat: Found in dense understory of mountain forests or scrubby hillsides.

Voice: Song is several buzzy notes on 1 pitch, ending in a lower-pitched downslur. Call is a loud "check."

Conservation: BBS: W ↓ C ⇓ CBC: →

Common Yellowthroat

Geothlypis trichas

Male

Female

Immature male

Identification: 5″ MALE: Yellow throat and upper breast; black mask with grayish-white border; buff flanks; yellow undertail coverts. FEMALE: Yellow throat and breast; olive-brown face and upperparts; whitish eye-ring; suggestion of eyebrow; brown wash on forehead. IMM—MALE: Partly developed mask often obscured by pale feather tips. FEMALE: Paler than adult female, with buffy-yellow throat; no brown on forehead. •There is much geographical variation in this species. Northern and eastern birds have whitish belly and yellow undertail coverts; southwestern birds have solid yellow underparts.

Feeding: Eats insects, spiders, and seeds gleaned from the ground or shrubs.

Nesting: Nest of coarse grasses, dead leaves, lined with fine grasses or hair, placed 1–2 ft. high in shrubbery. Eggs: 3–4, creamy white with brown marks; I: 12 days; F: 8–9 days, altricial; B: 1–2.

Other Behavior: Very abundant species.

Habitat: Dense brushy habitats near wet areas, drier habitats with dense understory.

Voice: Song sounds like "witchity, witchity, witchity," or "your money, your money, your money." Call is sharp "tchat, tchat."

Conservation: BBS: W ↑ C ↓ CBC: →

Wilson's Warbler

Wilsonia pusilla

Male

Female

Identification: 4¾" MALE: Black cap; yellow below; olive-green above. FEMALE: Has some black on crown, occasionally extensive. IMM— MALE: Like adult male, but sometimes duller. FEMALE: Does not have any black on crown. •Western birds are brighter yellow on face and underparts than eastern birds.

Feeding: Actively flycatches. Eats insects, berries.

Nesting: May be loosely colonial in ideal habitat. Nest of grasses, leaves, mosses, placed on the ground, usually at base of shrub. Eggs: 4–6, white with brown marks; I: 11–13 days; F: 8–10 days, altricial; B: 1.

Other Behavior: Frequently twitches tail and flicks wings. Stays low in undergrowth. More common in the West than the East.

Habitat: Willow and alder thickets near water, moist woodlands.

Voice: Song is a chattering trill that drops in pitch. Call is a flat low "chet."

Conservation: BBS: W ↓ C CBC: ↑

421

Canada Warbler
Wilsonia canadensis

Male

Immature female

Identification: 5¼" MALE: Necklace of black streaks across yellow breast; yellow "spectacles"; unmarked dark blue-gray back; white undertail coverts. FEMALE: Necklace is blurred and more subtle, especially on imm. female.

Feeding: Often flycatches. Feeds at low to middle levels in vegetation. Eats insects, spiders.

Nesting: Nest of weeds, leaves, and grasses, placed in tree stump or in roots of upturned tree, or sphagnum hummock. Eggs: 3–5, cream with brown marks; I: ?; F: ?, altricial; B: ?

Other Behavior: Frequently twitches tail. Breeding biology needs more study.

Habitat: Dense understory of mature deciduous or mixed woodlands, shrubby areas near streams and swamps.

Voice: Song is a musical warble that starts with a "chip" note. Call is a loud "chit."

Conservation: TREND UNKNOWN.

Red-faced Warbler

Cardellina rubrifrons

Identification: 5½" Red face, throat, and upper breast; black cap extends down sides of head; gray above; whitish area on nape and rump. **IMM:** Some birds have orange-red or pinkish faces.

Feeding: Feeds on insects gleaned from outer branches and trunks of conifers.

Nesting: Nest of pine needles and dead leaves is concealed on ground under log or shrub. Eggs: 3–4, white with brown spots; I: ?; F: ?, altricial; B: ?

Other Behavior: Little known about breeding biology. Needs more study.

Habitat: Mountain forests above 6,000 ft.

Voice: Song is variable series of clear ringing notes. Call is a low "tship."

Conservation: BBS: W ↑ C

Painted Redstart

Myioborus pictus

Identification: 5¾" Striking combination of jet-black head, chest, and upperparts; carmine-red breast; bold white wing and tail patches.

Feeding: Flits low onto tree trunk to snatch insects. Also flycatches. Eats insects, spiders.

Nesting: Nest is cup of grasses, weeds, and bark strips, placed on ground under rock, bank, or tree roots. Eggs: 3–7, creamy white with brown marks; I : 13–14 days; F: 9–13 days, altricial; B: 2.

Other Behavior: Frequently fans tail, revealing white outer tail feathers. Often polygynous.

Habitat: Pine-oak and pinyon-juniper forests, especially in mountain canyons above 6,000 ft.

Voice: Song is a musical warble. Call is whistled "chwee."

Conservation: BBS: W ⇓ C CBC: ↑

Yellow-breasted Chat
Icteria virens

Male

Identification: 7½" The largest warbler. MALE: White spectacles; black lores; white moustache stripe; yellow throat and breast; long tail; thick bill. FEMALE: Similar, with gray lores.

Feeding: Eats insects, berries, wild grapes, and other fruit. Forages low in shrubbery.

Nesting: Can be loosely colonial. Nest is a bulky cup of dead leaves, straw, weeds, and shredded bark lined with fine grasses, placed in shrub or small tree. Eggs: 3–5, white with brown marks; I: 11–12 days; F: 8–12 days, altricial; B: 2.

Other Behavior: Heard more than seen. Song is more reminiscent of a mockingbird's than a warbler's. In spring, males perform song flights.

Habitat: Dense thickets and brushy edges in dry or moist areas.

Voice: Song is an amazing assortment of whistles, rattles, squeaks, scolds, mews. Call is a grating "chack."

Conservation: BBS: W ↑ C ↓ CBC: ↓

Olive Warbler

Peucedramus taeniatus

Male

Female

Identification: 5¼" **MALE:** Tawny-orange head and throat; black patch extending through and broadening behind eye; white wing bars, base of primary feathers, and outer tail feathers. **FEMALE:** Similar pattern; olive-gray head; gray cheek patch; face and chest are yellow. **IMM:** Duller, especially imm. female, which has grayish cheek patch and buffy eyebrow.

Feeding: Forages for insects in the tops of trees. Creeps along pine branches and explores clusters of pine needles, probing for insects with its long bill.

Nesting: Nest of mosses, lichens, and pine needles, placed at end of pine branch. Eggs: 3–4, pale blue or white with dark smudges; I: ?; F: ?, altricial; B: ?

Other Behavior: Breeding biology needs more study. In the nonbreeding season may join mixed-species flocks containing other warbler species.

Habitat: Coniferous forests above 7,000 ft.

Voice: Song is loud "peter peter peter," like song of Tufted Titmouse. Call is whistled "peuw."

Conservation: TREND UNKNOWN.

Hepatic Tanager
Piranga flava

Male

Female

Identification: 7½" **MALE:** Brick-red with a **dark ear patch** and grayish tinge to wings and back; large dark gray bill. **FEMALE: All yellowish with a grayish cheek, grayish crown and back,** and grayish flanks; large dark gray bill. **IMM— MALE:** In 1st year, mostly yellow with some red patches; in 2nd year, mostly red with some patches of yellow. **FEMALE:** Like adult female. Imm. plumage kept 2 years.

Feeding: Forages in tree foliage for insects. Often catches flies in midair as well.

Nesting: Nest of grasses and weed stems lined with finer material, placed in the fork of horizontal tree branch 15–50 ft. above the ground. Eggs: 3–5, bluish with dark marks; I: ?; F: ?, altricial; B: ?

Other Behavior: Breeding biology needs more study. Nests in mountain forests up to 7,000 ft. The similar Summer Tanager is usually seen in lower valleys and along streams.

Habitat: Pine and oak woods in mountains, canyons.

Voice: Song is a string of varied whistles; call is a soft "chwick."

Conservation:
BBS: W ⇑ C

Summer Tanager
Piranga rubra

Female

Immature male

Male

Identification: 7½" **MALE:** Uniformly bright rose-red head and body; darker red wings and tail. **FEMALE:** Yellowish below; slightly darker above; no gray cheek patch or white wing bars. **IMM—MALE:** Patches of red and green over body. **FEMALE:** Like adult female. Imm. plumage kept 1 year.

Feeding: May catch insect prey in midair. Fond of eating bees and wasps, and will raid their nests. Eats fruit and berries. Sometimes comes to bird feeders for fruit, bread crumbs, and peanut butter mixtures.

Nesting: Nest of weed stems, bark, and coarse grasses lined with finer materials, placed on horizontal branch of tree 10–35 ft. above the ground. Eggs: 3–5, pale bluish green with dark marks; I: 12 days; F: ?, altricial; B: ?

Other Behavior: Usually concealed in tree foliage. More easily detected by song. Range in the East is diminishing. Where range overlaps with Scarlet Tanager's, these 2 species are aggressive to each other.

Habitat: Pine-oak woods, willows and cottonwoods along streams.

Voice: Song is a string of varied whistles; call is a rapid harsh "chchbit."

Conservation:
BBS: W ↑ C ↓ CBC: ↑

Western Tanager

Piranga ludoviciana

Greenish-morph female

Summer male

Grayish-morph female

Identification: 7" SUMMER—MALE: **Red face; yellow belly; black back, wings, and tail;** 2 wing bars, the upper broad and yellow, the lower thin and whitish. FEMALE: Two morphs: greenish yellow with gray back; and mostly gray with yellow only on head and undertail coverts. Both have brown wings with 2 light wing bars. WINTER—MALE: Similar to summer, but head yellowish with some red and some fine streaking. FEMALE: Like summer.

Feeding: Forages in foliage. Eats wasps and other insects, often catching them in midair. May come to bird feeders to eat halved oranges.

Nesting: Nest of twigs and rootlets lined with finer materials, placed on the outer limbs of trees 10–65 ft. above the ground. Eggs: 3–5, pale blue with dark marks; I: 13 days; F: 13–15 days, altricial; B: ?

Other Behavior: Some winter on West Coast, often around flowering eucalyptus.

Habitat: Coniferous or mixed forests.

Voice: Song is a series of 2- to 3-syllable slow phrases. Call is a slurred "pit-er-ic."

Conservation: BBS: W ↓ C ↓ CBC: ↑

Northern Cardinal

Cardinalis cardinalis

Male

Female

Identification: 8½" MALE: **All bright red with black around base of bill; large crest;** reddish bill. FEMALE: **Buffy below; grayish brown above; reddish bill,** crest, wings, and tail. Juveniles look like adult female but have dark bill.

Feeding: Feeds by hopping around on ground, gleaning food from low shrubbery and trees. Eats insects, spiders, wild fruits and berries, weed seeds. A favorite at bird feeders, where it prefers sunflower seed, safflower seed, cracked corn.

Nesting: Nest of twigs, bark strips, vines, leaves, rootlets, and paper lined with fine grass and hair, placed in dense shrubbery or among branches of small tree 1–15 ft. above ground. Eggs: 2–5, buff-white with dark marks; I: 12–13 days; F: 9–11 days, altricial; B: 1–4.

Other Behavior: At your bird feeder you may see mate-feeding, a highlight of the relationship between a pair of breeding cardinals that can occur as often as 4 times a minute. In this, the male picks up a seed, hops over to the female, and the two momentarily touch beaks as she takes the food. Mate-feeding will continue through the egg-laying and incubation phases of breeding. Both male and female sing.

Habitat: Shrubs near open areas, woods, suburban yards.

Voice: Song a series of clear repeated whistles that vary, like "whoit whoit whoit, cheer cheer cheer"; call a metallic "chip."

Conservation: BBS: W ↑ C ↑ CBC: ↓

Pyrrhuloxia
Cardinalis sinuatus

Male

Female

Identification: 8″ MALE: Gray with rose-red on face and central underparts, wings, and tail; long red-tipped crest; stubby bill orangish yellow. FEMALE: Gray with long red-tipped crest; some red on face, wings, and tail; stubby bill yellowish.

Feeding: Forages on the ground, eating weed and grass seeds, catkins, cactus fruit, mesquite beans, and insects. May come to bird feeders for sunflower seeds and fruit.

Nesting: Nest of thorny twigs, inner bark, coarse grass, and spiderweb lined with plant fibers, fine grass, horsehair, and rootlets, placed among the branches of mesquite or other thickets 5–20 ft. above the ground. Eggs: 2–5, gray-white or green-white with brown spots; I: 14 days; F: 10 days, altricial; B: 1.

Other Behavior: Male feeds female as part of courtship activities. During winter, found in small flocks and may wander to locate good food sources.

Habitat: Arid and semiarid areas with thorny shrubs and woodlands.

Voice: Song a series of clear repeated whistles that vary; call a metallic "chip."

Conservation:
BBS: W ↑ C ↓ CBC: ↓

Rose-breasted Grosbeak

Pheucticus ludovicianus

Summer male

Female

Immature male

Identification: 8″ SUMMER—MALE: **Black head and back; red triangle on breast;** white belly. **In flight, shows white patches on wings; rose-red "armpits"; white rump.** FEMALE: **Large pale bill; white eyebrow; heavy streaking on whitish breast;** 2 white wing bars. Yellow "armpits" in flight. Plumage similar in winter and on imm. WINTER—MALE: Similar to summer, but with brown edges to head and back feathers. IMM: Male looks similar to adult female, but with rosy triangle on buffy breast and reddish "armpits" (seen in flight). Imm. plumage kept until spring.

Feeding: Gleans food from tree foliage. Eats insects, seeds, tree buds, and some fruit. Comes to feeders for sunflower seed.

Nesting: Nest of coarse and fine twigs lined with horsehair, rootlets, and grasses, placed on branch of tree 5–25 ft. above the ground. Eggs: 3–6, pale blue with irregular brown spots; I: 12–14 days; F: 9–12 days, altricial; B: 1–2.

Other Behavior: Both male and female sing.

Habitat: Deciduous woods, mixed shrubs and trees.

Voice: Song a rapid series of melodious whistles, referred to as "a robin in a hurry"; call a distinctive squeak, like a sneaker on a gym floor.

Conservation:
BBS: W ⇑ C ↓ CBC: ↑

Black-headed Grosbeak

Pheucticus melanocephalus

Male

Female   Immature male

Identification: 8″ **MALE:** Black head; buffy orange breast and collar; bold white markings on black wing. In flight, shows white patches on wings and yellow "armpits." **FEMALE: Large bill; buffy eyebrow; light streaking on buffy breast; 2 white wing bars.** Yellow "armpits" in flight. **IMM:** Male similar to adult female, but buffier below and with no streaking. Female like adult female. Imm. plumage kept until spring.

Feeding: Forages in the foliage of trees, eating pine and other seeds, wild berries, insects, and spiders. Comes to bird feeders for sunflower seed, other types of seed, and fruit.

Nesting: Nest of twigs, rootlets, flower heads, and forb stems lined with stems and rootlets, placed in the fork of a tree or shrub 4–25 ft. above the ground. Eggs: 2–5, blue-white or green-white with brown spots; I: 12–13 days; F: 11–12 days, altricial; B: ?

Other Behavior: Both male and female incubate the eggs and will sing from the nest. Hybridizes with Rose-breasted Grosbeak where ranges meet in Great Plains.

Habitat: Deciduous forests, thickets, and pine-oak and pinyon-juniper woodlands.

Voice: Song similar to Rose-breasted Grosbeak's; call is a low "eek."

Conservation: BBS: W ↓ C ↑ CBC: ↓

Blue Grosbeak

Guiraca caerulea

Male

Immature in fall

Female

Immature male, 1st spring

Identification: 7″ **MALE: Dark blue overall, with 2 reddish-brown wing bars,** the upper 1 broader; large silvery bill; black feathers around base of bill. **FEMALE: Plain brown overall; dark wings and tail; 2 buffy-brown wing bars; large, gray, conical bill.** IMM: Fall male and female resemble adult female, but may be a more reddish brown. In spring, male gains some blue patches on body feathers. Imm. plumage kept 1 year.

Feeding: Forages on the ground, hopping about in search of insects; also gleans foliage. Eats spiders, seeds, and wild fruits.

Nesting: Nest of rootlets, grasses, twigs, snakeskins, cotton, and bark strips lined with rootlets, grasses, and tendrils, placed in shrub, vine tangle, or tree 3–12 ft. above the ground. Eggs: 2–5, pale blue; I: 11–12 days; F: 9–13 days, altricial; B: 2.

Other Behavior: Often twitches and rapidly spreads tail when agitated. On migration, can be found in association with buntings.

Habitat: Open areas with some shrubbery, such as roadsides, hedgerows, farmlands, prairies.

Voice: Song a warbled phrase of musical notes; call a loud "chink."

Conservation:
BBS: W ⇑ C ↓ CBC: ↓

Lazuli Bunting
Passerina amoena

Male

Female

Immature male, 1st spring

Identification: 5½" MALE: Bright sky-blue head and back; reddish breast; white belly; 2 white wing bars, upper broader and more noticeable. FEMALE: Grayish brown above; light below with buffy wash on breast; 2 faint wing bars; light bluish cast to wings, tail, and rump. IMM: Male in 1st spring has a blend of blue and brown feathers on head and back. Imm. female like adult female. Imm. plumage kept 1 year.

Feeding: Forages close to or on the ground, eating insects, the seeds of various grasses and wild oats, and wild lettuce.

Nesting: Nest of dried grasses and forbs lined with horsehair and fine grasses, placed in thicket, shrub, or small tree 1–10 ft. above the ground. Eggs: 3–5, light blue-white; I: 12 days; F: 10–15 days, altricial; B: 2–3.

Other Behavior: Hybridizes with Indigo Bunting. Males sometimes polygynous.

Habitat: Shrubs and low trees in open areas, often near water.

Voice: Song a rapid jumble of whistled notes, some occasionally burry; call a short "pit."

Conservation: BBS: W ↑ C ⇓ CBC: ⇓

Indigo Bunting

Passerina cyanea

Female

Summer male

Immature male, 1st spring

Identification: 5½" SUMMER—MALE: Deep blue overall; dark gray conical bill. FEMALE: Extremely plain brown, with faint wing bars and faint streaking; short, gray, conical bill. Keeps same plumage all year. WINTER—MALE: Brownish, with some blue on underparts, wings, and rump. IMM: Female like adult female. Male like adult female through winter, then a mixture of brown and blue feathers on body. Imm. plumage kept 1 year.

Feeding: Forages on the ground and in low foliage for insects, weed seeds, wild berries, and grains.

Nesting: Nest of dead leaves, weed stems, grasses, lined with finer grasses and downy material, placed in the fork of branch of shrub, tangle, or tree 2–10 ft. above the ground. Eggs: 2–6, white; I: 12 days; F: 10–12, altricial; B: 1–2.

Other Behavior: Male conspicuously sings from tops of trees and shrubs. Female can be very secretive. If you are anywhere near the nest, the birds will give "spit" call, do tail-flick, and be reluctant to approach the nest. Sometimes hybridizes with Lazuli Bunting.

Habitat: Brush and low trees near open areas like overgrown fields.

Voice: A short rapid series of whistles, many paired, like "tsee tsee tew tew teer teer"; call a short "spit."

Conservation: BBS: W ⇓ C ↓ CBC: ⇓

Varied Bunting

Passerina versicolor

Male

Female

Identification: 5″ **MALE: Dark blue face; reddish-brown nape; blue rump;** rest of body appears black in most lights, even though it includes blues and purples. **FEMALE: Strongly curved top to upper mandible; dull grayish-olive upperparts; gray-brown underparts; bluish-gray rump; 2 narrow buff wing bars.** **IMM:** Similar to adult female. Imm. plumage kept 1 year.

Feeding: Forages on the ground and in low foliage. Eats insects and seeds.

Nesting: Nest of stems, dried grasses, paper, and sometimes snakeskin lined with fine grasses, rootlets, and hair, placed in low foliage of bush, tangle, or tree 2–10 ft. above the ground. Eggs: 3–5, light blue; I: 12 days; F: ?, altricial; B: ?

Other Behavior: Breeding biology needs more study.

Habitat: Arid areas with thorny brush, such as dry washes.

Voice: Song a short warbled phrase; call a "tsink."

Conservation:
BBS: W ⇓ C ⇑

Painted Bunting

Passerina ciris

Female

Male

Immature male, 1st spring

Identification: 5½" **MALE:** Brilliantly colored with **blue head, red underparts, and a light green back and wings. FEMALE: Very plain; leaf-green above; lighter green below; conical gray bill.** **IMM:** Male in winter is like adult female and in spring may acquire some blue and red feathers. Imm. female is like adult female. Imm. plumage kept 1 year.

Feeding: Forages on the ground and in low foliage for the seeds of grasses and insects. May come to bird feeders for sunflower seeds and other seed mixes.

Nesting: Nest of forb stems, grasses, and leaves lined with hair, fine grasses, rootlets, and occasionally bits of snakeskin, placed in low foliage of tree or shrub 3–25 ft. above the ground. Eggs: 3–5, light blue-white or gray-white with brown spots; I: 11–12 days; F: 12–14 days, altricial; B: 2–4.

Other Behavior: Males are sometimes polygynous.

Habitat: Brush, clearcuts, mesquite, rangeland, thickets.

Voice: Song a musical warble; call a short "chit."

Conservation: BBS: W ↑ C ⇓ CBC: ⇓

438

Dickcissel
Spiza americana

Summer male

Summer female

Immature

Identification: 6½" SUMMER—MALE: Yellow breast with triangular black bib; yellow eyebrow; reddish brown shoulder. FEMALE: Similar to male, but lacks the black bib. Keeps same plumage all year. WINTER—MALE: Same as summer, but yellow tips to feathers on breast cover much of the black bib. IMM: Fine streaking on breast, with little or no yellow; brown crown with fine, dark streaks; dusky line off base of bill. Imm. plumage kept until spring.

Feeding: Forages for food on the ground, eating insects and all kinds of weed seeds and grain.

Nesting: Nest of weed stems, grasses, leaves, and occasionally cornstalk lined with rootlets, fine grasses, and hair, placed in tree or hedge 2–14 ft. above the ground. Eggs: 2–6, light blue; I: 12–13 days; F: 7–10 days, altricial; B: 1.

Other Behavior: Found in large flocks during migration and winter. During nesting season, many nests are destroyed by mowing machines; Dickcissel nests are also frequently parasitized by the Brown-headed Cowbird. Sings persistently during breeding.

Habitat: Prairies, weedy fields, grain fields.

Voice: Song is 2 short notes followed by buzzy notes, like "dick dick dickzizzel"; call is short "zzzt."

Conservation: BBS: W ↓ C ↓ CBC: ↓

439

Green-tailed Towhee
Pipilo chlorurus

Identification: 6½" **Gray face; reddish-brown cap; white chin;** unmarked back, wings, and tail are greenish.

Feeding: Forages on the ground by scratching under brush. Eats weed seeds, wild berries, insects, and may come to bird feeders for seed.

Nesting: Nest of twigs, grasses, bark, and stems lined with horsehair, rootlets, fine plant stems, placed on or near the ground under the cover of brush. Eggs: 2–5, white and heavily spotted; I: ?; F: ?, altricial; B: 2.

Other Behavior: May include notes of other birds in its song. When alarmed during breeding, will run with its tail raised high, drawing attention to itself and away from its nest.

Habitat: Dense shrubs, chaparral slopes, sage brush, manzanita. Summers in mountains; winters in lowlands and foothills.

Voice: Song 2–3 whistled notes followed by harsh trill, like "weeteer chrrrrrr"; call a catlike "meew."

Conservation: BBS: W ↓ C ↓ CBC: →

Eastern Towhee
Spotted Towhee

Pipilo erythrophthalmus   *Pipilo maculatus*

Eastern male

Eastern female

Spotted male

Spotted female

Identification: 8″ In both species **dark hood and back contrast with reddish-brown flanks and white belly.** MALE: Upperparts black. FEMALE: Upperparts reddish brown in the East, dark brown in the West. Spotted Towhee has white spots on the wings; Eastern Towhee has no spots.

Feeding: Hops backward, raking up leaf litter. Eats insects, spiders, lizards, snakes, weed and grass seeds, and wild berries. Comes to feeders for seed on ground.

Nesting: Nest of leaves, strips of bark, grasses, lined with fine grasses, placed on or near the ground in a scratched depression under brush. Eggs: 2–6, creamy with brown spots; I: 12–13 days; F: 10–12 days, altricial; B: 1–3.

Other Behavior: The distinctive "chewink" or "chweee" call note of both sexes is a good clue to their presence. In the spring, the male starts continually singing and countersinging with neighboring males. He courts the female with song and by displaying with wings and tail spread. During egg laying and incubation, the male rarely comes near the nest and the female is quite secretive. Both parents feed the nestlings.

Eastern   Spotted

Habitat: Open woods with shrub understory.

Voice: Eastern song is 2 whistles and a high trill, like "drink your teeee"; Spotted song is high trill. Call "chewink" or "chweee."

Conservation:
Eastern:
BBS: W ↑ C ↓
Spotted:
BBS: W ↑ C

California Towhee
Canyon Towhee
Pipilo crissalis   Pipilo fuscus

California

Canyon

Identification: California 9", Canyon 8½" Both species have **long tail with reddish-brown undertail coverts** and **buffy throat bordered by short streaks.** CALIFORNIA: **Uniformly dark gray-brown overall.** CANYON: **Dull brown with reddish-brown crown and central breast dot.**

California   Canyon

Feeding: California forages for food around buildings, parked cars, and tall grass. Canyon forages in tall grass and on brushy hillsides. Both eat insects, weed seeds, and grains and come to bird feeders for seed mixes.

Nesting: Both have nest of small twigs, grasses, plant stems, and inner bark lined with rootlets, horsehair, and leaves, placed on ground or in low foliage up to 12 ft. above ground. Eggs: 2–6, light blue with dark marks; I: 11 days; F: 8 days, altricial; B: 2–3.

Other Behavior: Both act tame. California is usually seen in pairs and males are very territorial. Canyon often visits campsites and picnic areas, looking for dropped food. California Towhee subspecies *P. c. eremophilus* is endangered in Inyo County.

Habitat: California: in scrub, suburban yards. Canyon: arid areas with brush, canyons.

Voice: California song is accelerating "chink" notes; call "chink." Canyon song a double-note trill; call "chillip."

Conservation: California: BBS: W ⇓ C ↓ CBC: ↓ Canyon: BBS: W ⇓ C ↓ CBC: ↓

Abert's Towhee

Pipilo aberti

Identification: 9 " Grayish brown above; buffy brown below; pale bill set off by black face.

Feeding: Forages on the ground by scratching in leaves for seeds and insects.

Nesting: Nest of plant stems, vines, and leaves lined with dried grasses, bark strips, placed on the ground or in low foliage up to 30 ft. high. Eggs: 2–5, pale blue or cream-white with dark marks; I: ?; F: 12–13 days, altricial; B: ?

Other Behavior: Lives on permanent year-round territories. Is being affected by cowbird parasitism and loss of streamside habitats.

Habitat: Cottonwoods, willows along streams.

Voice: Song a rapid "teek teek teek teek"; call a sharp "teek."

Conservation:
BBS: W ⇑ C CBC: ⇑

Sparrows are a group of small generally brown-streaked birds that are often found in grassy, weedy, or brushy areas. To some people, they may all look alike and seem hard to identify, but there are several things you can do to distinguish among them.

First, learn the most common species, which are shown on these Learning Pages. Knowing these will enable you to identify most of the sparrows that you see and give you a base from which you can begin to identify others. To find out more about these common species, see their full accounts.

Another aid to identification is to learn some of the more obvious clues that just a few species have. These include breast dots (on clear or streaked breasts), eye-rings, and white on the outer tail feathers (seen in flight).

Sparrows with Central Breast Dots

- **Always have dot on streaked breast:**
  Fox Sparrow, p. 464
  Song Sparrow, p. 465

- **Sometimes have dot on streaked breast:**
  Vesper Sparrow, p. 454
  Savannah Sparrow, p. 459

- **Always have dot on clear breast:**
  American Tree Sparrow, p. 448
  Lark Sparrow, p. 455
  Sage Sparrow, p. 457

Sparrows with White Eye-rings

Rufous-crowned Sparrow, p. 447
Brewer's Sparrow, p. 451
Field Sparrow, p. 452
Vesper Sparrow, p. 454
Sage Sparrow, p. 457
Grasshopper Sparrow, p. 461

Sparrows with White on Outer Tail Feathers

Cassin's Sparrow, p. 446
Vesper Sparrow, p. 454
Lark Sparrow, p. 455
Dark-eyed Junco, p. 472
Yellow-eyed Junco, p. 473

Other Common Birds That Look Like Sparrows

Several frequently seen birds resemble sparrows but are not related to them. The most common of these is the House Sparrow, which lives in cities, in suburbs, and on farms. It is a member of the Weaver Finch family.

Another is the female House Finch. One way to identify her is by her close association with the male, which has red on its head, breast, and rump. Both species come to bird feeders.

Male

House Sparrow, p. 507

Female

Female

House Finch, p. 499

MOST COMMONLY SEEN SPARROWS

These are among the most commonly seen sparrows. Many are more abundant in winter, when they have left their breeding grounds and are more likely to visit suburban yards and feeders.

Song Sparrow
Central spot on streaked breast.
P. 465.

Chipping Sparrow
Rusty cap, black eyeline.
P. 449.

Summer

Dark-eyed Junco
Black or gray hood, brown back, white belly. P. 472.

Fox Sparrow
Large; heavily streaked breast with central dot; reddish-brown tail.
P. 464.

Golden-crowned Sparrow
Black crown with large golden patch on forehead. P. 469.

White-crowned Sparrow
Bold black-and-white-streaked crown. P. 470.

Botteri's Sparrow
Cassin's Sparrow
Aimophila botterii   Aimophila cassinii

Botteri's

Cassin's

Identification: Botteri's 6", Cassin's 5½" Both have flat head, long rounded tail. **BOTTERI'S: Clear buffy breast; reddish-brown back** (grayer in S. Tex.) **with black streaks.** Lacks wing bars, white corners of tail, and flank streaking of Cassin's. **Best located and identified by song.** See Voice. **CASSIN'S: Clear pale breast; gray back with black marks; slight streaking along flanks; whitish wing bars on fresher fall through spring plumage.** In flight, note **white corners of tail.** Song differs from Botteri's. See Voice.

Feeding: Both species feed on the ground, eating insects and weed seeds. Cassin's occasionally eats flowers.

Nesting: Cassin's—Cuplike nest of grass lined with rootlets and hair, placed on ground or to 1 ft. high in shrub or cactus. Eggs: 3–5, white; I: ?; F: ?, altricial; B: ? Botteri's—Breeding biology needs more study.

Other Behavior: Both seen briefly flying above grass tops, then dropping down. Cassin's does song in flight as it rises up, then flutters down; courtship chases with "tzee tzee" call. Both secretive when not breeding.

Botteri's   Cassin's

Habitat: Tallgrass areas with shrubs.

Voice: Botteri's song accelerating notes, "tsp tsp tsptsp tstststs." Cassin's song short trill with 1–2 short notes at start and end, "tup tup trrrrr tew tew."

Conservation:
Botteri's:
BBS: W ⇓ C
Cassin's:
BBS: W ↑ C ⇓ CBC: ↑

Rufous-winged Sparrow
Rufous-crowned Sparrow
Aimophila carpalis   Aimophila ruficeps

Rufous-winged   Rufous-crowned

Identification: 5½" Both species have **clear gray breast; whitish throat; gray face; thin rufous eyeline; rufous crown.** Songs differ. See Voice. RUFOUS-WINGED: Limited to S. Ariz. **Two black whisker marks off base of bill; thin eyeline starts at bill; small rufous patch on shoulder is sometimes visible.** RUFOUS-CROWNED: **One black whisker mark off base of bill; thin eyeline starts behind eye; conspicuous whitish eye-ring.**

R.-winged   R.-crowned

Feeding: Both eat insects and seeds on ground. Rufous-winged may also catch insects in air or glean them from shrubs.

Nesting: Rufous-winged's nest cuplike, made of plant stems lined with fine grasses and hair, placed in tree, shrub, or cactus 1–6 ft. high. Eggs: 2–5, bluish white; I: 13 days; F: 8–10 days, altricial; B: 2. Rufous-crowned's nest cuplike, of grasses, twigs, and bark lined with hair and fine grasses, placed on ground or in tree or shrub 1–3 ft. high. Eggs: 3–4, white; I: ?; F: ?, altricial; B: 1–2.

Other Behavior: Timing of Rufous-winged breeding varies; may be triggered by rainfall.

Habitat: Rufous-winged: grass areas with shrubs. Rufous-crowned: rocky hillsides.

Voice: Rufous-winged song "chip yoor teeeee"; call "seep." Rufous-crowned song bubbling; call "deer."

Conservation: Rufous-winged: BBS: W ⇑ C CBC: ↓ Rufous-crowned: BBS: W ⇑ C ⇓ CBC: ↑

American Tree Sparrow

Spizella arborea

Identification: 6″ **Clear gray breast with central black dot; gray face;** thin rufous eyeline; **rufous crown; white wing bars; 2-toned bill —** upper bill dark, lower bill yellow. In winter, gray edges to crown feathers may slightly obscure rufous color.

Feeding: Feeds mostly on ground, eating weed seeds, but may also eat seeds on shrubs and trees. At feeders, eats seed scattered on ground or on a tray.

Nesting: Cuplike nest of grasses and bark strips lined with softer materials, placed on ground or in shrub 1 ft. high. Eggs: 3–5, pale greenish or bluish white; I: 12–13 days; F: 9–10 days, altricial; B: 1.

Other Behavior: Most often seen in winter, when the birds migrate south and gather into small flocks as they feed. Females tend to winter farther south than males. Groups of 30–50 birds remain on fairly fixed winter territories, breaking up into smaller flocks within that area.

Habitat: Summers in subarctic scrub; winters in weedy fields, brushy edges, open woodlands, gardens.

Voice: Main winter sound is a 3-note call, "tseedle-eet."

Conservation: CBC: ⇓

Chipping Sparrow

Spizella passerina

Winter

Summer

Juvenile

Identification: 5½" SUMMER: **Clear gray breast; bright rufous crown; whitish eyebrow; strong black eyeline;** black bill. WINTER: **Head is buffier and less distinctly colored; brown crown with fine black streaks; buffy eyebrow; indistinct eyeline;** grayish bill; gray rump. JUV: Finely streaked breast; finely streaked crown; buffy face. Late-brood birds may partially arrest molt into adult winter plumage, creating plumages intermediate between juvenal and winter adult.

Feeding: Eats insects and seeds on ground. May hawk insects in air. Sometimes comes to feeders.

Nesting: Cuplike nest of grasses, placed on branch of tree 3–10 ft. high. Eggs: 3–4, pale blue with dark blotches; I: 11–12 days; F: 7–10 days, altricial; B: 2.

Other Behavior: Male arrives first on territory and sings from exposed perches. Territories are about ½ acre. When the female arrives, mating is often seen, as is nest building, which is done by the female as the male follows her to and from the nest.

Habitat: Grassy areas, open woods, lawns, parks.

Voice: Song a continuous rapid trill, 2–3 seconds long.

Conservation:
BBS: W ⇓ C ↑ CBC: ↑

Clay-colored Sparrow

Spizella pallida

Identification: 5½" **Clear light gray breast; brown crown with fine black streaks and whitish central stripe; whitish eyebrow; buffy cheek patch outlined above and below with black; gray collar;** long notched tail; faint whisker stripe; unstreaked buffy rump. **Imm:** Like adult, but with buffy eyebrow and buffy band across breast. Imm. plumage kept through winter.

Feeding: Feeds mostly on the ground, eating weed seeds, insects, and some flowers.

Nesting: Cuplike nest of grasses and weed stems lined with finer grasses and hair, placed on ground or in shrub up to 5 ft. high. Eggs: 3–5, pale aqua with dark marks; I: 11–14 days; F: 7–9 days, altricial; B: 1–2.

Other Behavior: Males advertise small territories of slightly less than an acre by singing from exposed perches. Range expanding eastward.

Habitat: Summers in open brushy areas, often near water. In winter, also in weedy fields.

Voice: Song is 2–5 buzzes, given relatively slowly.

Conservation: BBS: W ↓ C ↓ CBC: ⇓

Brewer's Sparrow

Spizella breweri

Identification: 5½" **Clear gray breast; dark brown crown with fine black streaks; gray eyebrow; distinct white eye-ring;** brown cheek patch outlined above and below with black; faint whisker stripe; long notched tail. Generally quite drab compared to similar Clay-colored Sparrow.

Feeding: In summer, eats a large number of insects on ground; also eats weed seeds.

Nesting: Cuplike nest of grasses lined with hair and rootlets, placed in sagebrush, shrub, or cactus up to 4 ft. high. Eggs: 3–4, blue-green with dark marks; I: 13 days; F: 8–9 days, altricial; B: 2.

Other Behavior: Except for some singing by the males, generally quite inconspicuous on the breeding ground, where most activities take place under cover of vegetation. More conspicuous in migration and winter, when they may be seen feeding with other sparrow species. They often bathe in shallow streams or puddles and then may fly to shrubbery and sing in a canarylike fashion as a group.

Habitat: Brushy areas, sagebrush, desert scrub.

Voice: Long (up to 10 seconds) canarylike song is distinctive.

Conservation: BBS: W ⇓ C ⇓ CBC: ↑

Field Sparrow

Spizella pusilla

Identification: 5½" **Clear buffy to light gray breast; bright pink bill; rufous crown; conspicuous white eye-ring;** grayish face with rufous eyeline and variably sized rufous ear patch.

Feeding: Feeds on the ground, eating mostly insects in summer and weed seeds the rest of the year. May come to feeders where seed is scattered on the ground.

Nesting: Cuplike nest of grasses, placed on ground or up to 5 ft. high in shrub or small tree. Eggs: 3–4, pale blue with dark markings; I: 10–11 days; F: 8 days, altricial; B: 1–3.

Other Behavior: Each male has his own distinct and consistent version of song. In a field with several males, you can then recognize individuals and watch as they outline territories by singing from several prominent perches. Territories are about 2–6 acres. You can tell when females arrive on the territories, for male singing drops off markedly. Watch for the female as she builds the nest. Nest failures due to storms and predation are frequent, but the birds usually just renest in the same area.

Habitat: Open areas with scattered shrubs and small trees.

Voice: Song a series of downslurred whistles that gradually increase in speed, like a bouncing ball. Calls are "chip" and a trill.

Conservation:
BBS: W C ⇓ CBC: ⇓

Black-chinned Sparrow

Spizella atrogularis

Male

Identification: 5½" Gray overall with reddish-brown back and wings; back streaked with black; pink bill. **Summer—Male:** Black chin and throat. **Female:** Brownish-gray crown; dark gray chin. **Winter—Male:** Dark gray to blackish chin and throat. **Female:** No darker areas on chin and throat. **Imm:** Like winter female. Imm. plumage kept through winter.

Feeding: Feeds in brush and on ground, eating seeds and insects.

Nesting: Cuplike nest of grasses and weed stems lined with finer grasses and hair, placed in low shrub. Eggs: 2–5, light blue; I: 13 days; F: ?, altricial; B: 1, possibly more.

Other Behavior: Very little is known about the behavior of this species. This is a good opportunity for further observations.

Habitat: Sagebrush, shrubby hillsides.

Voice: Song is a few whistled notes followed by a trill.

Conservation:
BBS: W ⇓ C CBC: ↑

Vesper Sparrow
Pooecetes gramineus

Identification: 6″ Finely streaked breast with no central dot; white eye-ring; small chestnut shoulder patch that is not always visible; medium-length notched tail. **IN FLIGHT:** Note white outer tail feathers.

Feeding: Feeds on the ground, eating insects, weed seeds, and grain.

Nesting: Cuplike nest of grasses and rootlets, placed on the ground in a slight depression. Eggs: 3–5, creamy to greenish white with darker marks; I: 11–13 days; F: 7–12 days, altricial; B: 2.

Other Behavior: Male sings from highest perches within territory, such as fence posts, shrubs, or tree limbs; often sings at dusk. Territory size is 1–2 acres. The male may do flight song over the territory during courtship. Frequently seen dust bathing.

Habitat: Dry fields with sparse vegetation, occasionally beach grass, sagebrush, forest clearings, or agricultural fields.

Voice: Song is 2 pairs of slurred whistles, the 2nd pair higher-pitched, followed by trills.

Conservation:
BBS: W ↓ C ↑ CBC: ↓

Lark Sparrow
Chondestes grammacus

Identification: 6½" Easily recognized by its striking red-brown cheek patch and crown stripes; clear gray breast with central dot. IN FLIGHT: Note long rounded tail with white corners. JUV: Juvenal plumage sometimes kept into fall. Face and tail pattern resemble adult, but breast and crown streaked.

Feeding: Feeds on ground, eating mostly weed seeds and some insects. May be seen feeding in small flocks during summer and large flocks during winter.

Nesting: Cuplike nest of grasses lined with finer grasses and rootlets, placed usually on ground. Eggs: 4–5, white with dark marks; I: 11–12 days; F: 9–10 days, altricial; B: 1.

Other Behavior: Males defend immediate area around nest, but leave territory to feed with other Lark Sparrows. In courtship, male struts around female with wings half-open and fluttering and bill pointed up. Song may be given from the ground, from perches, or in flight. Also known to sing at night.

Habitat: Open woods, farmland, roadsides, open residential areas.

Voice: Complex song of trills, clear notes, and buzzes; call a sharp "tsip," sometimes given in a series.

Conservation: BBS: W ↓ C ⇓ CBC: ⇓

Black-throated Sparrow

Amphispiza bilineata

Adult

Immature

Identification: 5″ Black throat and breast; gray crown and ear patch; bright white eyebrow and malar streak. IN FLIGHT: Note black tail with white outer feathers. IMM: Like adult, but chin and throat white; upper breast finely streaked with black. Imm. plumage kept 1 year.

Feeding: Feeds mostly on the ground, eating insects, weed and grass seeds, and some green vegetation.

Nesting: Loose cuplike nest of grasses and weed stems lined with hair, placed 1–3 ft. high in shrub or cactus. Eggs: 3–4, pale bluish white; I: ?; F: ?, altricial; B: ?

Other Behavior: Males may defend territories against Sage Sparrows as well as other Black-throated Sparrows. After breeding and throughout winter, look for Black-throated Sparrows in small flocks of 5–20 birds, often feeding with other species of sparrows such as Brewer's, Chipping, Sage, and White-crowned.

Habitat: Arid and semiarid regions with sage, cactus, creosote, or mesquite.

Voice: Song varies, but often is a few clear whistles followed by trills.

Conservation:
BBS: W ↑ C ⇓ CBC: ↓

Sage Sparrow
Amphispiza belli

Interior race

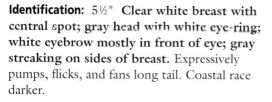

Coastal race

Identification: 5½" **Clear white breast with central spot; gray head with white eye-ring; white eyebrow mostly in front of eye; gray streaking on sides of breast.** Expressively pumps, flicks, and fans long tail. Coastal race darker.

Feeding: Feeds on ground, eating mostly insects and, in winter, seeds.

Nesting: Cuplike nest of twigs, grasses, bark, lined with finer materials, placed on the ground or up to 3 ft. high in shrub. Eggs: 3–4, bluish white; I: 13 days; F: 9–11 days, altricial; B: 1–2.

Other Behavior: Notice how each male has a consistent song, which enables you to recognize individuals when they are singing. Female sits tight on nest even when approached closely.

Habitat: Inland: dry flatlands with sparse vegetation. On the coast: chaparral.

Voice: Song is a soft high-pitched series of notes.

Conservation: BBS: W ↓ C ⇓ CBC: ⇓ San Clemente Island subspecies in Calif. is threatened, possibly due to habitat destruction by feral goats and pigs on the island.

Lark Bunting

Calamospiza melanocorys

Summer male

Winter male

Female

Identification: 7" SUMMER—MALE: **All black with large white wing patch;** conical blue-gray bill. FEMALE: **Brown-streaked breast; conical blue-gray bill; long white patch on brown wings.** Looks similar in winter. WINTER—MALE: **Similar to summer female, but with black chin and white patch on black wings. IN FLIGHT: Large white wing patches obvious.**

Feeding: Feeds on the ground, eating seeds and insects.

Nesting: Loose cup of grasses and weed stems lined with down, placed on ground near clump of grass. Eggs: 3–6, pale blue-green with darker marks; I: 12 days; F: 8–9 days, altricial; B: 1–2.

Other Behavior: Male does flight song over territory, rising to 20–30 feet, circling, and then slowly descending. Territories are small and many males may be seen displaying at the same time and fairly close to each other. These birds gather into large flocks during migration and reach wintering grounds by late summer. Loss of prairie habitat has reduced their range in northern and eastern portions.

Habitat: Prairies, sparsely vegetated areas with some shrubs, feedlots, plowed fields.

Voice: Song is a mixture of trills and whistles; call is a whistled "toohee."

Conservation: BBS: W ⇑ C ↓ CBC: ⇓

Savannah Sparrow

Passerculus sandwichensis

"Belding's Sparrow"

Identification: 5½" **Streaked breast; variable yellowish eyebrow; thin white central stripe in brown crown; short notched tail.** Streaking on breast may form a central dot. •Varies geographically. *P. s. beldingi*, "Belding's Sparrow," on S. Calif. coast, is darkest.

Feeding: Feeds on ground, eating mostly seeds but also insects, spiders, and snails in summer. Sometimes jumps backward to scrape away ground debris and uncover food.

Nesting: Small cuplike nest of grasses and moss lined with hair or finer grasses, placed on the ground. Eggs: 4–5, blue-green or white with dark marks; I: 12 days; F: 14 days, altricial; B: 1–2.

Other Behavior: Males at times may have more than one mate. Females may also lay eggs in other pairs' nests. This sparrow runs along the ground like a small vole to avoid possible danger and, when flying, stays close to grass tops.

Habitat: A variety of moist tallgrass areas — meadows, beaches, lake and river edges; varied habitats in winter.

Voice: Song is several short notes followed by 2 rapid, high-pitched, buzzy trills, the 2nd one lower-pitched, like "tsit tsit tsit zeee zaaay."

Conservation: BBS: W ↑ C ↓ CBC: ↓

459

Baird's Sparrow

Ammodramus bairdii

Identification: 5½" Buffy overall with black markings; black-streaked crown has a buffy-orange central stripe that broadens at back and extends to nape; rich buffy eyebrow; 2 dark streaks on either side of pale throat; short black streaks on upper breast form a necklace (not always present); wing and back feathers have black centers. Song is distinctive, see Voice. Flat head, large bill, and short tail typical of the genus.

Feeding: In summer, eats insects, especially grasshoppers and spiders; in winter, eats mostly weed seeds.

Nesting: Cuplike nest of grasses, placed on ground. Eggs: 3–5, white with darker marks; I: 11–12 days; F: 8–10 days, altricial; B: 1.

Other Behavior: Males defend territories of 1–2 acres, and neighboring males may interact with short vertical flights. Each male has several song perches around his territory. These sparrows rarely fly, preferring to walk among the grasses. Secretive.

Habitat: Prairie, rangelands, meadows.

Voice: Song is 1–4 high-pitched short notes followed by a warbling trill.

Conservation: BBS: W ↑ C ⇓ CBC: ↓ Threatened in Can., where there is a loss of its breeding habitat of short-grass prairie.

Grasshopper Sparrow

Ammodramus savannarum

Identification: 5″ Clear buffy breast and flanks; brown crown with thin whitish central stripe; whitish eye-ring; usually an orange-yellow spot before eye. Varies geographically; darkest subspecies in Fla.

Feeding: Eats many insects, including grasshoppers. Also eats weed and grass seeds.

Nesting: Cuplike, slightly covered-over nest of grasses lined with hair, placed on ground at the base of a grass clump. Eggs: 4–5, creamy white with dark speckles; I: 11–12 days; F: 9 days, altricial; B: 2.

Other Behavior: Look for male singing from weed tops or fence posts. Song may occur during day or night and female often answers with her own trill. Male occasionally chases female in courtship. Several pairs may nest together in a loose colony.

Habitat: Prairie, dry weedy fields, old pastures, hayfields.

Voice: Song a very high-pitched buzz with 1 or more introductory notes, like "tik-zzzzzzz."

Conservation: BBS: W ⇓ C ⇓ CBC: ↓ Florida subspecies, *A. s. floridanus,* is endangered.

Le Conte's Sparrow

Ammodramus leconteii

Identification: 5″ Dark crown with a white central stripe; reddish-brown streaks on gray nape; buffy upper breast and flanks with dark streaks, especially on sides of breast and flanks; orange to buffy-orange face surrounding a gray ear patch. Flat head and short tail typical of the genus. Fine streaking on upper breast of juveniles may be retained on adults into winter.

Feeding: Feeds on the ground, eating grass and weed seeds, as well as insects.

Nesting: Cuplike nest of grasses, placed on or just above the ground. Eggs: 3–5, light gray with darker marks; I: 12–13 days; F: 8–10 days, altricial; B: 2.

Other Behavior: May sing during day or night. Often runs through grasses, rather than flying over them, to avoid danger.

Habitat: Marshes, wet meadows, weedy fields.

Voice: Song a high-pitched buzz with accents at start and end, like "tika-zzzzzz-tzt."

Conservation:
BBS: W ↑ C ↓ CBC: ↑

Nelson's Sharp-tailed Sparrow
Ammodramus nelsoni

Identification: 5″ Bright buffy face surrounds diffuse gray ear patch; dark crown with a gray central stripe that widens into a gray, unstreaked nape; dark back with white stripes; breast and flanks buffy with blurry streaking on flanks and little or none on breast. Chin usually light buff. Flat head and short tail typical of the genus.

Feeding: Feeds on the ground, eating grass and weed seeds, as well as insects.

Nesting: Loosely woven nest of grasses, placed on ground or in dense grasses. Eggs: 3–7, light green with dark marks; I: 11 days; F: 10 days, altricial; B: 1–2.

Other Behavior: This species breeds in the West but winters along the southeast coast. In winter it may be difficult to distinguish from the similar Salt Marsh Sharp-tailed Sparrow.

Habitat: Freshwater marshes, wet meadows, lakeshores.

Voice: Song a faint, raspy trill with a soft introductory note, like "cata-tseeeee."

Conservation: BBS: w ⇓ c ↑

Fox Sparrow

Passerella iliaca

Eastern race

Western mountain race

Northwest race

Identification: 7" Large sparrow; whitish underparts boldly streaked with brown or rufous and with an irregular central dot on breast; reddish-brown rump and tail. •Varies geographically. Subspecies of the Pacific Northwest have dark brown heads and backs; subspecies of western mountains have gray heads and backs; primarily eastern subspecies has rufous streaking on its gray head and back.

Feeding: Feeds on the ground, eating seeds, fruits, and insects. Often jumps forward and back, pulling aside ground debris to uncover food items beneath. May come to feeders where seed is scattered on the ground.

Nesting: Cuplike nest of grasses, lichens, and leaves lined with hair, fur, and rootlets, placed on ground under small tree or shrub. Eggs: 4–6, light blue-green with darker marks; I: 11–14 days; F: 7–12 days, altricial; B: 1–2.

Other Behavior: Males may have 1–3 versions of their song which are distinctive to each male. Males with more than 1 version tend to go through their complete repertoire before repeating any version.

Habitat: Deciduous or coniferous woods, brushy areas, woods edges.

Voice: Song is a short series of clear melodious whistles; more melodic than that of most other sparrows.

Conservation:
BBS: W ↓ C CBC: ↓

Song Sparrow

Melospiza melodia

Identification: 6" Whitish breast with brown streaks and a dark central dot; reddish-brown crown with a gray central stripe; gray eyebrow; white throat bordered by heavy brown marks off the base of the bill; long rounded tail.
•Varies geographically, with paler subspecies in the Southwest and darker subspecies along the West Coast.

Feeding: Feeds on ground, eating seeds, insects, and some fruit. May come to feeders with seed scattered on the ground.

Nesting: Cuplike nest of grasses and occasionally leaves, placed on ground or in shrub or weeds 1–4 ft. high. Eggs: 3–5, greenish white with dark marks; I: 12–13 days; F: 10 days, altricial; B: 2–3.

Other Behavior: Males define territories of ½–1½ acres by giving song from prominent perches. Male chases female when she first arrives on territory, and reduces amount of his singing. Later courtship involves male diving at female and her giving a trill-like call.

Habitat: Dense shrubs at the edge of open areas such as fields, lawns, or streams.

Voice: Song is a few repeated notes followed by a rich and varied warble. Calls include "tsip" and "tchump."

Conservation:
BBS: W ↓ C ↑ CBC: ↓

Lincoln's Sparrow

Melospiza lincolnii

Identification: 5½" **Buffy wash across upper breast and flanks is finely streaked with black; clear white belly; reddish-brown crown with thin gray central stripe;** broad gray eyebrow; buffy lines off base of bill; distinct buffy eye-ring.

Feeding: Feeds on ground, scratching backwards with both feet to uncover seeds and insects.

Nesting: Cuplike nest of grasses lined with hair or feathers, placed on ground at the base of a grass clump or shrub. Eggs: 4–5, pale green with darker marks; I: 11–12 days; F: 9–12 days, altricial; B: 1–2.

Other Behavior: Males sing from perches and defend territories of about 1–2 acres. Females may give a "zeezeezee" call, and this stimulates the male to dive at her and may lead to mating. Males sometimes do flight songs over their territories. Generally secretive, especially on wintering grounds.

Habitat: Summers in bogs and wet meadows; winters in weedy fields and shrub edges.

Voice: Song a mixture of musical trills and buzzy notes; somewhat like a House Wren's. Calls include "tsup" and "zeee."

Conservation: BBS: W ⇑ C ⇑ CBC: ↓

Swamp Sparrow

Melospiza georgiana

Winter

Summer

Immature

Identification: 5½" SUMMER: **Rich reddish-brown wings with no wing bars; reddish-brown crown,** sometimes with fine black streaks and thin lighter central stripe; **white throat and belly; gray breast,** sometimes with indistinct streaking; buffy flanks; gray eyebrow and nape. WINTER: Like summer, but **crown heavily streaked with brown and black and with a gray central stripe; flanks darker brownish buff.** IMM: Like winter adult, but buffy (rather than gray) eyebrow and nape, and indistinct streaking on breast. Imm. plumage kept until spring.

Feeding: Feeds on the ground, often in shallow water, eating insects and weed and grass seeds.

Nesting: Bulky cuplike nest of grasses, placed in cattails or shrub to 2 ft. high. Eggs: 4–5, pale green with dark marks; I: 12–15 days; F: 10–13 days, altricial; B: 1–2.

Other Behavior: Male Swamp Sparrows may sing at night as well as during the day. Also, after a few weeks of quiet in late summer, they can be heard again singing in fall.

Habitat: Summers in freshwater marshes, swamps, bogs; winters also in damp fields with tall grass.

Voice: Song is a slow musical trill on 1 pitch; calls include a sharp "chip."

Conservation:
BBS: W ⇑ C ↑ CBC: ↑

White-throated Sparrow

Zonotrichia albicollis

White morph

Tan morph

Identification: 6½" **Dark crown with buff or white central stripe; eyebrow white or tan with yellow mark at front; throat white; breast gray with a few faint streaks.** There are two morphs of this species: white and tan, based on the color of their eyebrows. Female may have less bold pattern on head, duller yellow before eye, grayer throat, and more streaking on breast. IMM: Indistinguishable from adult female in the field. Imm. plumage kept through winter.

Feeding: Feeds on the ground, eating weed seeds, grain, fruit, and insects. At feeders, eats cracked corn, sunflower seed, and millet from trays or scattered on the ground.

Nesting: Cuplike nest of grasses lined with hair and rootlets, placed on ground under small tree or shrub. Eggs: 4–6, light blue-green with dark marks; I: 11–14 days; F: 7–12 days, altricial; B: 1–2.

Other Behavior: Breeding pair usually contains 1 bird from each morph, either a tan female and a white male, or a white female and a tan male.

Habitat: Coniferous and mixed woods, brushy areas.

Voice: Song is 2 long whistled notes followed by 3–4 higher, quavering notes, like phrase "sweet sweet Canada Canada Canada." Calls are "tseeet" when birds are in flocks and "pink" in alarm.

Conservation: BBS: W ↑ C ⇓ CBC: ↓

Golden-crowned Sparrow
Zonotrichia atricapilla

Adult

Immature

Identification: 7" **Black crown with a bold golden patch in the center; gray face; white eye-ring; clear gray breast.** In early winter, crown pattern slightly obscured by lighter edges to feathers. IMM: Crown diffusely golden in front and brown in back; face light brown; white eye-ring; clear brownish-gray breast. Imm. plumage kept through winter.

Feeding: Feeds on or near ground, eating seeds, and buds, leaves, and flowers of summer plants; also insects and fruit. Comes to feeders where seed is scattered on ground or on tray.

Nesting: Large nest of grasses, ferns, sticks, lined with finer grasses and hair, placed on ground or bank in shallow depression. Eggs: 3–5, creamy white or light blue; I: ?; F: ?, altricial; B: 1 or possibly more.

Other Behavior: Often seen with White-crowned Sparrows in winter flocks. Male sings almost continuously during early breeding. Not much is known about breeding behavior.

Habitat: Summers in mountain thickets and shrubs; winters in brushy areas.

Voice: Song is 3–4 downslurred whistles, like phrase "oh dear me."

Conservation:
CBC: ↓

White-crowned Sparrow
Zonotrichia leucophrys

Adult *Z. l. gambelli*

Adult *Z. l. leucophrys*

Immature

Identification: 7" Boldly black-and-white-streaked head; no yellow dot before eye; pink-orange bill; gray face and nape; clear gray breast; whitish throat. **Imm:** Head pattern similar to adult, but colors of streaks are reddish brown and grayish brown instead of black and white. Imm. plumage kept through winter. •Several subspecies: *Z. l. gambelli* has a gray breast and whitish lores; *Z. l. leucophrys* has black lores.

Feeding: Feeds on ground, scratching back leaf debris with both feet as it looks for seeds and insects. Occasionally hawks insects. Comes to feeders with seed scattered on the ground.

Nesting: Bulky nest of grasses, twigs, plant stems, lined with finer grasses, hair, and feathers, placed on ground or in small tree or shrub. Eggs: 3–5, pale blue or green with darker spots; I: 11–15 days; F: 10 days, altricial; B: 1–4.

Other Behavior: In winter, often in flocks of 10–20 birds which often stay in the same area for many weeks. Often nests in residential areas. Has been expanding its winter range into the Northeast since about 1950.

Habitat: Varied; includes wet meadows, shrubby borders, woods, gardens, parks.

Voice: Song variable geographically. Often whistled notes and a trill; calls include a sharp "pink."

Conservation: BBS: W ↓ C ↓ CBC: ↓

470

Harris' Sparrow
Zonotrichia querula

Summer

Winter

Immature

Identification: 7½" Our largest sparrow. SUMMER: **Black on crown, surrounding bill, and on chin and throat;** gray face; pink-orange bill; white belly with streaking on flanks. WINTER: Like summer, but **lighter flecks in black on head; light brown face.** IMM: Similar to winter adult, but with little or no black on face; flecks of black on brown crown; chin and throat mostly white. Imm. plumage kept through winter.

Feeding: Feeds on the ground, eating mostly weed and grass seeds, grain, and small fruits. Also eats some insects. At feeders, eats seed scattered on the ground or on trays.

Nesting: Cuplike nest of mosses, grasses, weed stems, lined with finer grasses, placed in depression in ground. Eggs: 3–5, whitish with darker marks; I: 13 days; F: ?, altricial; B: 1.

Other Behavior: Harris' Sparrows breed far to the north and are mostly seen in winter in south-central states.

Habitat: Summers in the coniferous forest-tundra; winters in woods edges, brushy thickets.

Voice: Song is 3–4 quavering whistles, first on 1 pitch, then on another.

Conservation: CBC: ⇓

Dark-eyed Junco
Junco hyemalis

"Slate-colored" race

"Pink-sided" race

"Oregon" race

"Gray-headed" race

Identification: 6" In all plumages: **pale bill; dark eye; whitish belly; tail dark with conspicuous white outer feathers.** •Varies geographically. Eastern "Slate-colored" race is uniform dark gray (male) or brownish gray (female); western "Oregon" race has black (male) or gray (female) hood and brown back; western "Pink-sided" race has gray head and pinkish sides; "Gray-headed" race of the southern Rockies and Southwest is light gray with a reddish-brown back; "White-winged" race of north-central states has extensive white on tail and usually white wing bars.

Feeding: Feeds mostly on ground, eating weed and grass seeds. At feeders, eats seed on ground or on trays.

Nesting: Cuplike nest of grasses, moss, pine needles, lined with rootlets, placed in depression in ground near tall vegetation. Eggs: 3–6, gray or pale bluish with dark blotches; I: 12–13 days; F: 9–13 days, altricial; B: 1–2.

Other Behavior: Flocks return to same areas each winter. They are fixed in membership and have a hierarchy. Aggression at feeders is expression of dominance.

Habitat: Summers in woods, woods edges, bogs, mountains above tree level; winters in woods edges, brush.

Voice: Song is a short trill or series of trills on 1 or more pitches; calls include "tsip," "zeet," and "kew kew."

Conservation: BBS: W ⇑ C ⇑ CBC: ↓

Yellow-eyed Junco

Junco phaeonotus

Identification: 6½" Limited to S.E. Ariz. and S.W. N.Mex. **Grayish overall; reddish-brown back; bright orange-yellow eye;** bill dark above, light below; conspicuous white outer tail feathers.

Feeding: Feeds on ground, eating grass and weed seeds. Also eats some insects gleaned off leaves.

Nesting: Cuplike nest of fine grasses and hair, placed on ground or in small tree or shrub up to 10 ft. high. Eggs: 3–4, pale blue-gray; I: 15 days; F: 10 days, altricial; B: 2–3.

Other Behavior: Young form flocks after leaving parents and are joined later by adults after all breeding is done. Birds move to lower elevations in winter, but do not migrate long distances. Tends to walk, rather than hop as Dark-eyed Junco does.

Habitat: Conifer and pine-oak forests in mountains.

Voice: Song is a mixture of trills and whistled notes; call "tseet."

Conservation: CBC: ↑

McCown's Longspur
Calcarius mccownii

Summer male

Summer female

Identification: 6" In all plumages, note **dark central tail feathers and dark band at tail tip forming a T; reddish-brown shoulder patch, sometimes hidden; large bill.** Tips of folded wings extend over halfway down tail. SUMMER—MALE: **Gray head; black cap and whisker mark; black bib on upper breast.** FEMALE: **Brownish, with dark streaks on crown and back; may be a suggestion of black bib.** WINTER—MALE: **Like summer female, but with more black on bib.** FEMALE: **As in summer, but with pale breast and belly.**

Feeding: Feeds on ground, eating seeds and insects.

Nesting: Nest of grasses lined with finer grasses, placed in shallow depression in ground near grass clump or small plant. Eggs: 3–6, pale pink or pale green with darker spots; I: 12 days; F: 12 days, altricial; B: 1–2.

Other Behavior: Male does flight song on territory, rising up to 30 ft. and then gliding down with wings and tail spread and legs hanging down. Birds form large flocks during migration and in winter.

Habitat: Summers in short-grass plains; winters in plowed agricultural fields, dry lake beds.

Voice: Song is a series of short musical warbles. Call a "chitup chitup."

Conservation:
BBS: W ↑ C ⇑ CBC: ⇑

Lapland Longspur

Calcarius lapponicus

Summer female

Summer male

Winter female

Identification: 6″ Our most widespread longspur in winter. Although outer tail feathers are partially white, **in all plumages tail appears mostly dark, even in flight.** SUMMER—MALE: **Black crown, face, throat, and bib; reddish-brown nape; yellow bill.** FEMALE: **Brownish; dark streaks on crown and back; pale, streaked, chestnut collar; brown ear patch has dark outline on back edge; black flecking in area of bib.** WINTER—MALE: Like summer female. FEMALE: Like summer, but lacks chestnut collar and dark area of bib; may show substantial rufous on wings.

Feeding: Feeds on ground, eating seeds, insects, and spiders.

Nesting: Cuplike nest of grasses lined with finer grasses, hair, and feathers, placed in shallow depression in ground scraped out by birds. Eggs: 3–7, pale green to buff with dark marks; I: 12–13 days; F: 10–12 days, altricial; B: 1.

Other Behavior: Male does flight song display on territory.

Habitat: Summers in wet grassy areas of tundra; winters in open grassy areas, plowed agricultural lands, airports, occasionally beaches.

Voice: Song a rich warbling given during flight display. Calls a dry "tikerik tikerik" and a rich "tew."

Conservation: CBC: ⇑

475

Smith's Longspur

Calcarius pictus

Summer male

Winter

Identification: 6" In all plumages, outer tail feathers white and no band at tip of tail. SUMMER—MALE: Black-and-white "helmet"; buffy-orange throat, nape, and breast. FEMALE: Brownish; dark streaks on crown and back; small white shoulder, sometimes hidden. WINTER: Both sexes like summer female.

Feeding: Feeds on ground, eating seeds, insects, and spiders.

Nesting: Cuplike nest of grasses lined with finer grasses, hair, and feathers, placed in shallow depression in ground scraped out by birds. Eggs: 4–6, grayish with dark dots; I: 11–12 days; F: ?, altricial; B: 1.

Other Behavior: Often winters in wide-open short-grass areas, such as airport fields and pastures. Can be approached closely before it flies. Usually remains separate from other longspurs.

Habitat: Summers in grassy tundra; winters in open areas with short grass.

Voice: Song a series of warbles ending with phrase "wee-tew." Call a short dry clicking sound.

Conservation: CBC: ↑

476

Chestnut-collared Longspur

Calcarius ornatus

Summer male

Female

Identification: 5½" In all plumages, note triangular black area at base of mostly white tail. SUMMER—MALE: Black crown; buffy face and throat; chestnut collar; black breast and upper belly. FEMALE: Brown-streaked; best distinguishing characteristic is black triangle on tail. WINTER—MALE: Buffy edgings to feathers make summer pattern indistinct, but buffy throat and hint of black belly and chestnut crown are still visible. FEMALE: As in summer.

Feeding: Feeds on ground, eating seeds and some insects.

Nesting: Cuplike nest of grasses lined with finer grasses, hair, and feathers, placed in shallow depression in ground scraped out by birds. Eggs: 3–6, creamy with dark marks; I: 11–13 days; F: 10–12 days, altricial; B: 2.

Other Behavior: Male does flight display over territory while singing; glides down exposing white on fanned wings and tail.

Habitat: Short-grass prairies and cultivated fields.

Voice: Song is a musical twittering. Call is "tilip tilip."

Conservation:
BBS: W ↑ C ↓ CBC: ⇑

Snow Bunting

Plectrophenax nivalis

Summer female

Summer male

Winter male

Identification: 7" Summer—Male: Strikingly marked with white on head and body; black on back, wings, and tail; bill black. Female: Subtler version of male coloration. **Head is grayish white; dark areas on back, wings, and tail are brownish gray.** Winter: Crown black (male) or buffy (female); back streaked with buff and black; buffy ear patch; white belly; flanks and breast washed with buff; bill yellow-orange. In Flight: Note long white wings with black outer portions.

Feeding: Feeds on ground, eating seeds, leaf buds, and insects.

Nesting: Nest of moss, grasses, and earth, placed on ground in rocky area. Eggs: 3–9, creamy blue or gray; I: 10–16 days; F: 10–17 days, altricial; B: 1–2.

Other Behavior: In winter, can be seen bathing in snow. May burrow into snow to keep warm. Stays in large flocks throughout winter, roosting on ground or perching on telephone wires.

Habitat: Summers in arctic tundra and rocky shores; winters in open fields, roadsides, beaches.

Voice: Song is a musical warble. Calls include a short whistled "tew" and soft buzzy notes.

Conservation: CBC: ⇓

Bobolink

Dolichonyx oryzivorus

Summer female

Summer male

Winter

Identification: 7″ SUMMER—MALE: Black head and black body with bold buffy-white nape. In flight note white rump. FEMALE: Buffy, with brown streaks on back and flanks; dark streaks on crown; dark eyeline behind eye. WINTER: Both sexes like summer female, but buffier. In all plumages, note sharply pointed tail feathers.

Feeding: Feeds on the ground, eating insects, weed and grass seeds. Also eats cultivated rice crops in the South.

Nesting: Nest of coarse grass and sedge lined with finer material, placed on the ground. Eggs: 4–6, cinnamon with brown blotches; I: 12 days; F: 10–14 days, altricial; B: 1.

Other Behavior: Loss of hayfield breeding habitat is due to urban development, reforestation, and loss of dairy farms. Studies show that early cutting of hayfields, before Bobolinks fledge, can kill more than 80% of young. When hayfields are on conservation lands, conservation commissions can help by setting a policy to delay cutting until after Bobolink young have adequately fledged. Studies in North recommend this cutting be after July 20 or in August.

Habitat: Hayfields and grasslands.

Voice: Song is a long bubbling sound given by male in flight; call a "pink."

Conservation: BBS: W ↓ C ⇓ CBC: ↓ Populations have declined due to loss of grassland breeding habitat and hunting during the last century to protect rice crops.

479

Red-winged Blackbird

Agelaius phoeniceus

Male

Female

Identification: 8½″ **MALE: All black with a red shoulder patch bordered by yellow.** Males in central Calif. have no yellow on shoulder patch; they are sometimes called Bicolored Blackbirds. **FEMALE: Brown above and heavily streaked brown below; sharp-pointed bill; buffy-to-whitish eyebrow.** IMM—MALE: Similar to adult female, but darker and with an orangish shoulder patch bordered by white. FEMALE: Like adult female. Imm. plumage kept 1 year.

Feeding: Eats insects, weed seeds. Comes to bird feeders singly or in large flocks for cracked corn, seed mixes.

Nesting: Nest of reeds and grasses lined with finer material, placed in reeds and grasses or shrubs 3–8 ft. high. Eggs: 3–5, pale greenish blue with dark marks; I: 11 days; F: 11 days, altricial; B: 2–3.

Other Behavior: Males hold territories of ⅛–¼ acre, which they defend by singing from perches with wings spread open and red shoulder patches exposed. They can also conceal the red patch, showing only the yellow border. Males are polygynous, averaging 3 mates per breeding season. Huge communal roosts in winter.

Habitat: Marshes and meadows.

Voice: Song a loud "okaleee"; calls include "check," "tseert," and, given only by female, a "ch'ch'ch'chee chee chee."

Conservation: BBS: W ↑ C ↓ CBC: ↑

Tricolored Blackbird
Agelaius tricolor

Male

Female

Identification: 8½" MALE: All black with a red shoulder patch bordered by white. FEMALE: Blackish brown above and on belly; heavily streaked dark brown only on chest; sharp-pointed thick-based bill; buffy-to-whitish eyebrow. IMM—MALE: Similar to adult female, but darker and with an orangish shoulder patch bordered by white. FEMALE: Like adult female. Imm. plumage kept 1 year.

Feeding: Feeds on the ground, eating insects, grains, and weed seeds. Flocks may feed in agricultural grain fields, cattle feedlots, horse and cattle ranches, dumps.

Nesting: Nest of coarse reeds and grasses lined with finer material, placed in reeds above ground or water, or on ground. Eggs: 3–4, pale greenish blue with dark marks; I: 11–13 days; F: 11–14 days, altricial; B: 2.

Other Behavior: Lives in large flocks throughout the year. In winter, flocks are nomadic, may feed and roost with other blackbird species. Breeding colonies have ranged from 100 to 200,000 birds in past. Numbers are declining now due to marsh drainage and habitat destruction.

Habitat: Freshwater marshes with cattails and dense shrubs, grain fields.

Voice: Song a harsh "onkazreeee"; call "chup."

Conservation: BBS: W ⇑ C CBC: ⇑

Eastern Meadowlark
Western Meadowlark

Sturnella magna   Sturnella neglecta

Eastern

Western

Identification: 9" Both species are **brownish above and yellow below with a black V on breast. Best distinguished by voice.** See Voice. IN FLIGHT: Note **white outer tail feathers and quick flutters followed by short glides.** Mostly indistinguishable in the field, except by song and range. In the Western Meadowlark, the yellow on the throat extends slightly up onto the cheek; in the Eastern, it does not. Hybrids occur in Midwest.

Feeding: Both feed on the ground, eating insects, grain, and weed seeds.

Nesting: Both have a domed nest of coarse grass lined with finer grass, placed in natural or scraped depression on the ground. Eggs: 3–7, white with dark marks; I: 13–15 days; F: 11–12 days, altricial; B: 1–2.

Other Behavior: Occasionally hybridize where ranges overlap. Both form winter flocks of up to 100 or more birds that feed and roost together. Western is expanding range in Northeast. Eastern is declining because of loss of breeding habitat as grasslands become converted to suburbs. Also, mowing of fields destroys many nests.

Eastern   Western

Habitat: Meadows, grasslands.

Voice: Eastern song 2–8 high-pitched whistles, "seeoo seeyeer"; call a "dzeert." Western song a short phrase of lower-pitched flutelike notes; call is low "chup."

Conservation:
Eastern:
BBS: W ↑ C ↓ CBC: ⇓
Western:
BBS: W ↓ C ↓ CBC: ⇓

Yellow-headed Blackbird

Xanthocephalus xanthocephalus

Male   Female

Identification: 9½" MALE: **Bright yellow hood; black body;** white patch on wing shows in perched and flying bird. FEMALE: **Grayish brown overall, except for yellow chin and breast;** white streaks on upper belly. IMM—MALE: Like adult female, except: more orangish yellow on breast; no white streaking on belly; and, in flight, shows thin white patches on upperwings. FEMALE: Like adult female. Imm. plumage kept 1 year.

Feeding: Feeds on the ground, eating insects, grass and weed seeds. Forages in fields, agricultural areas, meadows, ranches, farms.

Nesting: Nest of water-soaked reeds and grasses lined with softer material, placed in vegetation up to 7 ft. above water. Eggs: 3–5, pale greenish gray with dark marks; I: 11–13 days; F: 9–12 days, altricial; B: 2.

Other Behavior: In fall and winter, joins with other blackbirds, European Starlings, and Brown-headed Cowbirds in large mixed flocks that roost in marshes.

Habitat: Summers in marshes; winters in grain fields.

Voice: Song is short choked notes, interspersed with a long buzz; call is a low "krrt."

Conservation:
BBS: W ⇑ C ↑ CBC: ⇓

483

Rusty Blackbird
Euphagus carolinus

Summer male

Summer female

Winter male

Winter female

Identification: 9″ SUMMER—MALE: Appears dull black overall; pale yellow eye; slightly shorter tail and longer bill than similar male Brewer's Blackbird. FEMALE: Dark grayish to black; pale yellow eye; may have brown edges to wing feathers. WINTER—MALE: Like summer, but feathers edged with rusty brown on head, back, and wings; black rump. FEMALE: Buffy underparts; buffy eyebrow; rusty back; gray rump. Birds of both sexes in their first fall tend to be rustier and buffier than in following years. Summer plumage acquired by wearing off of lighter tips to feathers.

Feeding: Feeds on the ground and in very shallow water, eating insects, crustaceans, fish, grain, and weed seeds.

Nesting: Nest of grass, moss, and mud lined with finer material, placed in shrub or tree 2–20 ft. above the ground. Eggs: 4–5, pale greenish with dark marks; I: 14 days; F: 11–14 days, altricial; B: ?

Other Behavior: Forms huge winter flocks with other blackbirds and starlings.

Habitat: Summers in spruce bogs, wet woods; winters in woods and fields near water.

Voice: Song a squeaky "chugalasqueeek"; call a "chek."

Conservation: BBS: W ⇓ C CBC: ⇓

Brewer's Blackbird
Euphagus cyanocephalus

Male

Female

Identification: 9″ MALE: Black, with purplish gloss on head and greenish gloss on body; pale yellow eye; slightly longer tail and shorter bill than similar male Rusty Blackbird. May have minimal brownish-gray edges to body feathers in fall. FEMALE: Grayish brown; dark eye.

Feeding: Feeds on the ground, eating grain, weed seeds, fruit, and insects.

Nesting: Nest of twigs, grass, and a matrix of mud or cow dung lined with finer material, placed on or just above the ground in vegetation. Eggs: 3–7, pale gray with dark marks; I: 12–14 days; F: 13–14 days, altricial; B: 1–2.

Other Behavior: In fall and winter, forms huge flocks often mixed with other blackbirds, starlings, and Brown-headed Cowbirds. These flocks forage during the day in agricultural areas. Communal roosts in marshes may number in the tens of millions.

Habitat: Wet meadows, rivers, stream margins bordered by dense shrubs, cultivated areas, parks, desert oases, urban areas, roadsides.

Voice: Song is a squeaky "kasqueek"; call a "chick."

Conservation: BBS: W ↓ C ↑ CBC: ↓

485

Great-tailed Grackle

Quiscalus mexicanus

Male

Female

Identification: 18″ MALE: Large all-black bird with purplish gloss on flattish head and on back; long tail is folded up on the sides; bright yellow eye. FEMALE: Buffy brown below; darker above, with slight greenish iridescence; yellow eye; 2–4″ shorter than male. IMM— MALE: Lacks gloss of adult; tail flat rather than folded; eye is dark, changing to yellow by spring. FEMALE: Paler than adult; may have more contrast on face, with light eyebrow and dark eyeline; eye is dark, changing to yellow by spring. Imm. plumage kept 1 year. •In S. Calif. and W. Ariz., birds much smaller; female breast very pale.

Feeding: Eats insects, grain, fruit, crustaceans, fish, bird eggs. Visits bird feeders for seed and grain.

Nesting: Nest of grasses, reeds, and mud or cow dung lined with finer material, placed in marsh plant or tree. Eggs: 3–4, bluish green with dark marks; I: 13–14 days; F: 20–23 days, altricial; B: 1–2.

Other Behavior: Nests colonially, sometimes in the thousands. Forms huge winter roosts.

Habitat: Open land with some trees; parks, ranches, urban areas.

Voice: Song a spectacular series of whistles, hisses, and ratchety sounds.

Conservation: BBS: W ⇑ C ⇑

Common Grackle
Quiscalus quiscula

Male, purple

Male, bronze

Identification: 12″ MALE: **Black with iridescence on head, back, and belly; tail folded up at edges mostly during breeding; yellow eye.** Iridescence on body is purplish on birds from Southeast to S. New England, bronze on birds elsewhere. Smaller, shorter tail and smaller bill than similar Boat-tailed and Great-tailed Grackles. FEMALE: **Similar to male, but with shorter flat tail and less iridescence.**

Feeding: Feeds mostly on ground, eating insects, weed seeds, grains, minnows, small crayfish, rodents, and birds. Comes to bird feeder for seed and cracked corn.

Nesting: Nest of grass, twigs, reeds, and mud lined with finer materials, placed in shrub or tree 3–30 ft. above the ground or water. Eggs: 4–7, pale greenish brown with dark marks; I: 13–14 days; F: 12–16 days, altricial; B: 1.

Other Behavior: During courtship, male flies with tail held in V. Forms huge winter roosts, often mixed with Red-winged Blackbirds and cowbirds, that can number in tens of millions of birds and be a nuisance if located near urban areas. Large flocks may damage grain crops.

Habitat: Open areas with some trees; city parks, urban yards, farmland.

Voice: Song a short series of harsh sounds ending in a squeak, like "grideleeek"; calls a "chaack" and "chaaah."

Conservation: BBS: W ↓ C ↓ CBC: ↑

Bronzed Cowbird

Molothrus aeneus

Male

Female, Texas subspecies

Identification: 8" MALE: Black overall, with bluish iridescence on wings and tail; long, dark, conical bill; flat forehead; red eye. FEMALE: Similar bill, profile, and eye color; subspecies in Southwest grayish brown overall; in Tex., dull black overall.

Feeding: Feeds mostly on the ground, eating insects, grains, and weed seeds. Can also be seen on the backs of cattle, picking off ticks and other parasites.

Nesting: No nest. Eggs: Usually 1 per host nest, pale greenish blue; I: 10–13 days; F: 11 days, altricial; B: ?

Other Behavior: Female lays usually 1 egg per nest in the nests of other bird species, especially orioles. She usually removes 1 of the eggs of the host species, replacing it with her own egg. The cowbird egg hatches 1 day earlier than the others. The cowbird nestling is larger than the young of the host, gets more of the food, and may crowd the other young out of the nest. In most cases, some of the host young do fledge, although cowbird parasitism reduces their number. Some birds deal with cowbird parasitism by ejecting or destroying cowbird eggs, abandoning their nest, or building over the eggs and starting a new clutch.

Habitat: Urban lawns, agricultural fields, parks, open woods.

Voice: Song a series of squeaks; call a low "chuck."

Conservation: BBS: W ↓ C ⇑ CBC: ⇑

Brown-headed Cowbird
Molothrus ater

Male

Female

Identification: 7" MALE: **Dark brown head; glossy black body;** dark gray conical bill. FEMALE: **Grayish brown overall with very little distinct marking; dark gray conical bill;** faint streaking on breast.

Feeding: Feeds on the ground, eating grain, grass and weed seeds, and insects. Visits bird feeders.

Nesting: No nest. Eggs: Usually 1 per host nest, white with dark marks; I: 10–13 days; F: 9–11 days, altricial; B: ?

Other Behavior: See Bronzed Cowbird account for more information. Although 97% of cowbird eggs and nestlings fail to reach adulthood, the average cowbird pair replaces itself with 1.2 pairs, enough to keep the cowbird population expanding. Cowbird parasitism reduces the breeding success of many species and, in some cases, poses a severe threat to their survival. This is the case with Kirtland's Warbler, Golden-cheeked Warbler, Black-capped Vireo, and the Calif. subspecies of Bell's Vireo. Cowbirds have been recorded as successfully parasitizing 144 species. The fragmentation of forests, due to suburban development, gives cowbirds new access to many forest species.

Habitat: Pastures, woods edges, urban lawns, forest clearings.

Voice: Song is a liquid "bublucomseee"; call is high "pseeeseee" and "ch'ch'ch'ch."

Conservation: BBS: W ↓ C ↓ CBC: ⇓

Orchard Oriole
Icterus spurius

Male

Female

Immature male, 1st spring

Identification: 7" **MALE: Black hood, wings, and tail; reddish-brown belly and rump. FEMALE: Olive-green above; yellow below; 2 thin white wing bars. IMM—MALE:** In fall, similar to adult female. In next spring and summer, like adult female, but with black throat and upper breast, sometimes with a few reddish-brown feathers mixed in. **FEMALE:** Like adult female. Imm. plumage kept 1 year.

Feeding: Feeds in trees and shrubs, eating insects and fruit, tree blossoms. May come to hummingbird feeders.

Nesting: Shallow pouchlike nest of woven grass blades lined with finer materials, suspended from fork in branch of tree 6–20 ft. above the ground. Eggs: 3–7, pale grayish blue with dark marks; I: 12–14 days; F: 11–14 days, altricial; B: 1.

Other Behavior: Nests singly or in loose colonies. Males sing from trees. Often hidden in foliage, but not usually shy. Adults and young stay together until time for southward migration. Common cowbird host.

Habitat: Orchards, open woods, shade trees in towns, wetlands, parks, streamside groves.

Voice: Song a rapid series of whistled notes; call a short "chuk."

Conservation: BBS: W ⇑ C ⇓ CBC: → Population is declining due to loss of tropical forests on wintering grounds.

Hooded Oriole
Icterus cucullatus

Female

Male

Immature male, 1st spring

Identification: 7½" **MALE: Orange-to-yellow body** (Tex. birds orange, Calif. birds yellower); **black face and throat; long, thin, slightly downcurved bill; black wings. FEMALE: Uniformly greenish yellow below; long, thin, slightly downcurved bill;** gray wings with 2 wing bars; relatively long tail. **IMM—MALE:** In fall, like adult female; next spring and summer, like adult male, but with grayish-brown wings. **FEMALE:** Like adult female. Imm. plumage kept 1 year.

Feeding: Feeds in foliage, eating insects, berries, and flower nectar. Like other orioles, will come to sugar-water solutions such as hummingbird feeders.

Nesting: Nest of coarse grasses and palmetto or yucca fibers lined with finer material, suspended from branch 5–30 ft. above ground. In palm trees, sewn to underside of palm leaf. Eggs: 3–5, pale with splotches; I: 12–14 days; F: 14 days, altricial; B: 2–3.

Other Behavior: Range is expanding in Calif. following extensive planting of palm trees, a nesting habitat.

Habitat: Urban or rural areas, often with palms.

Voice: Song a rapid varied series of whistles; call a "weeet."

Conservation: BBS: W ↑ C ⇑ CBC: ↓

491

Baltimore Oriole
Bullock's Oriole
Icterus galbula   Icterus bullockii

Baltimore male

Baltimore female

Bullock's male

Bullock's female

Identification: 8½" Baltimore is mostly eastern, Bullock's is mostly western. **BALTIMORE—MALE: Black hood and back; orange body. FEMALE: Olive-yellow on rump; orange-yellow below; head and back mottled with black; throat variably blotched with black. IMM:** Female like adult. Male like adult female, but with orange-tipped lesser coverts. **BULLOCK'S—MALE: Orange face; black eyeline; large white wing patch. FEMALE: Yellowish head and breast; whitish belly. IMM:** Female like adult. Fall male yellowish with black throat and eyeline; spring male like adult male, but lacks white wing patch.

Feeding: Eats insects, fruits, flower nectar. Comes to bird feeders for orange halves and sugar solutions.

Nesting: Both use hanging nest of plant fibers suspended from branch 6–60 ft. high. Eggs: 4–6, pale bluish white with dark marks; I: 12–14 days; F: 12–14 days, altricial; B: 1.

Other Behavior: Male and female sing in both species.

Baltimore   Bullock's

Habitat: Deciduous trees near openings, such as parks, gardens, roads.

Voice: Song is 4–8 medium-pitched whistled notes; calls a 2-note "teetoo" and a rapid chatter, "ch'ch'ch'ch'ch."

Conservation:
Baltimore:
BBS: W ⇑ C ↓
Bullock's:
BBS: W ↓ C ↓

Scott's Oriole
Icterus parisorum

Male

Female

Immature male

Identification: 8″ MALE: **Black head, back, and breast; yellow belly;** yellow wing patch. FEMALE: **Greenish yellow below; darker above, with dark streaks on back; variable black mottling on throat.** IMM—MALE: Like adult male, but with mottled black hood and streaked back. FEMALE: Like adult female, but with little or no black on head and throat. Imm. plumage kept 1 year.

Feeding: Feeds in trees, shrubs, and on the ground, eating insects, small fruits, berries, and flower nectar. Comes to bird feeder sugar-water solutions.

Nesting: Hanging nest of yucca fibers and grass lined with finer material, suspended from yucca, pine, or other tree 4–20 ft. above the ground. Eggs: 2–4, pale blue with dark marks; I: 12–14 days; F: 14 days, altricial; B: 2.

Other Behavior: Males arrive on breeding grounds about a week before females. They forage in treetops, singing throughout the day. Females give softer version of song.

Habitat: Arid and semiarid woods, scrub, often with yuccas.

Voice: Song is clear whistled phrases; call a "chak."

Conservation:
BBS: W ↑ C ⇑ CBC: ↑

Gray-crowned Rosy-Finch
Leucosticte tephrocotis

Male

Identification: 6" MALE: Primarily brown; gray hindcrown; rosy on wings, flanks, belly, and rump. FEMALE: Brown overall with gray hindcrown.

Feeding: Eats insects and seeds of small tundra plants. Comes to bird feeders.

Nesting: Nest of moss, grass, hair, lichens, and rootlets lined with hair, fine grasses, and ptarmigan feathers, placed in crevice or cavity of rocks, cliff, or human structure up to 25 ft. above the ground. Eggs: 3–6, white; I: 12–14 days; F: 16–22 days, altricial; B: 1–2.

Other Behavior: During breeding, semicolonial, with much aggression between males. Males outnumber females throughout year. In winter, they form large flocks that roost together, often in large numbers of 1,000 or more in caves, mine shafts, abandoned Cliff Swallow nests.

Habitat: Summers on rocky mountaintops, well above tree line; winters at lower elevations, sometimes in urban areas.

Voice: Song a descending series of harsh notes, like "chew chew chew chew"; calls include a high "chip."

Conservation: CBC: ⇓

494

Black Rosy-Finch
Brown-capped Rosy-Finch

Leucosticte atrata   Leucosticte australis

Black male

Brown-capped male

Identification: 6" BLACK—MALE: Blackish body; light gray nape; rosy rump and wings. FEMALE: Dark overall; little or no gray on nape. BROWN-CAPPED—MALE: Primarily brown; dark crown; gray hindcrown faint or lacking; rosy on wings, flanks, belly, and rump. FEMALE: Grayish brown overall with no dark cap or crown.

Feeding: Eats insects and seeds of small tundra plants. Comes to bird feeders.

Nesting: Nest of moss, grass, hair, lichens, and rootlets lined with hair, fine grasses, and feathers, placed in rock crevices in talus slopes, cliffs, or human structure such as cabin or bridge. Eggs: 3–6, white; I: 12–14 days; F: 16–22 days, altricial; B: 1–2.

Other Behavior: Semicolonial breeders. Males outnumber females. Nomadic in winter. Form large communal roosts that may number more than 1,000. Roost in caves, mine shafts, tunnels, abandoned Cliff Swallow nests.

Black   Brown-cap.

Habitat: Summer on alpine areas and tundra; winter at lower elevations, farms, yards.

Voice: Song a descending series of harsh notes, like "chew chew chew chew"; calls include a high "chip."

Conservation:
Black:
CBC: ⇓
Brown-capped:
CBC: ⇓

495

Pine Grosbeak
Pinicola enucleator

Male

Female

Identification: 9″ **MALE:** Rose-red head, chest, and back; gray belly; black wing with 2 white wing bars; stubby black bill. **FEMALE:** Similar to male, but colored areas olive-yellow and restricted to head and rump. **IMM—MALE:** Like adult female, but head and rump orangish. **FEMALE:** Similar to adult female. Imm. plumage kept 1 year.

Feeding: Forages on ground and in foliage for the seeds, nuts, buds, and fruits of many trees, such as crabapples, maples, ashes, pines. Also eats insects. At bird feeders prefers sunflower seed.

Nesting: Nest of mosses, twigs, roots, lichens, and grasses lined with rootlets, fur, lichens, placed in shrub or tree 2–30 ft. above the ground. Eggs: 2–6, blue-green with dark marks; I: 13–15 days; F: 13–20 days, altricial; B: 1.

Other Behavior: Irruptive species; in some winters moves south of normal range in great numbers, generally when populations are high and food sources in North are scarce. May associate with Bohemian Waxwing flocks.

Habitat: Summers in coniferous woods, high montane forests; winters near fruit and seed trees.

Voice: Song a musical warble; call a 3-note whistle, with middle note highest, like "teeweetee."

Conservation:
BBS: W ↓ C CBC: ↑

Purple Finch

Carpodacus purpureus

Male

Female

Identification: 6" MALE: Upperparts, breast, and flanks raspberry red (brightest in summer); head uniformly covered with red; little or no brown streaking on breast or flanks. FEMALE: Well-defined pattern on face of broad white eyebrow, brown eyeline, and white cheek; broad, blurry, brown streaking underneath; no streaking on undertail coverts. IMM: Male and female like adult female. Male may sing and breed in this plumage. Imm. plumage kept 1 year. See Voice for distinctive flight call.

Feeding: Forages on the ground and above in foliage for seeds and buds of trees and weeds, berries, and insects. Comes to bird feeders for sunflower seed and millet.

Nesting: Nest of twigs, grasses, rootlets, moss, bits of snakeskin, and string lined with horsehair, moss, and rootlets, placed on branch of tree 5–60 ft. high. Eggs: 3–6, light green-blue with dark marks; I: 13 days; F: 14 days, altricial; B: 1–2.

Other Behavior: Irruptive in some winters.

Habitat: Mixed woods, coniferous forests, lower mountain slopes, suburban yards.

Voice: Song an extended musical warble; call in flight a short "pik."

Conservation: BBS: W ↓ C ⇓ CBC: ↑

Cassin's Finch
Carpodacus cassinii

Male (l.), female (r.)

Identification: 6″ Often raises crown feathers giving it a spiky crest. **MALE: Rich red crown contrasts sharply with brown on rest of head; back brown; belly white with no obvious brown streaking;** bill relatively long. **FEMALE: Faint facial pattern of light eyebrow, brown ear patch, and light cheek; thin, well-defined brown streaking underneath; streaks on undertail coverts;** bill relatively long; often a faint eye-ring. **IMM:** Male and female like adult female. Male may sing and breed in this plumage. Imm. plumage kept 1 year. Similar House Finch has much shorter bill.

Feeding: Forages on the ground and in foliage for seeds and buds. Also eats insects, wild berries, and rock salt.

Nesting: Semicolonial. Nest of stems, twigs, lichens, lined with grasses, placed in branch of conifer, cottonwood, or other tree. Eggs: 3–6, blue-green with dark marks; I: 12–14 days; F: 14 days, altricial; B: ?

Other Behavior: Breeds at higher elevations than Purple Finch. In winter, moves to lower elevations.

Habitat: Conifers, in upper mountain forests.

Voice: Song an extended musical warble; call in flight a 2–3 part "teeyup" or "chideeyup."

Conservation:
BBS: W ↑ C CBC: ⇓

House Finch
Carpodacus mexicanus

Male

Yellowish male

Female

Identification: 5½" MALE: **Red on head and upper breast; broad brown streaking on lower breast and flanks.** In some regions, red replaced with yellow or orange. FEMALE: **Uniformly brown-streaked head; broad brown streaking on breast and belly;** white undertail coverts usually unstreaked. Short bill helps distinguish from much larger-billed Cassin's Finch.

Feeding: Forages on ground and in trees, eating weed seeds, blossoms, fruits, and buds. Can monopolize bird feeders, where it prefers sunflower seed.

Nesting: Nest of twigs, grasses, leaves, and debris, placed in variety of artificial and natural cavities, such as foundation plantings, vines, hanging planters, and occasionally birdhouses. Eggs: 2–6, bluish white with speckles; I: 12–16 days; F: 11–19 days, altricial; B: 1–3.

Other Behavior: Forms winter flocks. Native to western states. Was introduced to the East in New York City area in 1940 when pet dealers, being arrested for illegally selling House Finches as "Hollywood Finches," released the birds. Has since spread throughout much of East. Range still expanding.

Habitat: Urban areas, suburbs, parks, canyons, semidry brush country.

Voice: Song a musical warble often ending with a harsh downslurred "jeeer." Female and male both sing.

Conservation:
BBS: W ↓ C ⇑ CBC: ↑

Red Crossbill
White-winged Crossbill
Loxia curvirostra   Loxia leucoptera

Red male

White-winged male

Red female

White-winged female

Identification: 6″ Both species have **long bills with tips crossed.** RED—MALE: Red-to-orange body; black wings and tail; no white wing bars. FEMALE: Grayish with olive tinge; no wing bars. WHITE-WINGED—MALE: Pinkish-red body; black wings with 2 white wing bars. FEMALE: Grayish with olive tinges on head and back; yellowish on breast and rump; black wings with 2 white wingbars; some streaking on back and flanks.

Feeding: Both extract conifer seeds by forcing scales of cones apart with bills and lifting out seeds with tongue. They also eat other seeds, insects, and road salt, often resulting in traffic casualties. Occasionally at feeders.

Nesting: Both have nests of twigs, rootlets, grasses, moss, bark, lichens, placed in tree branch 6–40 ft. (Red) or 3–70 ft. (White-winged) above the ground. Eggs: 2–5, greenish white or bluish white with dark marks. Red—I: 12–18 days; F: 15–20 days, altricial; B: 1–2. White-winged—I: 12–14 days; F: ?, altricial; B: ?

Other Behavior: Irruptive species, making large migrations beyond normal range in some winters.

Red   White-wing.

Habitat: Coniferous woods. Red prefers pines; White-winged uses spruce and pines.

Voice: Songs a rapid warble. Red flight call a "jip jip jip"; White-winged flight call a "chif-chif."

Conservation:
Red:
BBS: W ↓ C ↑ CBC: ↑
White-winged:
BBS: W ⇓ C ⇑ CBC: ↓

Common Redpoll
Hoary Redpoll
Carduelis flammea   Carduelis hornemanni

Common male

Hoary

Common female

Hoary

Identification: 5½" Both species recognized by their **red forecrown and black chin.** COMMON—MALE: Brown streaking on flanks and on pale rump; rose limited to central breast in winter, on breast and cheeks in summer. FEMALE: Lacks red on breast, but has brown streaks on sides of upper breast. HOARY—MALE: Whitish overall; little or no streaking on underparts, nape, or rump; rose on breast absent or faint. FEMALE: Similar to male, but with no rose tinge on breast. •Vast majority of redpolls seen south of Can. are Common Redpolls.

Feeding: Both eat seeds and buds of trees, grasses, weeds, and insects. Come to bird feeders for sunflower seed and thistle (niger) seed.

Nesting: Both have nests of twigs and grasses, placed in bush or on ground. Common—Eggs: 4–7, pale green or blue with dark marks; I: 10–11 days; F: 12 days, altricial; B: 1–2. Hoary—Eggs: 3–7, pale green or blue with dark marks; I: 11 days; F: 9–14 days, altricial; B: 1.

Other Behavior: Both are irruptive species.

Common   Hoary

Habitat: Summer in tundra; winter in brushy areas.

Voice: For both, song is a mixture of trills and buzzes; calls include a "chit chit" and a rising "sweeyeet."

Conservation:
Common:
BBS: W ⇑ C CBC: ↓
Hoary:
CBC: ↓

Pine Siskin
Carduelis pinus

Identification: 5 " Brown above, light below; brown-streaked overall; long pointed bill; yellow on the wings and base of tail, not always immediately visible in perched birds. IN FLIGHT: Yellow stripe down length of wing.

Feeding: Forages on the ground and in foliage for conifer cone seeds, weed seeds, insects, flower buds, and nectar. Comes to bird feeders, sometimes in large numbers, for sunflower and thistle (niger) seed.

Nesting: Nest of grasses, twigs, rootlets, bark strips, and lichens lined with feathers, fur, and rootlets, placed in tree branch 3–50 ft. above the ground. Eggs: 1–5, light green-blue with dark marks; I: 13 days; F: 14–15 days, altricial; B: 1–2.

Other Behavior: Irruptive species. Seen in large numbers in some years. Often found with goldfinches. Listen for buzzy "zrreeeee" call, a good clue to its presence.

Habitat: Coniferous or mixed woods, shrub thickets, suburban yards.

Voice: Song a mixture of trills and rapid warbles; calls include a "sweeyeet" and a buzzy, ascending "zrreeeee."

Conservation:
BBS: W ↓ C ↓ CBC: ⇑

Lesser Goldfinch
Carduelis psaltria

Male (western portion of range)

Male (eastern portion of range)

Female

Identification: 4½" MALE: Comes in 2 forms. In western half of range has a **black cap, green back, yellow belly, and white patch on wings.** In the eastern half of range is **black above, yellow below, and has a whitish patch on the wings. FEMALE: Greenish above; yellow below; yellow undertail coverts; black wings have a white patch seen in flight.** IMM: Female like adult female. Male has mixed green-and-black cap. Imm. plumage kept 1 year.

Feeding: Eats wide variety of seeds from trees, weeds, grasses, also flower buds and berries. Comes to bird feeders for sunflower and thistle (niger) seed.

Nesting: Nest of bark, moss, and plant stems lined with feathers, cotton, and plant down, placed in shrub or tree 2–30 ft. above the ground. Eggs: 3–6, light blue or blue-white; I: 12 days; F: ?, altricial; B: ?

Other Behavior: Found in small to large flocks in winter, often along with other goldfinches, Pine Siskins, and Dickcissels. Drawn to habitats that include a good water source.

Habitat: Woods edges, roadsides, gardens, parks.

Voice: Song a rapid series of repeated phrases from other birds' songs; call a "peeyeet."

Conservation:
BBS: W ↓ C ⇓ CBC: ↓

Lawrence's Goldfinch
Carduelis lawrencei

Male

Female

Identification: 4½" Both sexes **grayish overall.** MALE: **Black forehead and chin; yellow breast; yellow on wings.** FEMALE: **Yellowish cast on breast; yellow on wings.** There are only slight differences between summer and winter birds.

Feeding: Forages on ground and in low foliage for weed seeds and insects. Comes to bird feeders for sunflower seed and thistle (niger) seed.

Nesting: Nest of grasses, lichens, wool, hair, feathers, and flowers, placed in shrub or tree 3–40 ft. above the ground. Eggs: 3–6, light blue; I: ?; F: ?, altricial; B: ?

Other Behavior: Seeks out water sources in its dry environment. Erratic breeding distribution from year to year within its range. In winter, found in flocks, often with other goldfinches and Lark Sparrows.

Habitat: Arid grassy slopes, chaparral, open oak or pine woods.

Voice: Song is a bubbling twitter; call in flight is a distinctive "tinkoo."

Conservation: BBS: W ↓ C CBC: ⇓

American Goldfinch
Carduelis tristis

Summer female

Summer male

Winter

Identification: 5" SUMMER—MALE: Yellow body; black cap, wings, and tail. FEMALE: Yellowish green overall, with black wings and tail. WINTER—MALE: Yellowish brown, with yellow wash on face and chin; black wings with white wing bars. FEMALE: Grayish brown, with little yellow; dark brown wings with white wing bars.

Feeding: Feeds on the ground, on weed stalks and foliage, eating seeds, insects, berries. At bird feeders, prefers hulled sunflower and thistle (niger) seeds.

Nesting: Nest of strands from weeds and vines, downy filaments from wind-dispersed seeds, such as thistles, bound with caterpillar webbing, placed in shrub or tree 4–20 ft. above the ground. Eggs: 3–7, light blue; I: 12–14 days; F: 11–15 days, altricial; B: 1–2.

Other Behavior: During breeding, male does deep loop flight, an exaggeration of the normal looping flight of goldfinches, with the "perchicoree" call. Often done while circling his territory. Female builds nest and may start 2nd nest while fledged young are fed by male. In winter, found in flocks that wander in search of food.

Habitat: Open areas with some shrubs and trees, farms, suburban yards, gardens.

Voice: Two songs: a long canarylike song, and a short forceful warble; calls include "sweeyeet," "beerbee," and "perchicoree" flight call.

Conservation:
BBS: W ↓ C ↓ CBC: ↑

Evening Grosbeak
Coccothraustes vespertinus

Male, winter

Female, winter

Identification: 8″ **MALE:** Yellow body; darker head with a bright yellow eyebrow; black-and-white wings. Bill is yellow in winter, pale green during summer. **FEMALE:** Brownish gray overall, with yellow on nape; black-and-white wings. Bill is same as male's.

Feeding: Feeds mainly on seeds of trees such as box elder, sugar maples, pines, tulip poplars. Also eats fruit, buds, nuts, insects, tree sap, and road salt. At bird feeders prefers sunflower seed.

Nesting: Nest of lichens, twigs, roots, and mosses lined with rootlets and finer materials, placed at the end of a tree branch 20–100 ft. above the ground. Eggs: 2–5, blue or bluish green with dark marks; I: 11–14 days; F: 13–14 days, altricial; B: 2.

Other Behavior: Breeding range has expanded. Irruptive species, occurring in large numbers in some years. At those times, it is common at bird feeders, flocks devouring large quantities of sunflower seed. In spring, beak turns from yellow to light green and courtship begins. Watch for the male feeding female sunflower seeds.

Habitat: Summers in northern mixed and coniferous woods; winters in open areas with trees and shrubs, suburban yards.

Voice: Song a halting warble; call is a ringing "peeer" and when given by a flock is reminiscent of sleighbells.

Conservation:
BBS: W ⇑ C CBC: ⇑

506

House Sparrow

Passer domesticus

Female

Summer male

Fall male

Identification: 6" MALE: Black bib; gray crown and cheek; rich brown back and nape. After molt in fall, gray feather tips obscure the black bib. FEMALE: Grayish-brown breast; brown crown; buffy eyebrow.

Feeding: Forages on the ground and in foliage for insects, spiders, small fruit, weed seeds, waste grain, and crumbs. Comes to feeders.

Nesting: Nest of straw, weeds, trash, grass, lined with feathers and hair, placed in any natural or constructed crevice or cavity, such as birdhouse, under eaves of house, in signs or nooks of commercial buildings. Eggs: 3–7, white, light green, or light blue with dark marks; I: 10–14 days; F: 14–17 days, altricial; B: 2–3.

Other Behavior: Roosts in groups at night in fall and winter, and also during midday, when birds gather at fixed spot and chirp noisily for up to an hour. Also called English Sparrow because was introduced from England to N. America in middle of 19th century. Aggressively competes with our native cavity-nesting species of birds for nest spots. Will kill adult birds, nestlings, and eggs of other species in order to take over a birdhouse or cavity.

Habitat: Urban areas, parks, open farmland.

Voice: Song a repeated "chirup chireep chirup"; call "chilup."

Conservation: BBS: W ↓ C ↓ CBC: ↓

Glossary

Accipiter — A genus of hawks with generally short wings and long tails; they catch other birds in the air.

Air sac — A membrane that extends from the lungs and in grouse and prairie-chickens is often inflated during breeding displays.

Altricial — A pattern of development in which young birds are featherless and dependent upon the parents for food and warmth for the first few weeks of their life.

Breastband — A dark band of feathers across the breast of a bird.

Breeding range — The geographical area where a species regularly breeds.

Brood — All young from a single clutch of eggs.

Buteo — A genus of hawks with long broad wings and short tails; they catch mostly rodents.

Call — A short instinctive vocalization.

Cap — A darker area of feathers on the top of the head.

Cere — A raised fleshy area at the base of the upper mandible on hawks, eagles, falcons, and their relatives.

Chevrons — Small V-shaped dots on the underparts of some birds.

Clutch — A complete set of eggs laid for one brood.

Colonial — A term used to describe many pairs of birds nesting very close together.

Coverts — Small feathers that overlap the bases of larger feathers on the wings and tail.

Crest — Slightly longer feathers on the top of the head which, when raised, form a peak.

Ear patch — Darker feathers located just behind and below the eye around the area of the ear.

Ear tuft — Longer feathers on either side of the top of the head. These usually can be raised and lowered.

Eclipse plumage — A briefly held nonbreeding plumage of male ducks which resembles that of the female. It usually occurs in mid-summer.

Eyebrow — A stripe above the eye.

Eye comb — A brightly colored fleshy area over the eye; most common in grouse and prairie-chickens and used in their displays.

Eye crescent — An arc of lighter color above and/or below the eye.

Eye-ring — A lighter area encircling the eye.

Eye-stripe — A stripe on the head from the base of the bill to the eye and on behind the eye.

Facial disk — Feathers that radiate out from the eyes, especially in owls.

Flank — The side of the belly just below the wing.

Flight feathers — The largest feathers of the wings; called primaries and secondaries.

Gorget — The area of the throat on hummingbirds that is often iridescent on the males.

Hood — A plumage pattern in which the head of a bird is all dark and contrasts with lighter feathers on the body.

Hybrid — The result of two species interbreeding.

Immature — A young bird in between juvenile and adult stages.

Inner wing — The portion of the wing closest to the body.

Irruption — A rapid increase in population of a species.

Introduced — Term used to describe a species that was brought by humans to a geographical area outside its normal range.

Juvenal plumage — The first full set of feathers of a young bird after it loses its natal down.

Juvenile — A young bird in juvenal plumage.

Leading edge — The front edge; term often used when describing plumage on wings.

Lore — The area between the eye and the base of the bill.

Mandible — The upper or lower half of the bill.

Mirror — Term used in relation to gulls to refer to the small white dots at the tips of the wings.

Molt — A complete or partial shedding of feathers.

Morph — A regularly occurring color variation within a species that is not related to the sex, age, or seasonal plumage of the bird.

Moustache — Dark streaks on either side of the base of the bill along the sides of the throat.

Nape — The back of the head and neck.

Neck-ring — A darker area of feathering that encircles the throat.

Plumage — The complete set of a bird's feathers at a certain time.

Polyandrous — Pairing and mating with more than one male.

Polygynous — Pairing and mating with more than one female.

Precocial — A pattern of development in which young birds hatch with feathers and are able to move and feed themselves.

Primaries — The longest flight feathers; they are located on the outer half of the wing.

Rump — The top of the base of the tail.

Secondaries — Flight feathers located on the inner half of the wing; they are about half as long as the primaries.

Sideburn — A dark vertical mark behind the eye, especially on falcons.

Song — An extended complex vocalization that is in part learned.

Spectacles — Light eye-rings and lores, making the bird look like it is wearing a pair of glasses.

Speculum — A colored patch on the inner wing of ducks.

Territory — A defended area.

Trailing edge — The back edge; term often used when describing plumage on wings.

Underparts — The area of the body below the wings, including the belly, breast, and throat.

Upperparts — The area above the wings, including the back, nape, and top of the head.

Uppertail coverts — The small feathers that cover the top of the base of the tail.

Undertail coverts — The small feathers that cover the underside of the base of the tail.

Vent — The anal and reproductive opening.

Wattle — A fleshy bumpy area on the face of a bird; often hangs down, as in the wattle of a Wild Turkey.

Window — A lighter area of translucence in a wing, often at the base of the primaries.

Wing bar — A continuous lighter area at the tips of wing coverts.

Wing lining — The coverts of the underwing.

Wing-stripe — A lengthwise stripe on the upper surface of the wing.

Winter plumage — The plumage held during the winter months.

Winter range — The geographical range of the bird during winter.

Wrist — The point of the first bend in the wing.

Photo Credits

The letter or letters immediately following each page number refer to the position of the photograph on the page (T = top; B = bottom; L = left; C = center; R = right). A second number in parentheses after a credit indicates that the photograph also appears as a small silhouette in the Learning Pages or in the Quick Guide to the Most Common Birds. For example, 279L (xxiv) identifies the photo of the male Downy Woodpecker, shown in the Species Accounts on page 279 and in the Quick Guide on page xxiv.

Steve Bentsen: 47L, 50R, 109R, 136BR, 157L, 176R, 203L, 204BR, 212, 225 (xxiv), 229L, 246TR, 266R, 267, 272R, 277L, 277R, 306, 350R, 357, 431L, 434TL, 434TR, 437R, 438L, 438TR, 438BR, 441BR (xxi), 446R, 456L, 456R, 461T, 480R (xxi), 486R, 503L (xviii).

Rick and Nora Bowers: 127, 256R, 316, 341L, 342L, 344B, 387L, 387R, 388R, 390B, 409, 423, 427R, 433BR, 437L, 447L, 460, 470BL, 483L, 483R.

Lysle R. Brinker: 478BR, 501TL, 501BL, 501TR, 501BR.

Kathleen and Lindsey Brown: 79T, 283L, 350L (xxiii), 353 (xxiii), 354L (xxiii), 354R, 393L (xxii), 393R (xxii), 430L, 430R, 448, 459L, 465BR (445), 468R, 505TR (xviii), 505L (xviii).

Bill Burt: 131, 132.

William S. Clark: 95BL, 109TL (86), 110TL.

Cornell Laboratory of Ornithology: L. Page Brown — 99R; B. D. Cotrille — 426B; H. Cruickshank — 116R; Bill Dyer — 396BR; Lang Elliott — 340; Mike Hopiak — 249L; O. S. Pettingill — 116R, 196TL (189); Dwain Prellwitz — 116L; Stan Smith — 214R; Mary Tremaine — 122T; Fred K. Truslow — 285R, 293L.

Rob Curtis: 228L, 228R, 300R, 302L, 302R, 304 (287), 312, 313, 330, 343T, 348, 351, 355, 358, 363, 368T, 368B, 370BL, 374T, 374B, 376, 379, 396BL, 410BR, 412L, 416B, 417, 418L, 422T, 424, 427L, 464TR, 465TR (xx), 467TR, 467BR, 471BR, 475BR, 493L.

Dave Czaplak: 206BL.

Mike Danzenbaker: 3B, 8B, 10T, 10B, 12, 14L, 14TR, 14BR, 15L, 16L, 17L, 17R, 18, 27R, 40R, 43L (84), 49, 52T, 57B, 61T, 61B, 64T, 67T, 67B, 74T, 76B, 82TL, 82BL, 113, 121L, 121R, 123, 135, 142BL (141), 150, 152R, 162R

(141), 164B, 164T, 169T, 185L, 185R, 186R, 192TL (188), 192BR, 193TR, 194TL (189), 197TR, 198TL, 198BR, 200BL, 200BR, 201TL, 202L, 205BR, 207TR, 208L, 208R, 209TL, 209BL, 213TL, 216T, 216B, 246L, 249R, 251, 260L, 260R, 263L, 264L, 270R, 276L, 276R, 280R, 281R, 291L, 291R (286), 293R, 296, 297L (287), 300L, 301, 303, 309, 314R, 319, 335, 338, 341R, 343B, 359, 369T, 370BR, 382 (xxiii), 390TR, 391R, 410L, 434BR, 435L, 440, 451, 452, 455, 459TR, 461B, 462L, 462R, 464L (445), 466, 476B, 477B, 478TR, 479BR, 491BR, 493TR, 503BR (xviii), 506T (xviii).

Larry R. Ditto: 40L, 54T, 66B, 114L, 124, 139, 224B, 235, 244, 245R, 431R, 458BL, 484BL, 484BR.

Steven D. Faccio: 362 (xx).

Kenneth W. Fink: 6T, 35, 48B, 62B, 69BR, 71R, 79B, 137R, 169BL (140), 182BL, 190BL, 195TL (189), 195TR, 196BR, 198TR, 199TR, 199BR, 200TL, 201BL, 202TR, 205BL, 210TR, 219BR, 220TL, 223, 226, 233R, 243, 261R, 263R, 268, 270L (xxiv), 271L, 274L, 281L, 328, 329, 333R, 475TR, 484TL, 485L (xxii), 488L, 492BL (xix), 494, 496L, 496R, 498.

Sam Fried: 186L, 201BR, 207TL, 211BR, 215TL, 237, 282R, 305, 332B, 339L, 339R, 342R, 474B, 476T, 482R, 495B.

Gary K. Froehlich: 24TL, 24R, 25L, 59T, 59B, 76T, 90L (83), 91TR (85), 128L, 155L, 155BR, 181, 230, 310 (287), 486L.

W. Edward Harper: 115R, 122B, 197BR, 215TR, 317.

James R. Hill, III: 336L, 336R, 337B.

Joseph R. Jehl, Jr.: 183BR, 184BR, 190BR.

Kevin T. Karlson: 4T, 9T, 70BL, 70T, 72T, 118T, 118BL, 118BR, 167BL (140), 172T, 172B, 174B, 176L, 177L, 183T, 184T, 187, 257L, 403BR, 411R.

Peter LaTourrette: 308R, 326R (xxiv).

Stephen G. Maka: 37L, 87L (85), 170BL (140), 383.

Maslowski Photograph: 46, 48T, 107R, 119B, 126, 183BL, 184BL, 210L, 236L, 241BL, 266L, 269, 292, 311, 321, 322, 356, 360, 364, 365, 367, 378, 398B, 401R (394), 422B, 439T, 467L, 468L, 469L (445), 475L, 478R, 507BR.

Charles W. Melton: 119TR.

Arthur Morris/Birds as Art: 11T, 11B, 23L, 25R, 26L, 29, 30R, 36T, 36B, 37R, 38L, 41T, 45, 55B, 57T, 58B, 65T,

65B, 66T, 68T, 77T, 77B, 78T, 133, 142BR, 143TR, 144, 146L, 147 (140), 149, 151T (141), 151B, 152L, 153R, 156T, 156B, 159 (141), 160, 161T, 161BR, 165T, 165B, 166T, 166B, 168T, 168BL, 168BR, 170T, 170BR, 171T, 171BL, 173B, 175BL (140), 175TR, 175BR, 179TL, 179TR, 179BR, 180L, 180TR (141), 180BR, 182BR, 190TR, 191BR, 195BL (189), 196BL (189), 203BR, 205T, 206BR, 210BR, 213TR, 254L, 255L, 256L, 325, 366, 369B, 390TL, 401L (394), 403T, 408T, 408BR, 410TR, 413T, 418BR, 428TR, 432L, 449L (xx) (445), 458T.

Blair Nikula: 171BR, 207BL, 209TR, 391L.

Rod Norden: 13, 16R, 19, 20.

Wayne R. Petersen: 474T.

B. "Moose" Peterson: 81B, 326L.

Photo/Nats: Mary Clay — 262R; Sam Fried — 297R; Michael Goodman — 47TR; Don Johnston — 115L; Barbara Magnuson — 69T, 373L; John F. O'Connor — 55T.

B. J. Rose: 194BR, 250.

Ray Schwartz: 110R, 110BL.

Leroy Simon: 32R.

Arnold Small: 4B, 6B, 26R, 70BR, 71L, 72BR, 73B, 74B, 75B, 80T, 80B, 81T, 130, 179BL, 182T, 197BL, 199TL, 213BR, 275, 289, 290, 295L, 399R.

Brian E. Small: 78B, 155TR (141), 169BR, 202BR, 211TR, 229R, 258R, 262L, 265L, 265R, 271R, 274R, 278L, 278R, 280L, 307, 308L, 314TL, 318, 320, 332T (xxii), 345, 352L (xxiii), 370TR, 375, 377, 380 (xix), 381T, 381B, 385, 392T, 392B, 396T, 397T, 397B (395), 402T, 402BL, 403BL, 404B (395), 405 (395), 406T, 406BL (395), 406BR, 407T, 407B, 412TR, 412BR, 414T, 414B, 415, 418TR, 419T, 419B, 420T (394), 420BL (394), 421T (395), 421B, 425, 429L, 429TR, 429BR, 432BR, 433T, 433BL, 435TR, 435BR, 439BR, 446L, 449TR, 449BR, 450, 453, 454, 457T, 457B, 459BR, 463, 464BR (xx), 470T (xx) (445), 481R, 484TR, 489L (xxi), 493BR, 503TR, 504L, 504R.

Hugh P. Smith, Jr.: 23R, 63, 92R, 93R, 129, 136TR, 193BL, 194BL (189), 246BR, 258L, 259L (xix), 259R, 261L, 273R, 284, 349 (xxiii), 352R, 361, 373R, 384 (xxiv), 442T, 442B, 469R, 472BR (xxiii), 485R (xxii), 491L, 491TR, 492BR (xix), 499TL (xix), 499TR, 502 (xx), 505BR (xviii), 507L (xx) (444).

Lillian and Don Stokes: 7R, 24BL, 30L, 31, 33, 38R, 39L, 39R, 41B, 50L, 51, 53, 87R, 136L, 137L, 138, 157R, 163B,

173T, 279L (xxiv), 279TR, 279BR (xxiv), 337L, 499B (xix) (444).

John L. Tveten: 28, 34, 114R, 119TL, 146R, 158, 162L, 192BL (188), 192TR, 194TR, 196TR, 198BL (189), 200TR, 201TR, 204T, 211L, 221R, 480L (xxi), 487T.

Richard R. Veit: 62T, 193BR, 195BL.

Tom Vezo: 32L, 52B, 54B, 64B, 69BL, 72BL, 73T, 75T, 94BL, 117T, 117B, 142TR, 143L, 145T (140), 163T, 167T, 167BR, 177R, 204BL, 206TR, 247B, 272L, 273L, 294, 327, 402BR, 416T, 420BR, 443, 473.

VIREO: S. Bahrt — 346; R. Behrstock — 197TL; Rick and Nora Bowers — 127, 193TL, 234, 247T, 264R, 298, 426T; A. and S. Carey — 112, 232, 233L; R. J. Chandler — 178R, 371L, 371R; B. Chudleigh — 143BR; H. Clarke — 389, 398T; J. Concalosi — 148, 224T; A. Cruickshank — 91BL; H. Cruickshank — 190TL, 203TR, 219L, 458BR, 477T, 488R; Rob Curtis — 125, 239, 333T, 447R; T. Davis — 145B; J. Dunning — 154; Sam Fried — 161BL, 174T, 288; W. Greene — 60, 120, 236R, 257R, 285L, 344T (xxiii), 506B (xviii); Don Hadden — 15R; B. Henry — 487B, 500TL, 500BL, 500TR, 500BR; D. R. Herr — 94R; J. Hoffman — 315, 400; Steven Holt — 324; M. P. Kahl — 128R; Kevin T. Karlson — 3T, 5B, 9B; S. J. Lang — 5T, 134, 441TL, 479L, 479TR; G. Lasley — 253; P. LaTourrette — 481L; J. Maron — 178L; Arthur Morris/Birds as Art — 7L, 44, 68B, 82R, 142TL, 191BL, 199BL, 206TL, 209BR, 314BL, 323L, 428L, 465L, 470BR, 482L; S. Olioso — 334; O. S. Pettingill, Jr. — 497T (xix); R. L. Pitman — 22R, 27L, 217, 218, 219TR; B. Randall — 252T, 252B, 255R, 295R; D. Roby and K. Brink — 220R; F. K. Schleicher — 153L, 472TL; B. Schorre — 386, 408BL, 411L, 413B, 428BR, 432TR, 434BL, 436TR, 439BL, 490L, 490TR, 490BR, 492TL, 492TR; Johann Schumacher — 56, 283BR, 489R (xxi); H. P. Smith, Jr. — 222, 299 (286), 331, 388L; T. J. Ulrich — 227, 241L, 248, 404T, 471L, 472BL (xxiii) (445), 472TR (xxiii), 495T, 497B (xix); R. Villani — 175TL, 282L, 507TR (xx) (444); A. Walther — 191TL, 347 (xxiii); Doug Wechsler — 58T, 220BL, 221L (xxiv), 323R, 370TL; Brian K. Wheeler — 91L, 93BL, 96TR, 98L (84), 102TL, 103R, 107BL (86), 111L (86), 111R; J. R. Woodward — 8T, 441TR; D. and M. Zimmerman — 254R, 283TR (xxiv), 399L, 441BL (xxi), 471TR; T. Zurowski — 215B.

Index

Color Tab Index to Bird Groups

Quick Guide to the Most Common Birds

Seabirds — Loons, Grebes, Shearwaters, Pelicans, Cormorants

Heronlike Birds — Bitterns, Herons, Egrets, Ibises

Swans, Geese, Ducks — Whistling-Ducks, Swans, Geese, Ducks

Hawklike Birds — Osprey, Kites, Eagles, Hawks, Falcons

Chickenlike Birds — Pheasant, Grouse, Turkey, Quail

Marsh Birds — Rails, Gallinule, Moorhen, Coot, plus Cranes

Shorebirds — Plovers, Stilt, Avocet, Sandpipers, Dowitchers, Phalaropes

Gull-like Birds — Jaegers, Gulls, Terns, Skimmer, plus Alcids

Pigeonlike Birds — Pigeon, Doves

Owls and Other Nocturnal Birds — Owls, Nighthawks, Whip-poor-will

Swifts, Hummingbirds — Swifts, Hummingbirds, plus Kingfishers

Woodpeckers — Woodpeckers, Sapsuckers, Flickers

Flycatchers — Flycatchers, Phoebes, Kingbirds

Shrikes, Vireos — Shrikes, Vireos

Jays, Crows — Jays, Magpies, Crows, Ravens

Swallows — Martin, Swallows

Chickadees, Nuthatches, Wrens — Chickadees, Titmice, Nuthatches, Wrens

Thrushes, Mimics — Bluebirds, Thrushes, Robin, Catbird, Mockingbird, Thrashers

Warblers — Warblers, Redstarts, Ovenbird, Waterthrush, Chat

Tanagers, Grosbeaks, Buntings — Tanagers, Cardinal, Grosbeaks, Buntings

Sparrows — Towhees, Sparrows, Juncos, Longspurs

Blackbirds, Orioles — Blackbirds, Grackles, Cowbirds, Orioles

Finches — Finches, Crossbills, Redpolls, Goldfinches